Age of Night

VOLUME ONE:
BUSINESS BETWEEN BRIGANDS

Written and Illustrated by
Amanda Kahl

with Creative Contribution by
Matthew Woodle

For Molly,
Thank you
and enjoy the
adventure!
-A. Kahl

Age of Night Volume One: Business Between Brigands

By Amanda Kahl and Matthew Woodle

ISBN: 978-1456567330

PROLOGUE

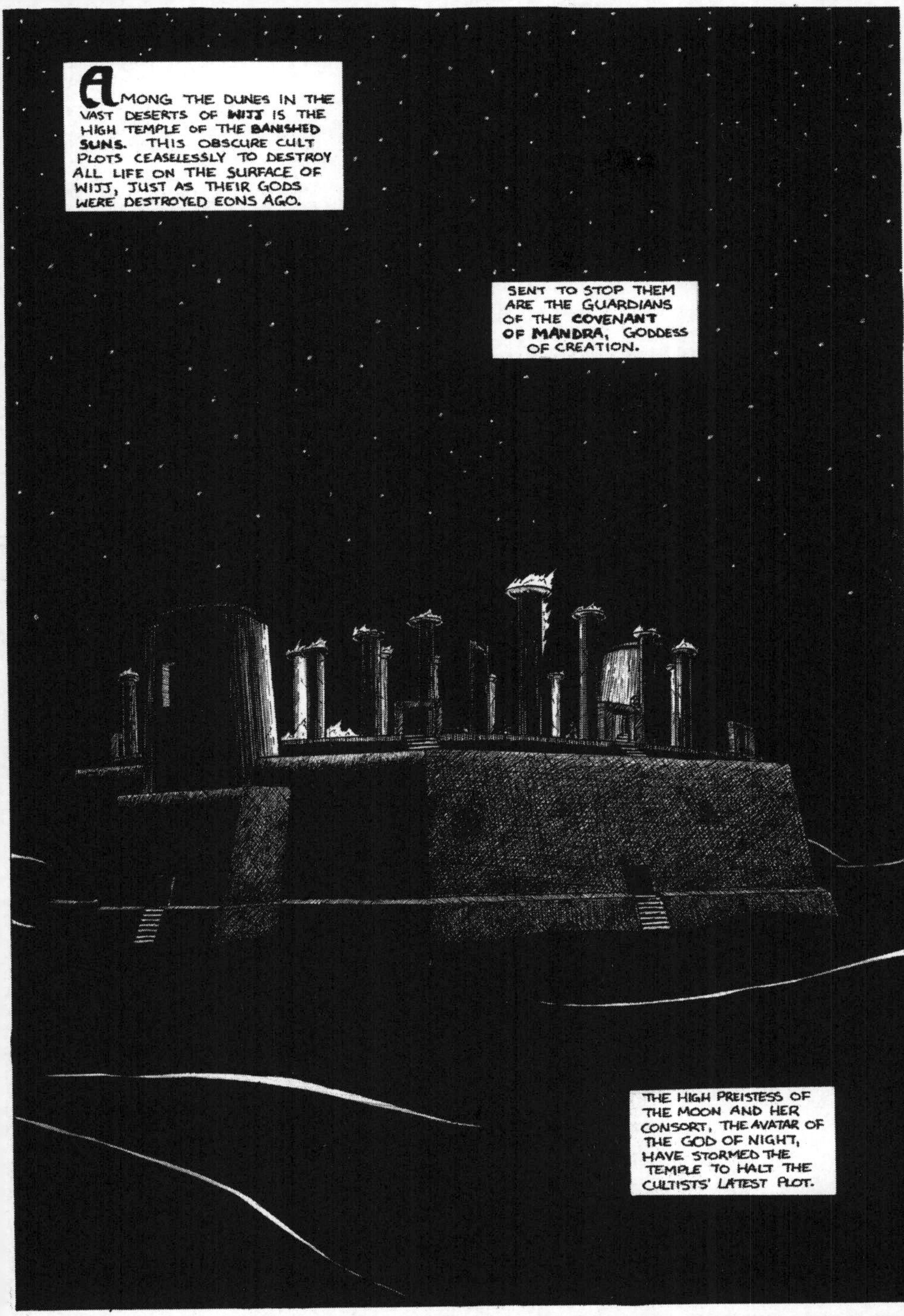
AMONG THE DUNES IN THE VAST DESERTS OF WIJJ IS THE HIGH TEMPLE OF THE BANISHED SUNS. THIS OBSCURE CULT PLOTS CEASELESSLY TO DESTROY ALL LIFE ON THE SURFACE OF WIJJ, JUST AS THEIR GODS WERE DESTROYED EONS AGO.
SENT TO STOP THEM ARE THE GUARDIANS OF THE COVENANT OF MANDRA, GODDESS OF CREATION.
THE HIGH PREISTESS OF THE MOON AND HER CONSORT, THE AVATAR OF THE GOD OF NIGHT, HAVE STORMED THE TEMPLE TO HALT THE CULTISTS' LATEST PLOT.

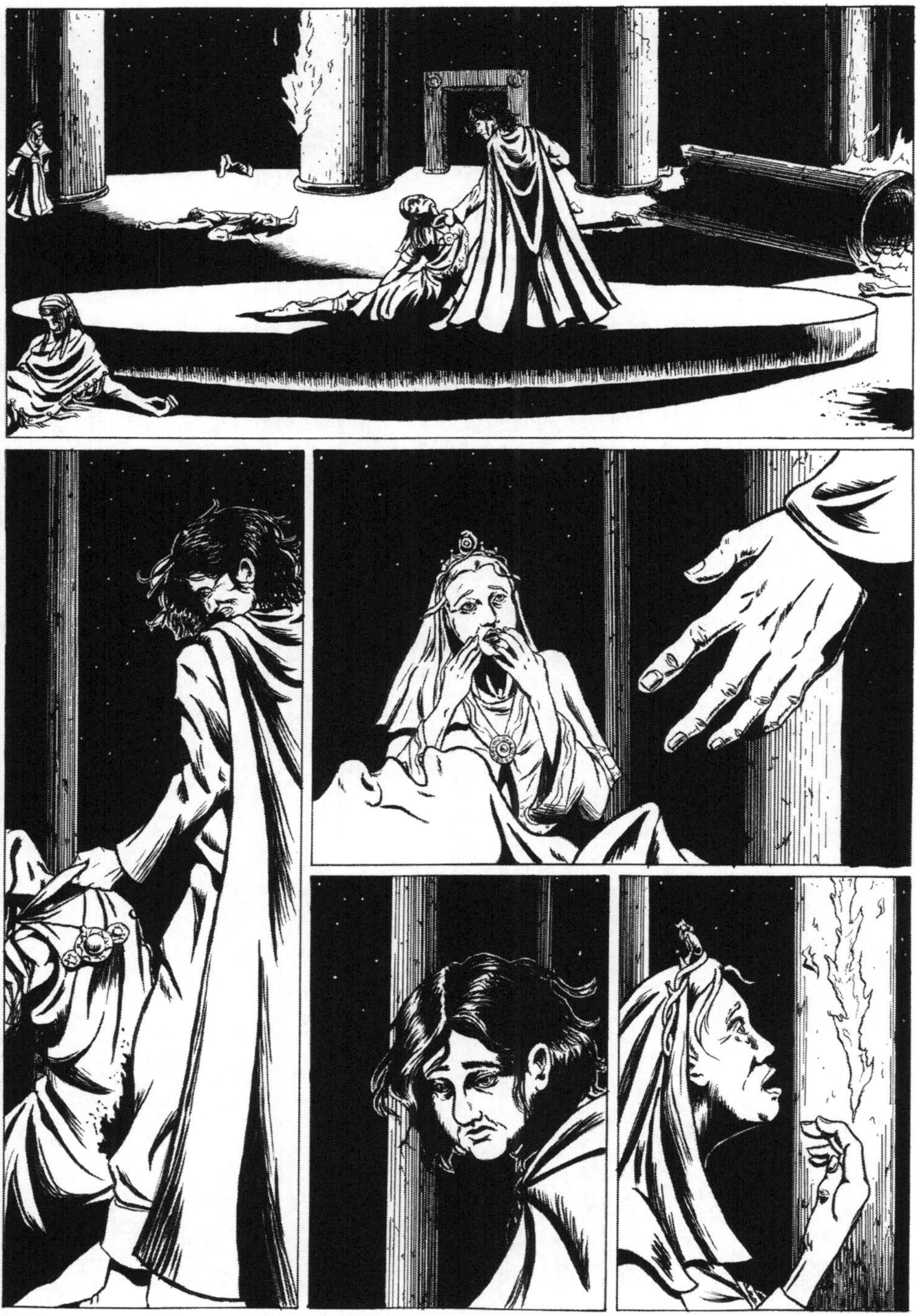

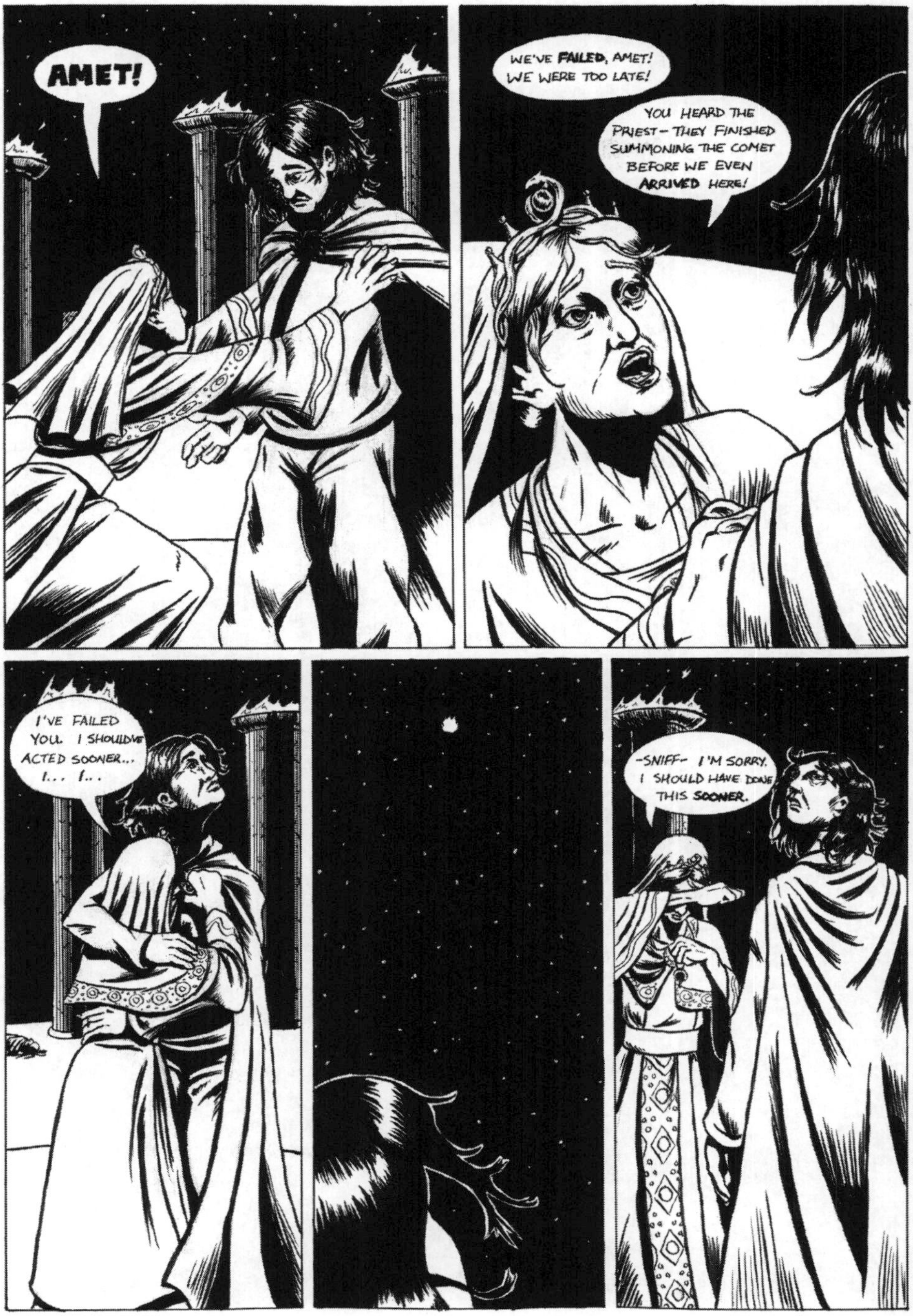
AMET!
WE'VE FAILED, AMET! WE WERE TOO LATE!
YOU HEARD THE PRIEST- THEY FINISHED SUMMONING THE COMET BEFORE WE EVEN ARRIVED HERE!
I'VE FAILED YOU. I SHOULD'VE ACTED SOONER... I... I...
-SNIFF- I'M SORRY. I SHOULD HAVE DONE THIS SOONER.

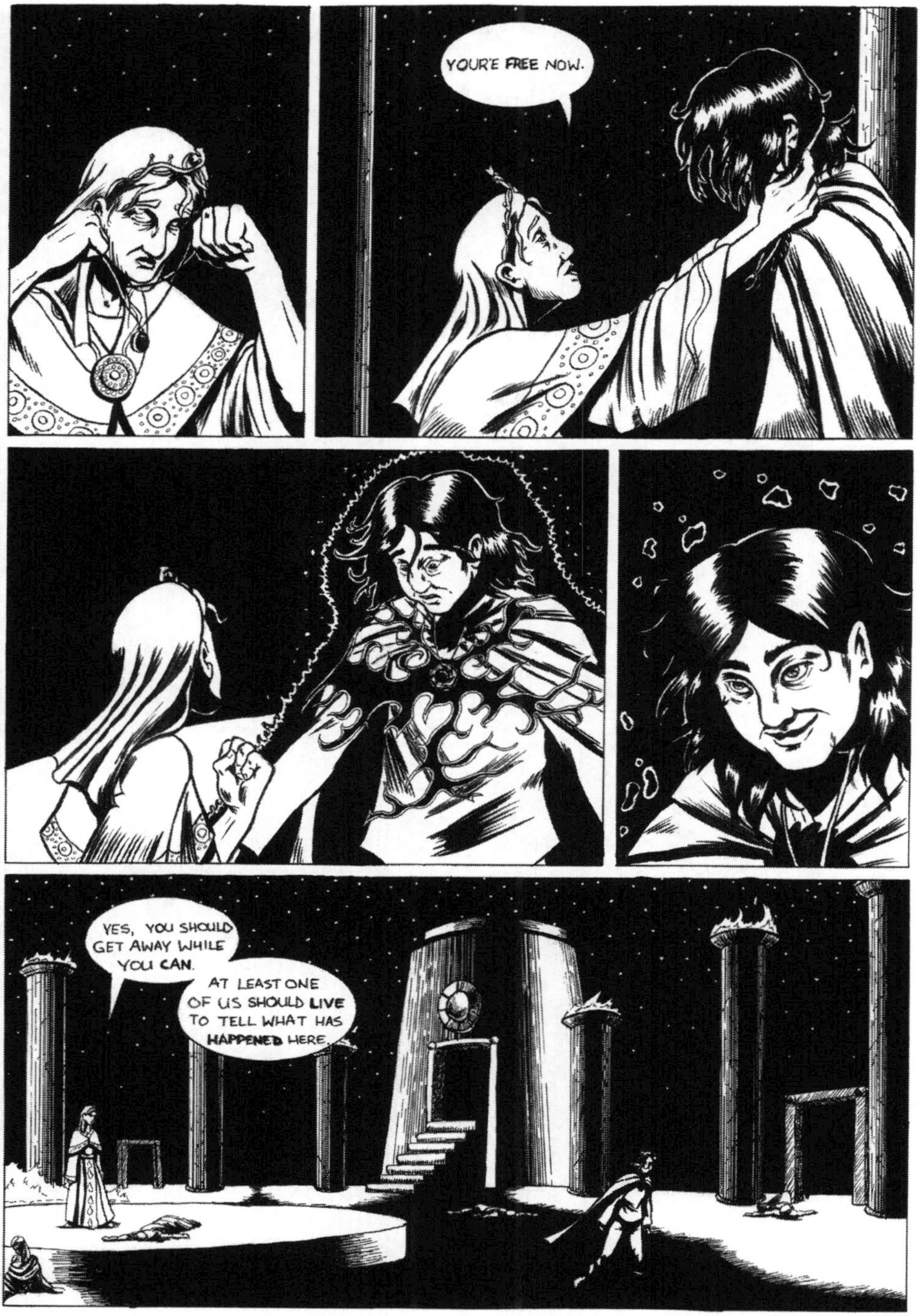
YOUR'E FREE NOW.
YES, YOU SHOULD GET AWAY WHILE YOU CAN.
AT LEAST ONE OF US SHOULD LIVE TO TELL WHAT HAS HAPPENED HERE.

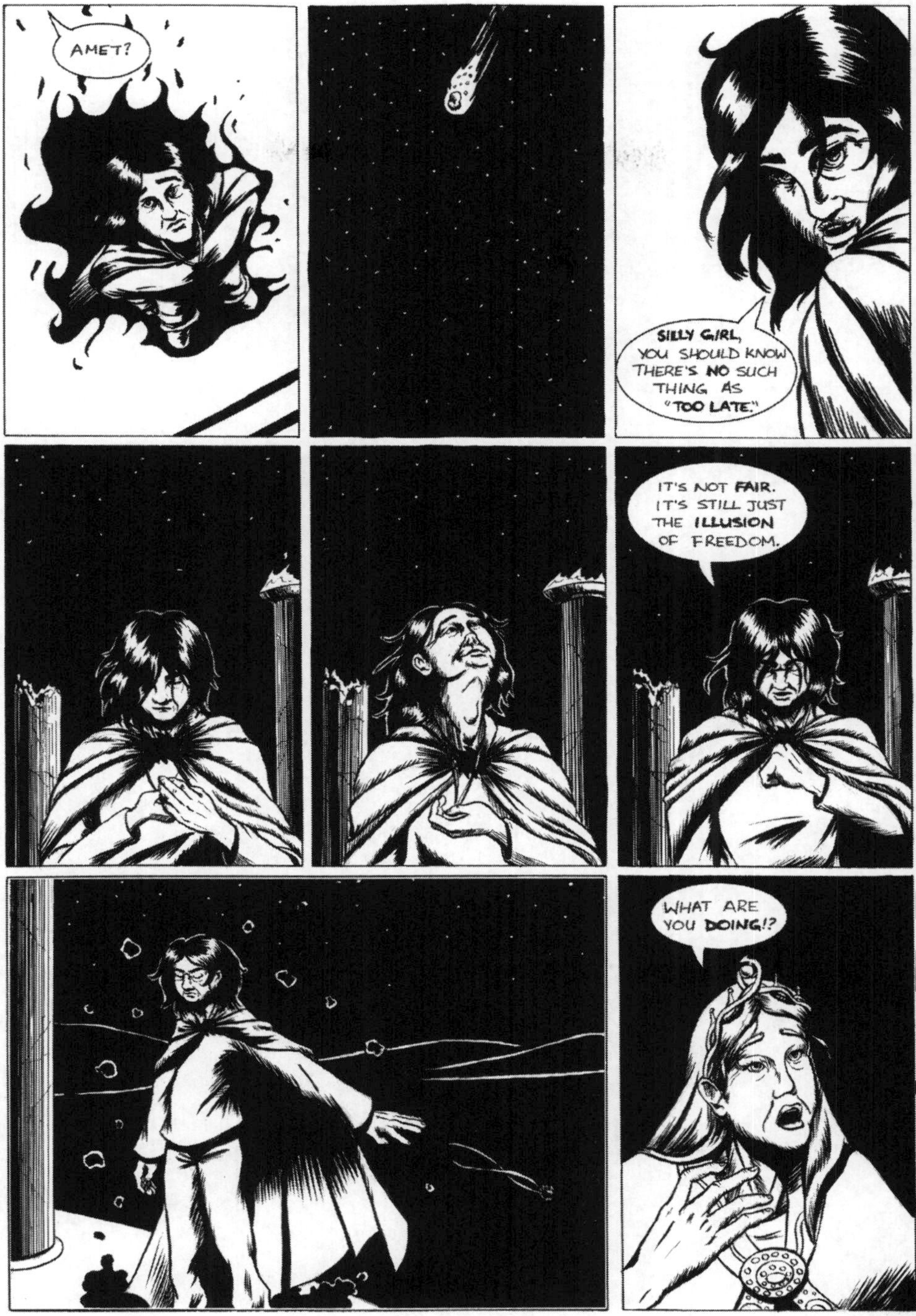
AMET?
SILLY GIRL, YOU SHOULD KNOW THERE'S NO SUCH THING AS "TOO LATE."
IT'S NOT FAIR. IT'S STILL JUST THE ILLUSION OF FREEDOM.
WHAT ARE YOU DOING!?

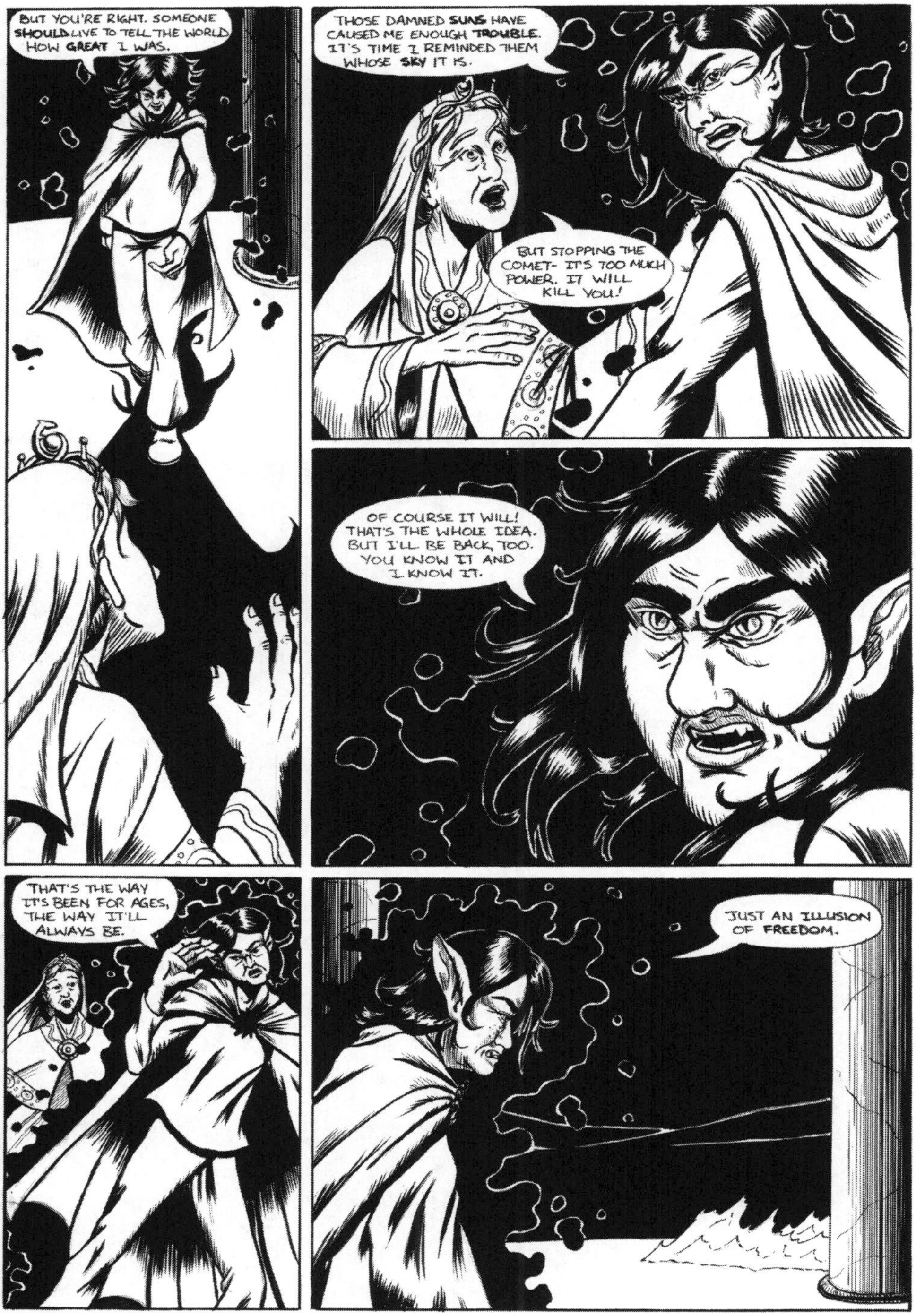
BUT YOU'RE RIGHT. SOMEONE SHOULD LIVE TO TELL THE WORLD HOW GREAT I WAS.
THOSE DAMNED SUNS HAVE CAUSED ME ENOUGH TROUBLE. IT'S TIME I REMINDED THEM WHOSE SKY IT IS.
BUT STOPPING THE COMET- IT'S TOO MUCH POWER. IT WILL KILL YOU!
OF COURSE IT WILL! THAT'S THE WHOLE IDEA. BUT I'LL BE BACK, TOO. YOU KNOW IT AND I KNOW IT.
THAT'S THE WAY IT'S BEEN FOR AGES, THE WAY IT'LL ALWAYS BE.
JUST AN ILLUSION OF FREEDOM.

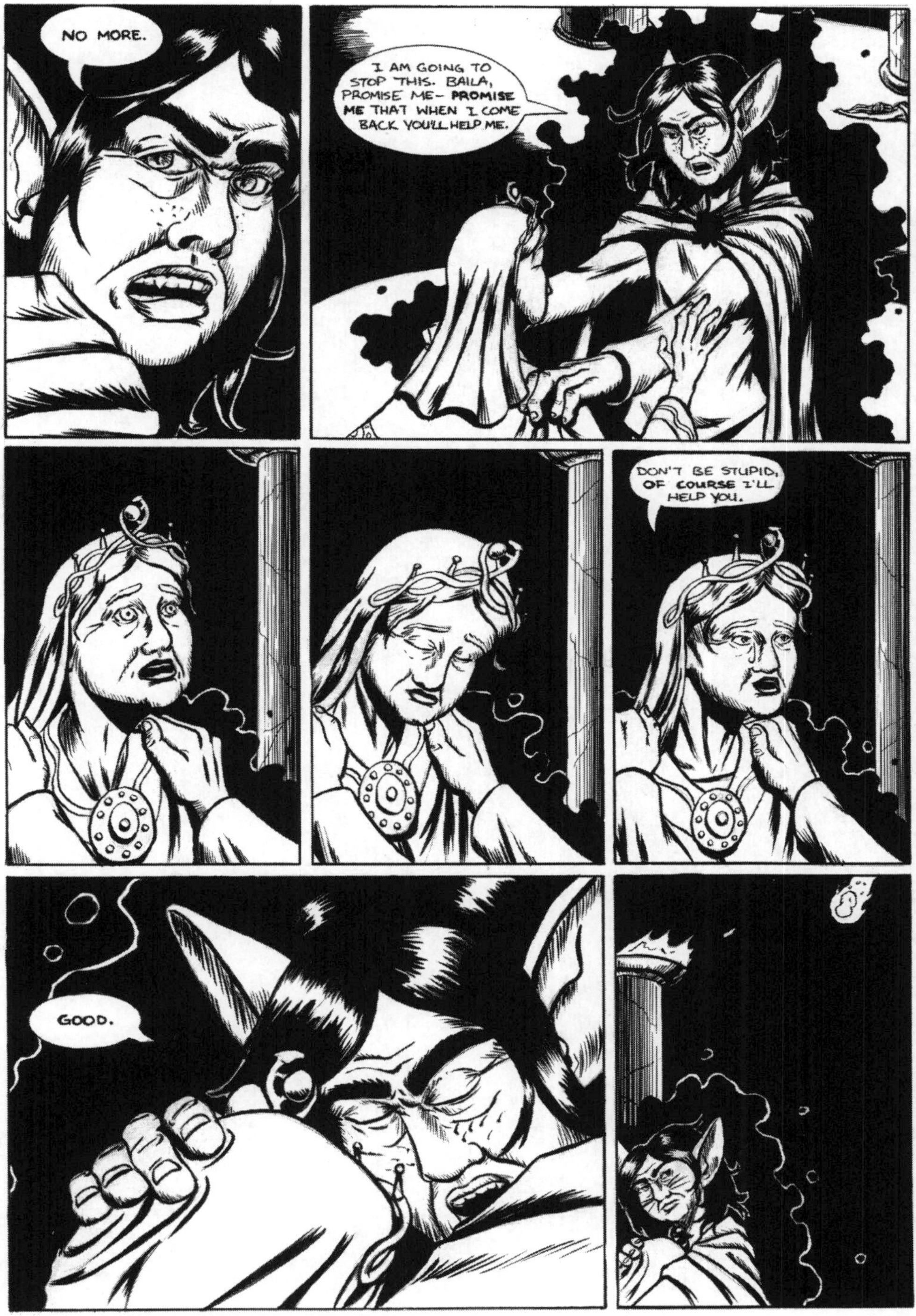
NO MORE.
I AM GOING TO STOP THIS. BAILA, PROMISE ME- PROMISE ME THAT WHEN I COME BACK YOU'LL HELP ME.
DON'T BE STUPID, OF COURSE I'LL HELP YOU.
GOOD.

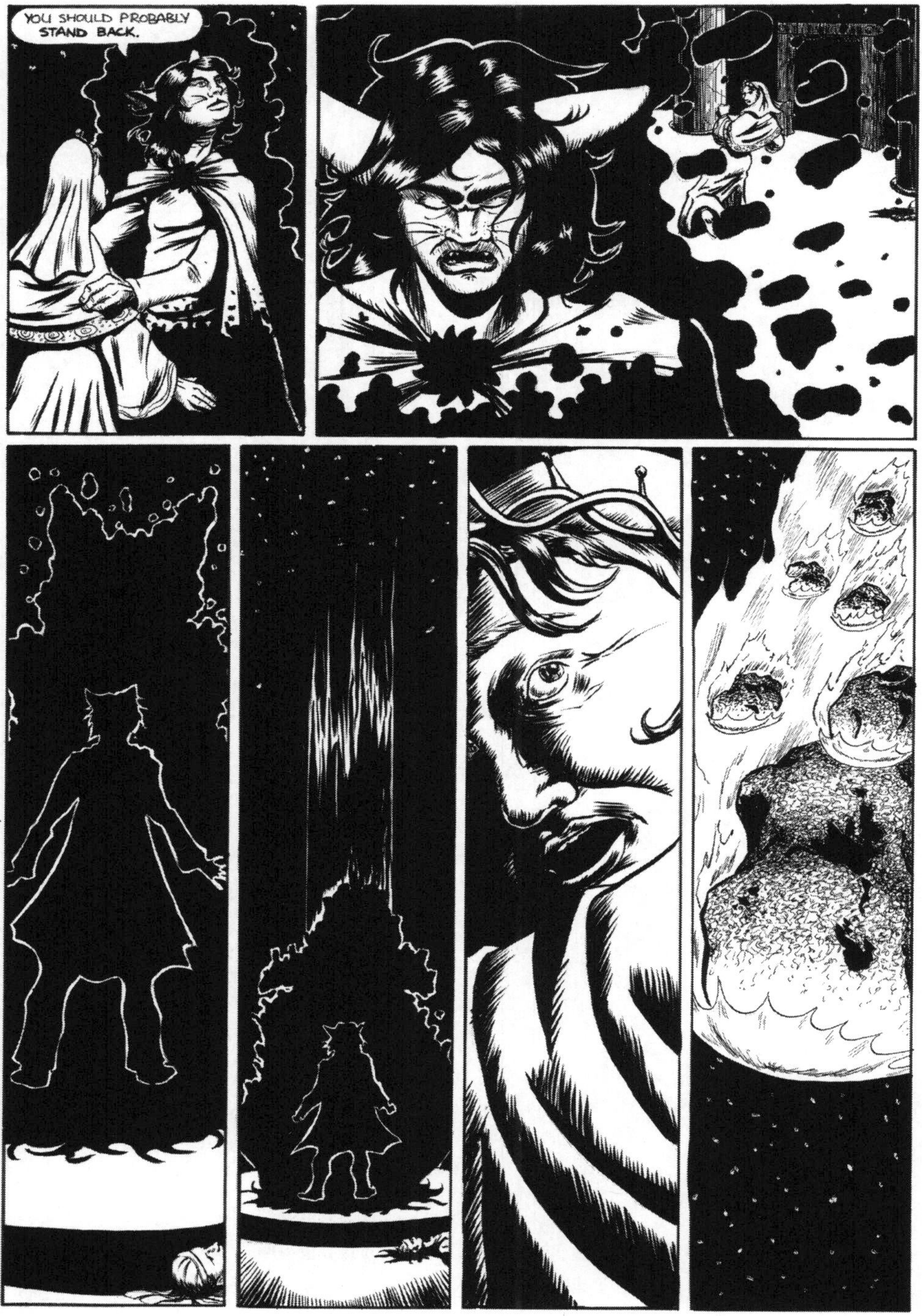
YOU SHOULD PROBABLY STAND BACK.

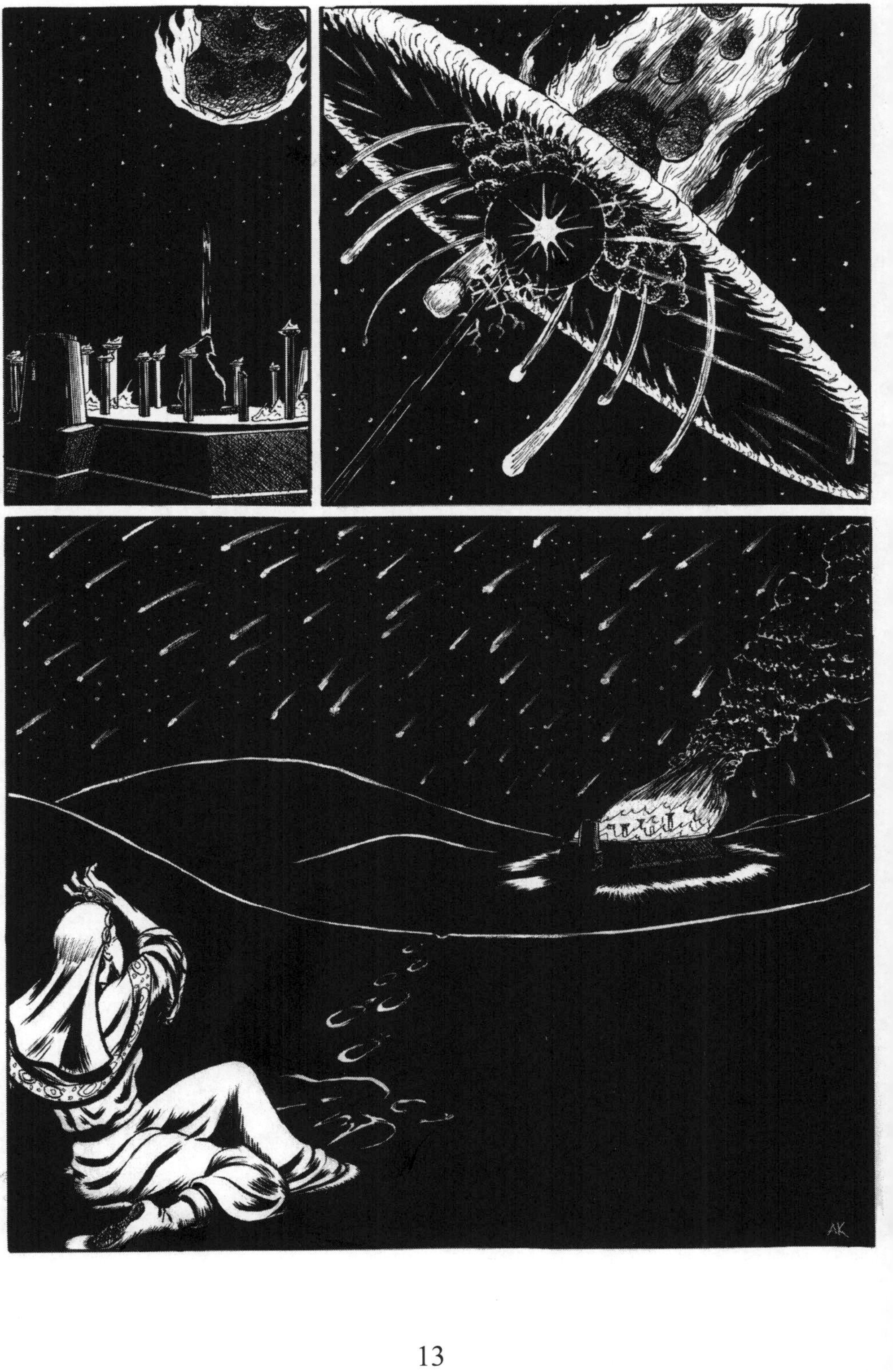
AK

CHAPTER I

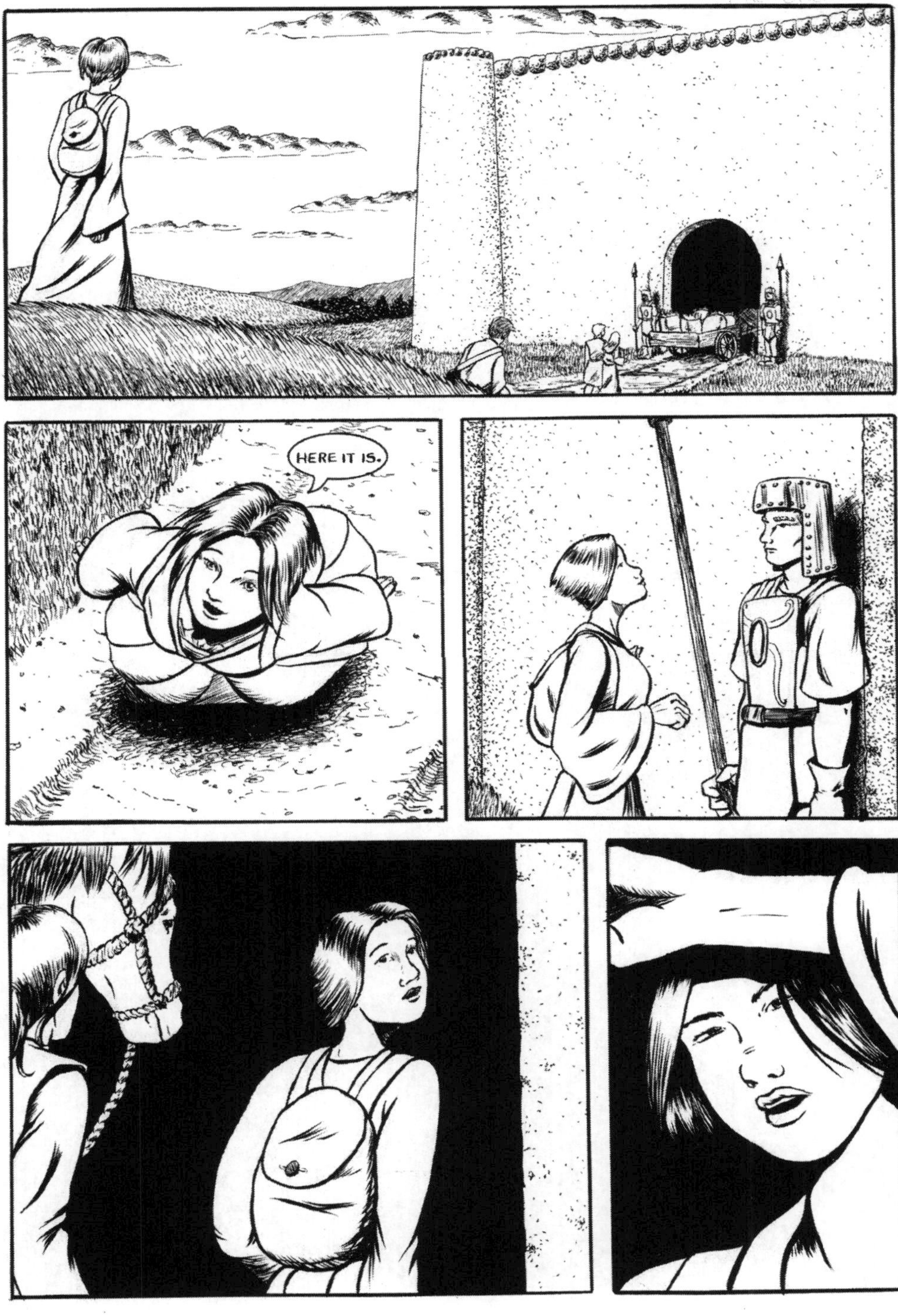
HERE IT IS.

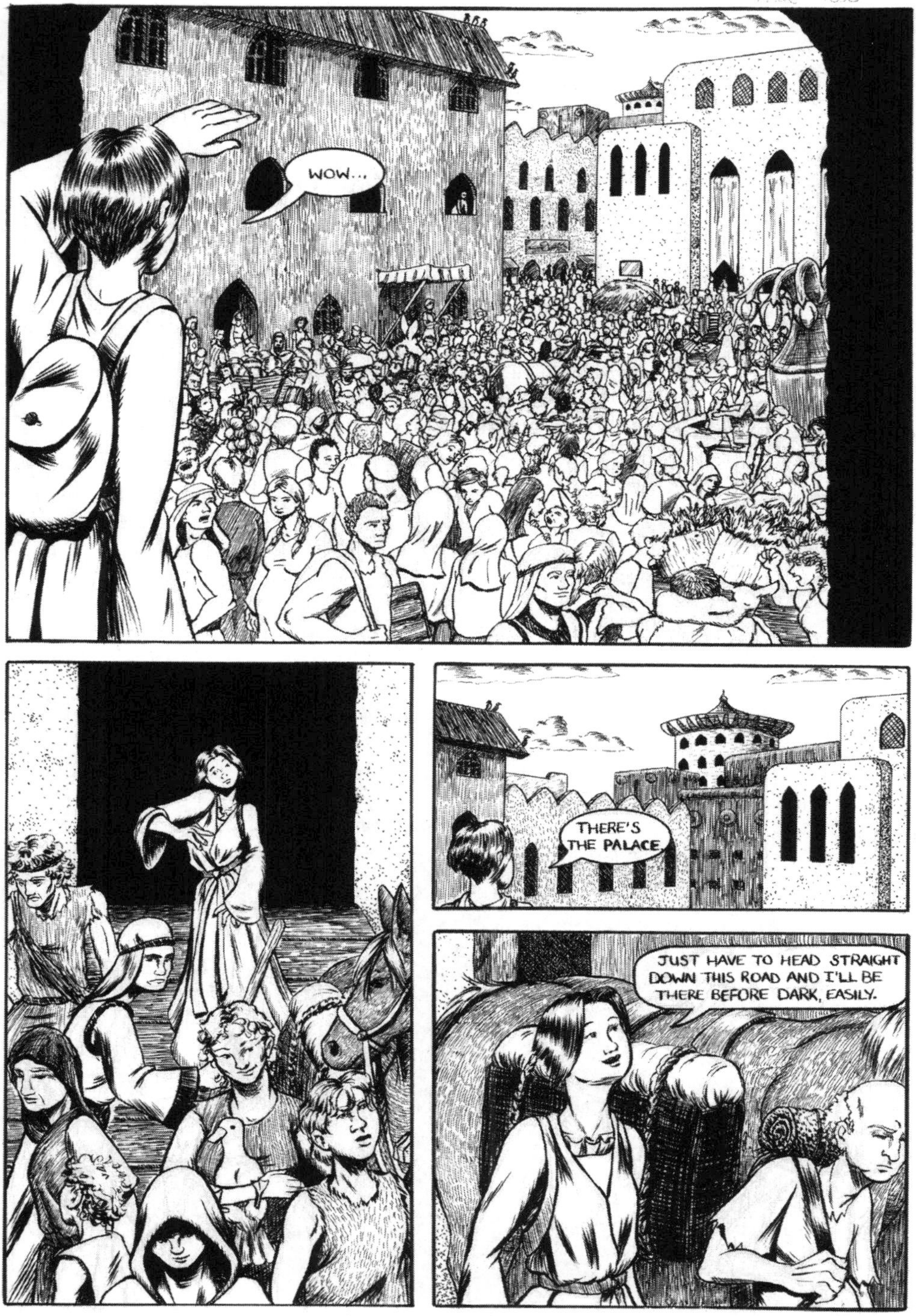
WOW...
THERE'S THE PALACE
JUST HAVE TO HEAD STRAIGHT DOWN THIS ROAD AND I'LL BE THERE BEFORE DARK, EASILY.

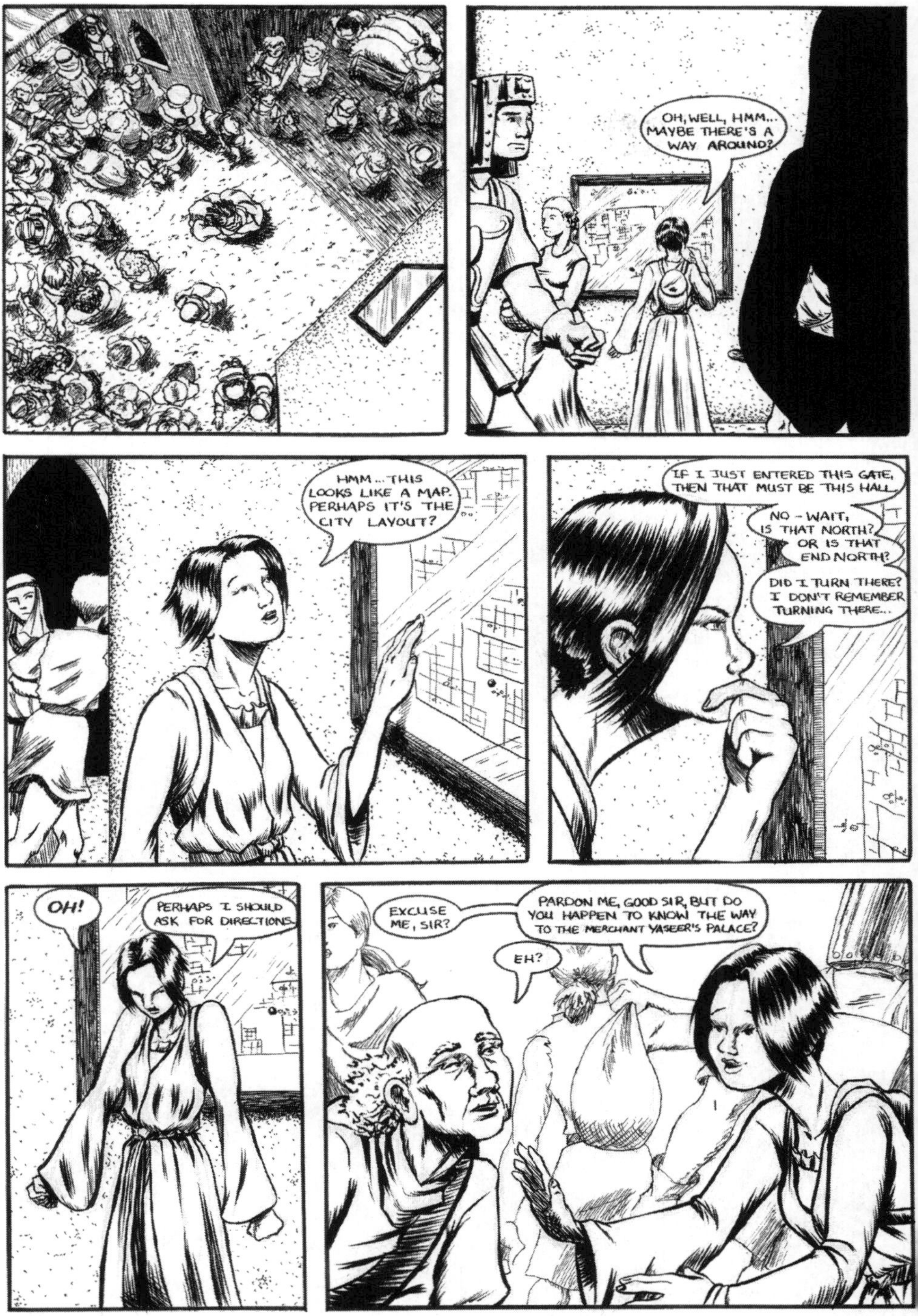
OH, WELL, HMM...
MAYBE THERE'S A
WAY AROUND?
HMM... THIS
LOOKS LIKE A MAP.
PERHAPS IT'S THE
CITY LAYOUT?
IF I JUST ENTERED THIS GATE,
THEN THAT MUST BE THIS HALL
NO - WAIT,
IS THAT NORTH?
OR IS THAT
END NORTH?
DID I TURN THERE?
I DON'T REMEMBER
TURNING THERE...
OH!
PERHAPS I SHOULD
ASK FOR DIRECTIONS.
EXCUSE
ME, SIR?
PARDON ME, GOOD SIR, BUT DO
YOU HAPPEN TO KNOW THE WAY
TO THE MERCHANT YASEER'S PALACE?
EH?

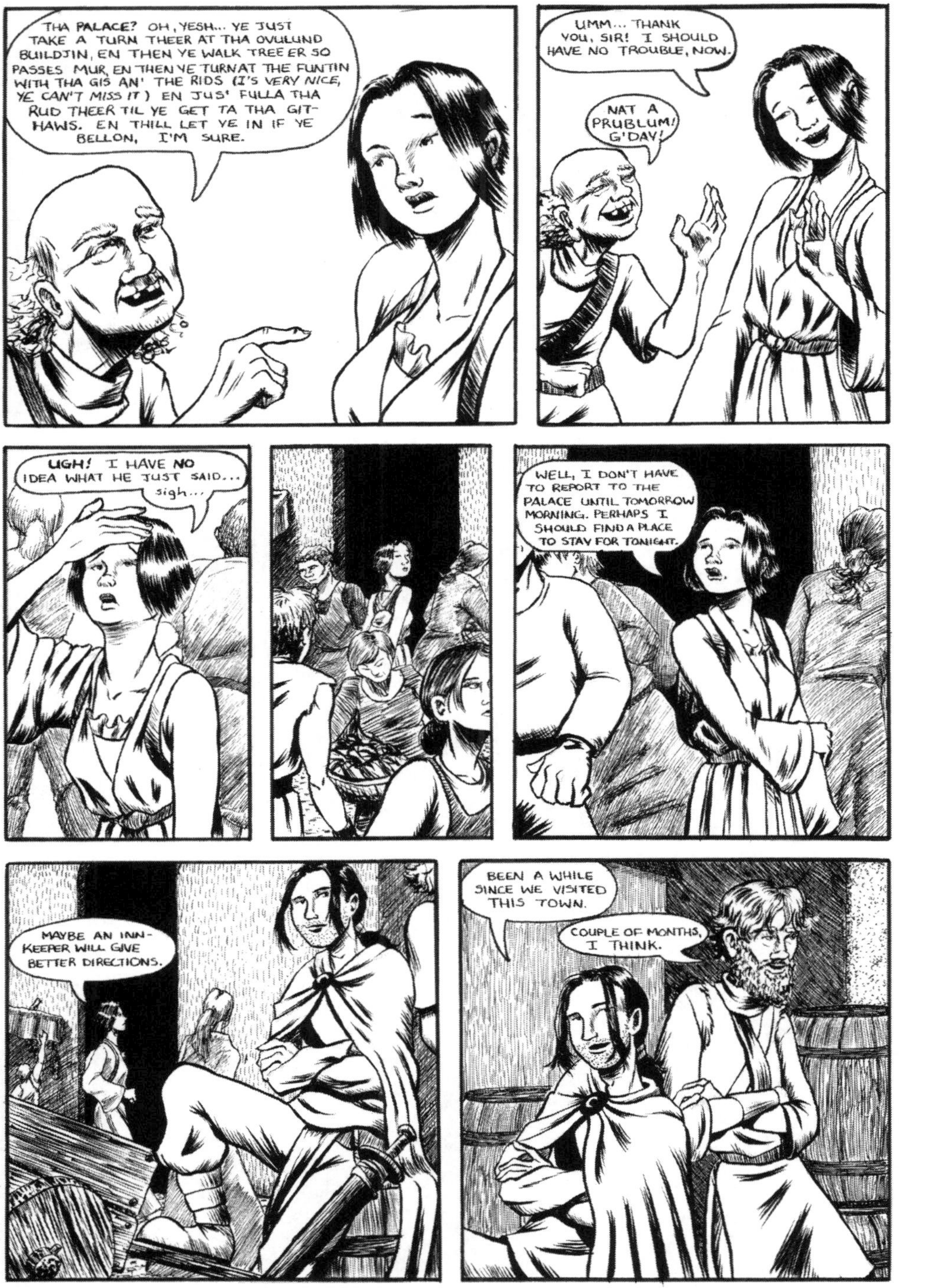
THA PALACE? OH, YESH... YE JUST TAKE A TURN THEER AT THA OVULUND BUILDJIN, EN THEN YE WALK TREE ER SO PASSES MUR, EN THEN YE TURN AT THE FUNTIN WITH THA GIS AN' THE RIDS (I'S VERY NICE, YE CAN'T MISS IT) EN JUS' FULLA THA RUD THEER TIL YE GET TA THA GIT-HAWS. EN THILL LET YE IN IF YE BELLON, I'M SURE.
UMM... THANK YOU, SIR! I SHOULD HAVE NO TROUBLE, NOW.
NAT A PRUBLUM! G'DAY!
UGH! I HAVE NO IDEA WHAT HE JUST SAID... sigh...
WELL, I DON'T HAVE TO REPORT TO THE PALACE UNTIL TOMORROW MORNING. PERHAPS I SHOULD FIND A PLACE TO STAY FOR TONIGHT.
MAYBE AN INN-KEEPER WILL GIVE BETTER DIRECTIONS.
BEEN A WHILE SINCE WE VISITED THIS TOWN.
COUPLE OF MONTHS, I THINK.

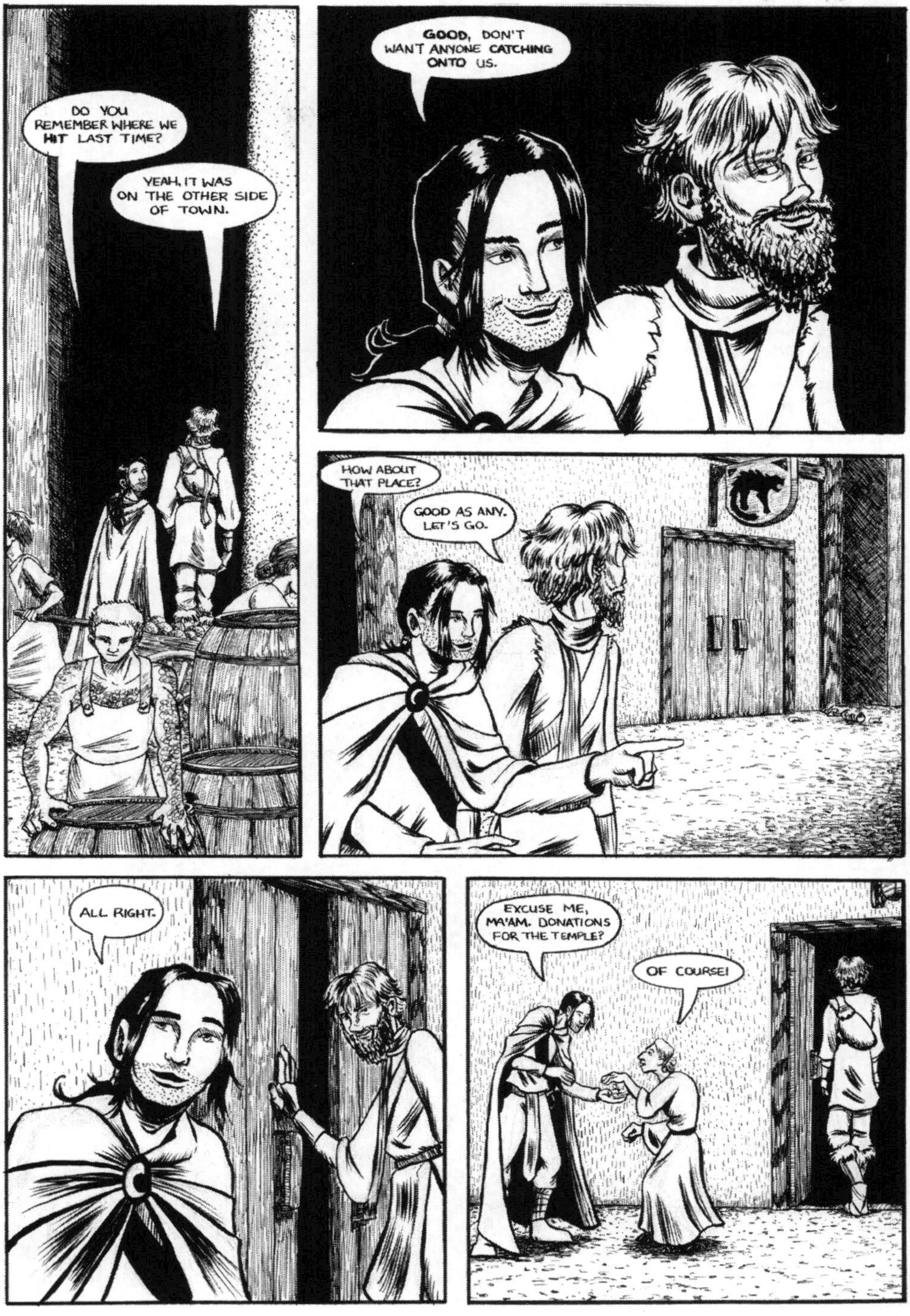
DO YOU REMEMBER WHERE WE HIT LAST TIME?
YEAH, IT WAS ON THE OTHER SIDE OF TOWN.
GOOD, DON'T WANT ANYONE CATCHING ONTO US.
HOW ABOUT THAT PLACE?
GOOD AS ANY. LET'S GO.
ALL RIGHT.
EXCUSE ME, MA'AM. DONATIONS FOR THE TEMPLE?
OF COURSE!

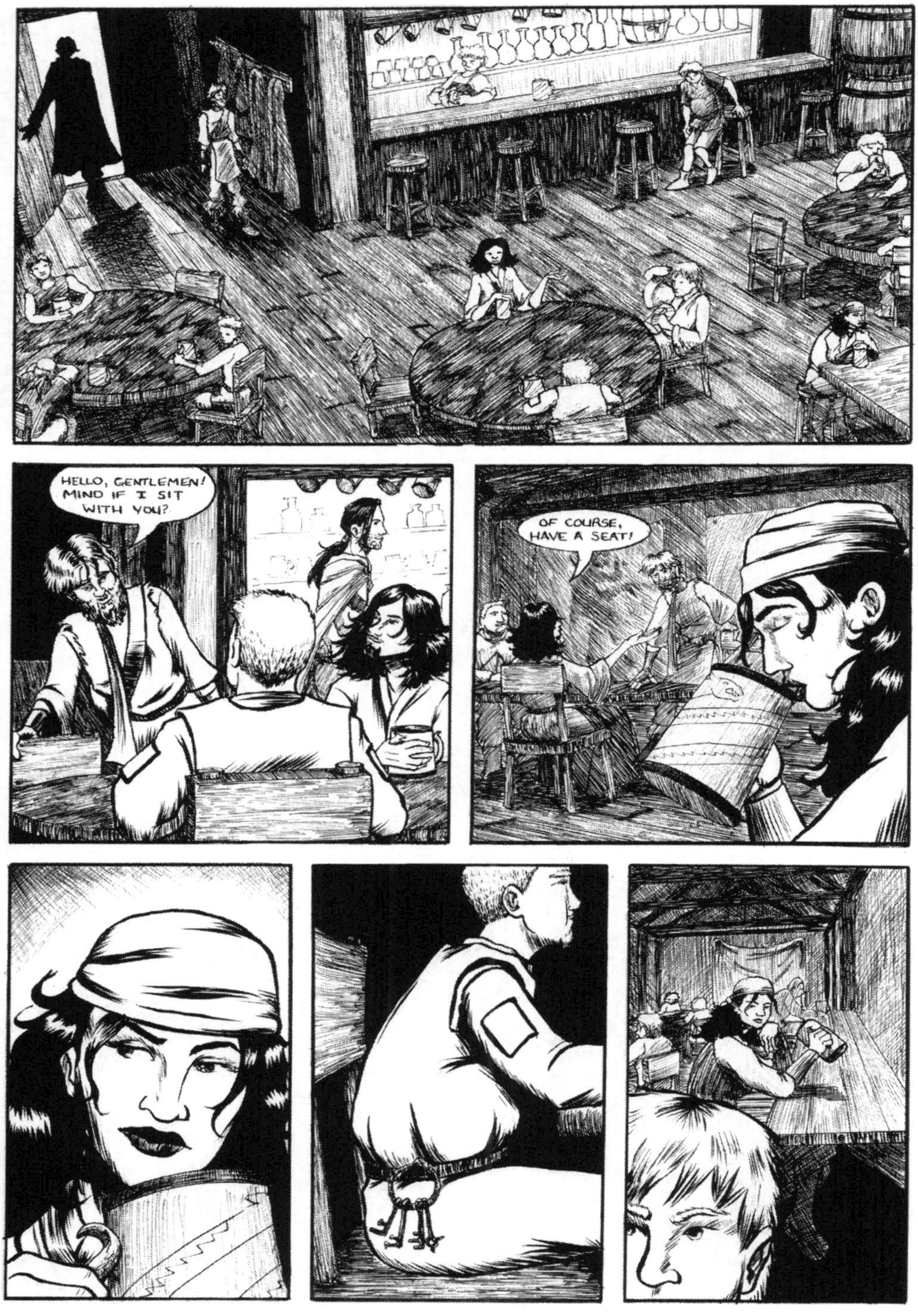
HELLO, GENTLEMEN! MIND IF I SIT WITH YOU?
OF COURSE, HAVE A SEAT!

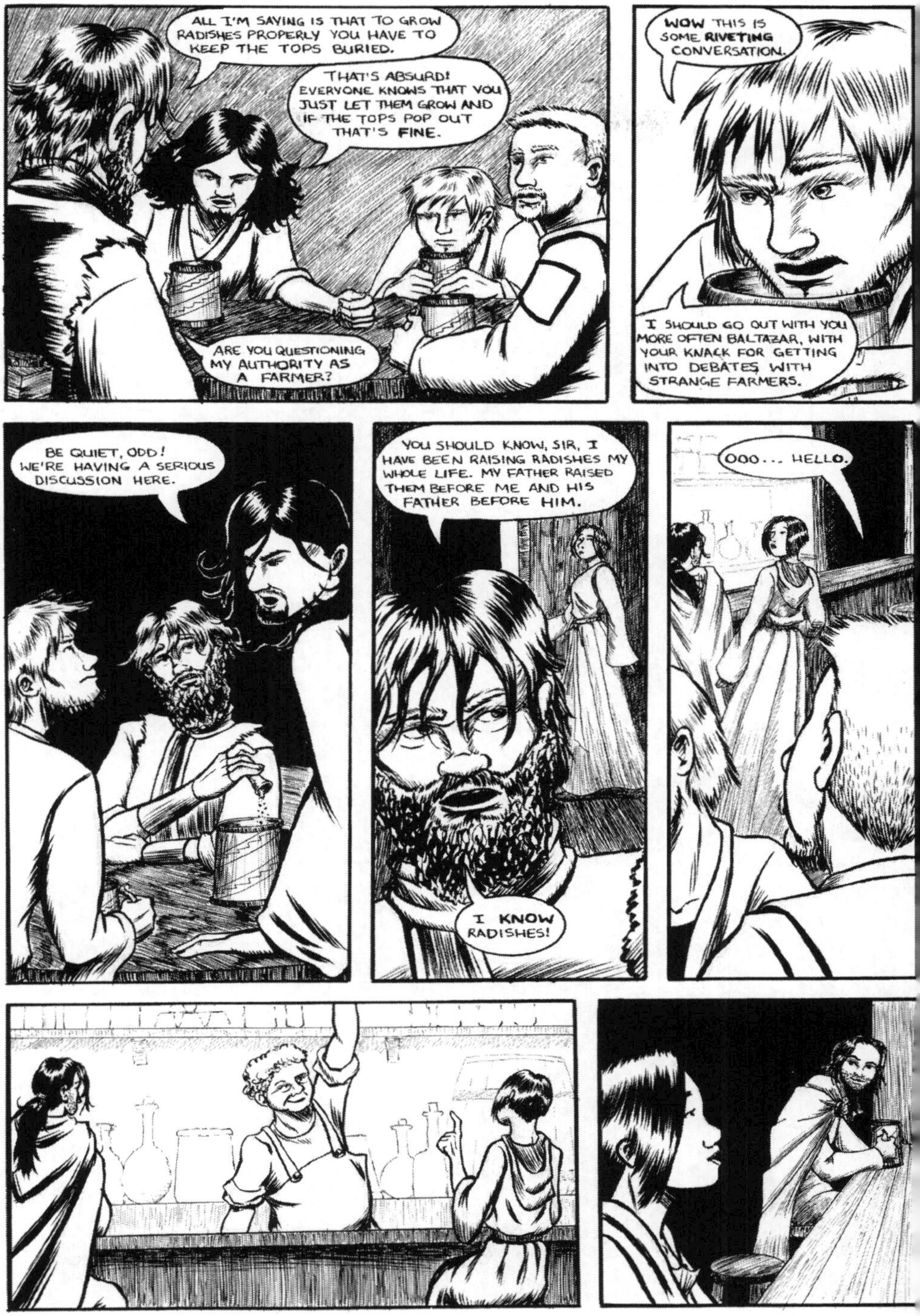
ALL I'M SAYING IS THAT TO GROW RADISHES PROPERLY YOU HAVE TO KEEP THE TOPS BURIED.
THAT'S ABSURD! EVERYONE KNOWS THAT YOU JUST LET THEM GROW AND IF THE TOPS POP OUT THAT'S **FINE**.
ARE YOU QUESTIONING MY AUTHORITY AS A FARMER?
WOW THIS IS SOME **RIVETING** CONVERSATION.
I SHOULD GO OUT WITH YOU MORE OFTEN BALTAZAR, WITH YOUR KNACK FOR GETTING INTO DEBATES WITH STRANGE FARMERS.
BE QUIET, ODD! WE'RE HAVING A SERIOUS DISCUSSION HERE.
YOU SHOULD KNOW, SIR, I HAVE BEEN RAISING RADISHES MY WHOLE LIFE. MY FATHER RAISED THEM BEFORE ME AND HIS FATHER BEFORE **HIM**.
I **KNOW** RADISHES!
OOO... **HELLO**.

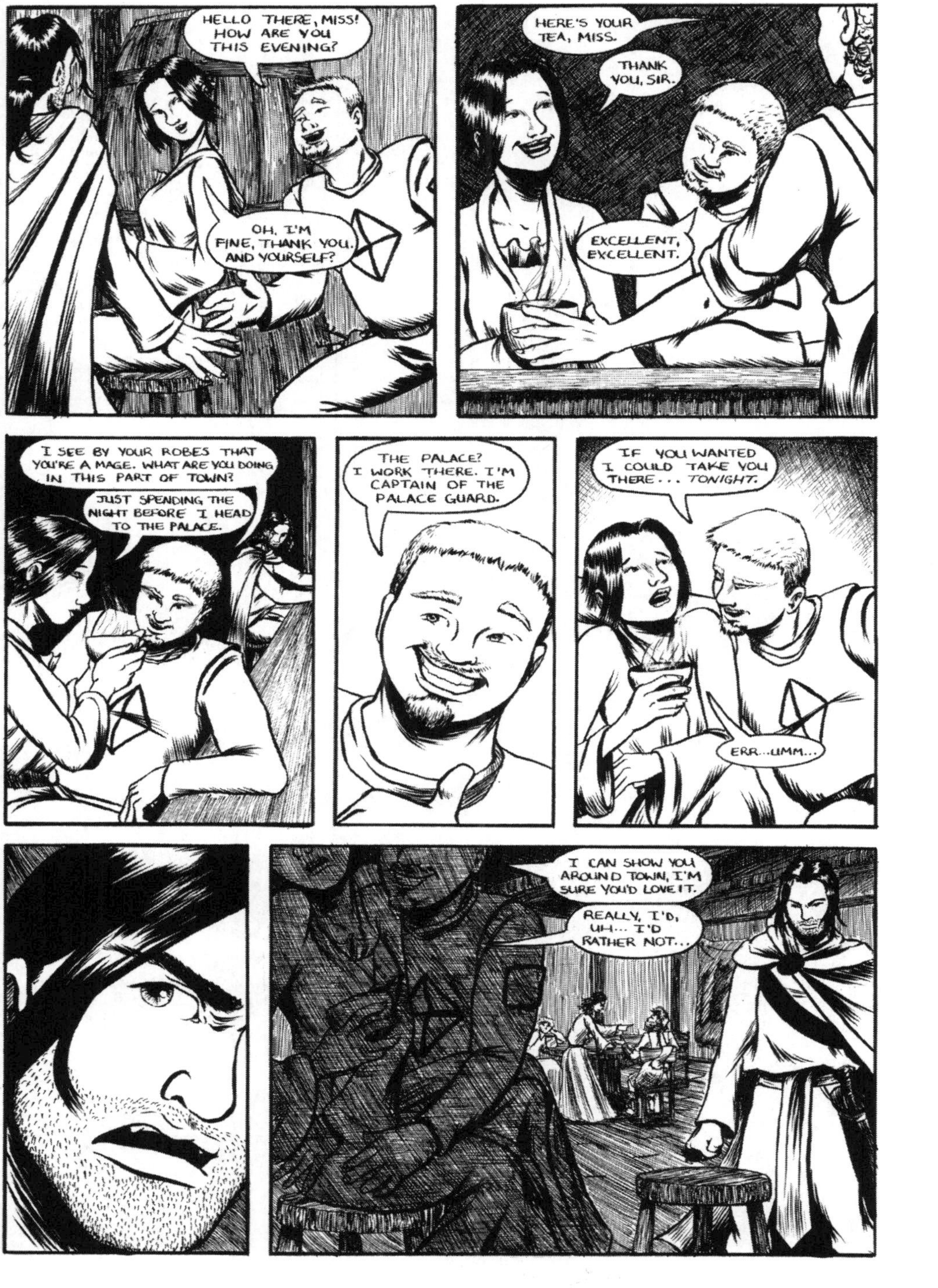
HELLO THERE, MISS! HOW ARE YOU THIS EVENING?
OH, I'M FINE, THANK YOU. AND YOURSELF?
HERE'S YOUR TEA, MISS.
THANK YOU, SIR.
EXCELLENT, EXCELLENT.
I SEE BY YOUR ROBES THAT YOU'RE A MAGE. WHAT ARE YOU DOING IN THIS PART OF TOWN?
JUST SPENDING THE NIGHT BEFORE I HEAD TO THE PALACE.
THE PALACE? I WORK THERE. I'M CAPTAIN OF THE PALACE GUARD.
IF YOU WANTED I COULD TAKE YOU THERE... TONIGHT.
ERR...UMM...
I CAN SHOW YOU AROUND TOWN, I'M SURE YOU'D LOVE IT.
REALLY, I'D, UH... I'D RATHER NOT...

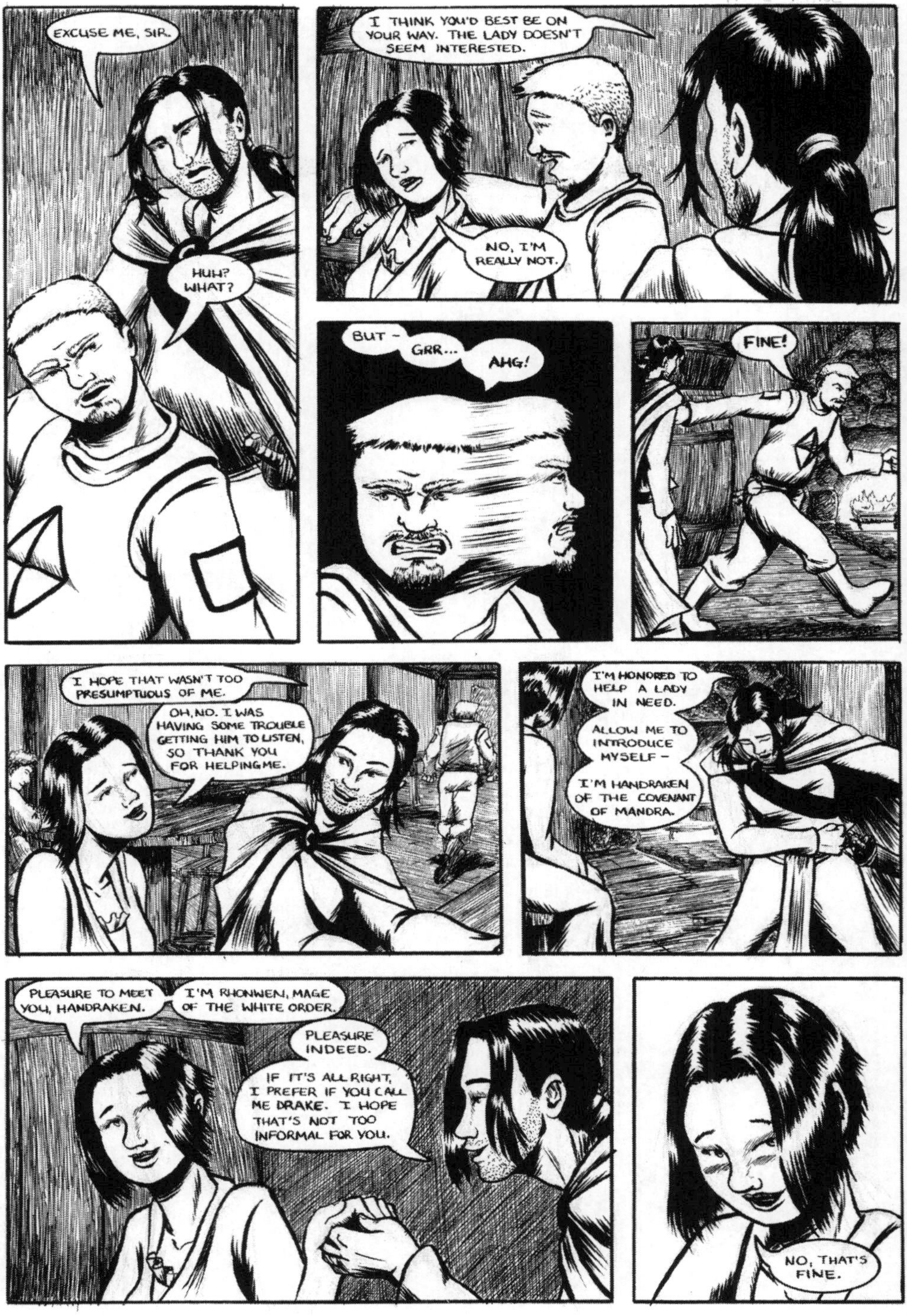
EXCUSE ME, SIR.
HUH? WHAT?
I THINK YOU'D BEST BE ON YOUR WAY. THE LADY DOESN'T SEEM INTERESTED.
NO, I'M REALLY NOT.
BUT -
GRR...
AHG!
FINE!
I HOPE THAT WASN'T TOO PRESUMPTUOUS OF ME.
OH, NO. I WAS HAVING SOME TROUBLE GETTING HIM TO LISTEN, SO THANK YOU FOR HELPING ME.
I'M HONORED TO HELP A LADY IN NEED.
ALLOW ME TO INTRODUCE MYSELF -
I'M HANDRAKEN OF THE COVENANT OF MANDRA.
PLEASURE TO MEET YOU, HANDRAKEN.
I'M RHONWEN, MAGE OF THE WHITE ORDER.
PLEASURE INDEED.
IF IT'S ALL RIGHT, I PREFER IF YOU CALL ME DRAKE. I HOPE THAT'S NOT TOO INFORMAL FOR YOU.
NO, THAT'S FINE.

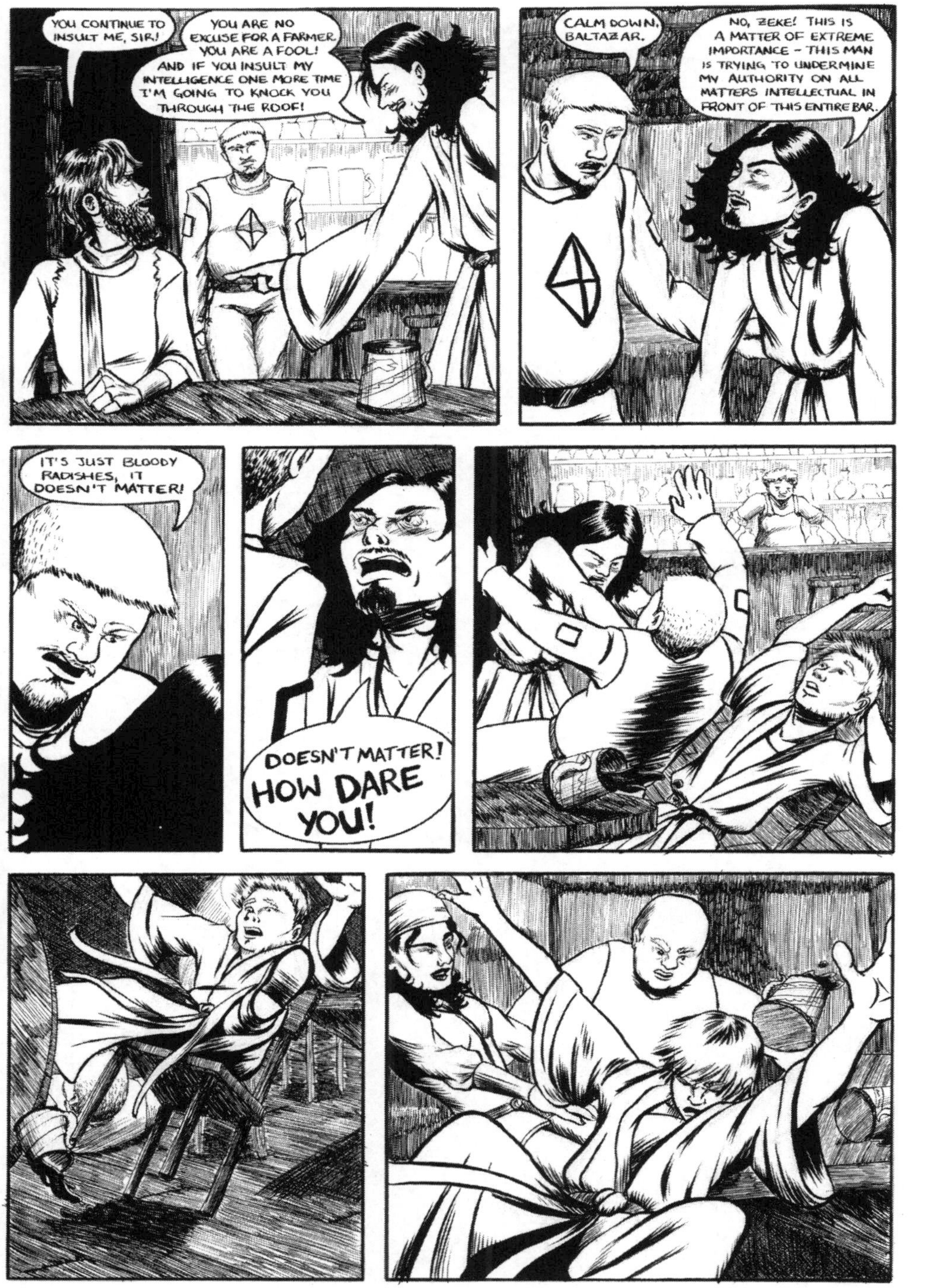

YOU CONTINUE TO INSULT ME, SIR!
YOU ARE NO EXCUSE FOR A FARMER. YOU ARE A FOOL! AND IF YOU INSULT MY INTELLIGENCE ONE MORE TIME I'M GOING TO KNOCK YOU THROUGH THE ROOF!
CALM DOWN, BALTAZAR.
NO, ZEKE! THIS IS A MATTER OF EXTREME IMPORTANCE - THIS MAN IS TRYING TO UNDERMINE MY AUTHORITY ON ALL MATTERS INTELLECTUAL IN FRONT OF THIS ENTIRE BAR.
IT'S JUST BLOODY RADISHES, IT DOESN'T MATTER!
DOESN'T MATTER! HOW DARE YOU!

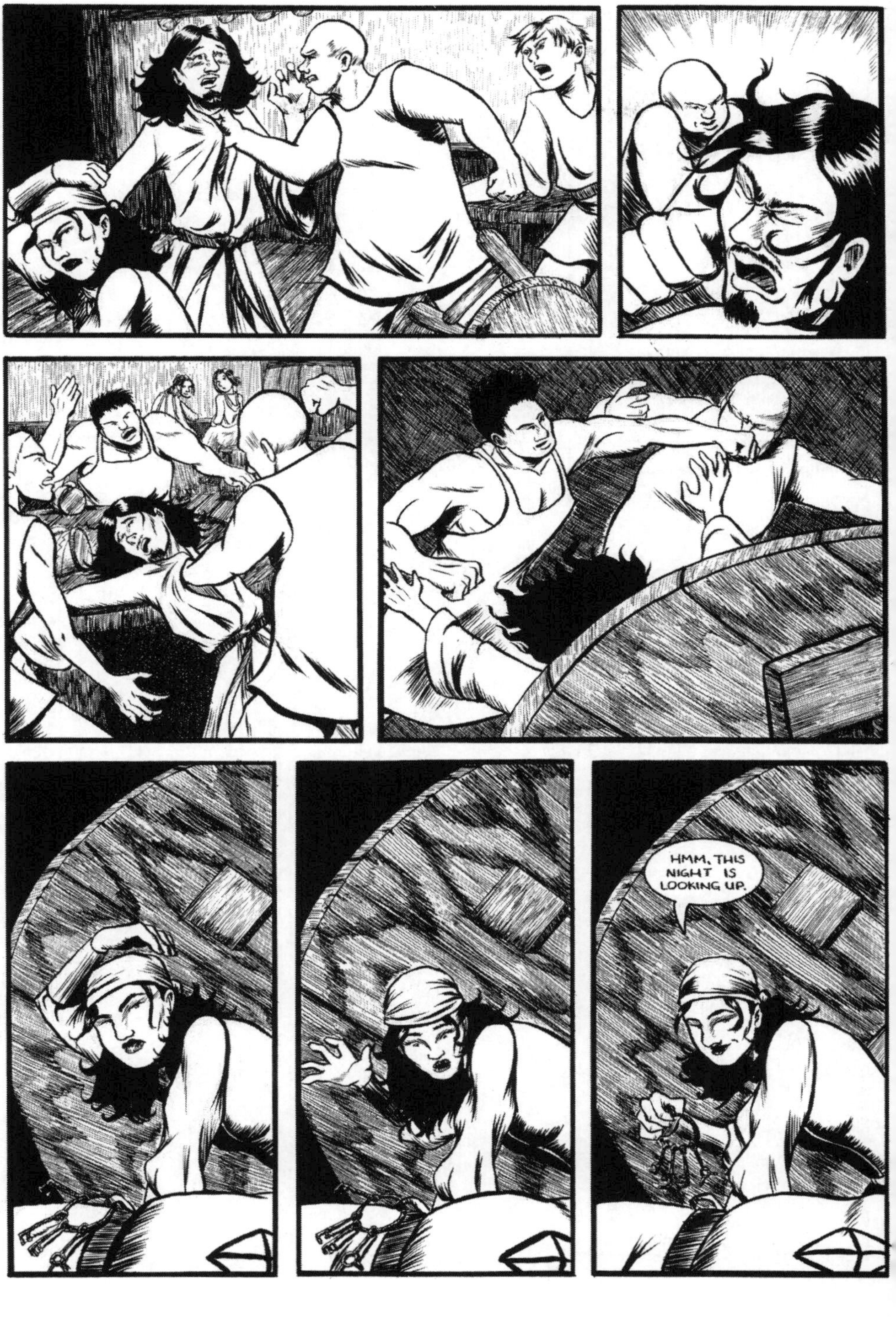
HMM, THIS NIGHT IS LOOKING UP.

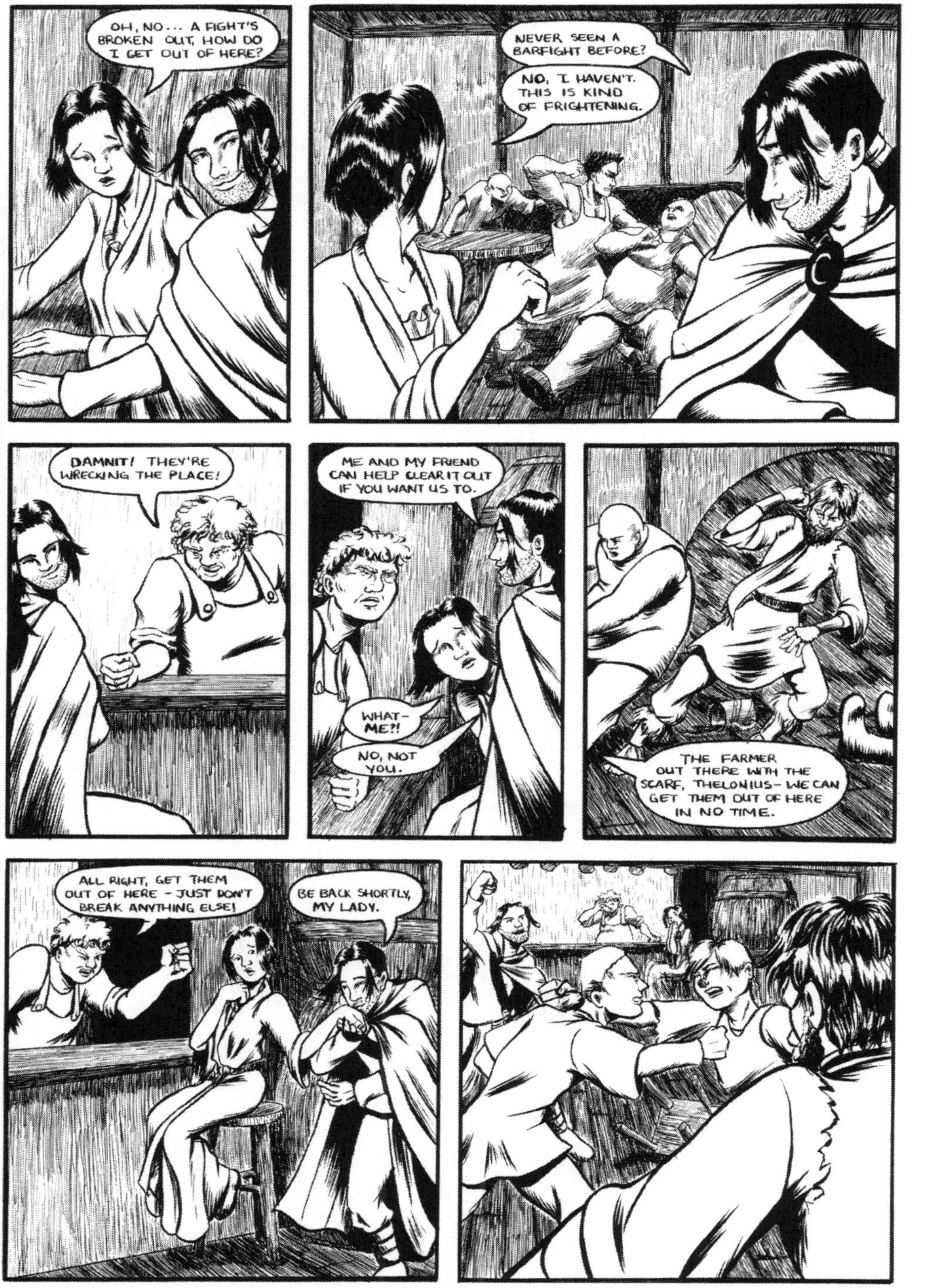
OH, NO... A FIGHT'S BROKEN OUT, HOW DO I GET OUT OF HERE?
NEVER SEEN A BARFIGHT BEFORE?
NO, I HAVEN'T. THIS IS KIND OF FRIGHTENING.
DAMNIT! THEY'RE WRECKING THE PLACE!
ME AND MY FRIEND CAN HELP CLEAR IT OUT IF YOU WANT US TO.
WHAT-ME?!
NO, NOT YOU.
THE FARMER OUT THERE WITH THE SCARF, THELONIUS- WE CAN GET THEM OUT OF HERE IN NO TIME.
ALL RIGHT, GET THEM OUT OF HERE - JUST DON'T BREAK ANYTHING ELSE!
BE BACK SHORTLY, MY LADY.

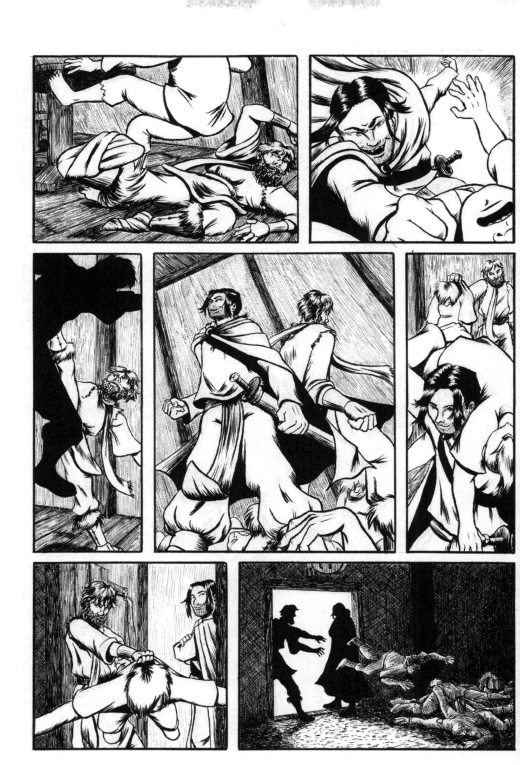

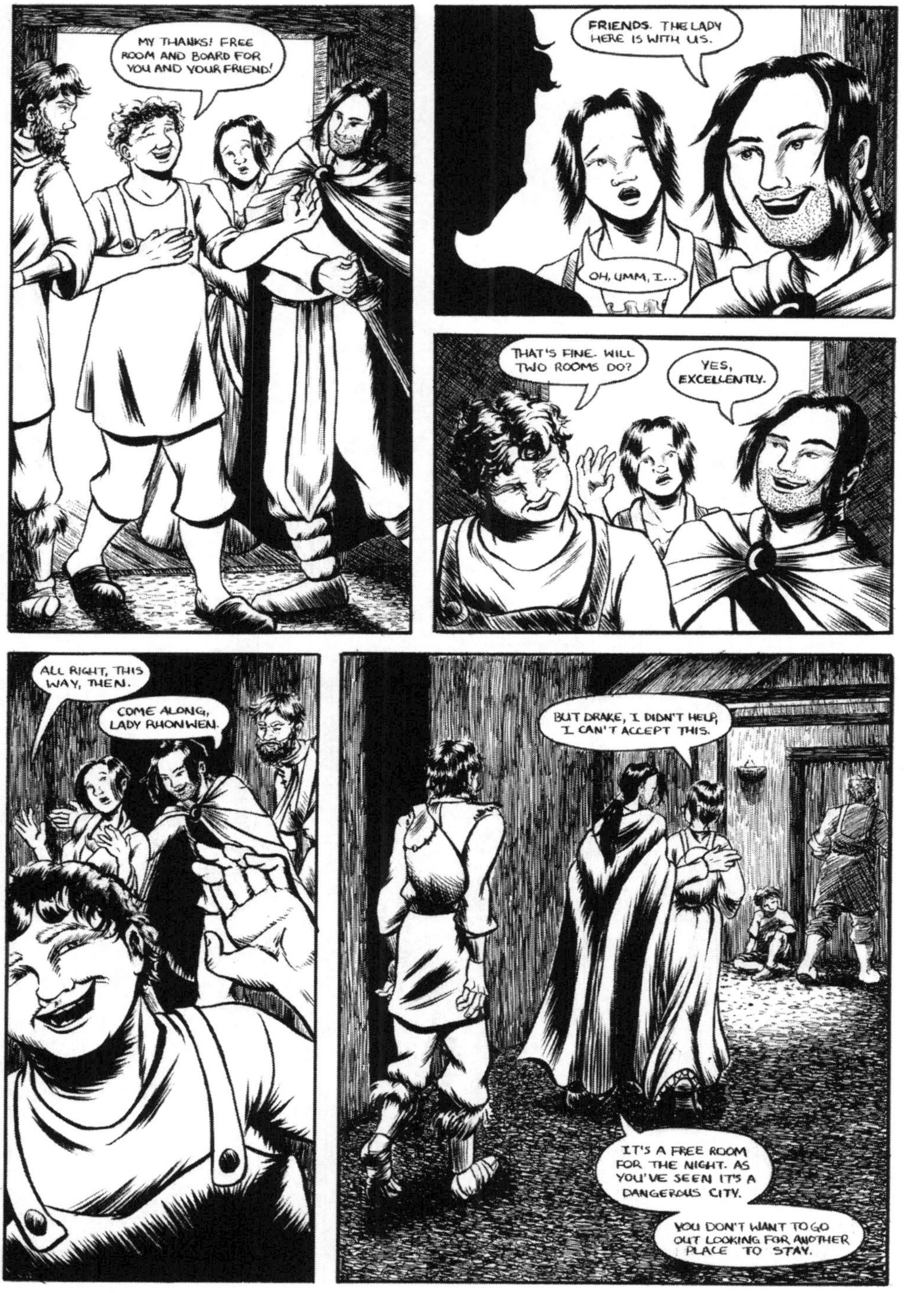
MY THANKS! FREE ROOM AND BOARD FOR YOU AND YOUR FRIEND!
FRIENDS. THE LADY HERE IS WITH US.
OH, UMM, I...
THAT'S FINE. WILL TWO ROOMS DO?
YES, EXCELLENTLY.
ALL RIGHT, THIS WAY, THEN.
COME ALONG, LADY RHONWEN.
BUT DRAKE, I DIDN'T HELP, I CAN'T ACCEPT THIS.
IT'S A FREE ROOM FOR THE NIGHT. AS YOU'VE SEEN IT'S A DANGEROUS CITY.
YOU DON'T WANT TO GO OUT LOOKING FOR ANOTHER PLACE TO STAY.

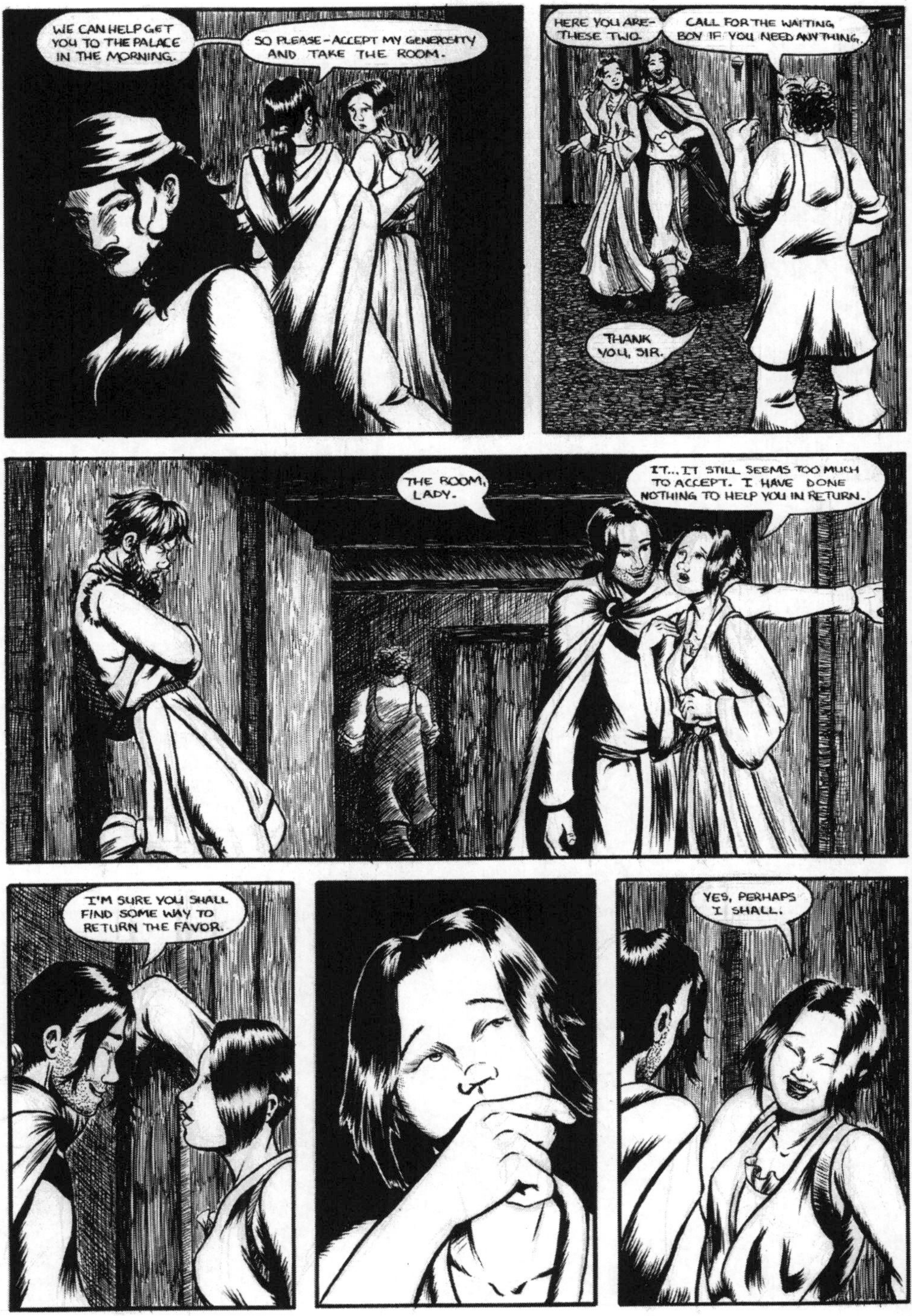
WE CAN HELP GET YOU TO THE PALACE IN THE MORNING.
SO PLEASE - ACCEPT MY GENEROSITY AND TAKE THE ROOM.
HERE YOU ARE - THESE TWO.
CALL FOR THE WAITING BOY IF YOU NEED ANYTHING.
THANK YOU, SIR.
THE ROOM, LADY.
IT... IT STILL SEEMS TOO MUCH TO ACCEPT. I HAVE DONE NOTHING TO HELP YOU IN RETURN.
I'M SURE YOU SHALL FIND SOME WAY TO RETURN THE FAVOR.
YES, PERHAPS I SHALL.

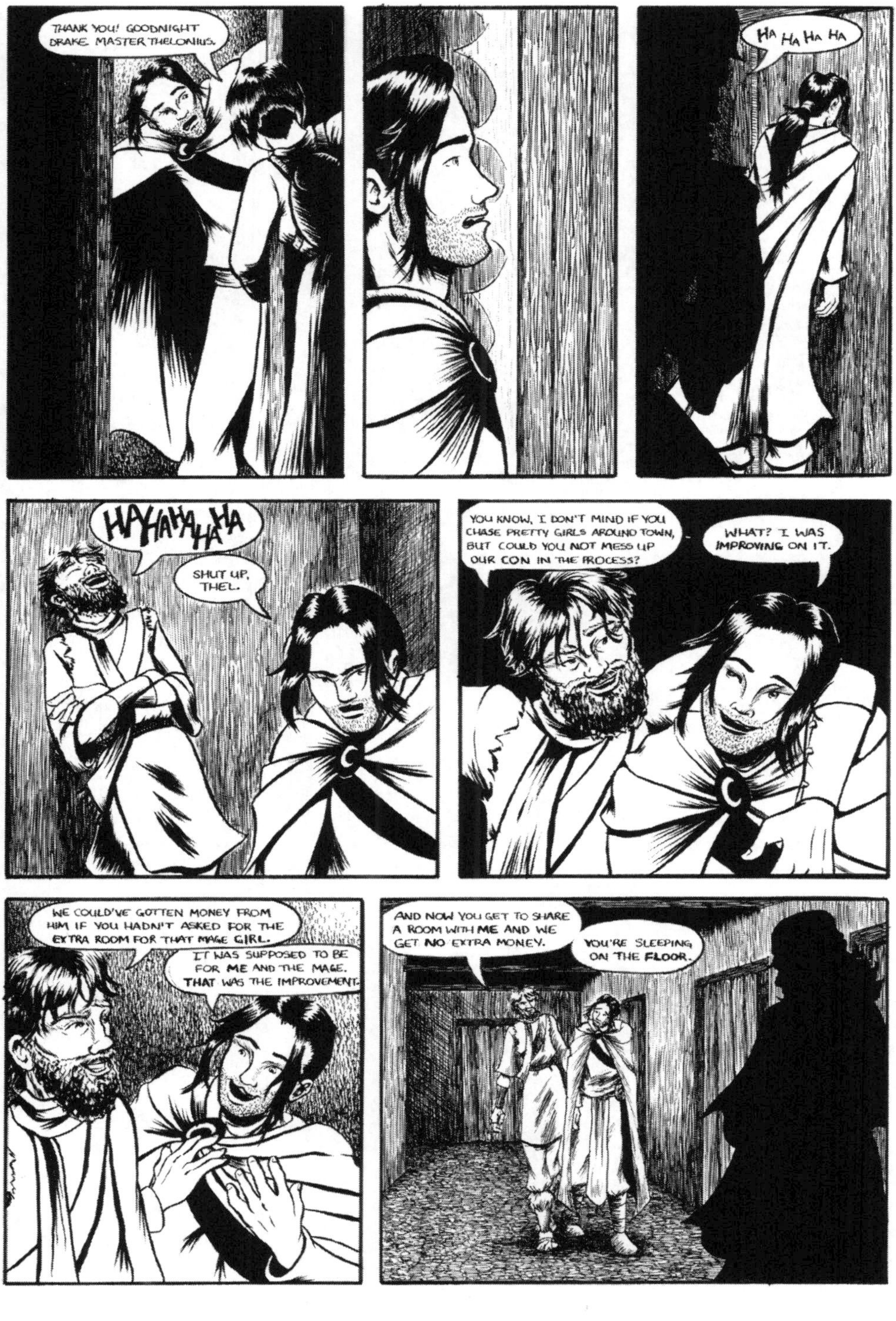
THANK YOU! GOODNIGHT DRAKE. MASTER THELONIUS.
HA HA HA HA
HAHAHAHAHA
SHUT UP, THEL.
YOU KNOW, I DON'T MIND IF YOU CHASE PRETTY GIRLS AROUND TOWN, BUT COULD YOU NOT MESS UP OUR CON IN THE PROCESS?
WHAT? I WAS IMPROVING ON IT.
WE COULD'VE GOTTEN MONEY FROM HIM IF YOU HADN'T ASKED FOR THE EXTRA ROOM FOR THAT MAGE GIRL.
IT WAS SUPPOSED TO BE FOR ME AND THE MAGE. THAT WAS THE IMPROVEMENT.
AND NOW YOU GET TO SHARE A ROOM WITH ME AND WE GET NO EXTRA MONEY.
YOU'RE SLEEPING ON THE FLOOR.

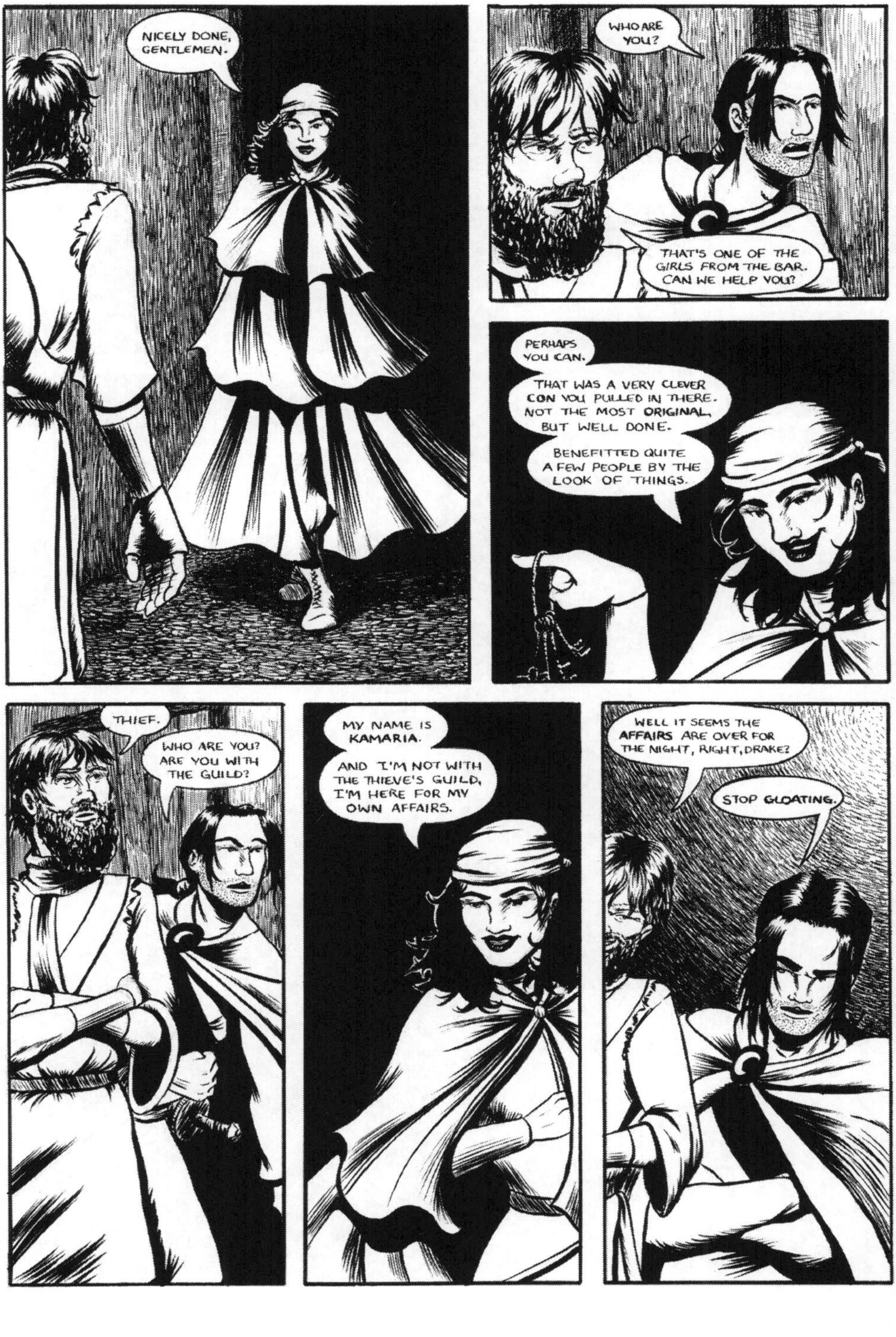
NICELY DONE, GENTLEMEN.
WHO ARE YOU?
THAT'S ONE OF THE GIRLS FROM THE BAR. CAN WE HELP YOU?
PERHAPS YOU CAN.
THAT WAS A VERY CLEVER CON YOU PULLED IN THERE. NOT THE MOST ORIGINAL, BUT WELL DONE.
BENEFITTED QUITE A FEW PEOPLE BY THE LOOK OF THINGS.
THIEF.
WHO ARE YOU? ARE YOU WITH THE GUILD?
MY NAME IS KAMARIA.
AND I'M NOT WITH THE THIEVE'S GUILD, I'M HERE FOR MY OWN AFFAIRS.
WELL IT SEEMS THE AFFAIRS ARE OVER FOR THE NIGHT, RIGHT, DRAKE?
STOP GLOATING.

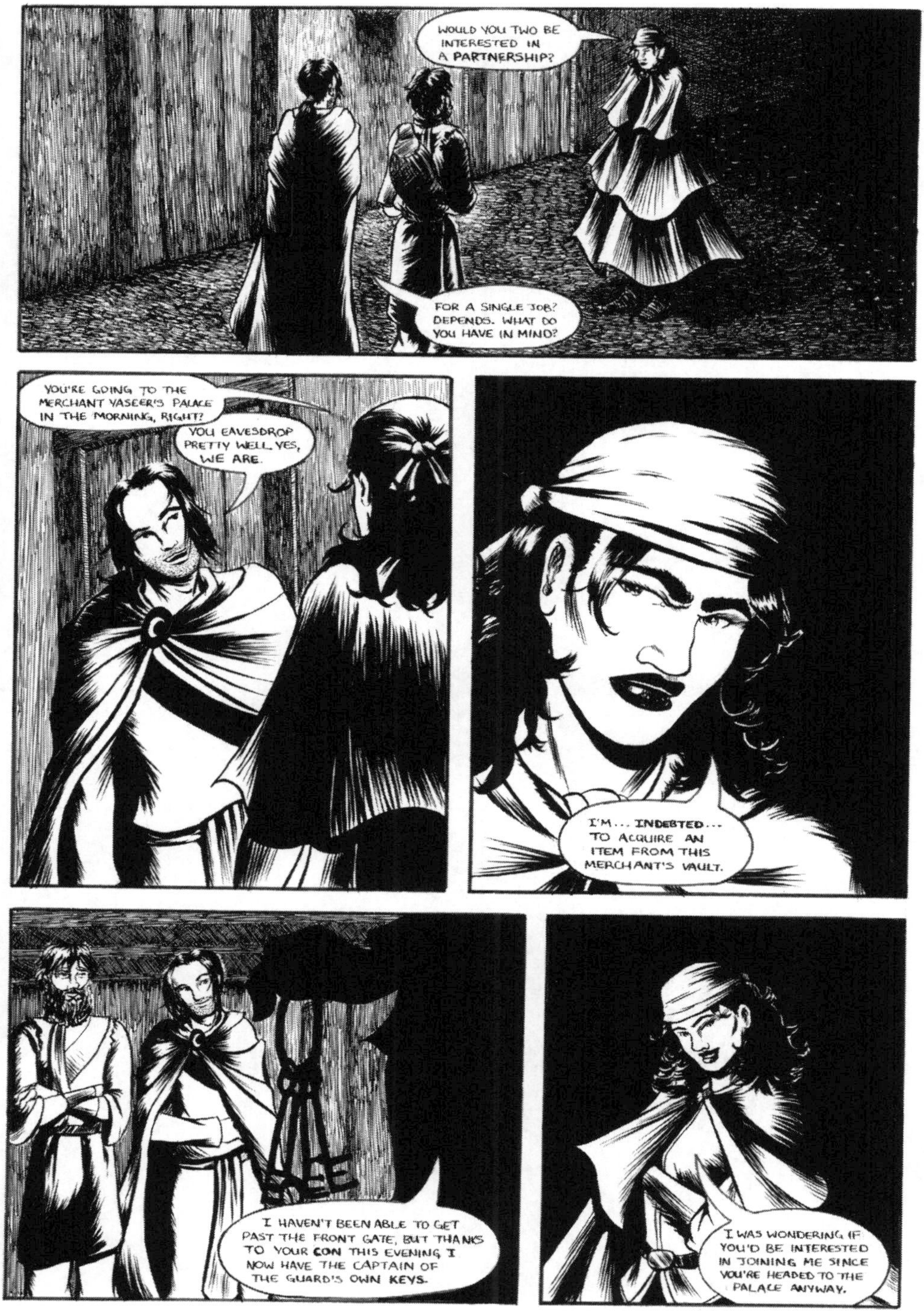
WOULD YOU TWO BE INTERESTED IN A PARTNERSHIP?
FOR A SINGLE JOB? DEPENDS. WHAT DO YOU HAVE IN MIND?
YOU'RE GOING TO THE MERCHANT YASEER'S PALACE IN THE MORNING, RIGHT?
YOU EAVESDROP PRETTY WELL. YES, WE ARE.
I'M... INDEBTED... TO ACQUIRE AN ITEM FROM THIS MERCHANT'S VAULT.
I HAVEN'T BEEN ABLE TO GET PAST THE FRONT GATE, BUT THANKS TO YOUR CON THIS EVENING I NOW HAVE THE CAPTAIN OF THE GUARD'S OWN KEYS.
I WAS WONDERING IF YOU'D BE INTERESTED IN JOINING ME SINCE YOU'RE HEADED TO THE PALACE ANYWAY.

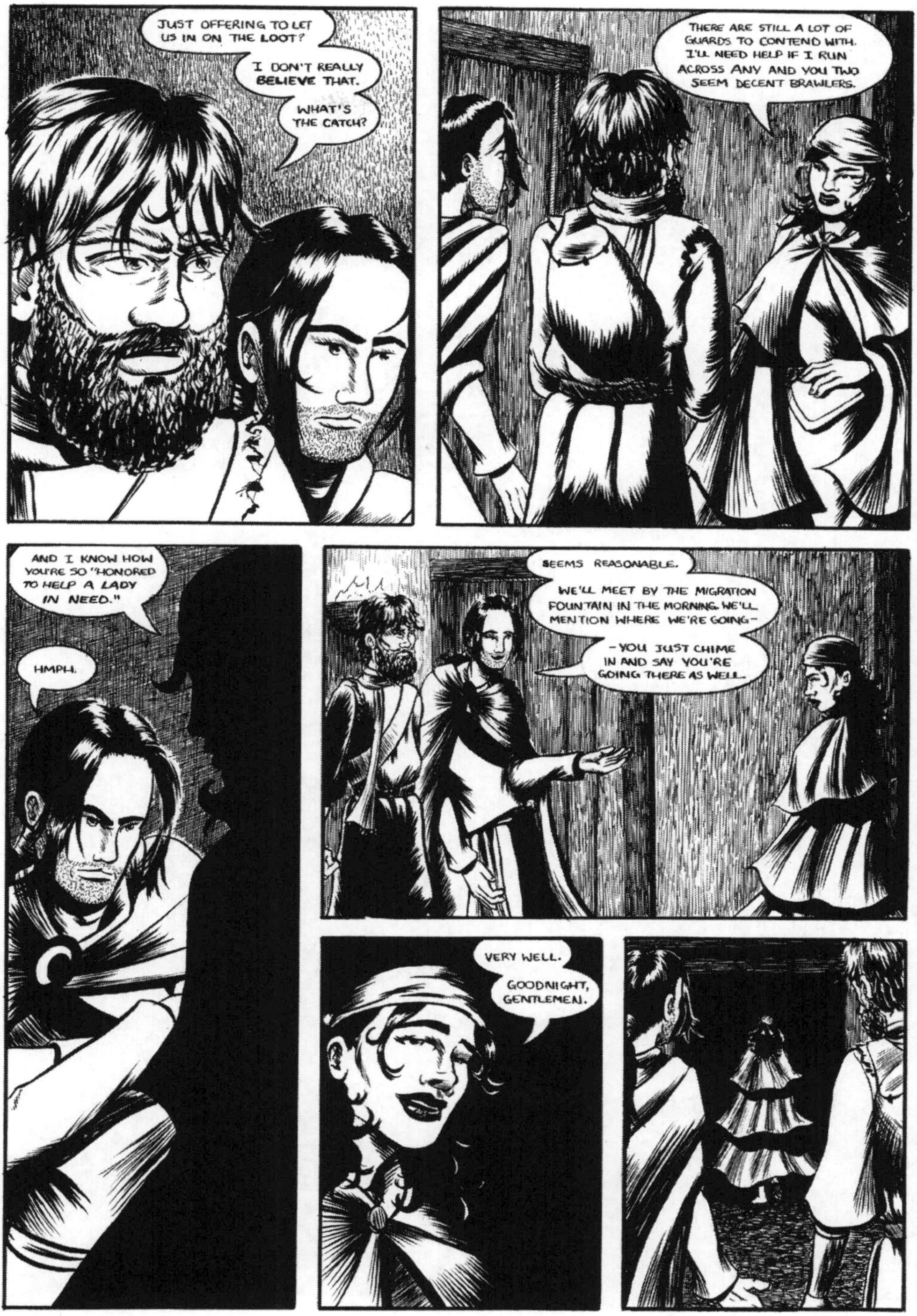
JUST OFFERING TO LET US IN ON THE LOOT?
I DON'T REALLY BELIEVE THAT.
WHAT'S THE CATCH?
THERE ARE STILL A LOT OF GUARDS TO CONTEND WITH. I'LL NEED HELP IF I RUN ACROSS ANY AND YOU TWO SEEM DECENT BRAWLERS.
AND I KNOW HOW YOU'RE SO "HONORED TO HELP A LADY IN NEED."
HMPH.
SEEMS REASONABLE.
WE'LL MEET BY THE MIGRATION FOUNTAIN IN THE MORNING. WE'LL MENTION WHERE WE'RE GOING—
—YOU JUST CHIME IN AND SAY YOU'RE GOING THERE AS WELL.
VERY WELL.
GOODNIGHT, GENTLEMEN.

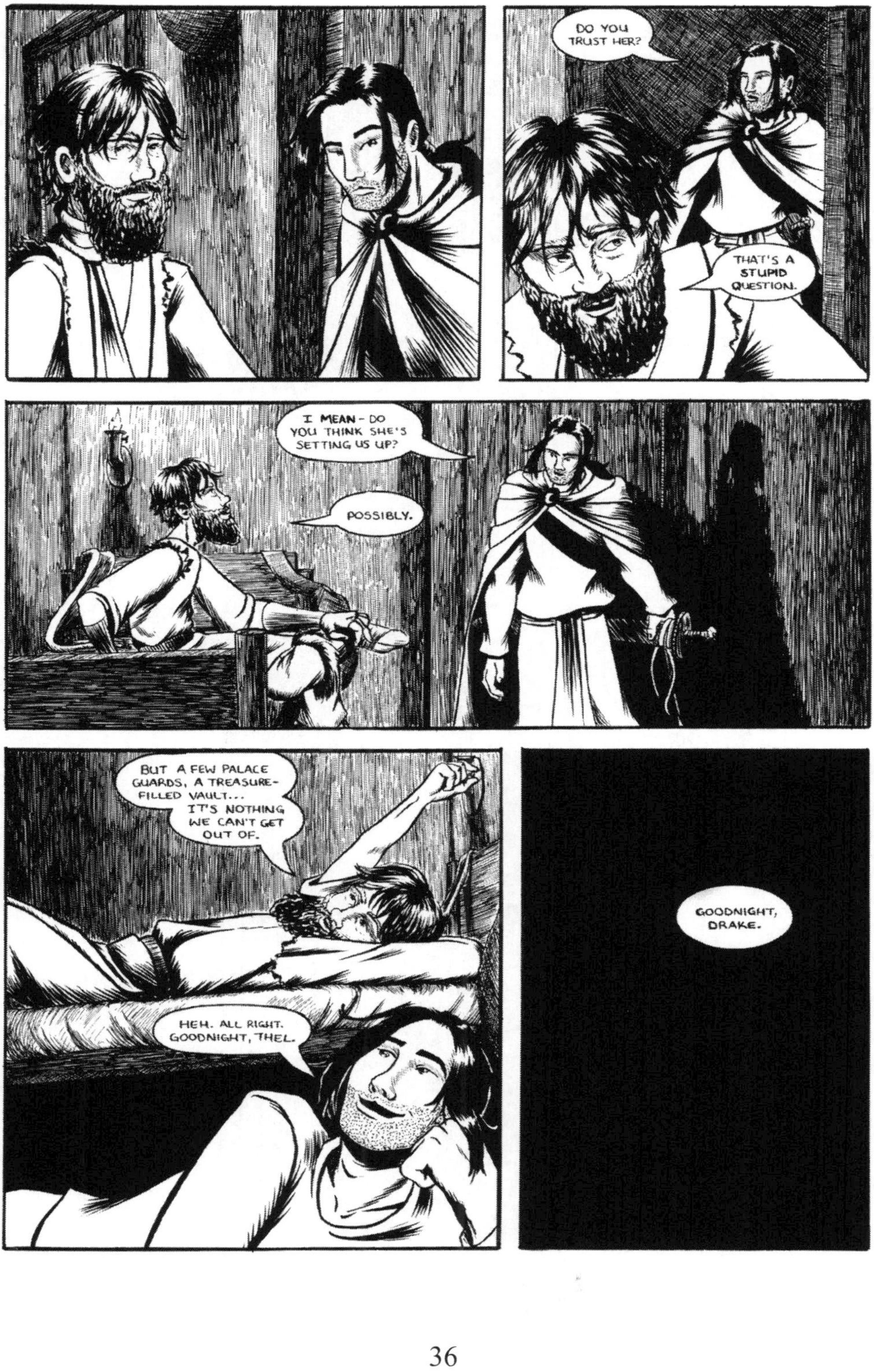
DO YOU TRUST HER?
THAT'S A STUPID QUESTION.
I MEAN - DO YOU THINK SHE'S SETTING US UP?
POSSIBLY.
BUT A FEW PALACE GUARDS, A TREASURE-FILLED VAULT...
IT'S NOTHING WE CAN'T GET OUT OF.
HEH. ALL RIGHT. GOODNIGHT, THEL.
GOODNIGHT, DRAKE.

CHAPTER II

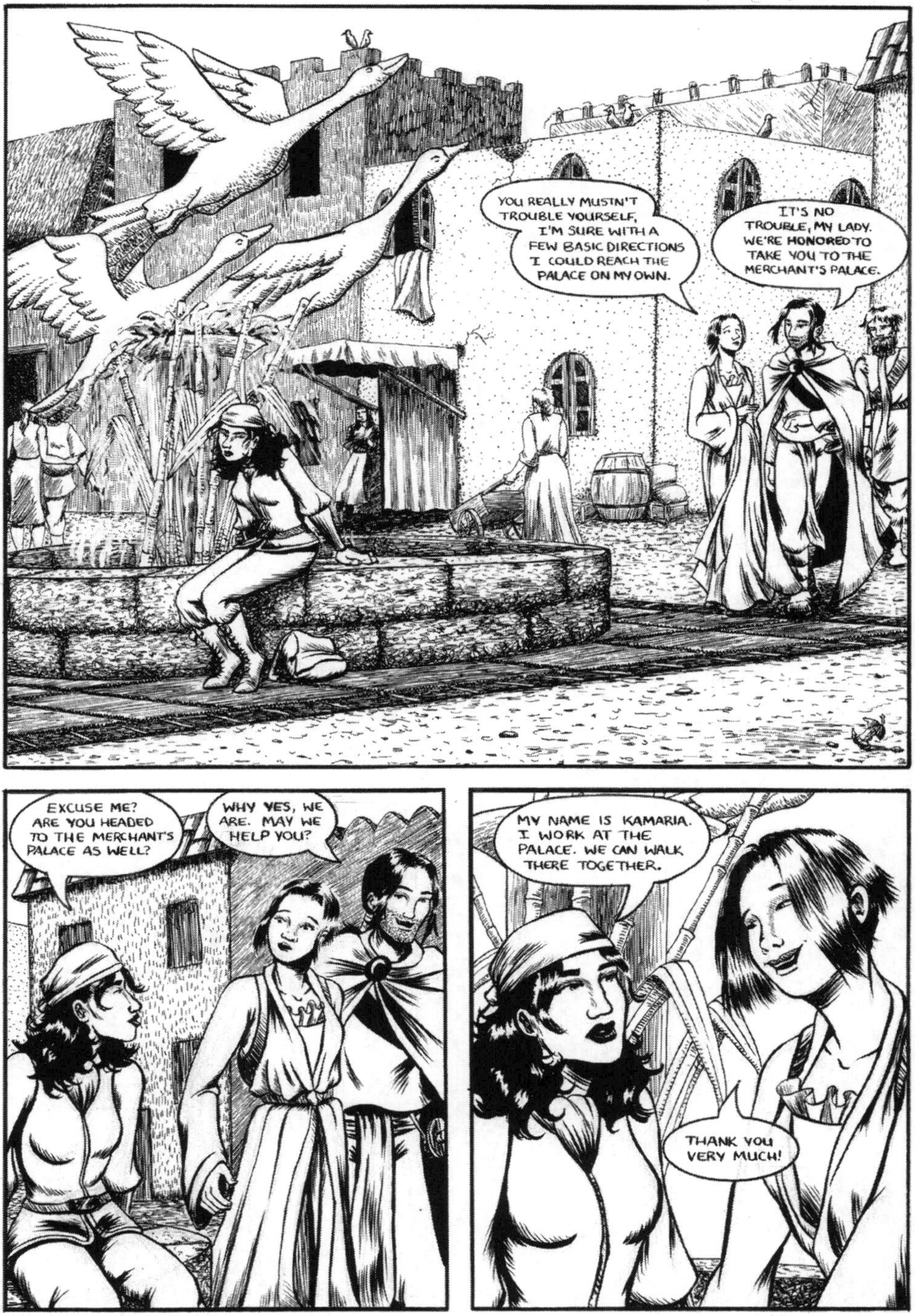
YOU REALLY MUSTN'T TROUBLE YOURSELF, I'M SURE WITH A FEW BASIC DIRECTIONS I COULD REACH THE PALACE ON MY OWN.
IT'S NO TROUBLE, MY LADY. WE'RE HONORED TO TAKE YOU TO THE MERCHANT'S PALACE.
EXCUSE ME? ARE YOU HEADED TO THE MERCHANT'S PALACE AS WELL?
WHY YES, WE ARE. MAY WE HELP YOU?
MY NAME IS KAMARIA. I WORK AT THE PALACE. WE CAN WALK THERE TOGETHER.
THANK YOU VERY MUCH!

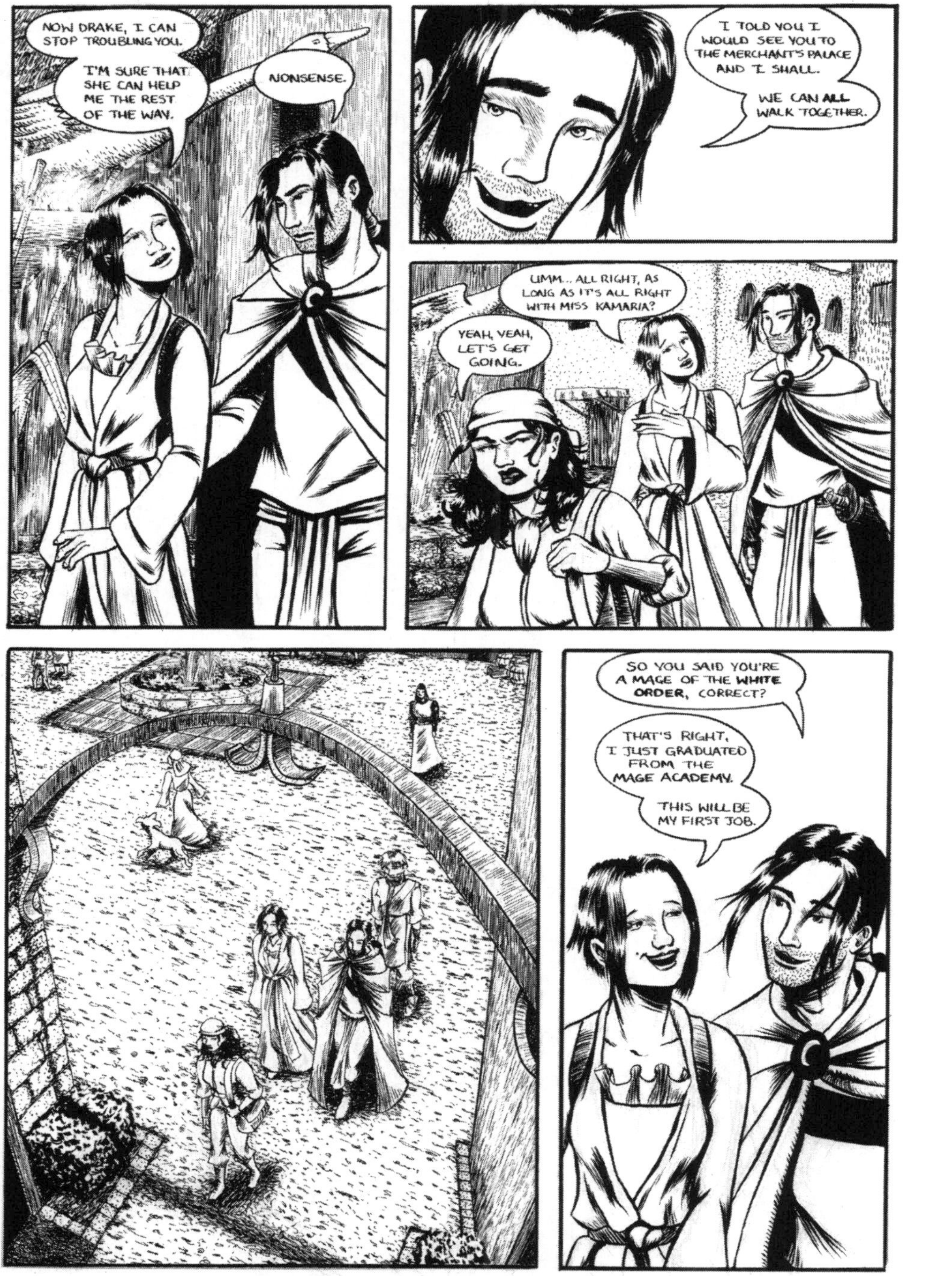
NOW DRAKE, I CAN STOP TROUBLING YOU.
I'M SURE THAT SHE CAN HELP ME THE REST OF THE WAY.
NONSENSE.
I TOLD YOU I WOULD SEE YOU TO THE MERCHANT'S PALACE AND I SHALL.
WE CAN **ALL** WALK TOGETHER.
UMM... ALL RIGHT, AS LONG AS IT'S ALL RIGHT WITH MISS KAMARIA?
YEAH, YEAH, LET'S GET GOING.
SO YOU SAID YOU'RE **A MAGE OF THE WHITE ORDER**, CORRECT?
THAT'S RIGHT, I JUST GRADUATED FROM THE **MAGE ACADEMY**.
THIS WILL BE MY FIRST JOB.

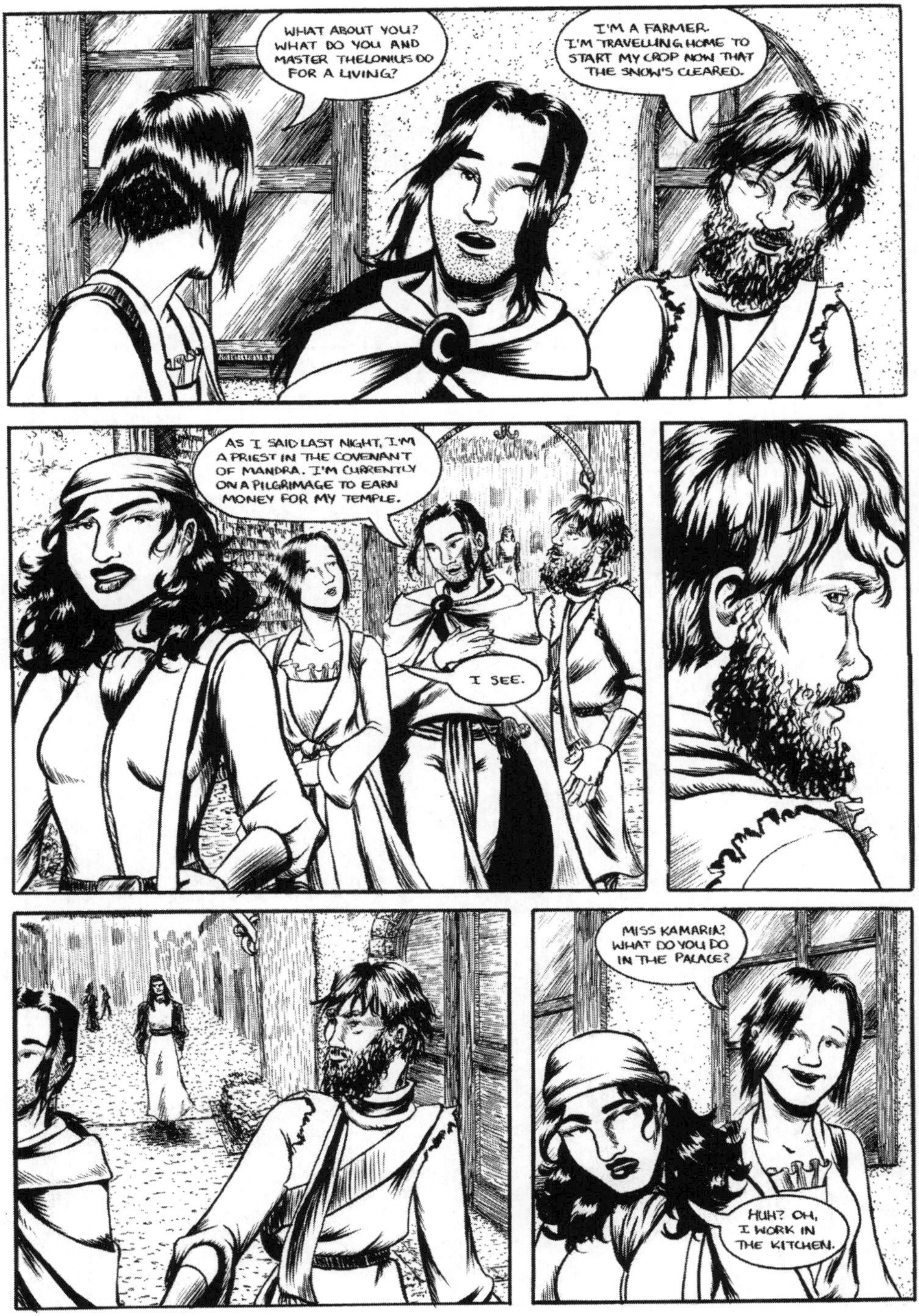
WHAT ABOUT YOU? WHAT DO YOU AND MASTER THELONIUS DO FOR A LIVING?
I'M A FARMER. I'M TRAVELLING HOME TO START MY CROP NOW THAT THE SNOW'S CLEARED.
AS I SAID LAST NIGHT, I'M A PRIEST IN THE COVENANT OF MANDRA. I'M CURRENTLY ON A PILGRIMAGE TO EARN MONEY FOR MY TEMPLE.
I SEE.
MISS KAMARIA? WHAT DO YOU DO IN THE PALACE?
HUH? OH, I WORK IN THE KITCHEN.

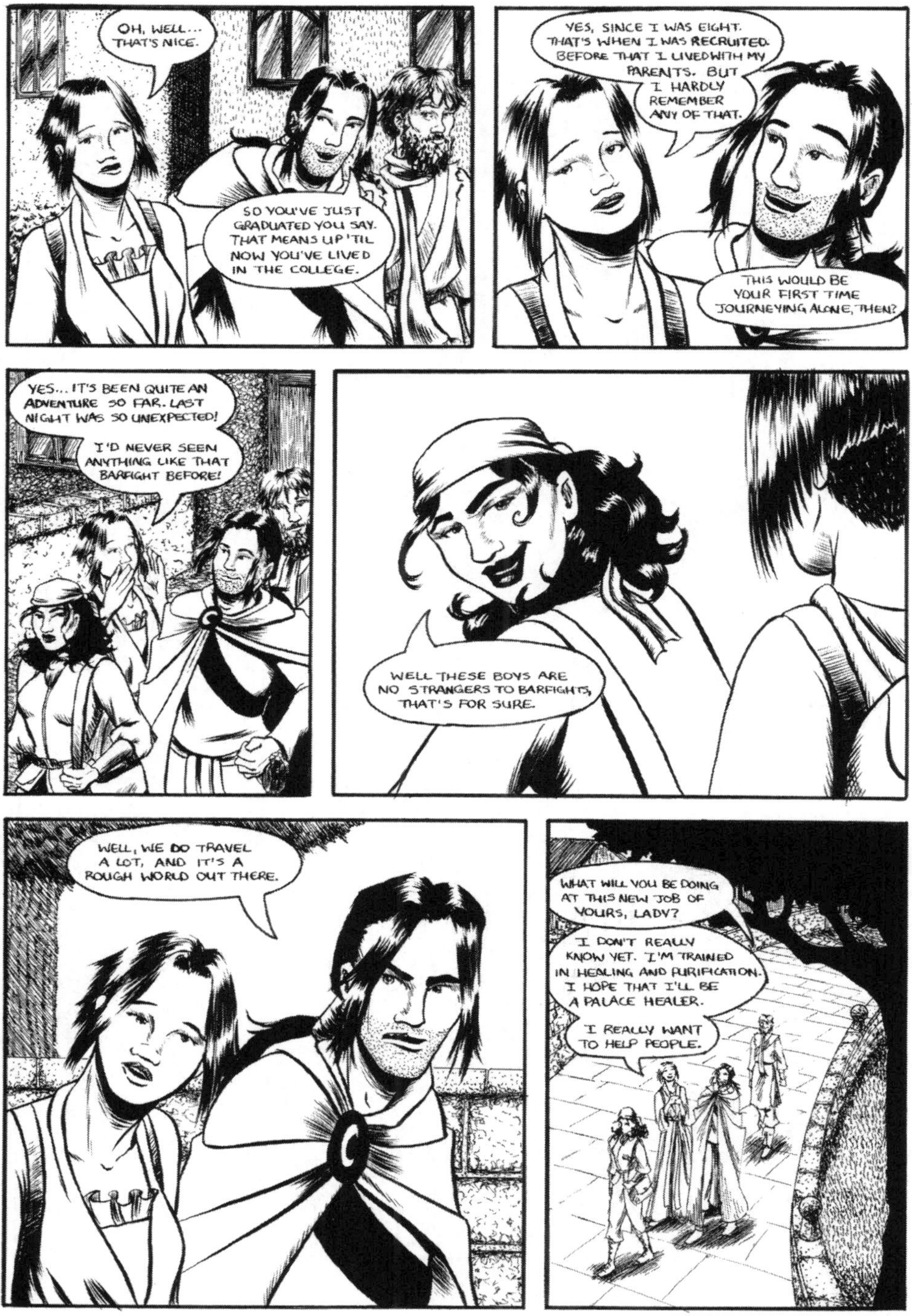
OH, WELL... THAT'S NICE.
SO YOU'VE JUST GRADUATED YOU SAY. THAT MEANS UP 'TIL NOW YOU'VE LIVED IN THE COLLEGE.
YES, SINCE I WAS EIGHT. THAT'S WHEN I WAS RECRUITED. BEFORE THAT I LIVED WITH MY PARENTS. BUT I HARDLY REMEMBER ANY OF THAT.
THIS WOULD BE YOUR FIRST TIME JOURNEYING ALONE, THEN?
YES... IT'S BEEN QUITE AN ADVENTURE SO FAR. LAST NIGHT WAS SO UNEXPECTED!
I'D NEVER SEEN ANYTHING LIKE THAT BARFIGHT BEFORE!
WELL THESE BOYS ARE NO STRANGERS TO BARFIGHTS, THAT'S FOR SURE.
WELL, WE DO TRAVEL A LOT, AND IT'S A ROUGH WORLD OUT THERE.
WHAT WILL YOU BE DOING AT THIS NEW JOB OF YOURS, LADY?
I DON'T REALLY KNOW YET. I'M TRAINED IN HEALING AND PURIFICATION. I HOPE THAT I'LL BE A PALACE HEALER.
I REALLY WANT TO HELP PEOPLE.

SO A RICH MERCHANT GETS HIS OWN MAGE FOR WHENEVER HE HAS A STOMACHACHE WHILE THE POOR ARE LEFT TO GROW ILL AND DIE UNATTENDED.

WONDERFUL NEW SOCIETY THE MAGES HAVE PLANNED FOR US.

I, UH —

YOU DON'T HAVE TO ANSWER TO HER, RHONWEN.

A LOT OF PEOPLE ARE BITTER ABOUT THEIR LIVES AND LIKE TO BLAME OTHERS FOR IT.

THE MAGES ARE JUST A POPULAR TARGET RIGHT NOW.

HERE'S THE MAIN GATE.

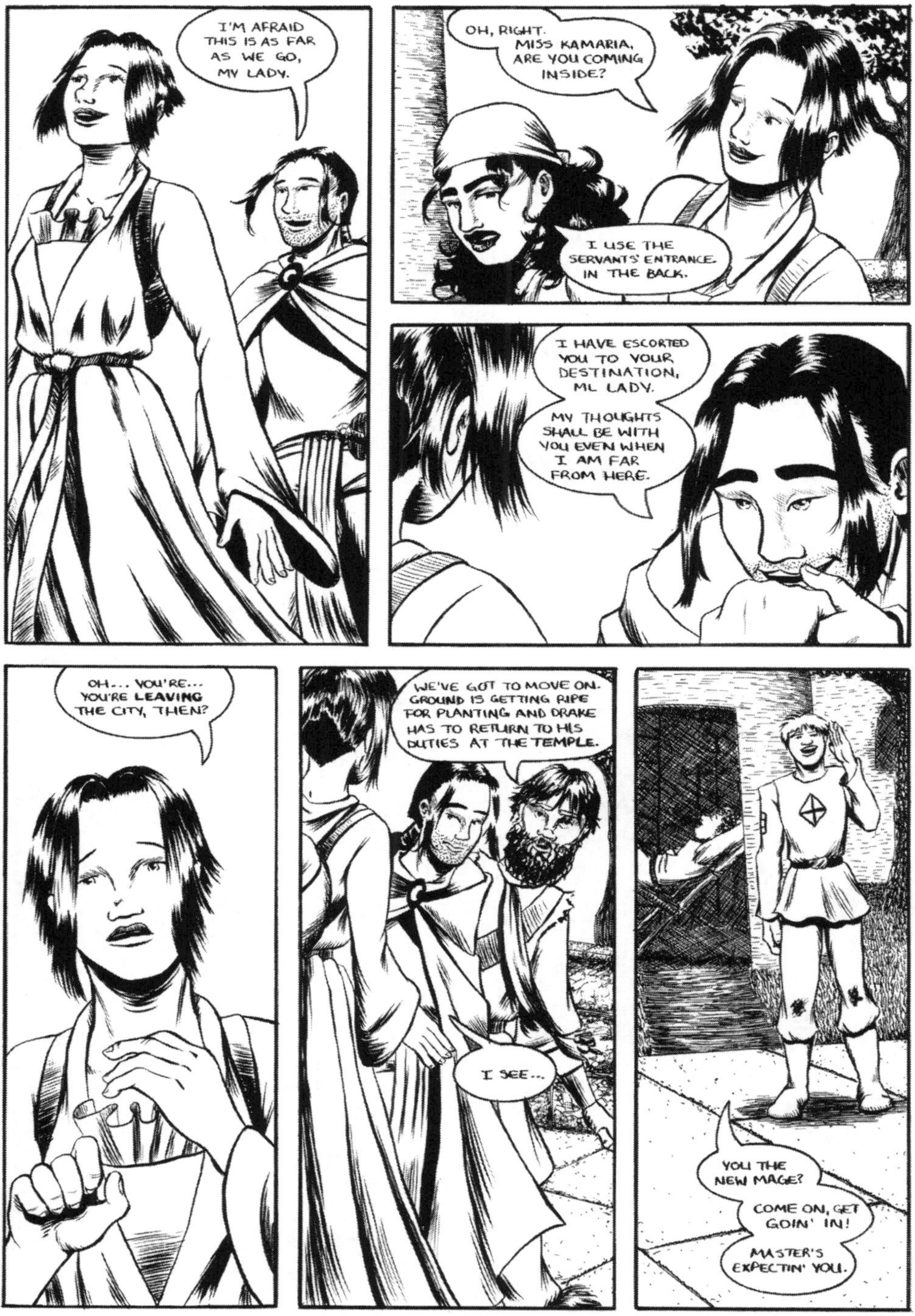
I'M AFRAID THIS IS AS FAR AS WE GO, MY LADY.
OH, RIGHT. MISS KAMARIA, ARE YOU COMING INSIDE?
I USE THE SERVANTS' ENTRANCE IN THE BACK.
I HAVE ESCORTED YOU TO YOUR DESTINATION, ML LADY.
MY THOUGHTS SHALL BE WITH YOU EVEN WHEN I AM FAR FROM HERE.
OH... YOU'RE... YOU'RE **LEAVING** THE CITY, THEN?
WE'VE GOT TO MOVE ON. GROUND IS GETTING RIPE FOR PLANTING AND DRAKE HAS TO RETURN TO HIS DUTIES AT THE **TEMPLE**.
I SEE...
YOU THE NEW MAGE?
COME ON, GET GOIN' IN!
MASTER'S EXPECTIN' YOU.

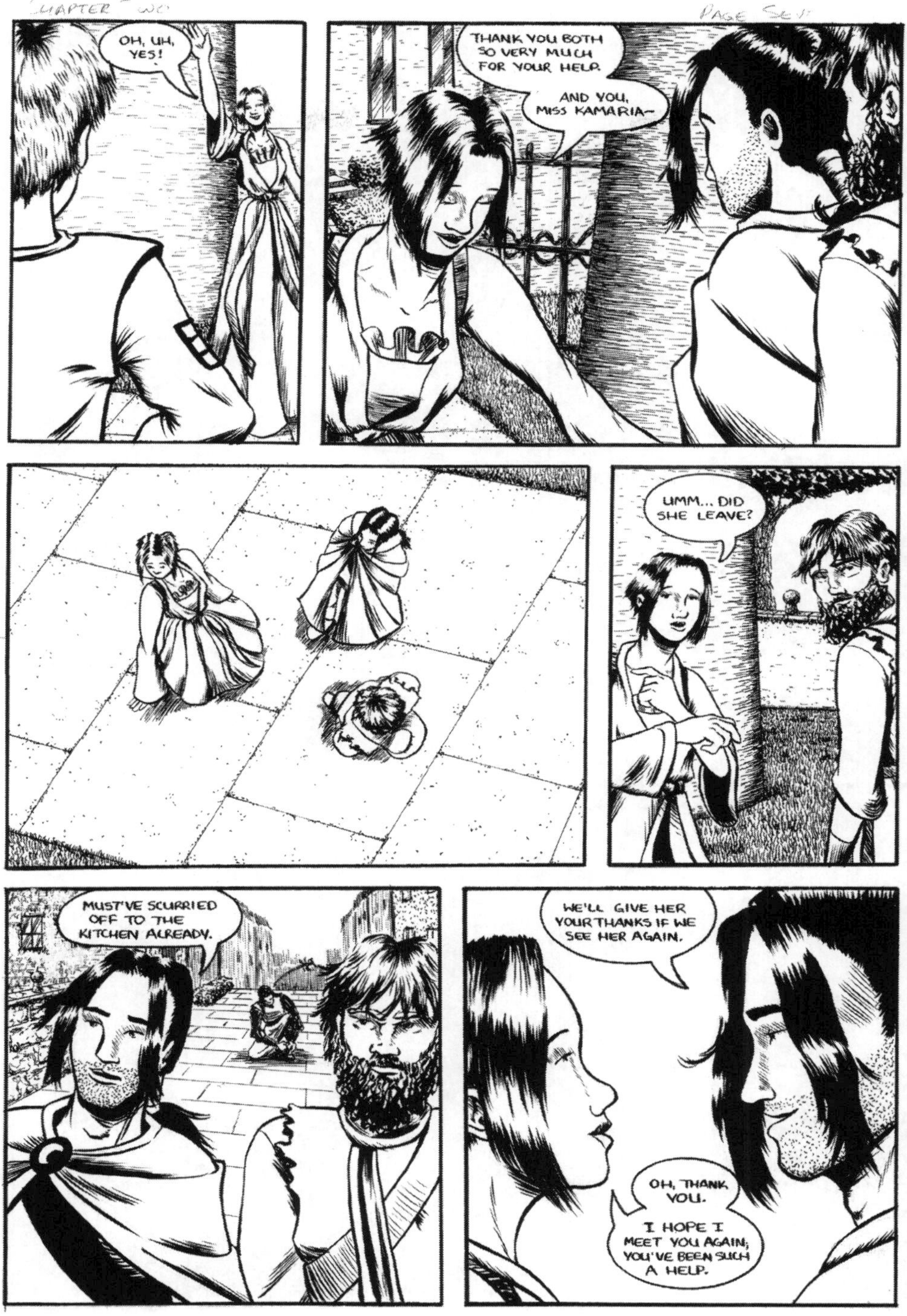
OH, UH, YES!
THANK YOU BOTH SO VERY MUCH FOR YOUR HELP.
AND YOU, MISS KAMARIA~
UMM... DID SHE LEAVE?
MUST'VE SCURRIED OFF TO THE KITCHEN ALREADY.
WE'LL GIVE HER YOUR THANKS IF WE SEE HER AGAIN.
OH, THANK YOU.
I HOPE I MEET YOU AGAIN; YOU'VE BEEN SUCH A HELP.

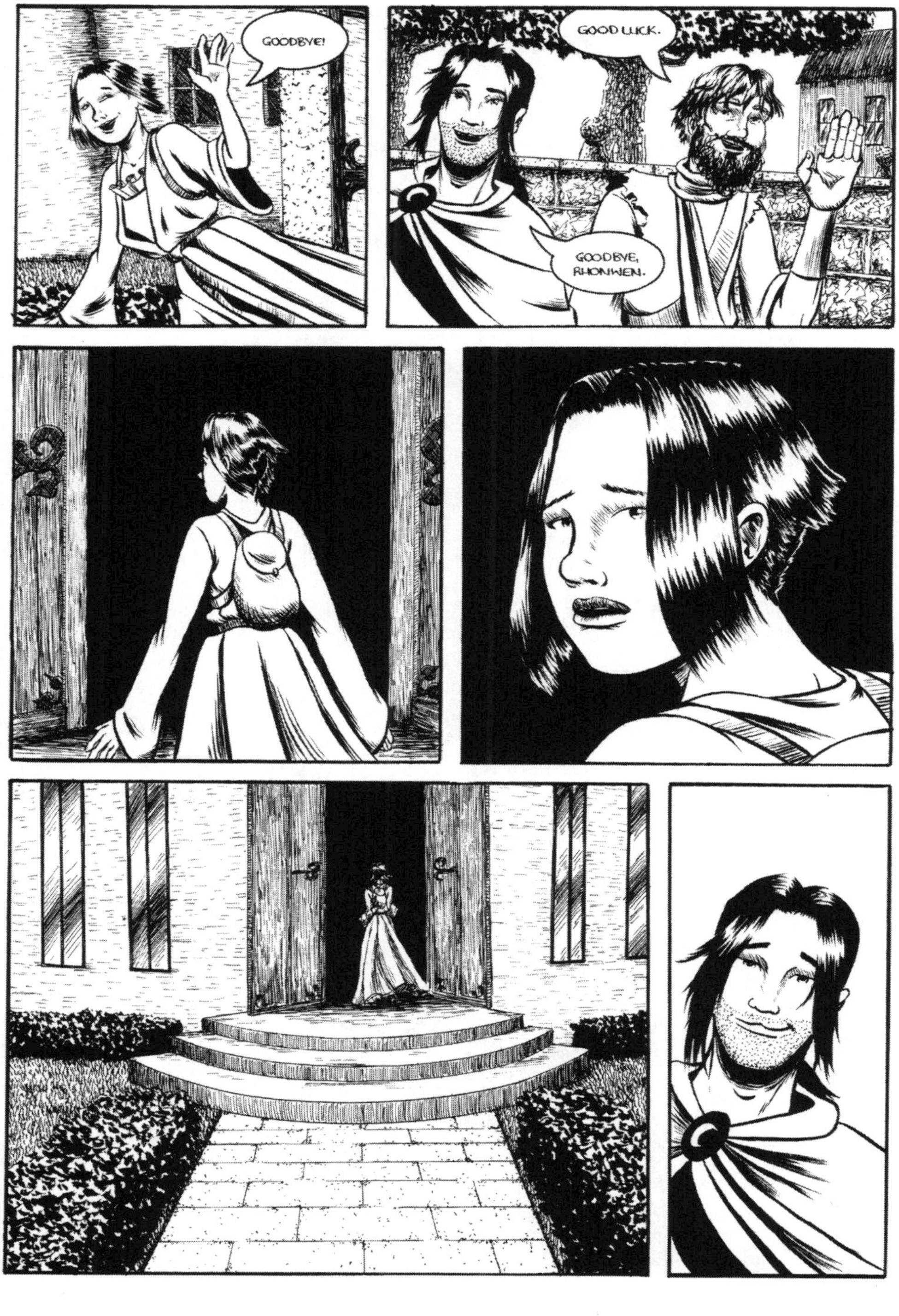
GOODBYE!
GOOD LUCK.
GOODBYE, RHONWEN.

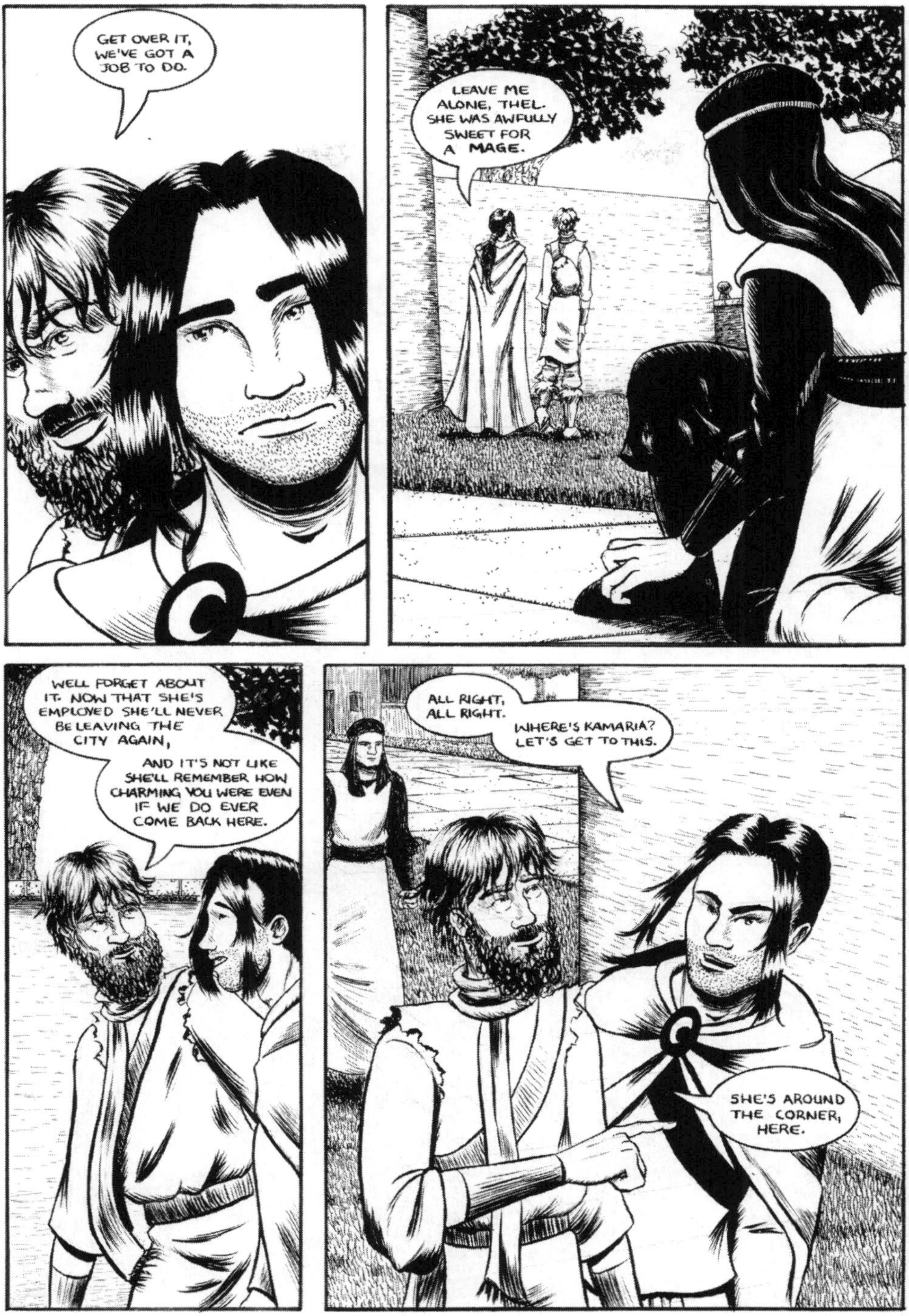
GET OVER IT, WE'VE GOT A JOB TO DO.
LEAVE ME ALONE, THEL. SHE WAS AWFULLY SWEET FOR A MAGE.
WELL FORGET ABOUT IT. NOW THAT SHE'S EMPLOYED SHE'LL NEVER BE LEAVING THE CITY AGAIN,
AND IT'S NOT LIKE SHE'LL REMEMBER HOW CHARMING YOU WERE EVEN IF WE DO EVER COME BACK HERE.
ALL RIGHT, ALL RIGHT.
WHERE'S KAMARIA? LET'S GET TO THIS.
SHE'S AROUND THE CORNER, HERE.

WHAT TOOK YOU TWO SO LONG?
DRAKE HAD TO SAY GOODBYE TO HIS SWEETHEART.
LET'S GET THIS OVER WITH.
YOU GOT THE WAY IN?
YES, RIGHT THROUGH HERE.
I'M PRETTY SURE THIS IS THE KEY FOR IT...
HERE WE GO, GENTLEMEN.

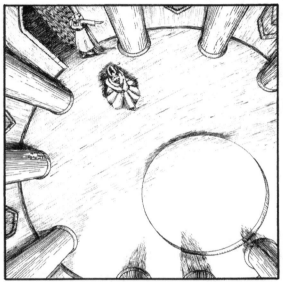

WE REALLY MUST HURRY. MY GUESTS ARE WAITING.

BIGGEST PARTY I'VE THROWN THIS YEAR.

YOU MUST BE THE MAGE RHONWEN OF THE WHITE ORDER.

I'M GLAD TO HAVE YOU IN MY SERVICE.

THE HONOR IS MINE, MASTER YASEER.

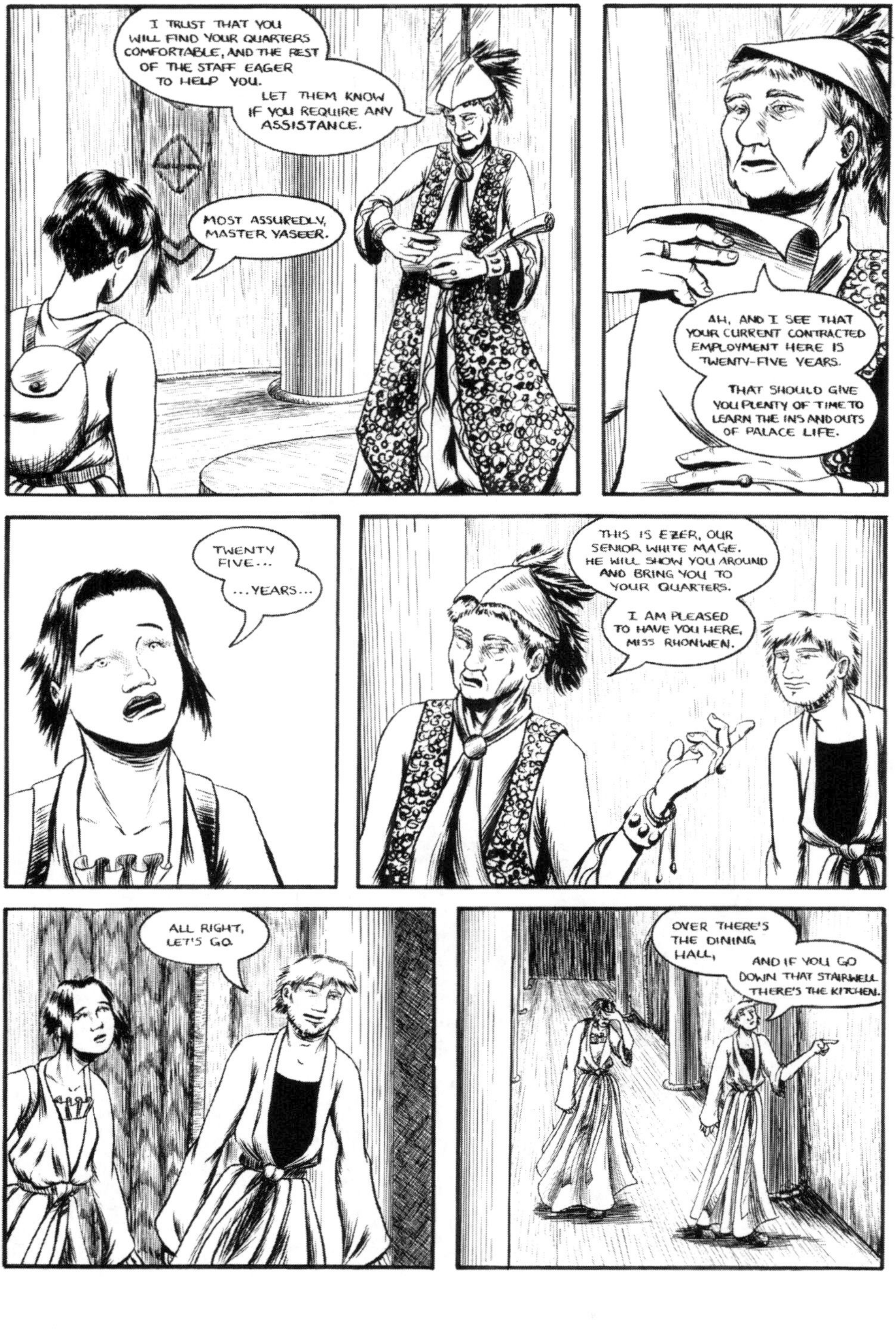
I TRUST THAT YOU WILL FIND YOUR QUARTERS COMFORTABLE, AND THE REST OF THE STAFF EAGER TO HELP YOU.
LET THEM KNOW IF YOU REQUIRE ANY ASSISTANCE.
MOST ASSUREDLY, MASTER YASEER.
AH, AND I SEE THAT YOUR CURRENT CONTRACTED EMPLOYMENT HERE IS TWENTY-FIVE YEARS.
THAT SHOULD GIVE YOU PLENTY OF TIME TO LEARN THE INS AND OUTS OF PALACE LIFE.
TWENTY FIVE...
...YEARS...
THIS IS EZER, OUR SENIOR WHITE MAGE. HE WILL SHOW YOU AROUND AND BRING YOU TO YOUR QUARTERS.
I AM PLEASED TO HAVE YOU HERE, MISS RHONWEN.
ALL RIGHT, LET'S GO.
OVER THERE'S THE DINING HALL,
AND IF YOU GO DOWN THAT STAIRWELL THERE'S THE KITCHEN.

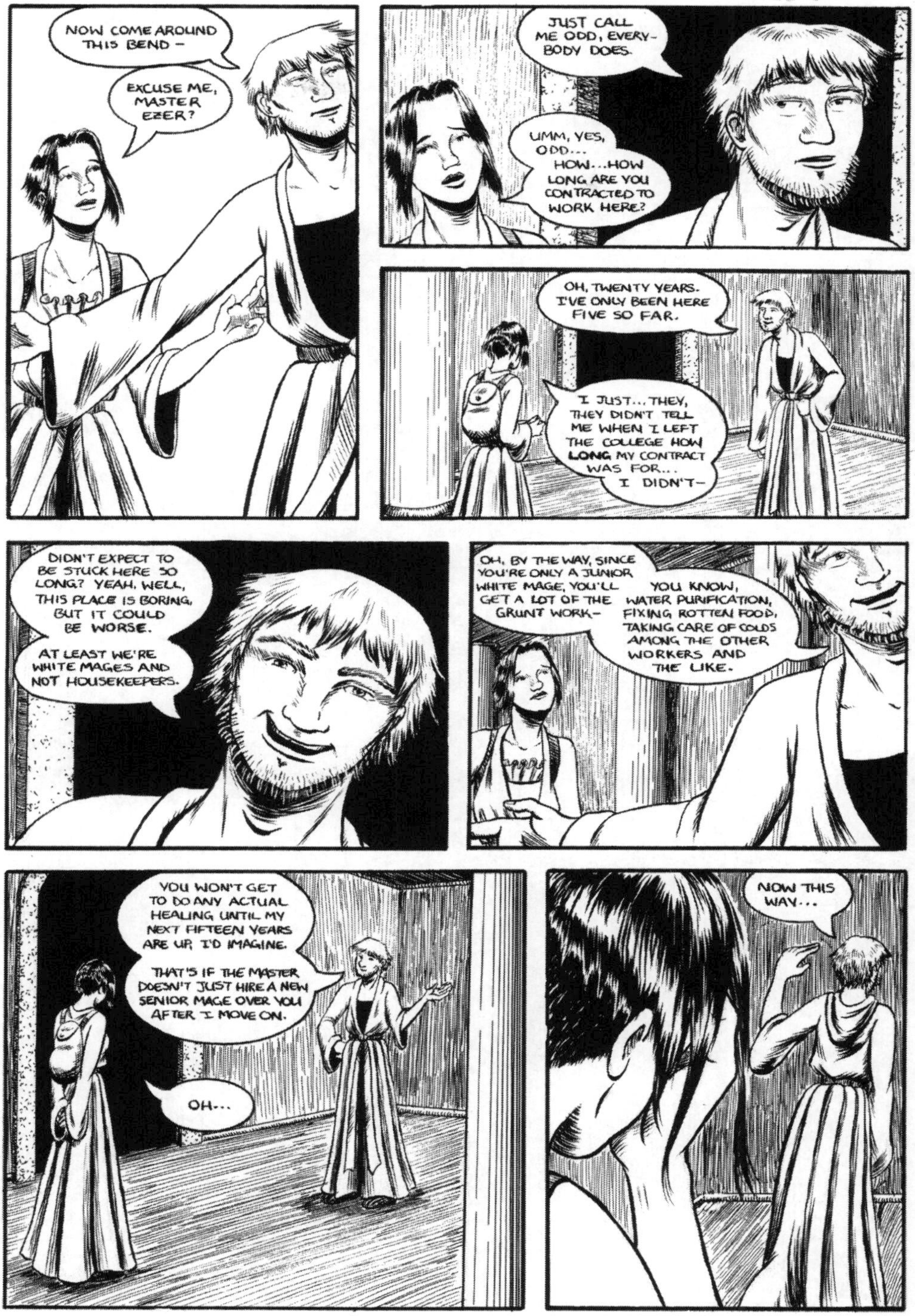
NOW COME AROUND THIS BEND—
EXCUSE ME, MASTER EZER?
JUST CALL ME ODD, EVERYBODY DOES.
UMM, YES, ODD... HOW...HOW LONG ARE YOU CONTRACTED TO WORK HERE?
OH, TWENTY YEARS. I'VE ONLY BEEN HERE FIVE SO FAR.
I JUST... THEY, THEY DIDN'T TELL ME WHEN I LEFT THE COLLEGE HOW LONG MY CONTRACT WAS FOR... I DIDN'T—
DIDN'T EXPECT TO BE STUCK HERE SO LONG? YEAH, WELL, THIS PLACE IS BORING, BUT IT COULD BE WORSE.
AT LEAST WE'RE WHITE MAGES AND NOT HOUSEKEEPERS.
OH, BY THE WAY, SINCE YOU'RE ONLY A JUNIOR WHITE MAGE, YOU'LL GET A LOT OF THE GRUNT WORK—
YOU KNOW, WATER PURIFICATION, FIXING ROTTEN FOOD, TAKING CARE OF COLDS AMONG THE OTHER WORKERS AND THE LIKE.
YOU WON'T GET TO DO ANY ACTUAL HEALING UNTIL MY NEXT FIFTEEN YEARS ARE UP, I'D IMAGINE.
THAT'S IF THE MASTER DOESN'T JUST HIRE A NEW SENIOR MAGE OVER YOU AFTER I MOVE ON.
OH...
NOW THIS WAY...

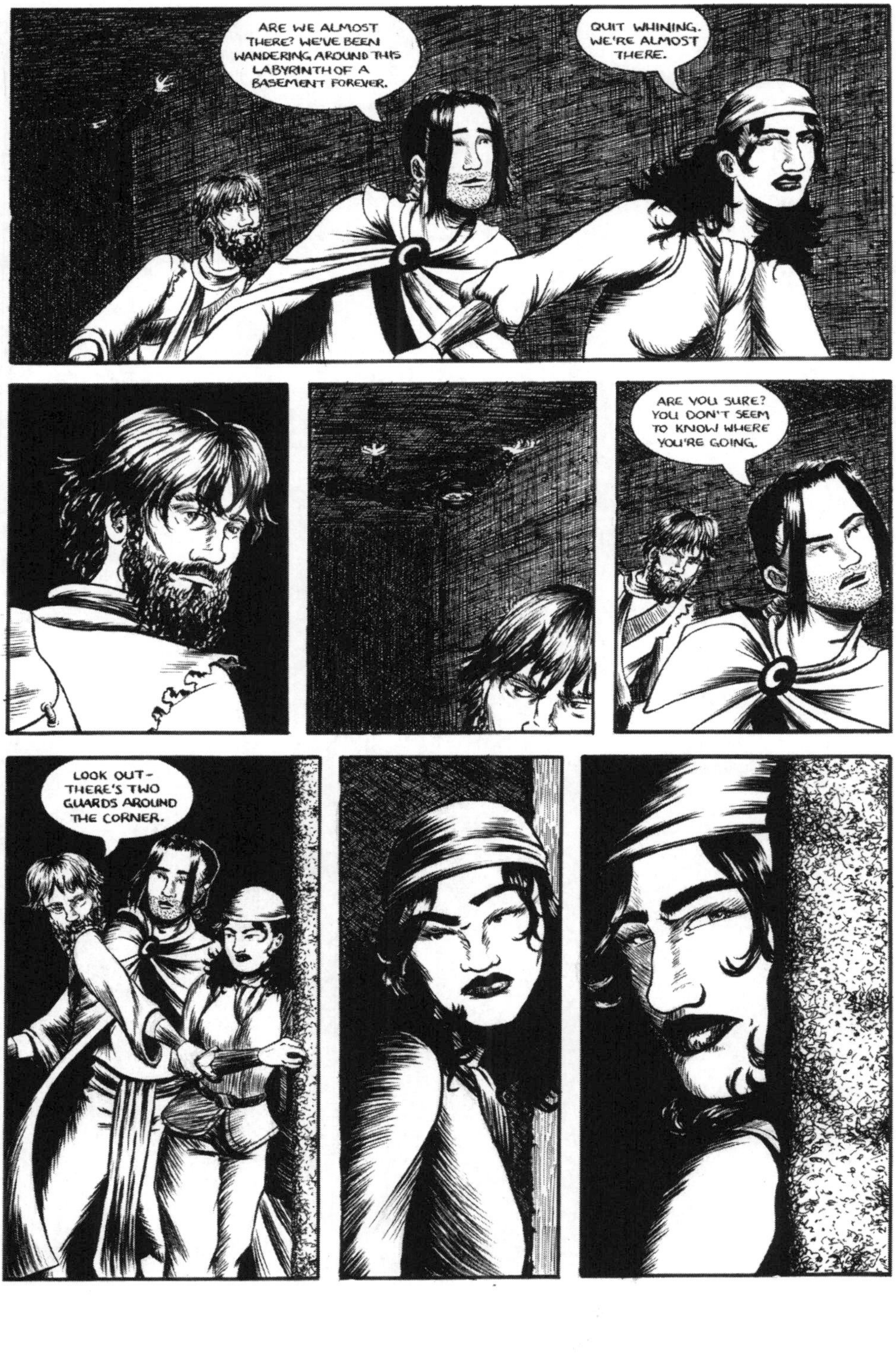
ARE WE ALMOST THERE? WE'VE BEEN WANDERING AROUND THIS LABYRINTH OF A BASEMENT FOREVER.
QUIT WHINING. WE'RE ALMOST THERE.
ARE YOU SURE? YOU DON'T SEEM TO KNOW WHERE YOU'RE GOING.
LOOK OUT- THERE'S TWO GUARDS AROUND THE CORNER.

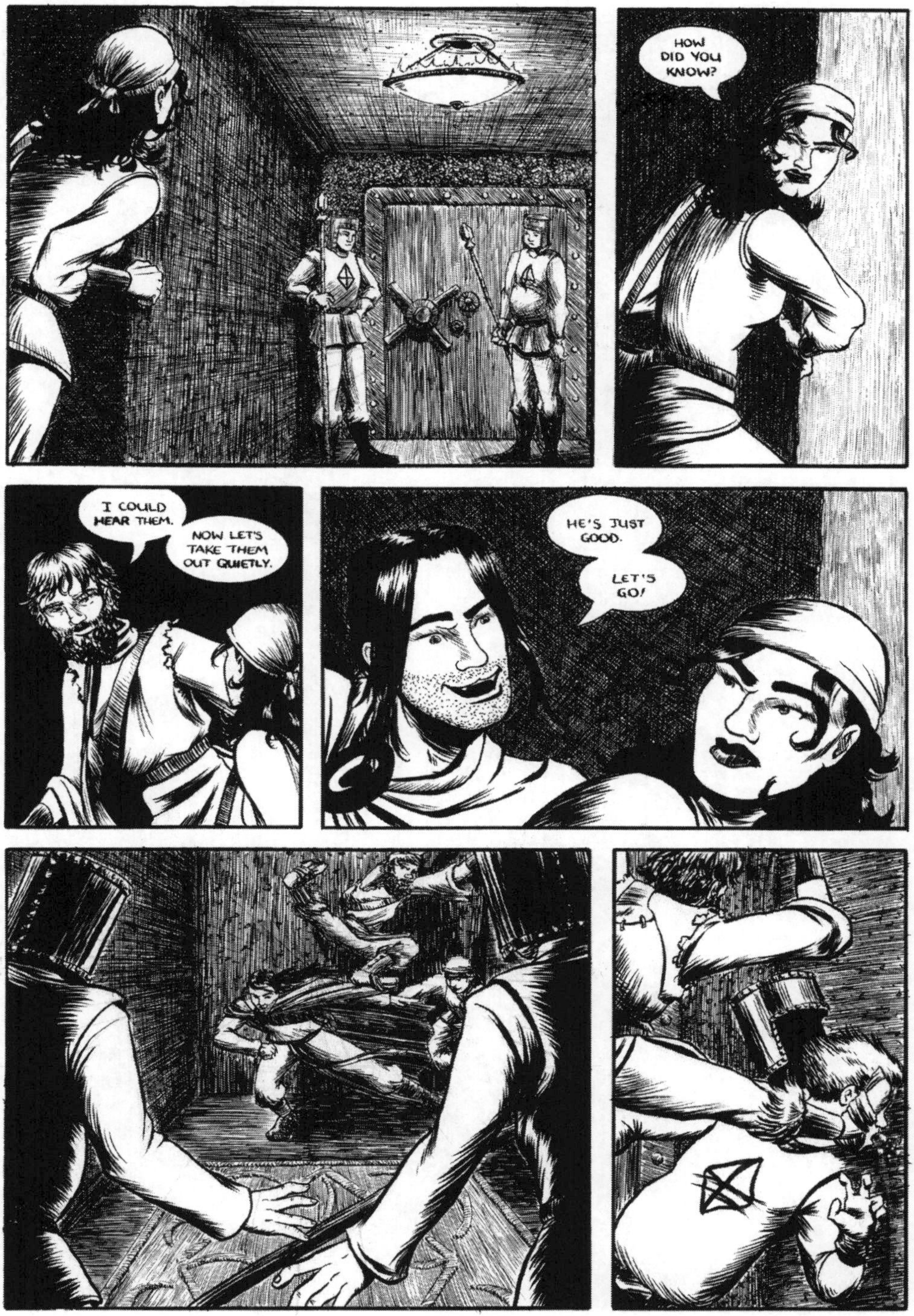
HOW DID YOU KNOW?
I COULD HEAR THEM.
NOW LET'S TAKE THEM OUT QUIETLY.
HE'S JUST GOOD.
LET'S GO!

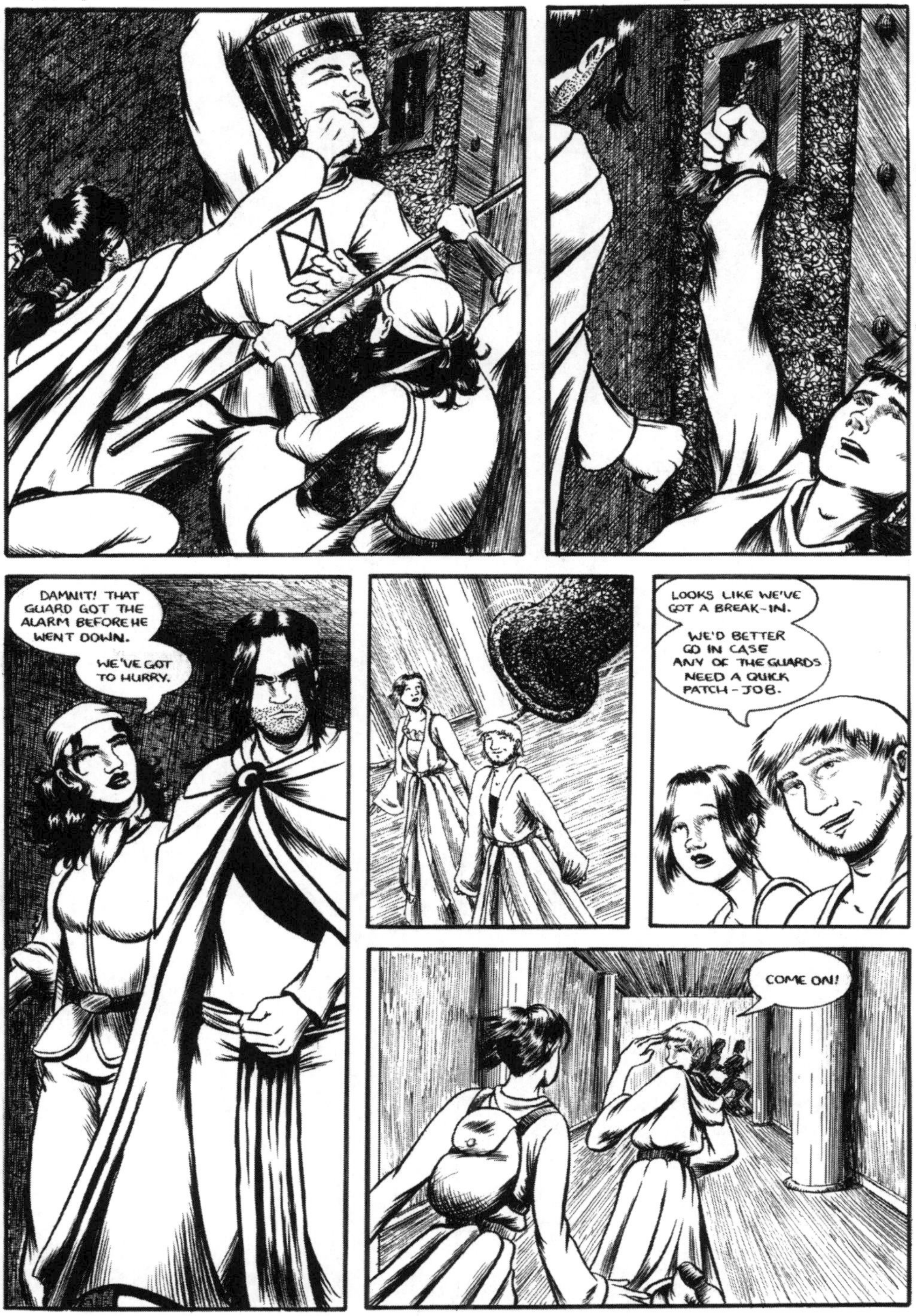
DAMNIT! THAT GUARD GOT THE ALARM BEFORE HE WENT DOWN.
WE'VE GOT TO HURRY.
LOOKS LIKE WE'VE GOT A BREAK-IN.
WE'D BETTER GO IN CASE ANY OF THE GUARDS NEED A QUICK PATCH-JOB.
COME ON!

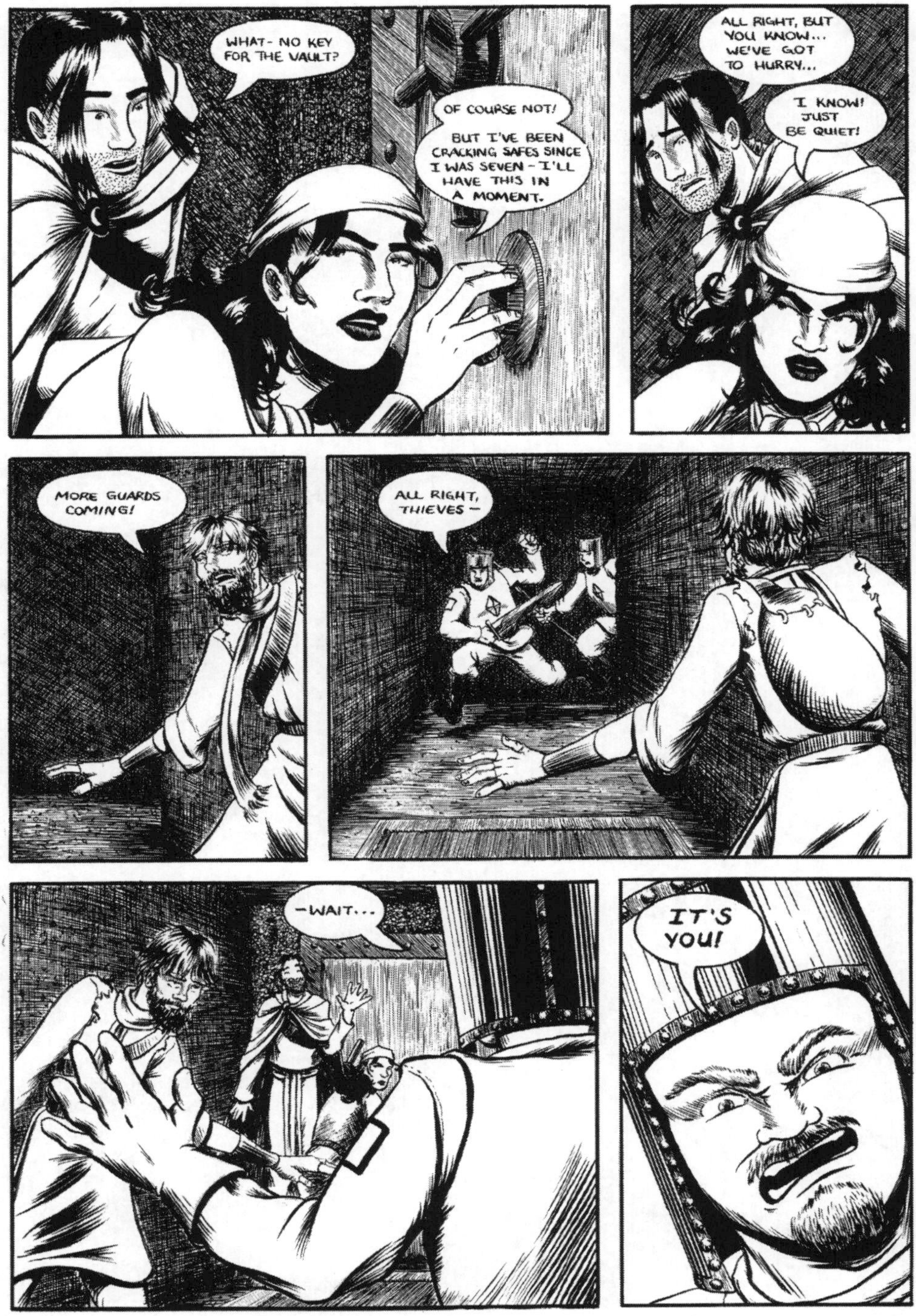
WHAT- NO KEY FOR THE VAULT?
OF COURSE NOT!
BUT I'VE BEEN CRACKING SAFES SINCE I WAS SEVEN - I'LL HAVE THIS IN A MOMENT.
ALL RIGHT, BUT YOU KNOW... WE'VE GOT TO HURRY...
I KNOW! JUST BE QUIET!
MORE GUARDS COMING!
ALL RIGHT, THIEVES -
-WAIT...
IT'S YOU!

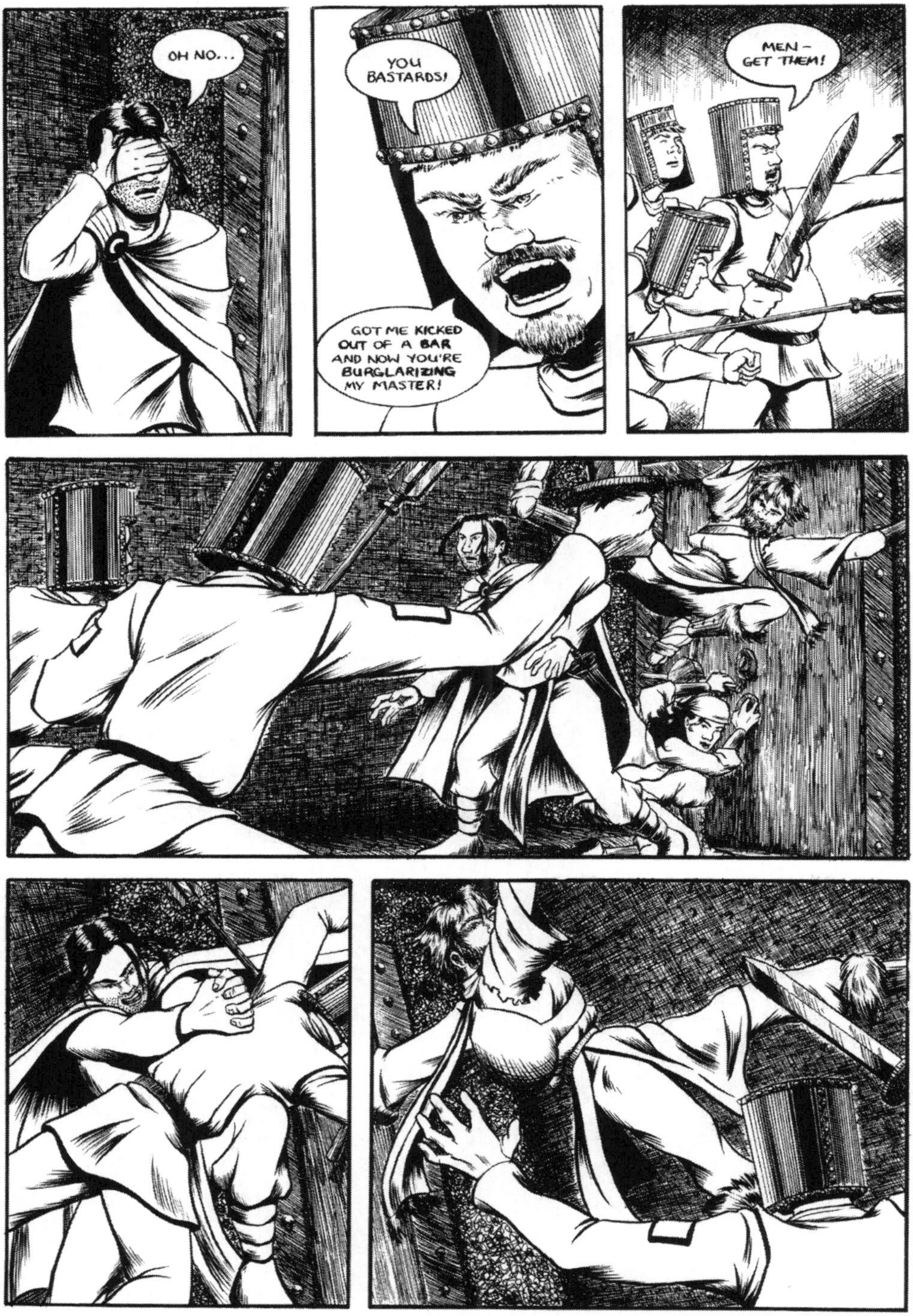
OH NO...
YOU BASTARDS!
GOT ME KICKED OUT OF A BAR AND NOW YOU'RE BURGLARIZING MY MASTER!
MEN- GET THEM!

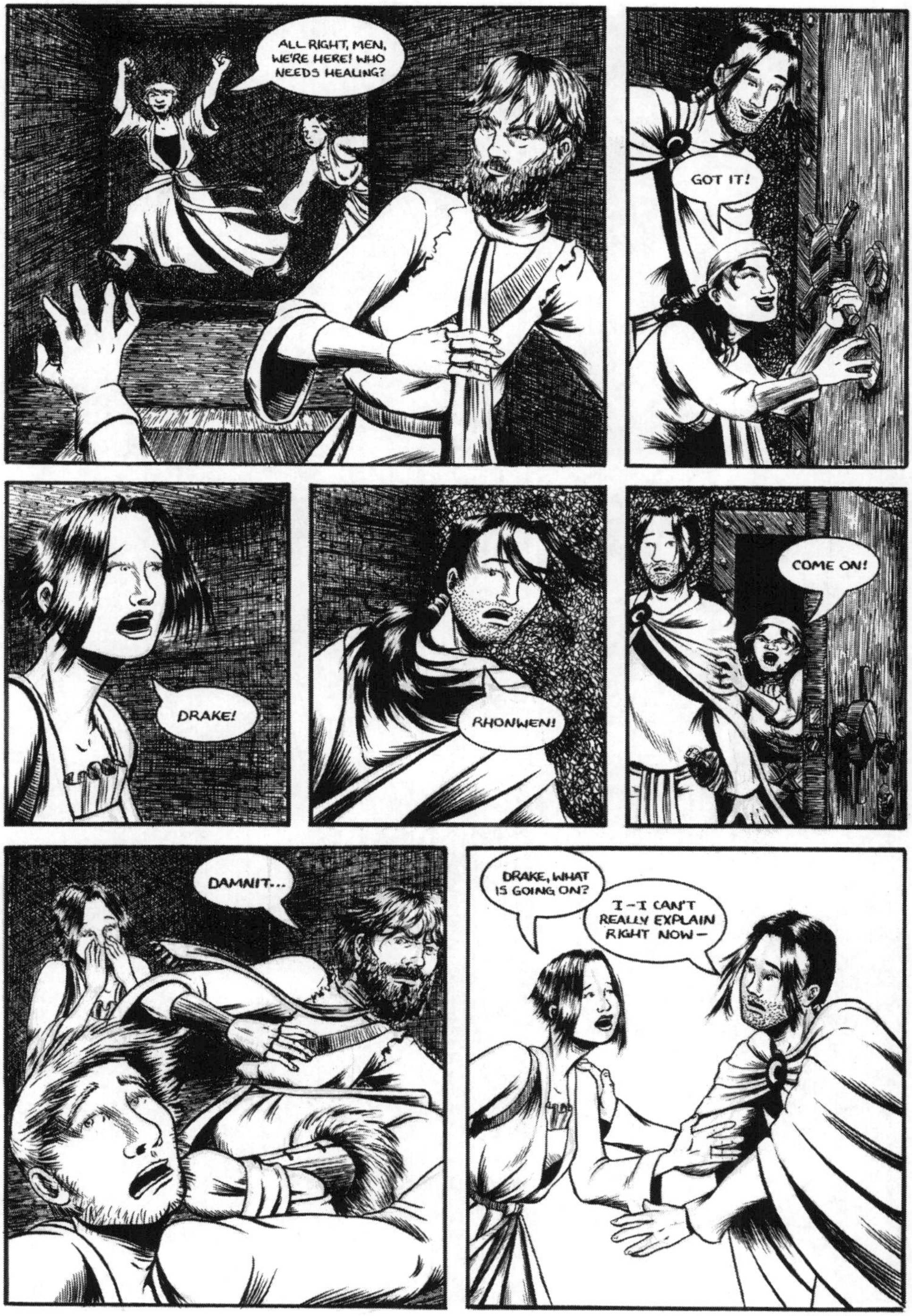
ALL RIGHT, MEN, WE'RE HERE! WHO NEEDS HEALING?
GOT IT!
DRAKE!
RHONWEN!
COME ON!
DAMNIT...
DRAKE, WHAT IS GOING ON?
I-I CAN'T REALLY EXPLAIN RIGHT NOW-

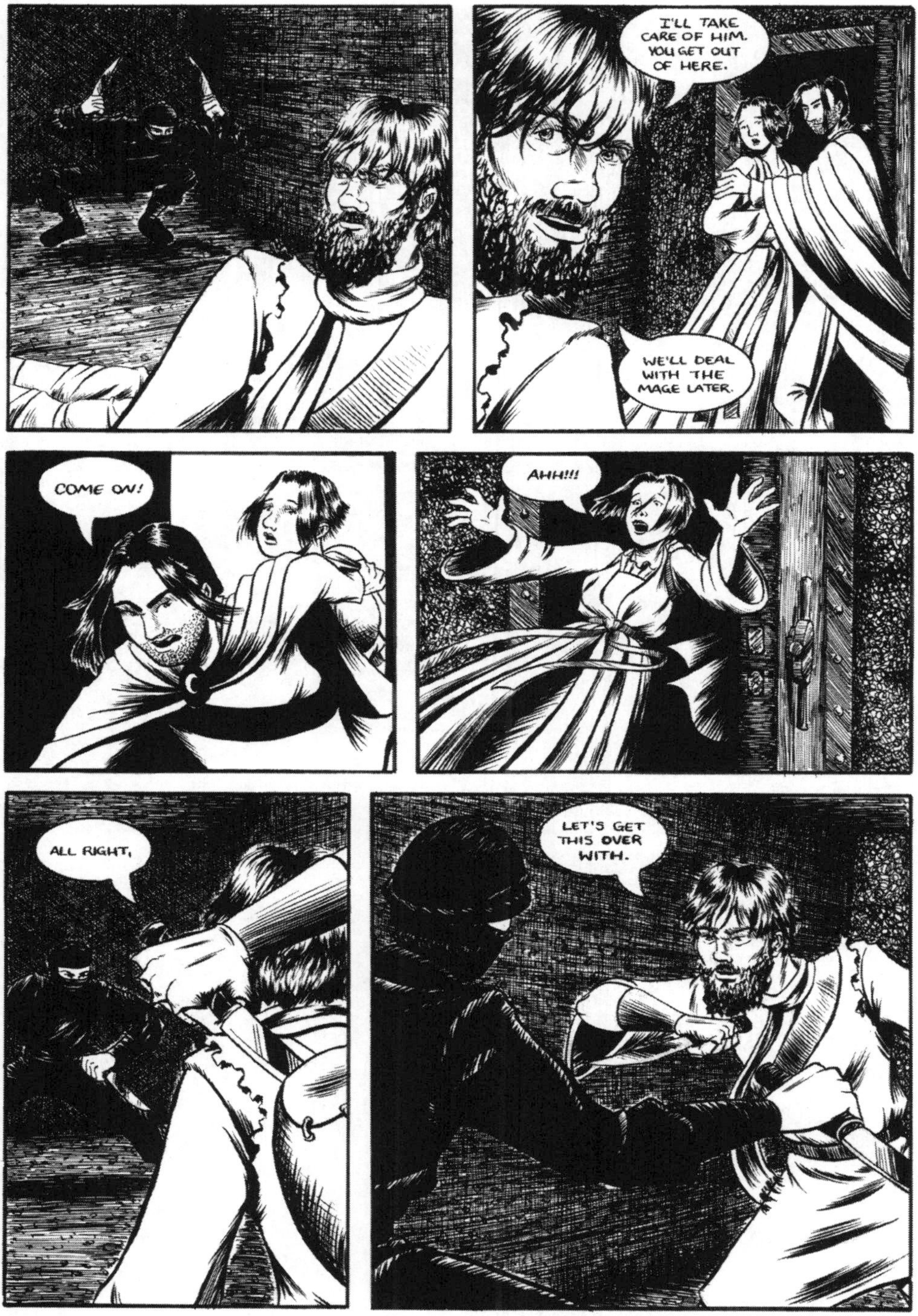
I'LL TAKE CARE OF HIM. YOU GET OUT OF HERE.
WE'LL DEAL WITH THE MAGE LATER.
COME ON!
AHH!!!
ALL RIGHT,
LET'S GET THIS OVER WITH.

CHAPTER III

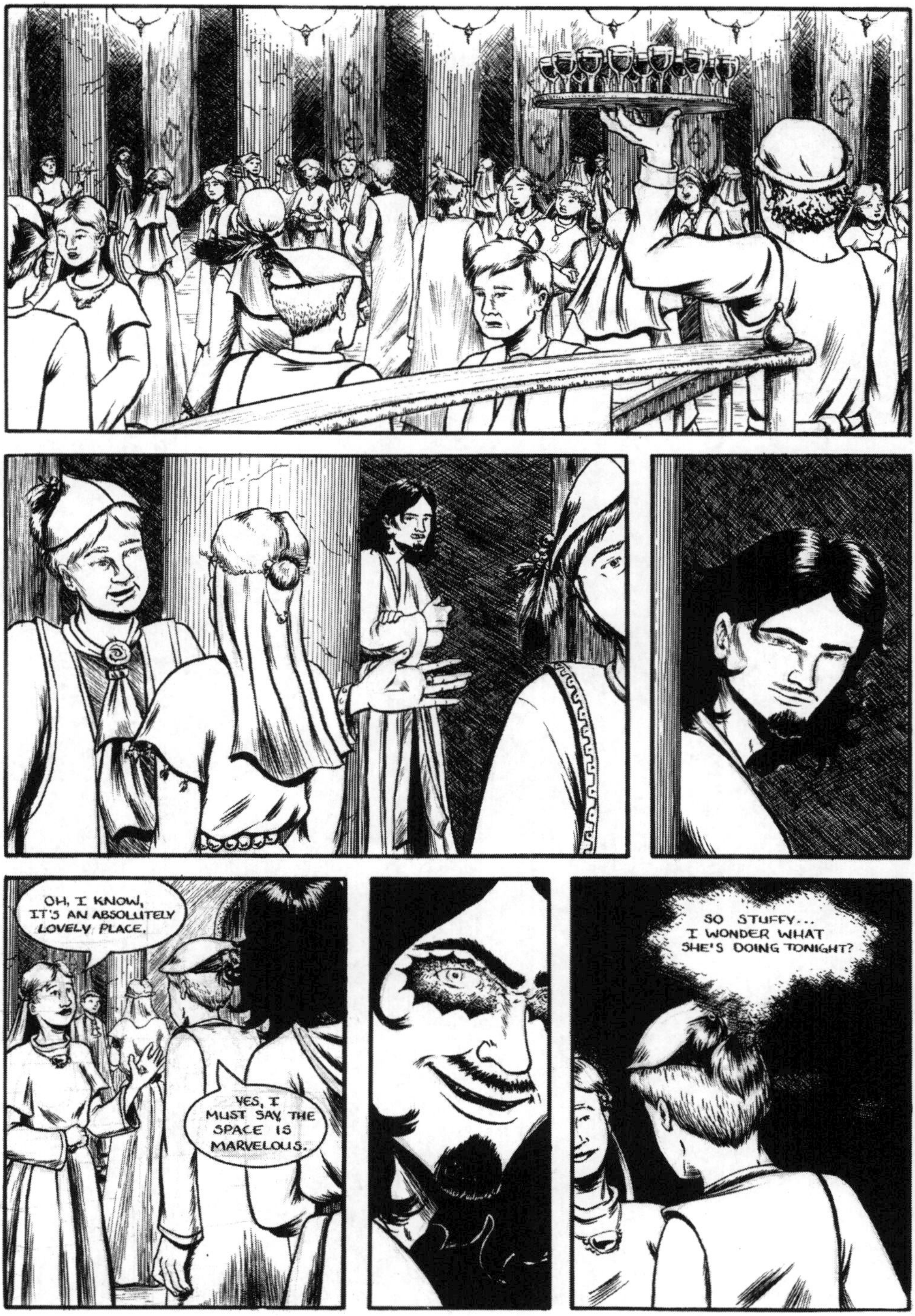
OH, I KNOW, IT'S AN ABSOLUTELY LOVELY PLACE.
YES, I MUST SAY, THE SPACE IS MARVELOUS.
SO STUFFY... I WONDER WHAT SHE'S DOING TONIGHT?

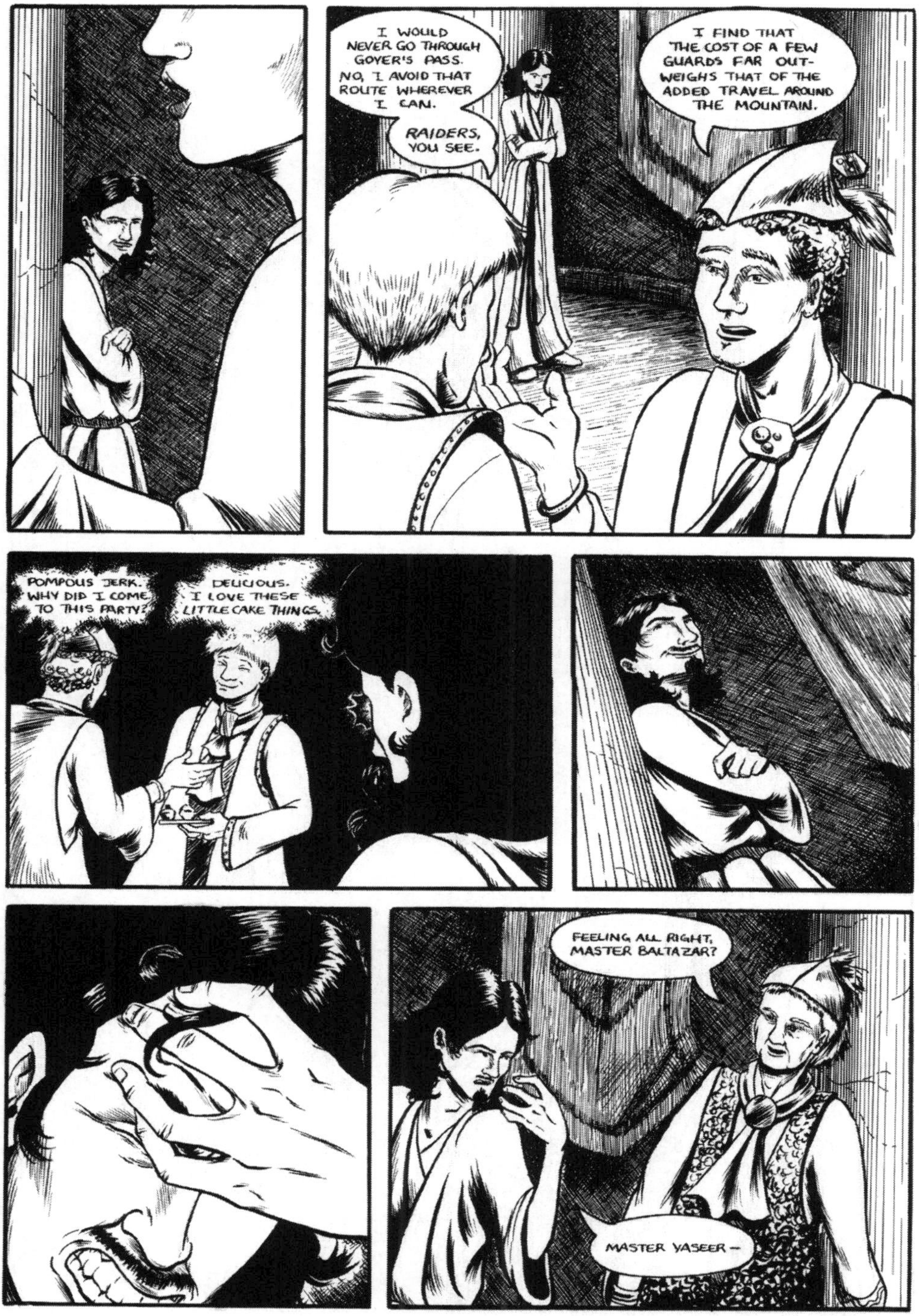
I WOULD NEVER GO THROUGH GOYER'S PASS.
NO, I AVOID THAT ROUTE WHEREVER I CAN.
RAIDERS, YOU SEE.
I FIND THAT THE COST OF A FEW GUARDS FAR OUT-WEIGHS THAT OF THE ADDED TRAVEL AROUND THE MOUNTAIN.
POMPOUS JERK. WHY DID I COME TO THIS PARTY?
DELICIOUS. I LOVE THESE LITTLE CAKE THINGS.
FEELING ALL RIGHT, MASTER BALTAZAR?
MASTER YASEER —

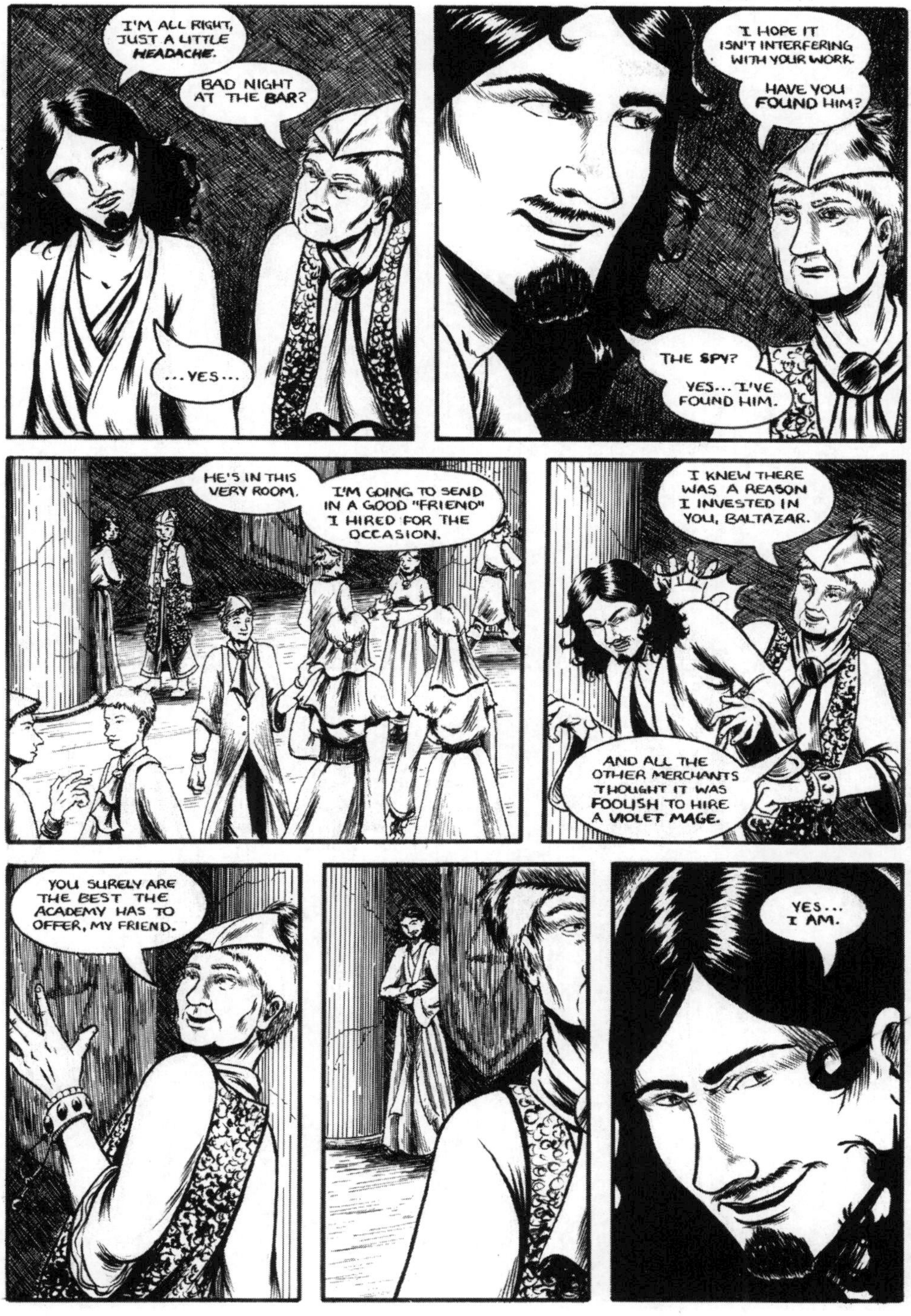
I'M ALL RIGHT, JUST A LITTLE HEADACHE.
BAD NIGHT AT THE BAR?
...YES...
I HOPE IT ISN'T INTERFERING WITH YOUR WORK.
HAVE YOU FOUND HIM?
THE SPY?
YES... I'VE FOUND HIM.
HE'S IN THIS VERY ROOM.
I'M GOING TO SEND IN A GOOD "FRIEND" I HIRED FOR THE OCCASION.
I KNEW THERE WAS A REASON I INVESTED IN YOU, BALTAZAR.
AND ALL THE OTHER MERCHANTS THOUGHT IT WAS FOOLISH TO HIRE A VIOLET MAGE.
YOU SURELY ARE THE BEST THE ACADEMY HAS TO OFFER, MY FRIEND.
YES... I AM.

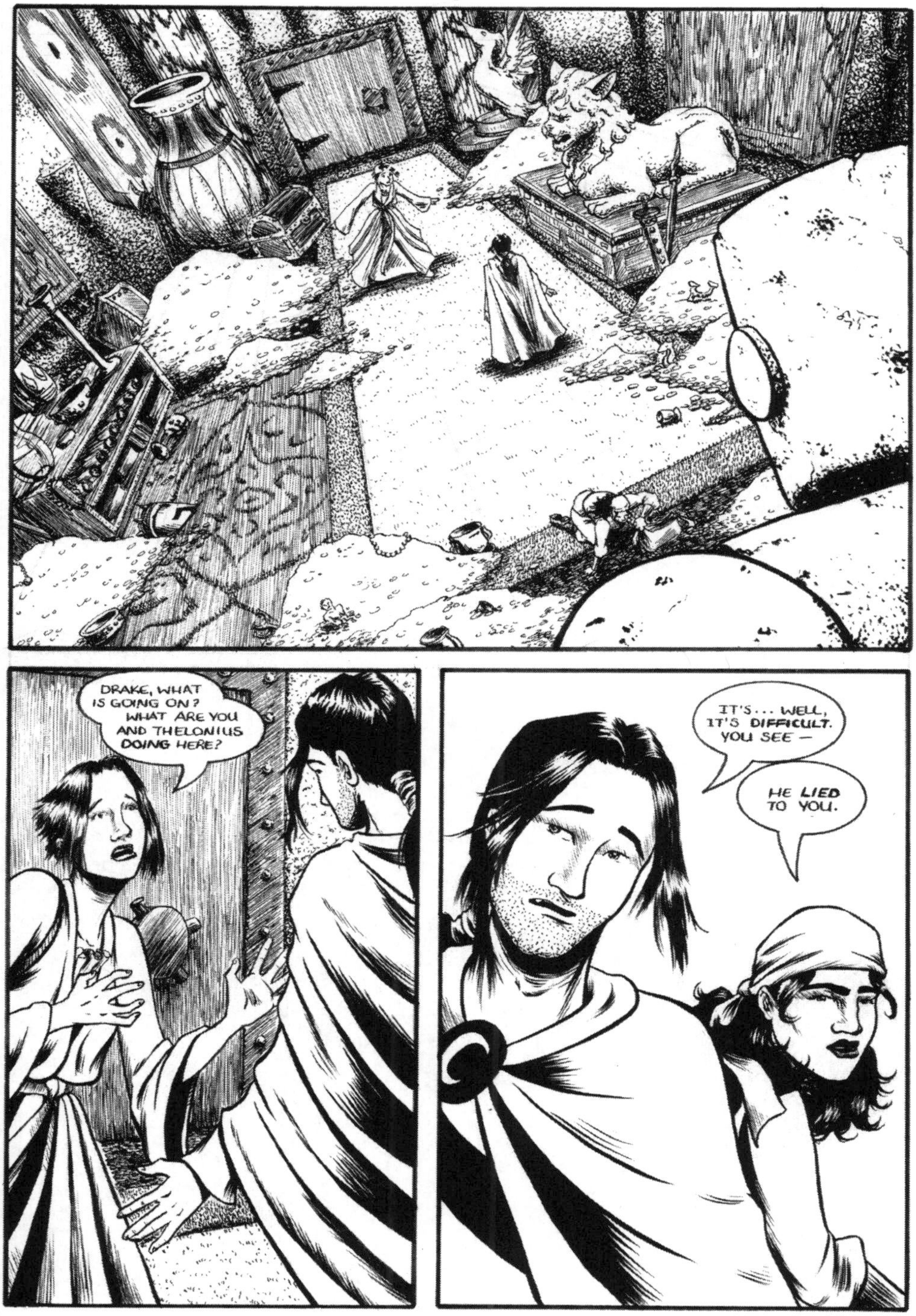
DRAKE, WHAT IS GOING ON? WHAT ARE YOU AND THELONIUS DOING HERE?
IT'S... WELL, IT'S DIFFICULT. YOU SEE —
HE LIED TO YOU.

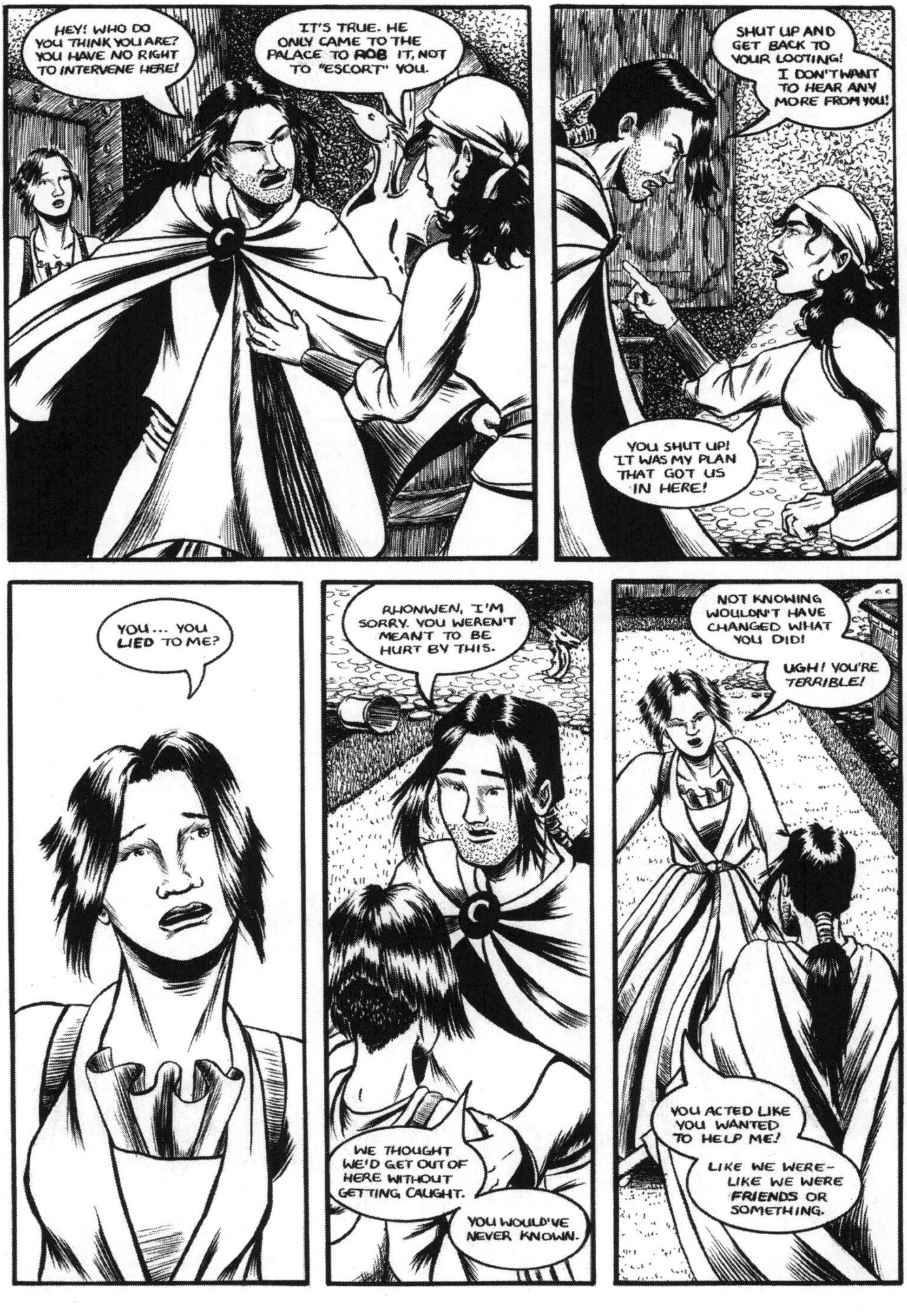
HEY! WHO DO YOU THINK YOU ARE? YOU HAVE NO RIGHT TO INTERVENE HERE!
IT'S TRUE. HE ONLY CAME TO THE PALACE TO ROB IT, NOT TO "ESCORT" YOU.
SHUT UP AND GET BACK TO YOUR LOOTING!
I DON'T WANT TO HEAR ANY MORE FROM YOU!
YOU SHUT UP! IT WAS MY PLAN THAT GOT US IN HERE!
YOU... YOU LIED TO ME?
RHONWEN, I'M SORRY. YOU WEREN'T MEANT TO BE HURT BY THIS.
WE THOUGHT WE'D GET OUT OF HERE WITHOUT GETTING CAUGHT.
YOU WOULD'VE NEVER KNOWN.
NOT KNOWING WOULDN'T HAVE CHANGED WHAT YOU DID!
UGH! YOU'RE TERRIBLE!
YOU ACTED LIKE YOU WANTED TO HELP ME!
LIKE WE WERE- LIKE WE WERE FRIENDS OR SOMETHING.

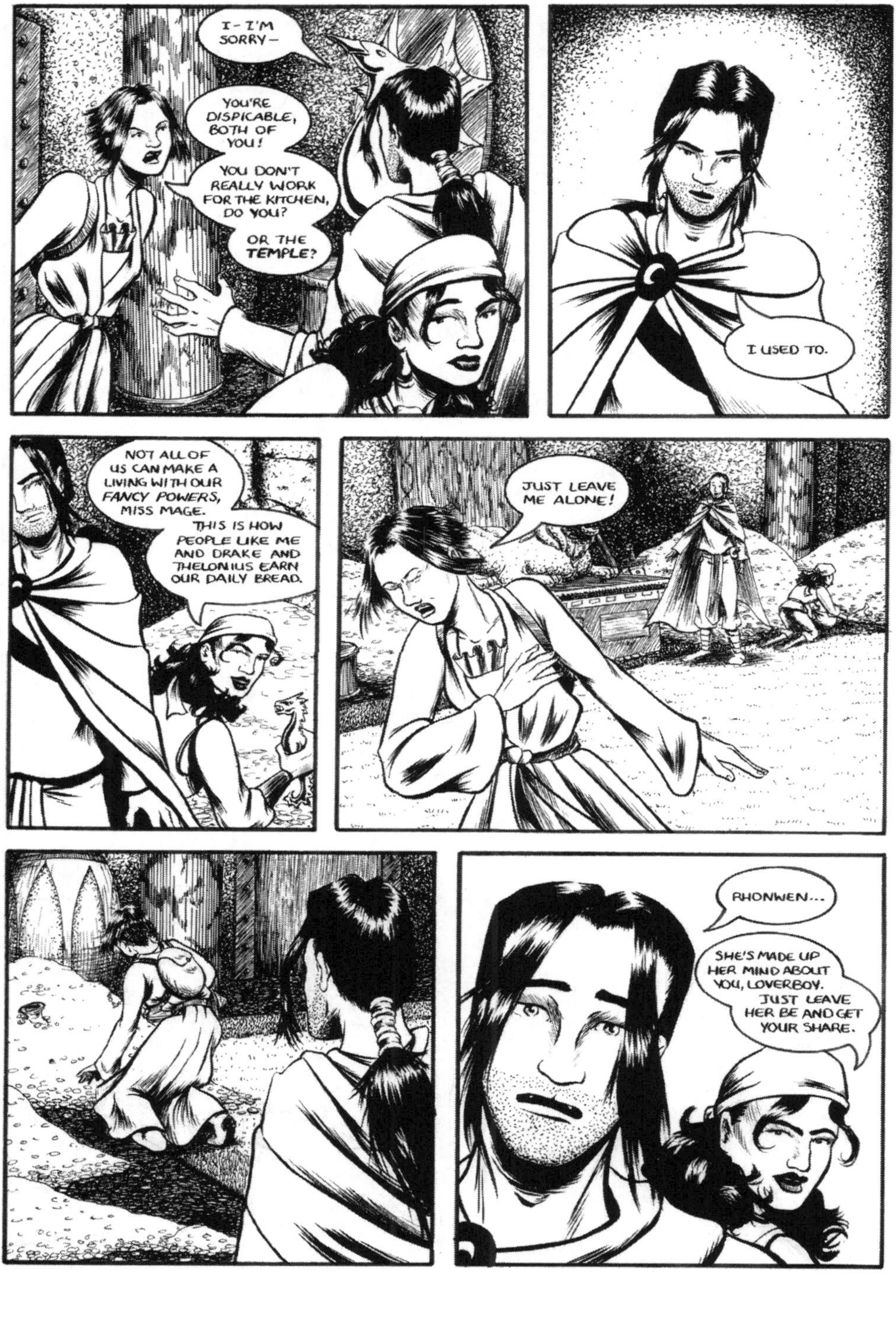

I- I'M SORRY-
YOU'RE DISPICABLE, BOTH OF YOU!
YOU DON'T REALLY WORK FOR THE KITCHEN, DO YOU?
OR THE TEMPLE?
I USED TO.
NOT ALL OF US CAN MAKE A LIVING WITH OUR FANCY POWERS, MISS MAGE.
THIS IS HOW PEOPLE LIKE ME AND DRAKE AND THELONIUS EARN OUR DAILY BREAD.
JUST LEAVE ME ALONE!
RHONWEN...
SHE'S MADE UP HER MIND ABOUT YOU, LOVERBOY.
JUST LEAVE HER BE AND GET YOUR SHARE.

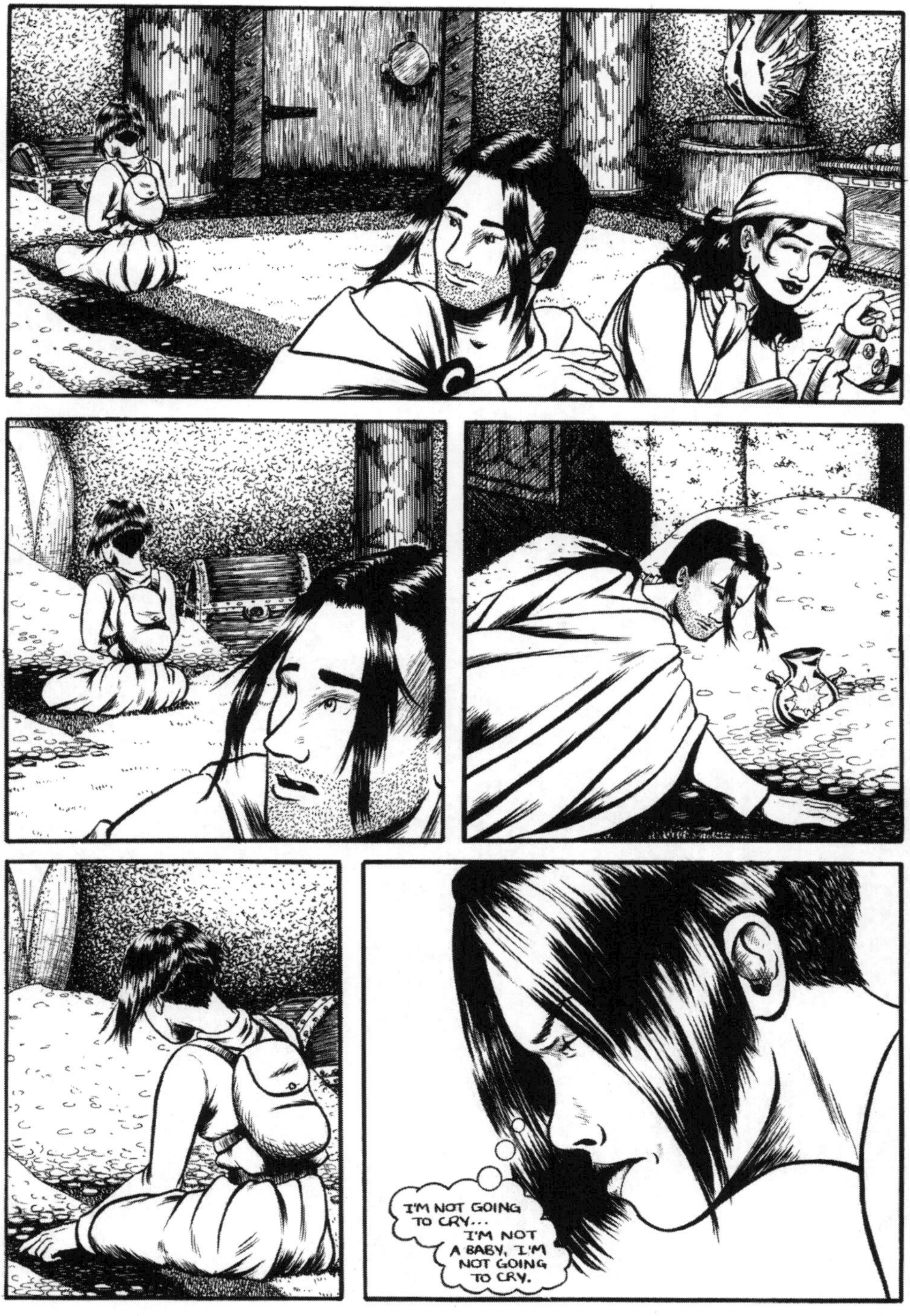
I'M NOT GOING TO CRY... I'M NOT A BABY, I'M NOT GOING TO CRY.

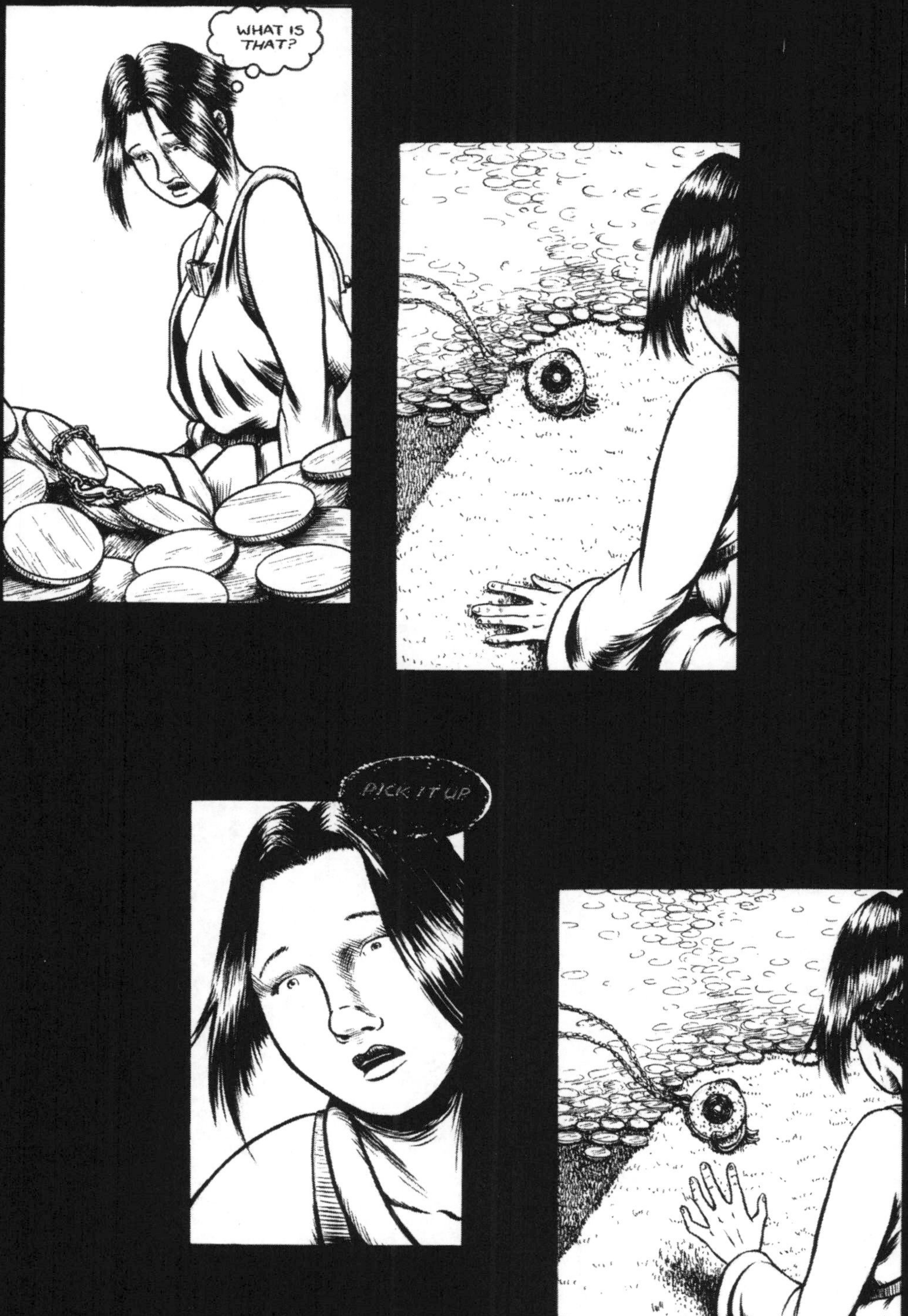
WHAT IS THAT?
PICK IT UP

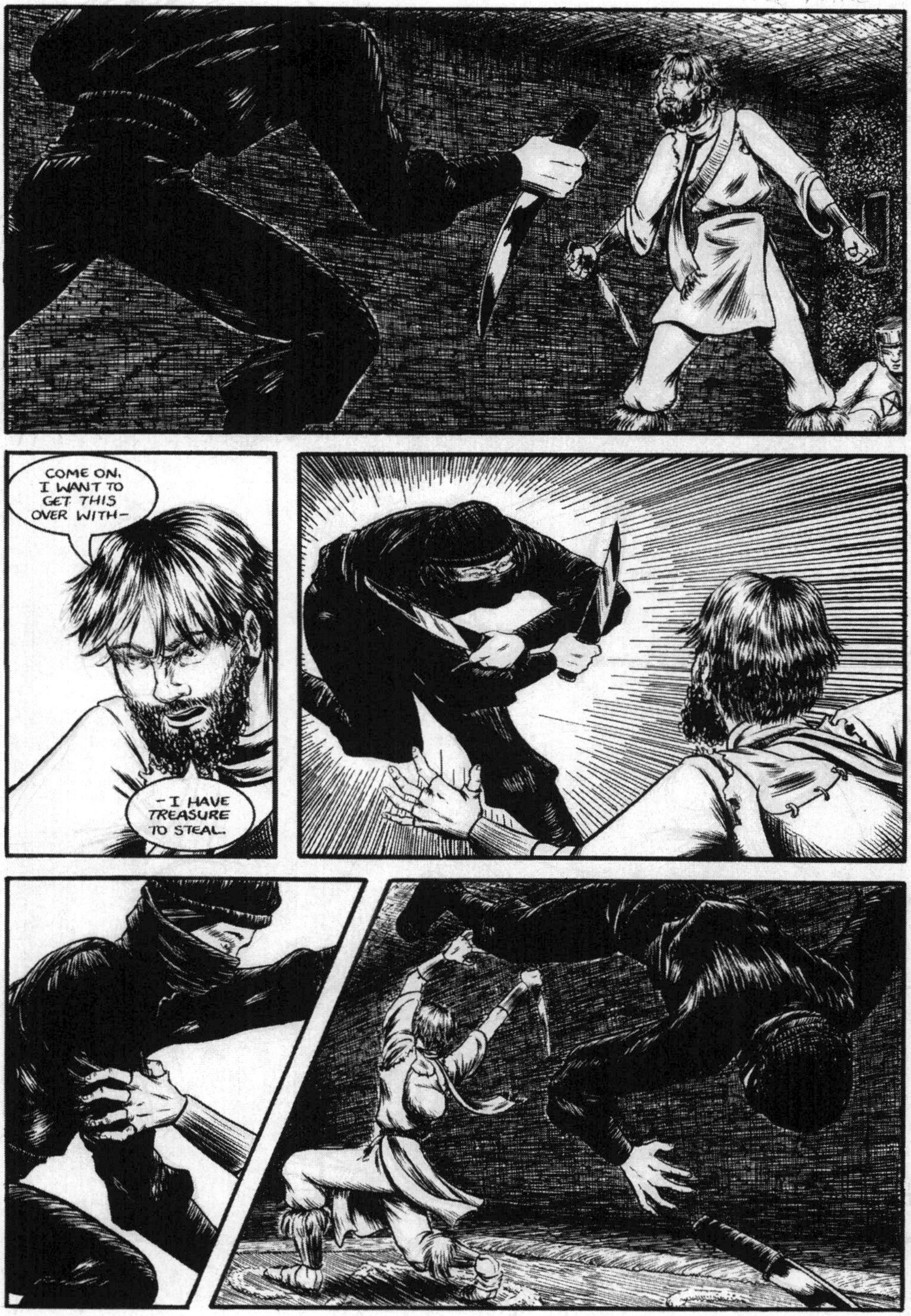
COME ON. I WANT TO GET THIS OVER WITH-
-I HAVE TREASURE TO STEAL.

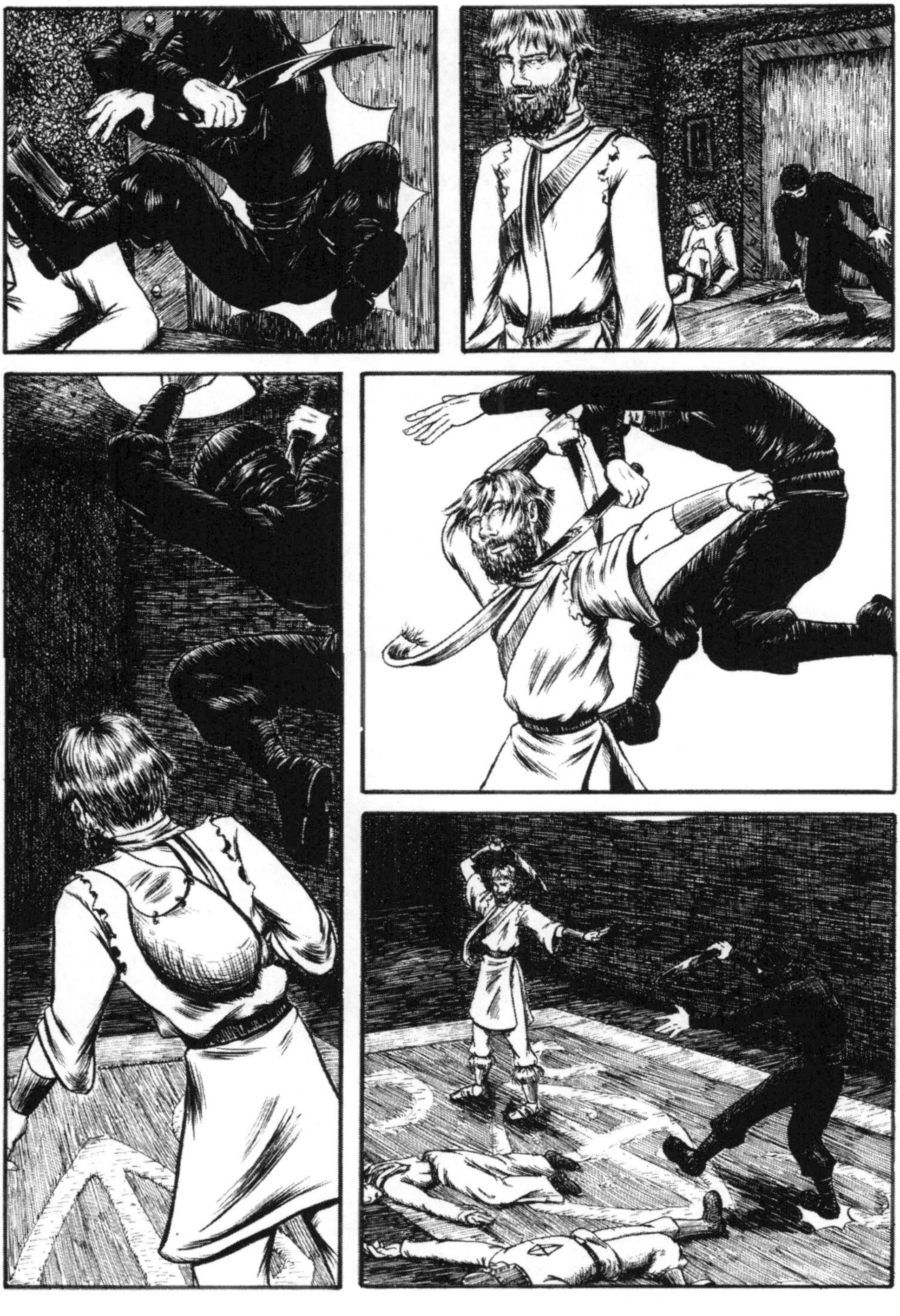

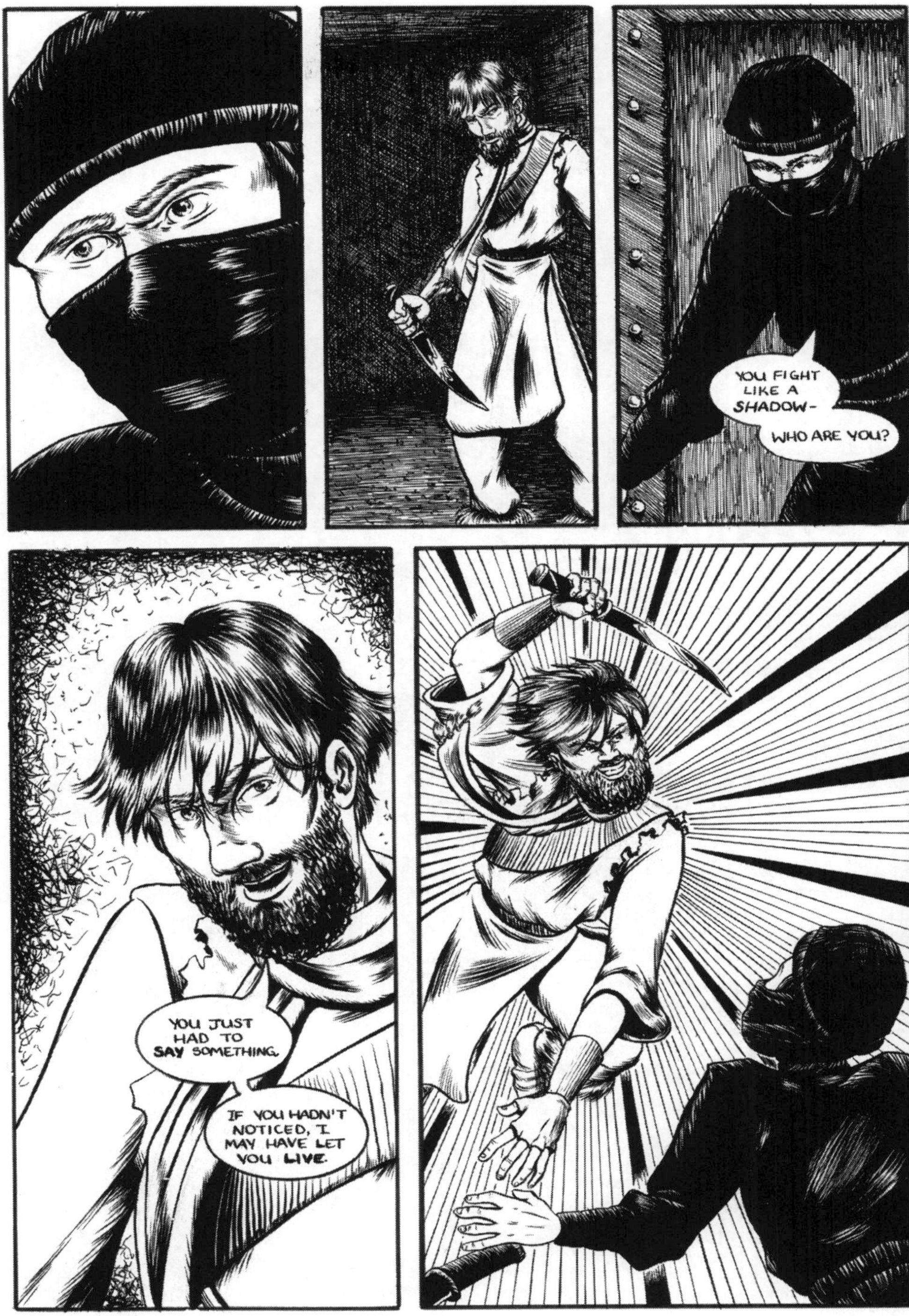
YOU FIGHT LIKE A SHADOW-
WHO ARE YOU?
YOU JUST HAD TO SAY SOMETHING.
IF YOU HADN'T NOTICED, I MAY HAVE LET YOU LIVE.

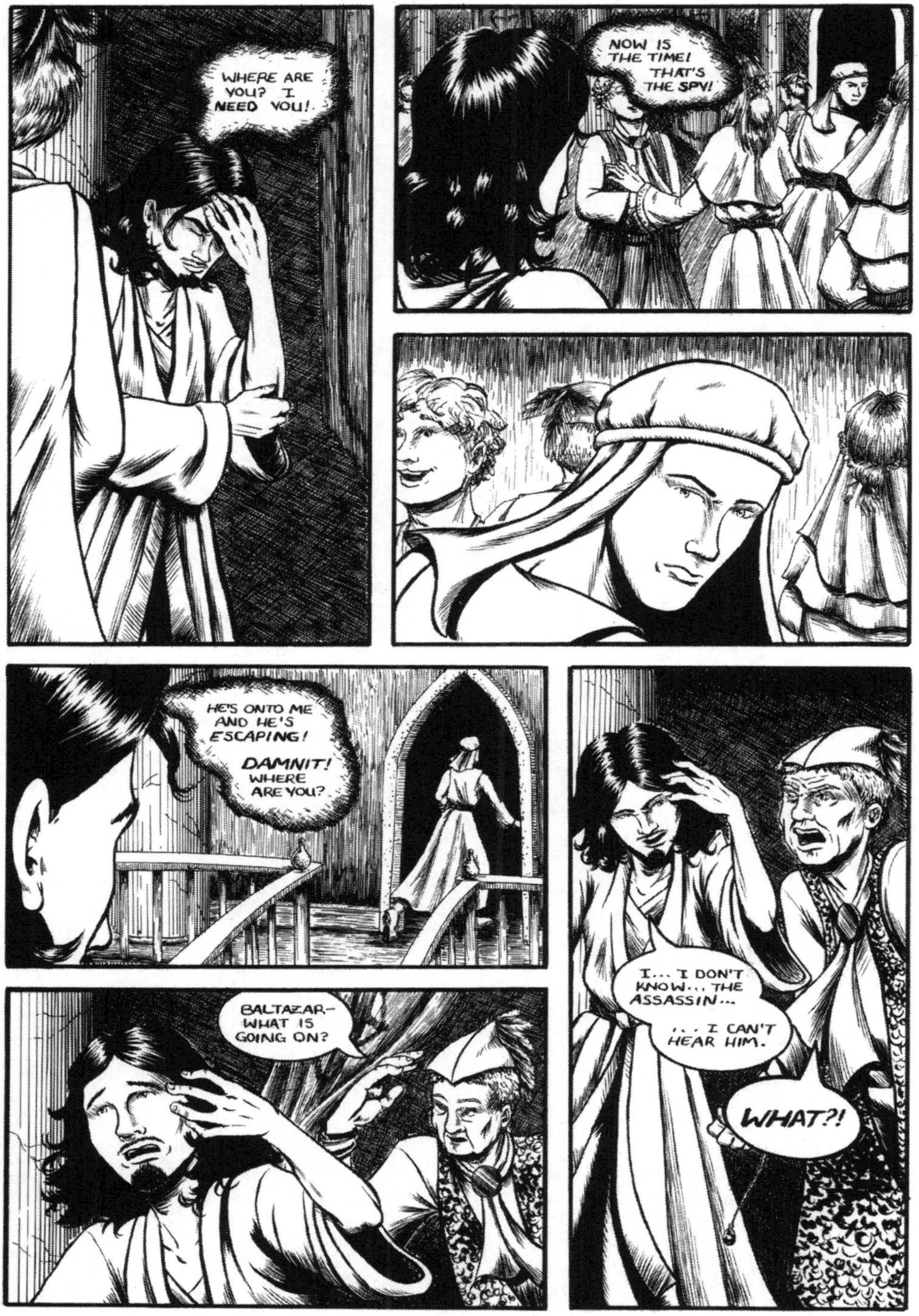
WHERE ARE YOU? I NEED YOU!
NOW IS THE TIME! THAT'S THE SPY!
HE'S ONTO ME AND HE'S ESCAPING!
DAMNIT! WHERE ARE YOU?
BALTAZAR- WHAT IS GOING ON?
I... I DON'T KNOW... THE ASSASSIN...
... I CAN'T HEAR HIM.
WHAT?!

UGLY THING, ISN'T IT?

DON'T INSULT GOLEMS – IT'S BAD LUCK.

PFT! I'M NOT REALLY CONCERNED WITH THOSE SUPERSTITIONS.

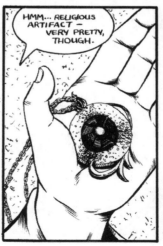

HMM... RELIGIOUS ARTIFACT – VERY PRETTY, THOUGH.

OH, WHAT AM I DOING? I SHOULDN'T TOUCH ANY OF THIS!

THE MASTER WILL BE SO —

— AHH!

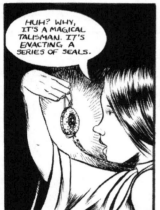

HUH? WHY, IT'S A MAGICAL TALISMAN. IT'S ENACTING A SERIES OF SEALS.

ARE YOU ALL RIGHT?

I... I DON'T KNOW, I —

AAHRGH!!!

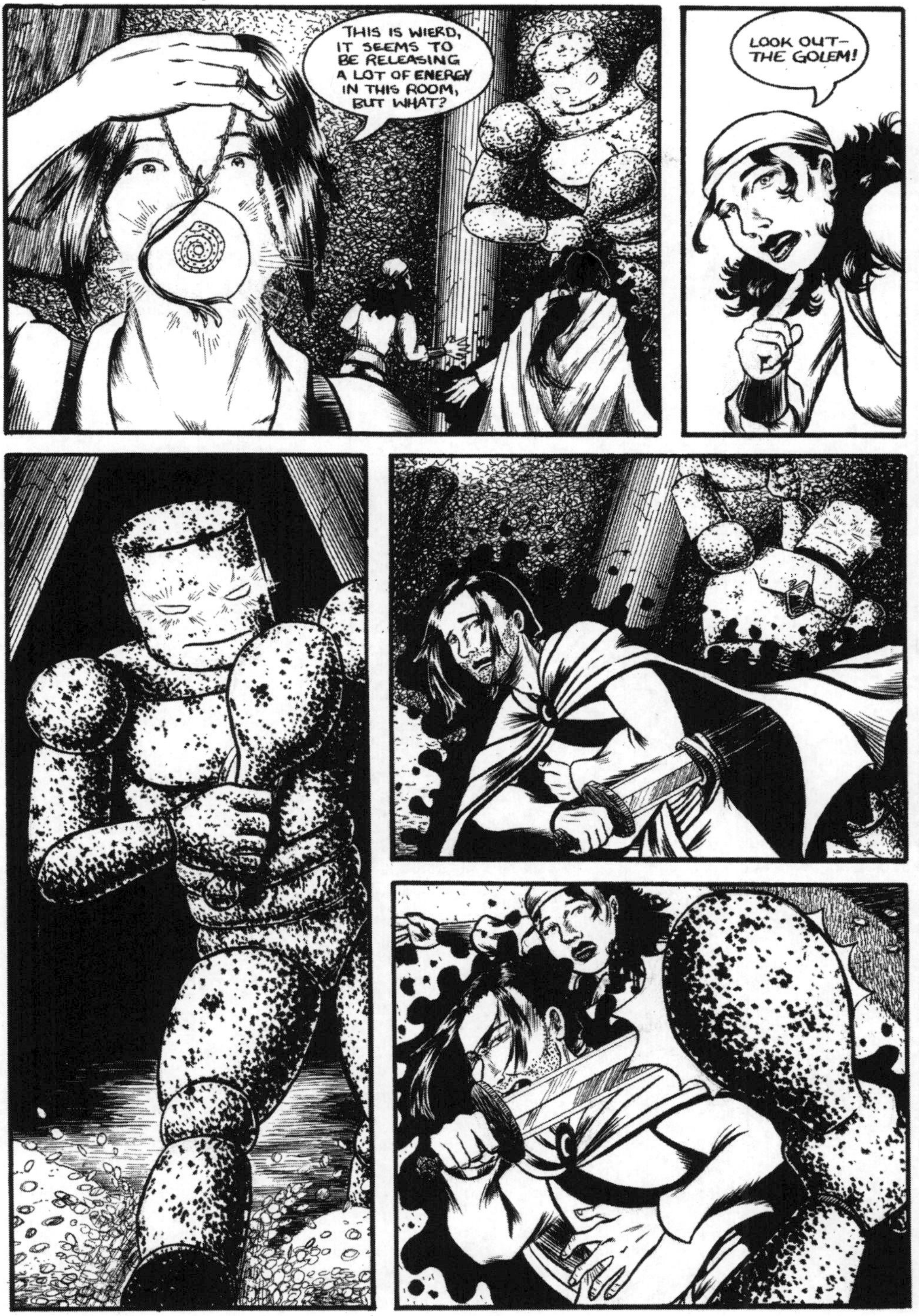
THIS IS WIERD, IT SEEMS TO BE RELEASING A LOT OF ENERGY IN THIS ROOM, BUT WHAT?
LOOK OUT- THE GOLEM!

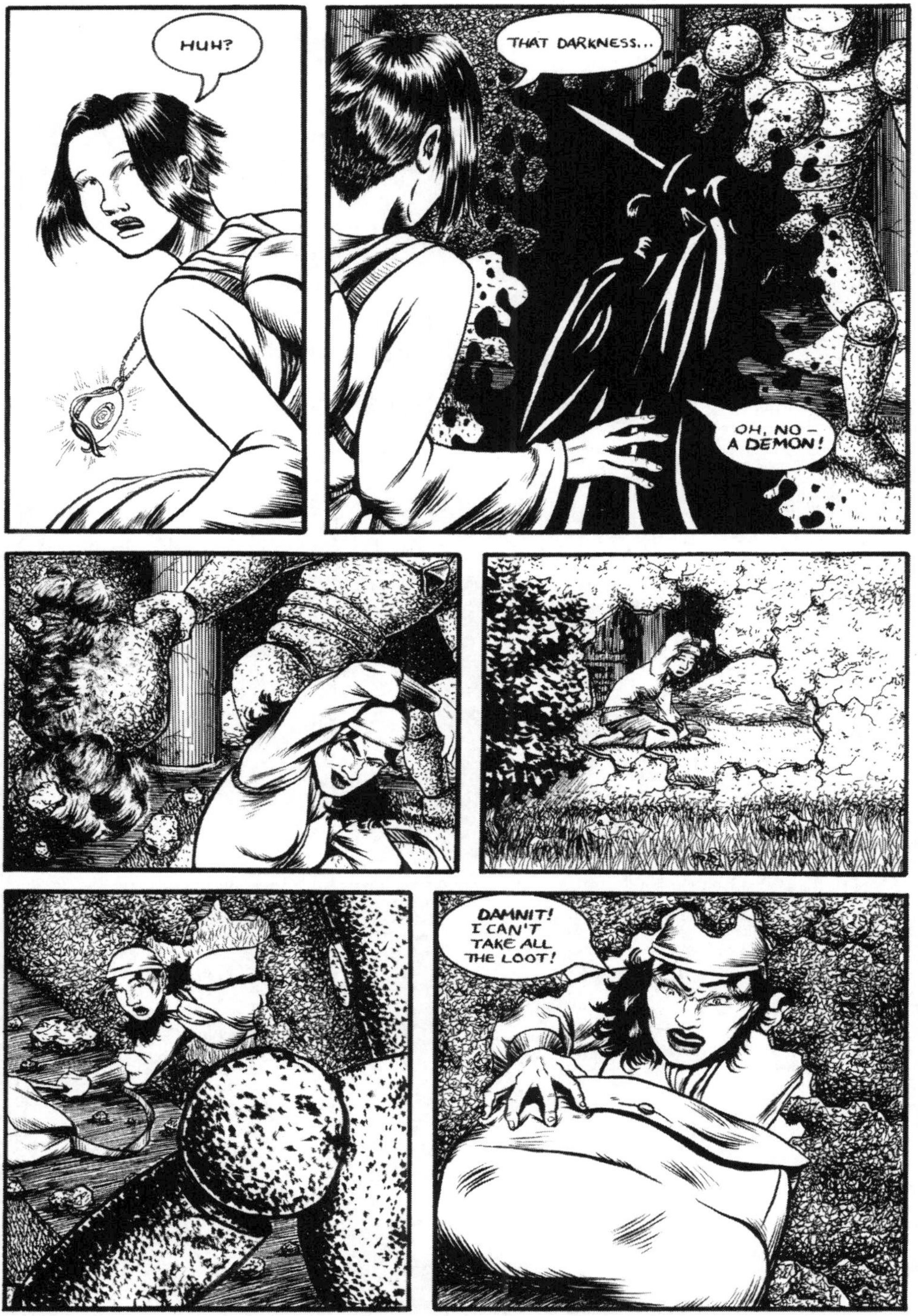
HUH?
THAT DARKNESS...
OH, NO - A DEMON!
DAMNIT! I CAN'T TAKE ALL THE LOOT!

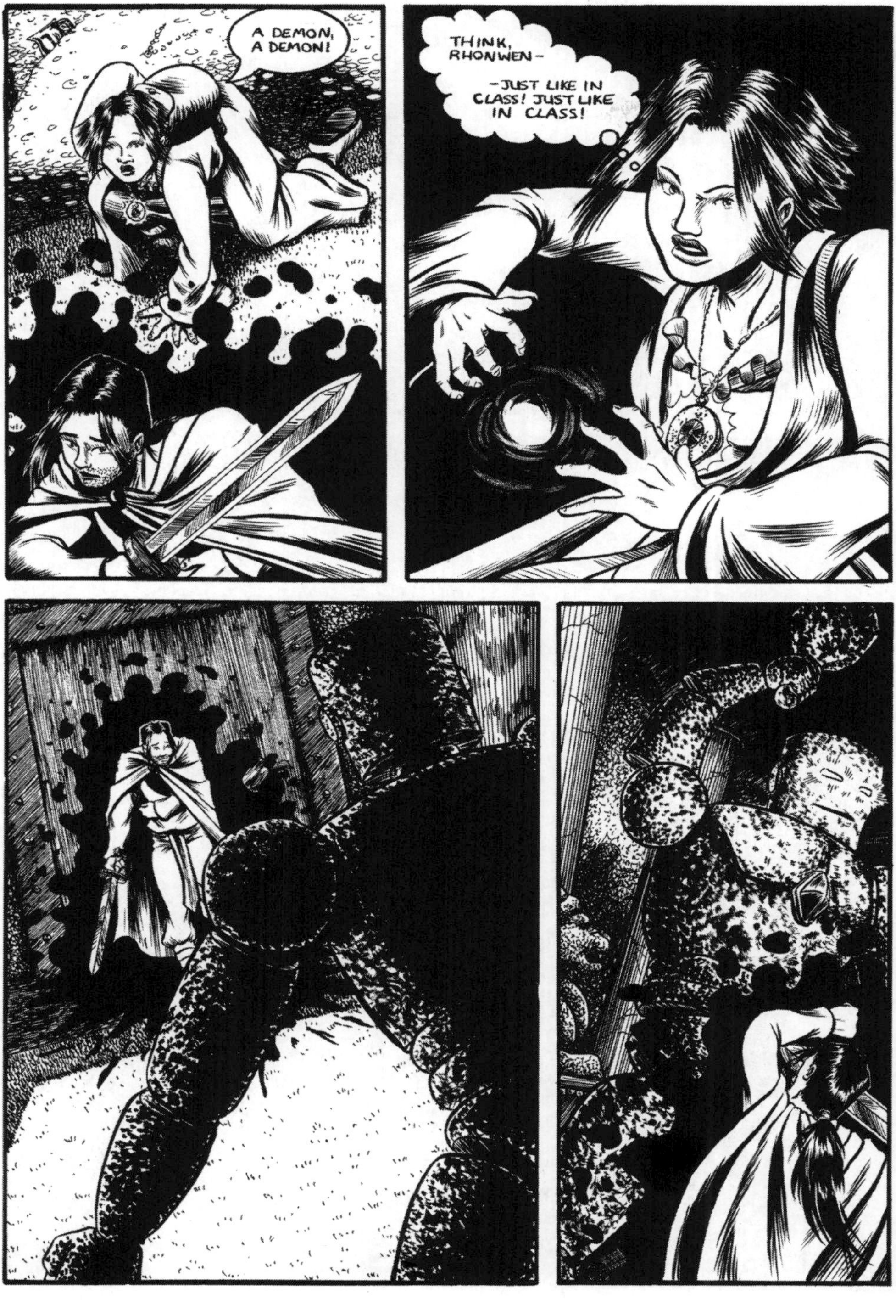
A DEMON, A DEMON!
THINK, RHONWEN-
-JUST LIKE IN CLASS! JUST LIKE IN CLASS!

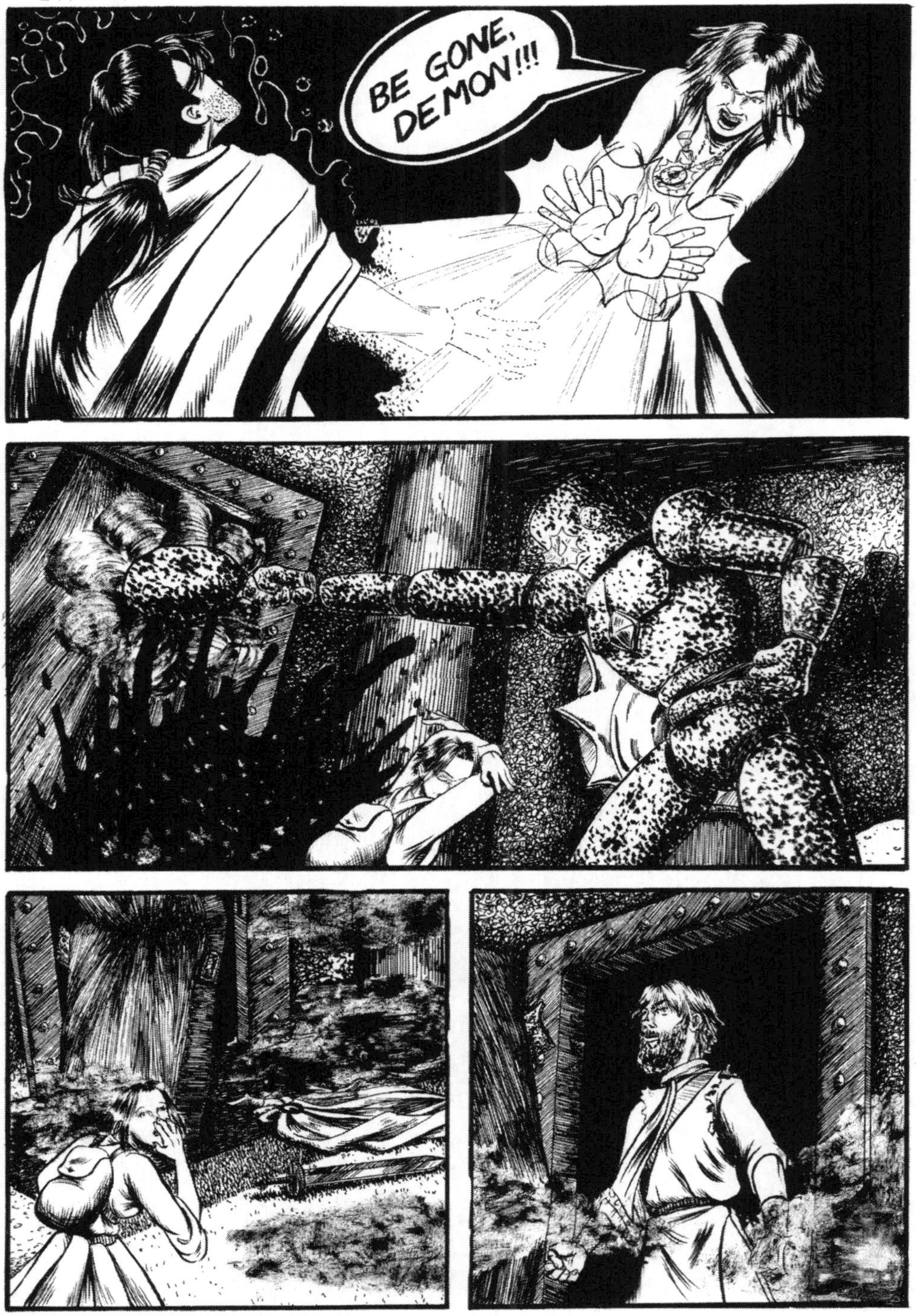
BE GONE, DEMON!!!

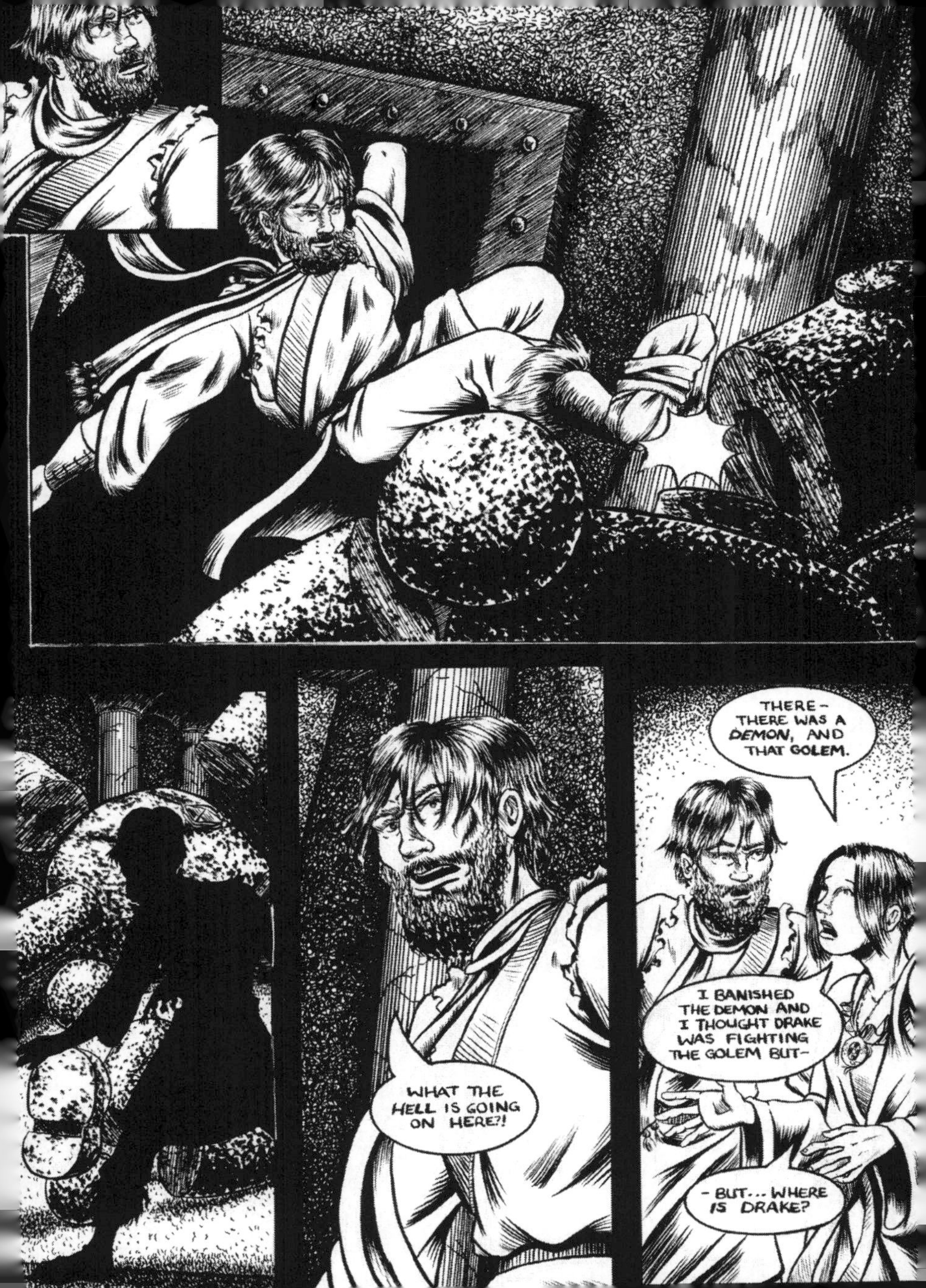
WHAT THE HELL IS GOING ON HERE?!
THERE- THERE WAS A DEMON, AND THAT GOLEM.
I BANISHED THE DEMON AND I THOUGHT DRAKE WAS FIGHTING THE GOLEM BUT-
- BUT... WHERE IS DRAKE?

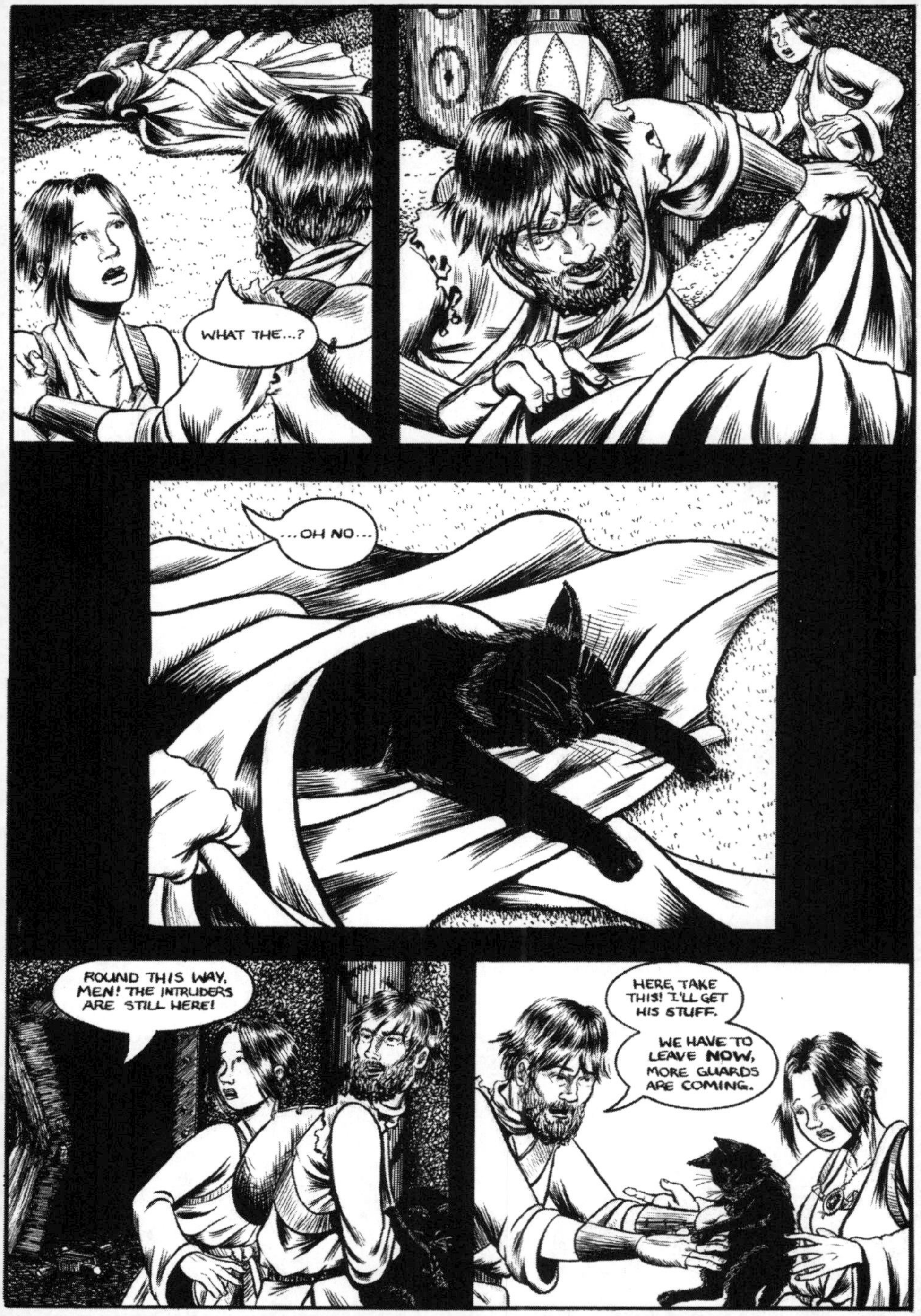
WHAT THE...?
...OH NO...
ROUND THIS WAY, MEN! THE INTRUDERS ARE STILL HERE!
HERE, TAKE THIS! I'LL GET HIS STUFF.
WE HAVE TO LEAVE NOW, MORE GUARDS ARE COMING.

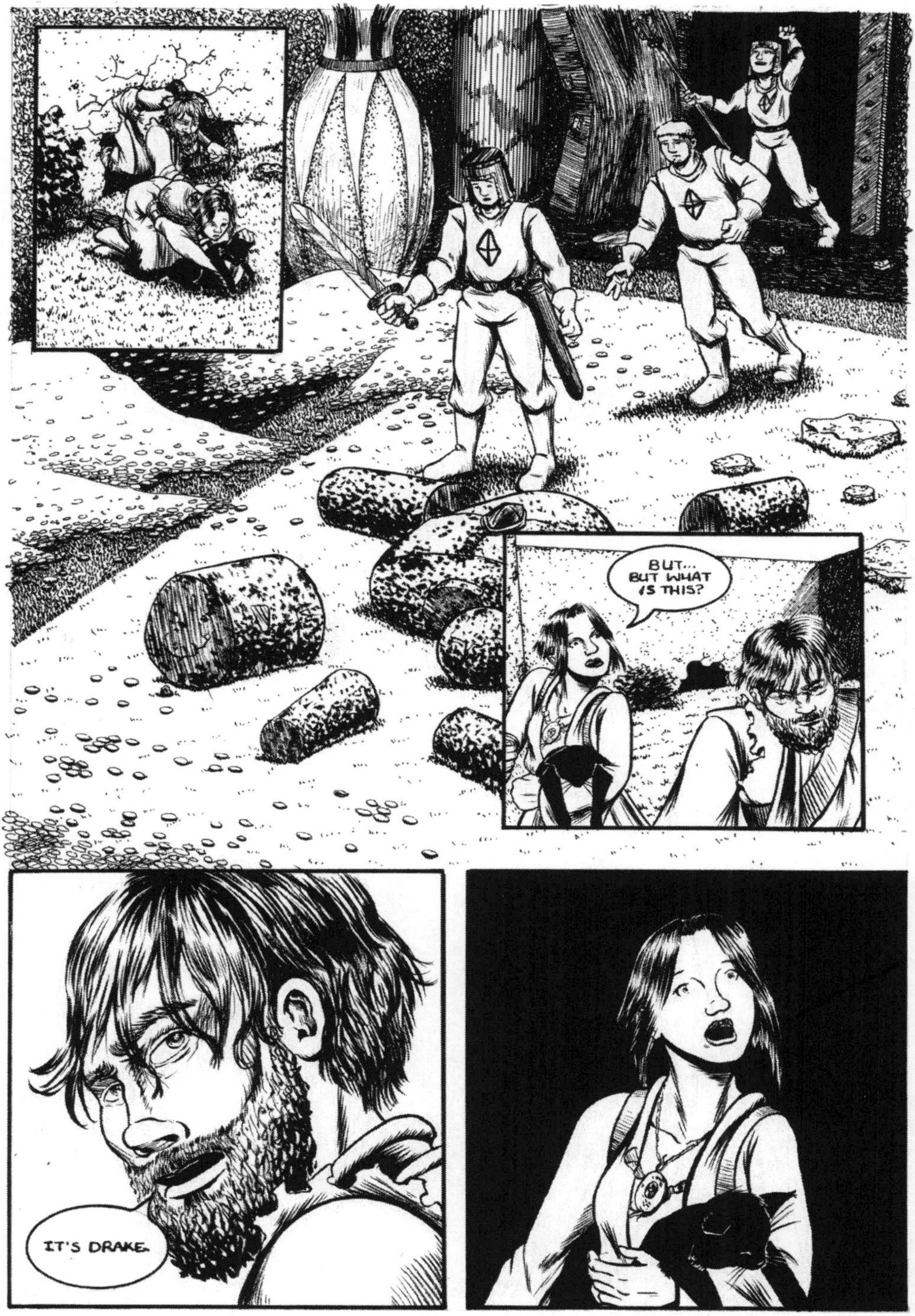
BUT... BUT WHAT IS THIS?
IT'S DRAKE.

CHAPTER IV

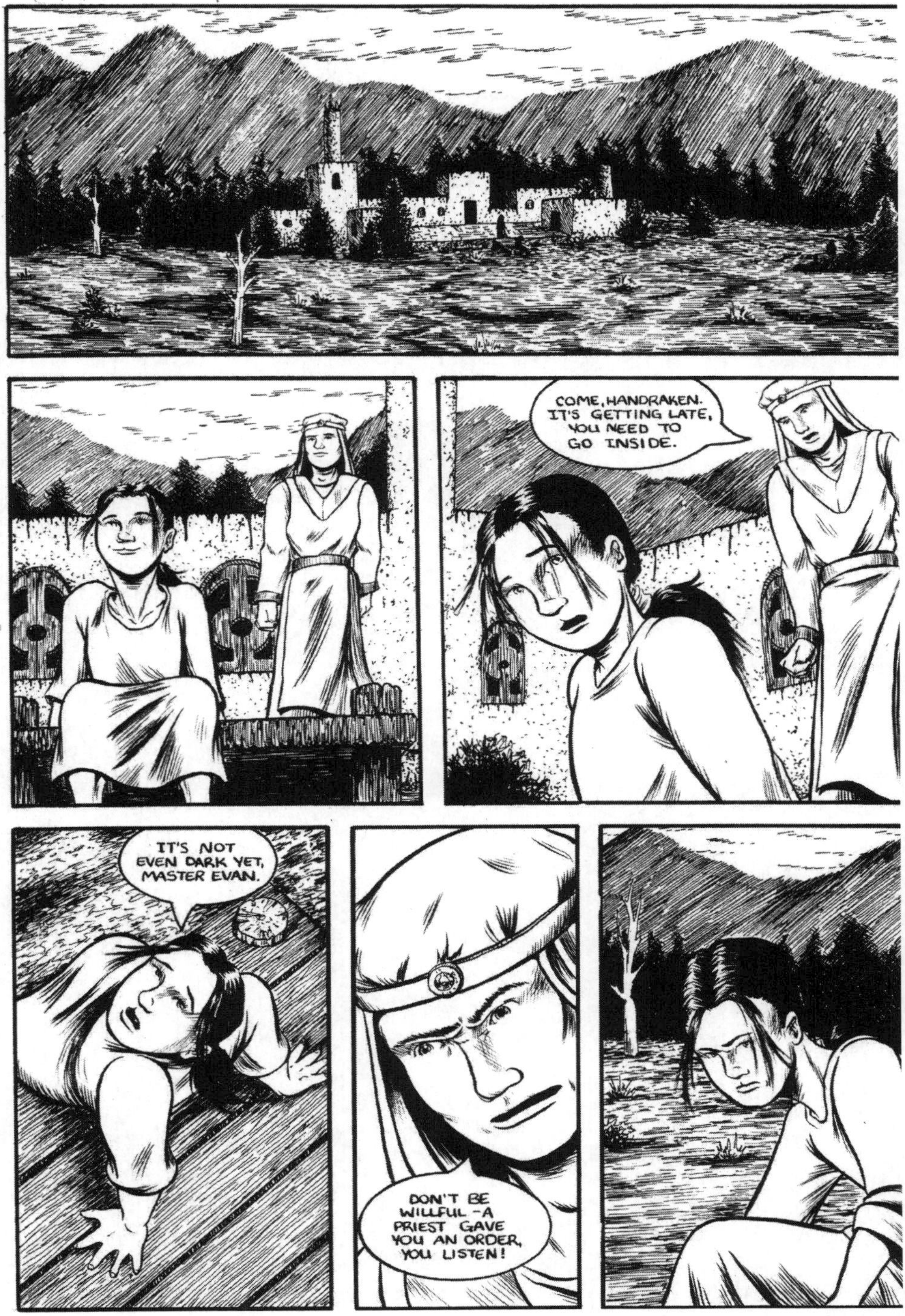
COME, HANDRAKEN. IT'S GETTING LATE, YOU NEED TO GO INSIDE.
IT'S NOT EVEN DARK YET, MASTER EVAN.
DON'T BE WILLFUL - A PRIEST GAVE YOU AN ORDER, YOU LISTEN!

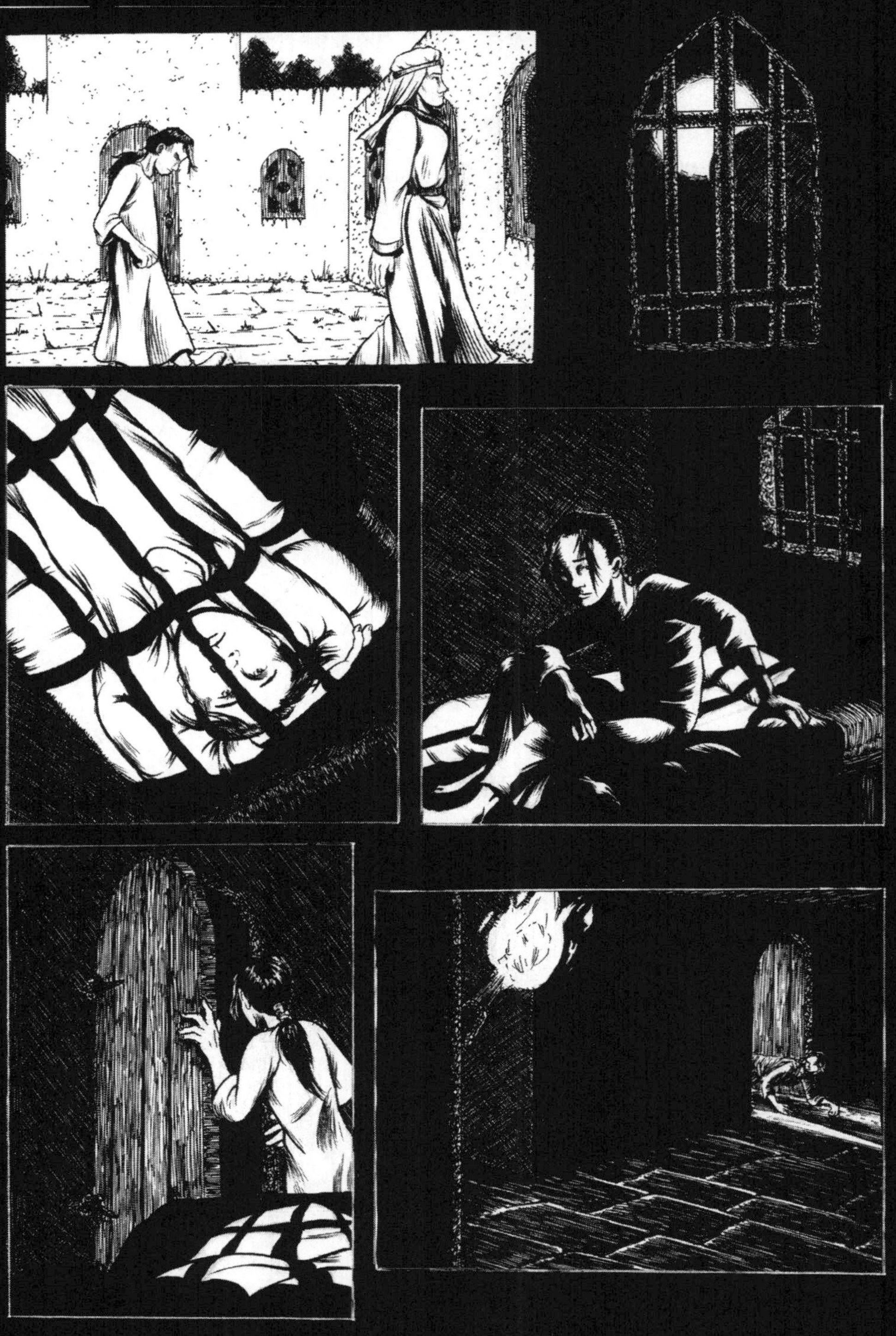

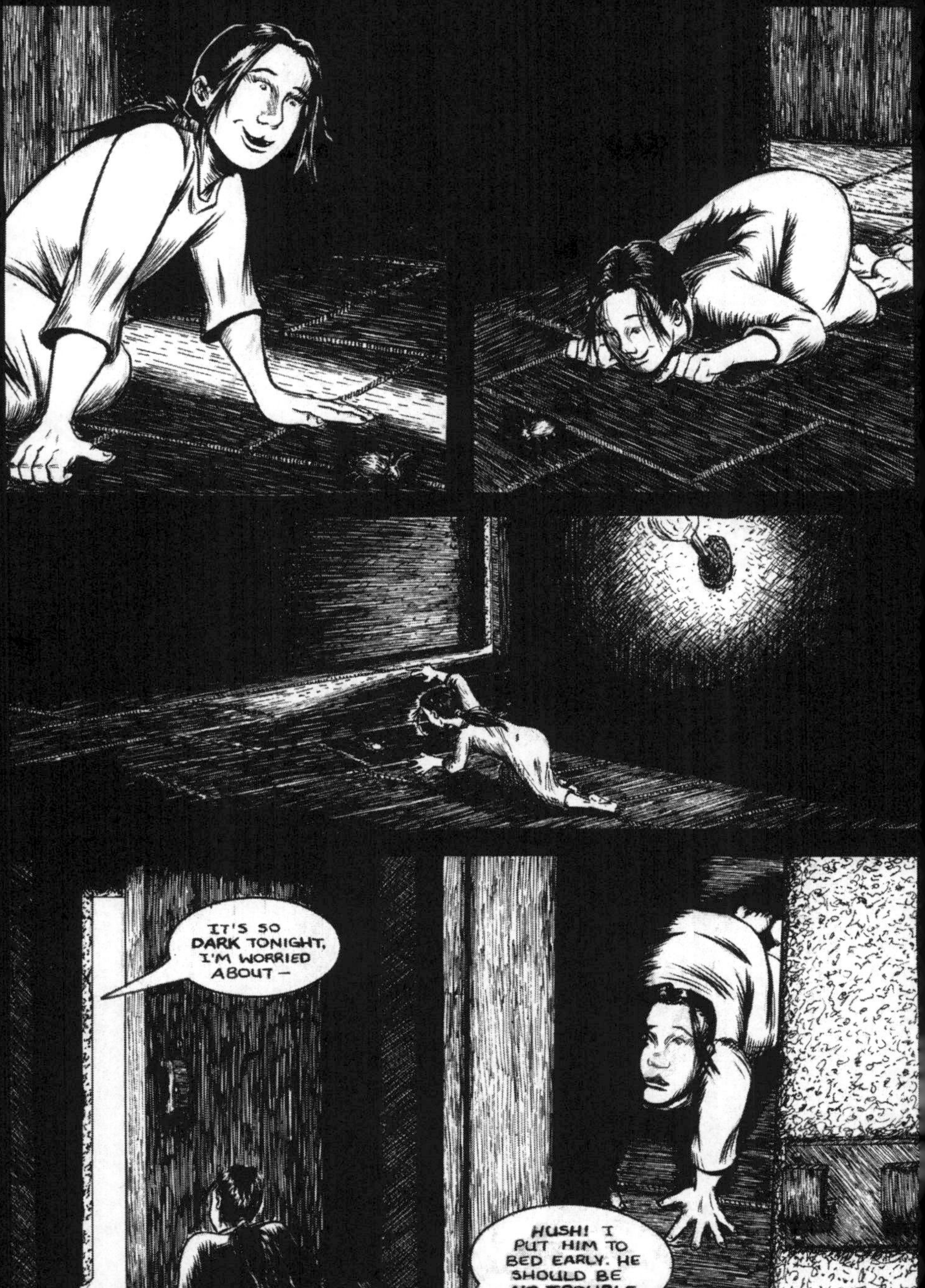
IT'S SO DARK TONIGHT, I'M WORRIED ABOUT—
HUSH! I PUT HIM TO BED EARLY. HE SHOULD BE NO TROUBLE.

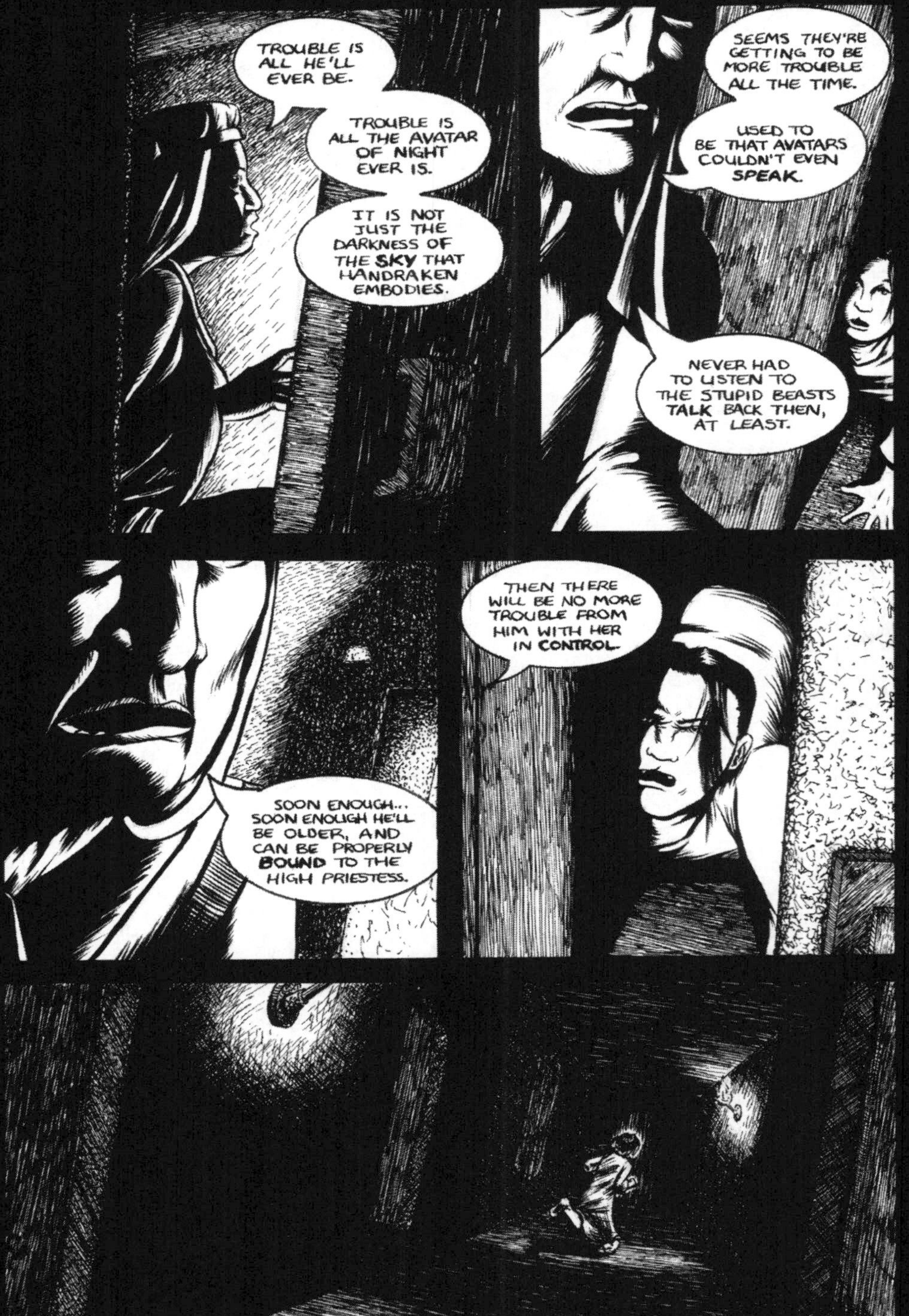
TROUBLE IS ALL HE'LL EVER BE.
TROUBLE IS ALL THE AVATAR OF NIGHT EVER IS.
IT IS NOT JUST THE DARKNESS OF THE SKY THAT HANDRAKEN EMBODIES.
SEEMS THEY'RE GETTING TO BE MORE TROUBLE ALL THE TIME.
USED TO BE THAT AVATARS COULDN'T EVEN SPEAK.
NEVER HAD TO LISTEN TO THE STUPID BEASTS TALK BACK THEN, AT LEAST.
SOON ENOUGH... SOON ENOUGH HE'LL BE OLDER, AND CAN BE PROPERLY BOUND TO THE HIGH PRIESTESS.
THEN THERE WILL BE NO MORE TROUBLE FROM HIM WITH HER IN CONTROL.

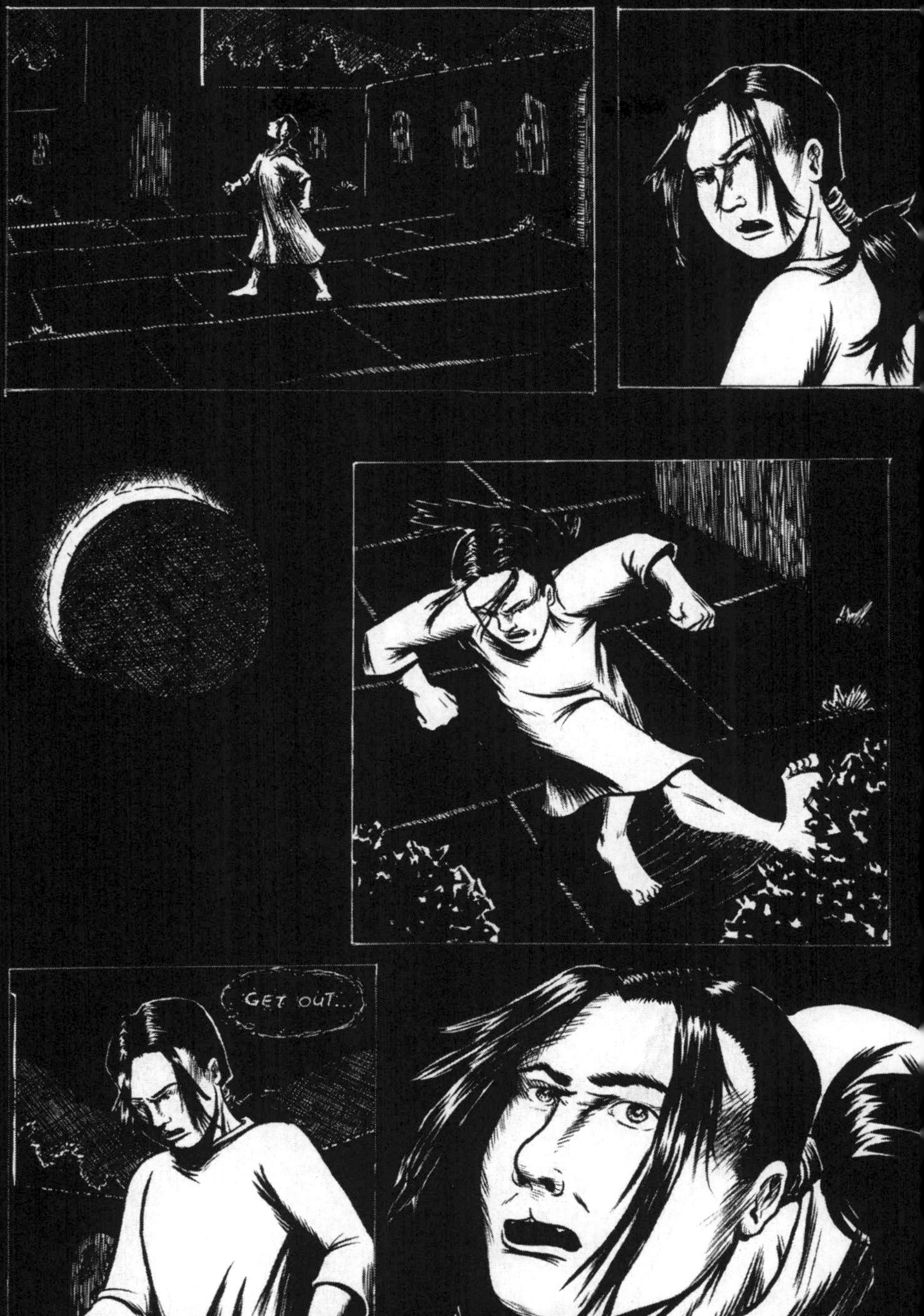
GET OUT...

RUN AWAY
RAAGH!!!

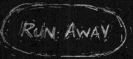

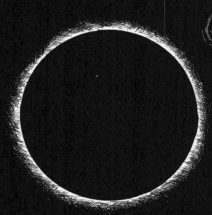

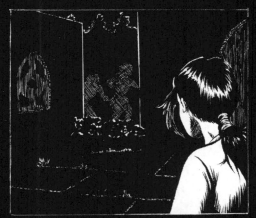

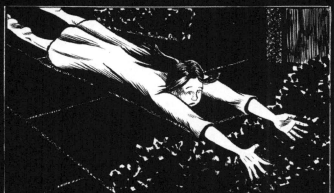

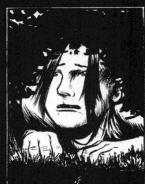

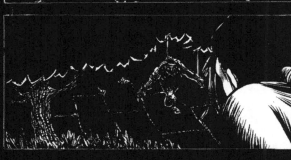

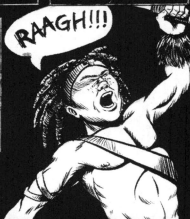

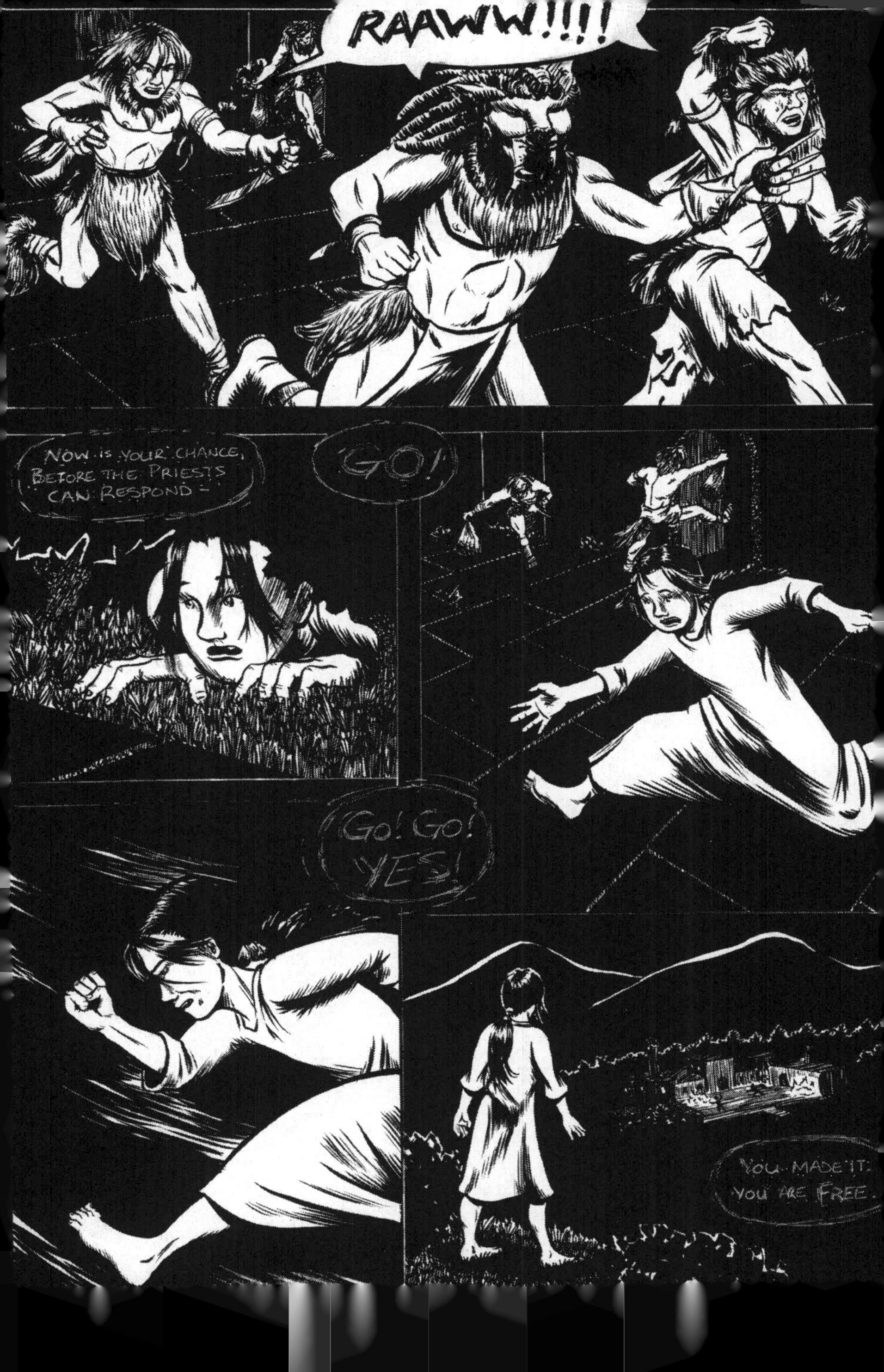
RAAWW!!!!
NOW IS YOUR CHANCE, BEFORE THE PRIESTS CAN RESPOND -
GO!
GO! GO! YES!
YOU MADE IT. YOU ARE FREE.

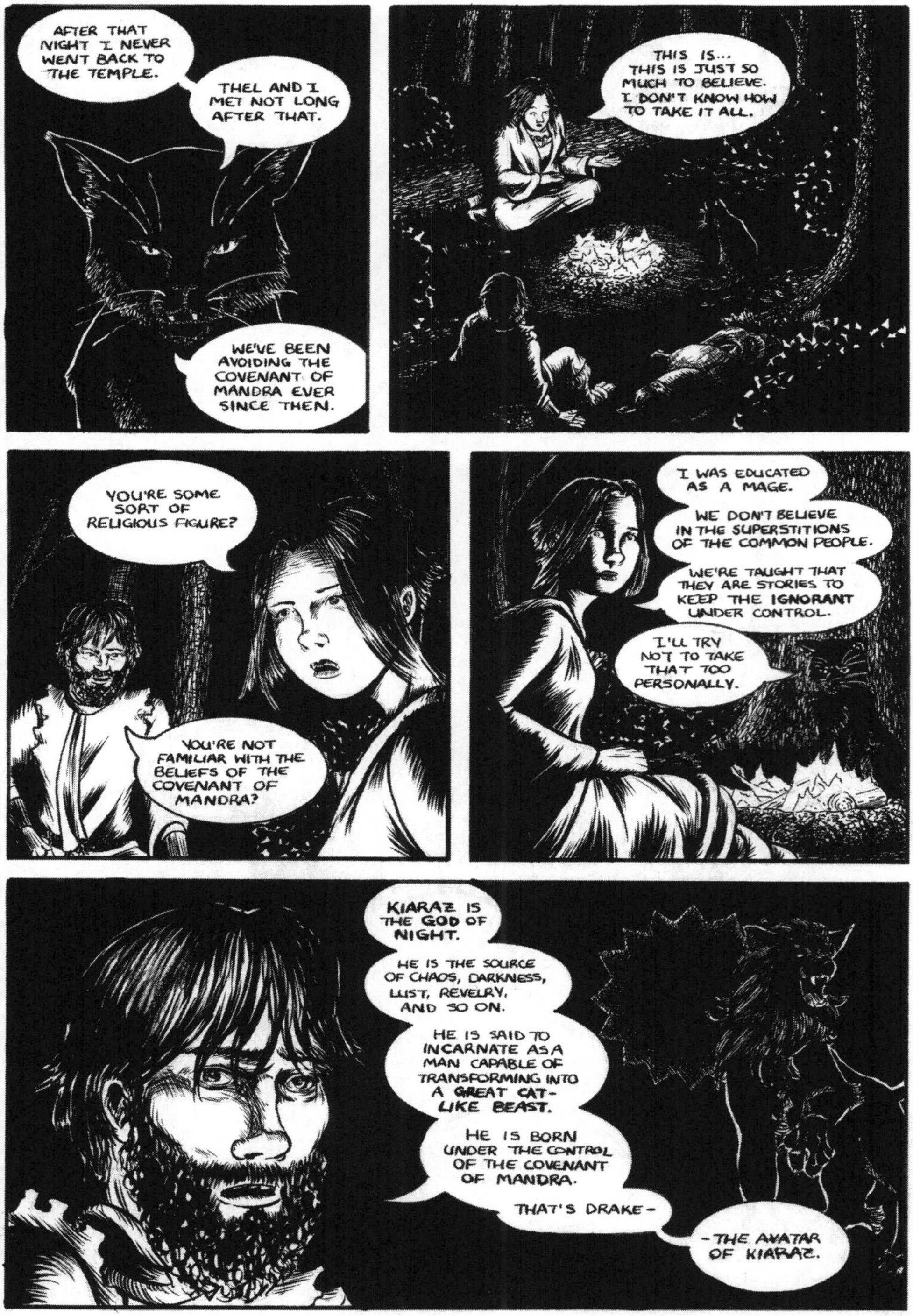
AFTER THAT NIGHT I NEVER WENT BACK TO THE TEMPLE.
THEL AND I MET NOT LONG AFTER THAT.
WE'VE BEEN AVOIDING THE COVENANT OF MANDRA EVER SINCE THEN.
THIS IS... THIS IS JUST SO MUCH TO BELIEVE. I DON'T KNOW HOW TO TAKE IT ALL.
YOU'RE SOME SORT OF RELIGIOUS FIGURE?
YOU'RE NOT FAMILIAR WITH THE BELIEFS OF THE COVENANT OF MANDRA?
I WAS EDUCATED AS A MAGE.
WE DON'T BELIEVE IN THE SUPERSTITIONS OF THE COMMON PEOPLE.
WE'RE TAUGHT THAT THEY ARE STORIES TO KEEP THE IGNORANT UNDER CONTROL.
I'LL TRY NOT TO TAKE THAT TOO PERSONALLY.
KIARAZ IS THE GOD OF NIGHT.
HE IS THE SOURCE OF CHAOS, DARKNESS, LUST, REVELRY, AND SO ON.
HE IS SAID TO INCARNATE AS A MAN CAPABLE OF TRANSFORMING INTO A GREAT CAT-LIKE BEAST.
HE IS BORN UNDER THE CONTROL OF THE COVENANT OF MANDRA.
THAT'S DRAKE-
-THE AVATAR OF KIARAZ.

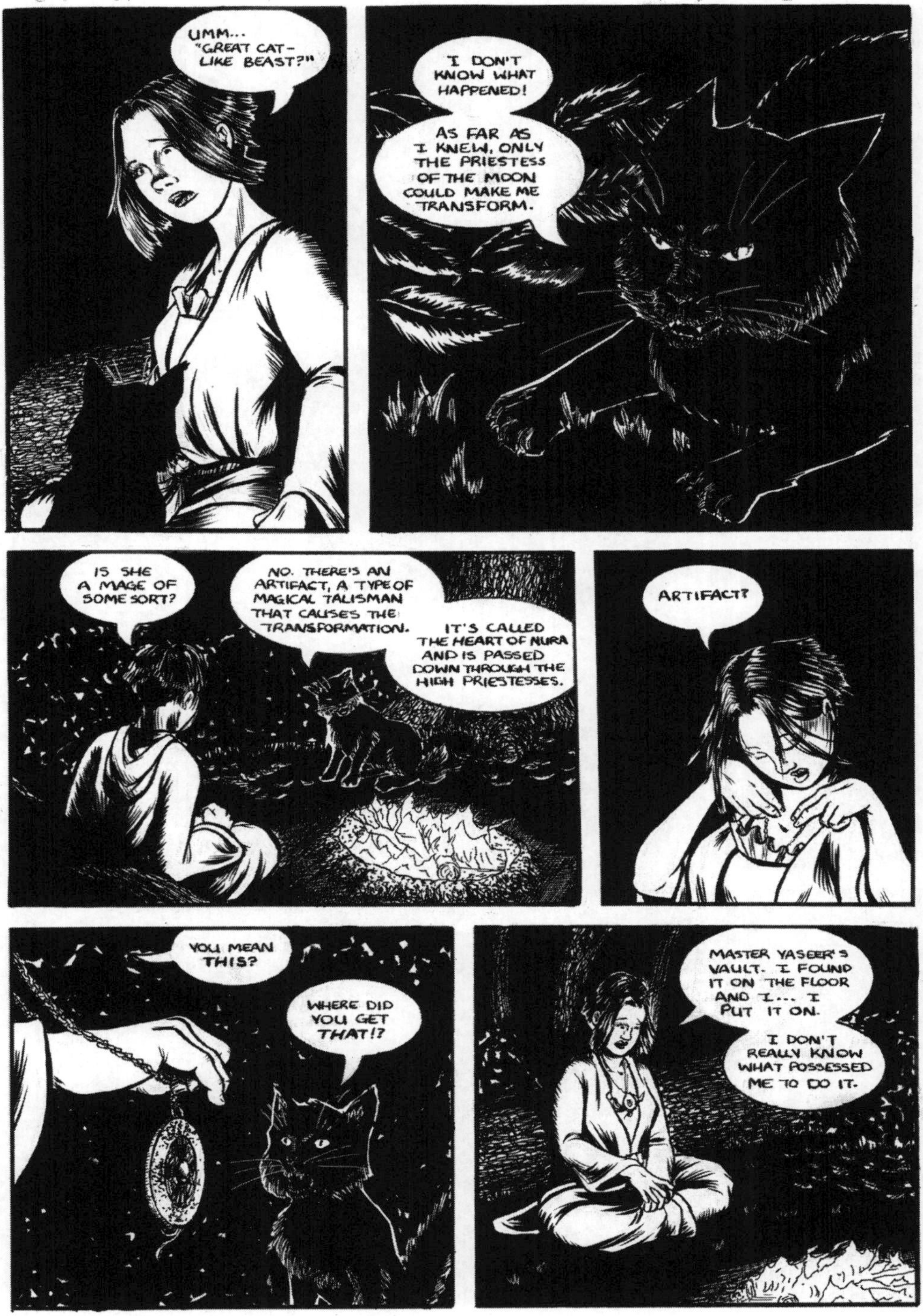
UMM... "GREAT CAT-LIKE BEAST?"
I DON'T KNOW WHAT HAPPENED!
AS FAR AS I KNEW, ONLY THE PRIESTESS OF THE MOON COULD MAKE ME TRANSFORM.
IS SHE A MAGE OF SOME SORT?
NO. THERE'S AN ARTIFACT, A TYPE OF MAGICAL TALISMAN THAT CAUSES THE TRANSFORMATION.
IT'S CALLED THE HEART OF NURA AND IS PASSED DOWN THROUGH THE HIGH PRIESTESSES.
ARTIFACT?
YOU MEAN THIS?
WHERE DID YOU GET THAT!?
MASTER YASEER'S VAULT. I FOUND IT ON THE FLOOR AND I... I PUT IT ON.
I DON'T REALLY KNOW WHAT POSSESSED ME TO DO IT.

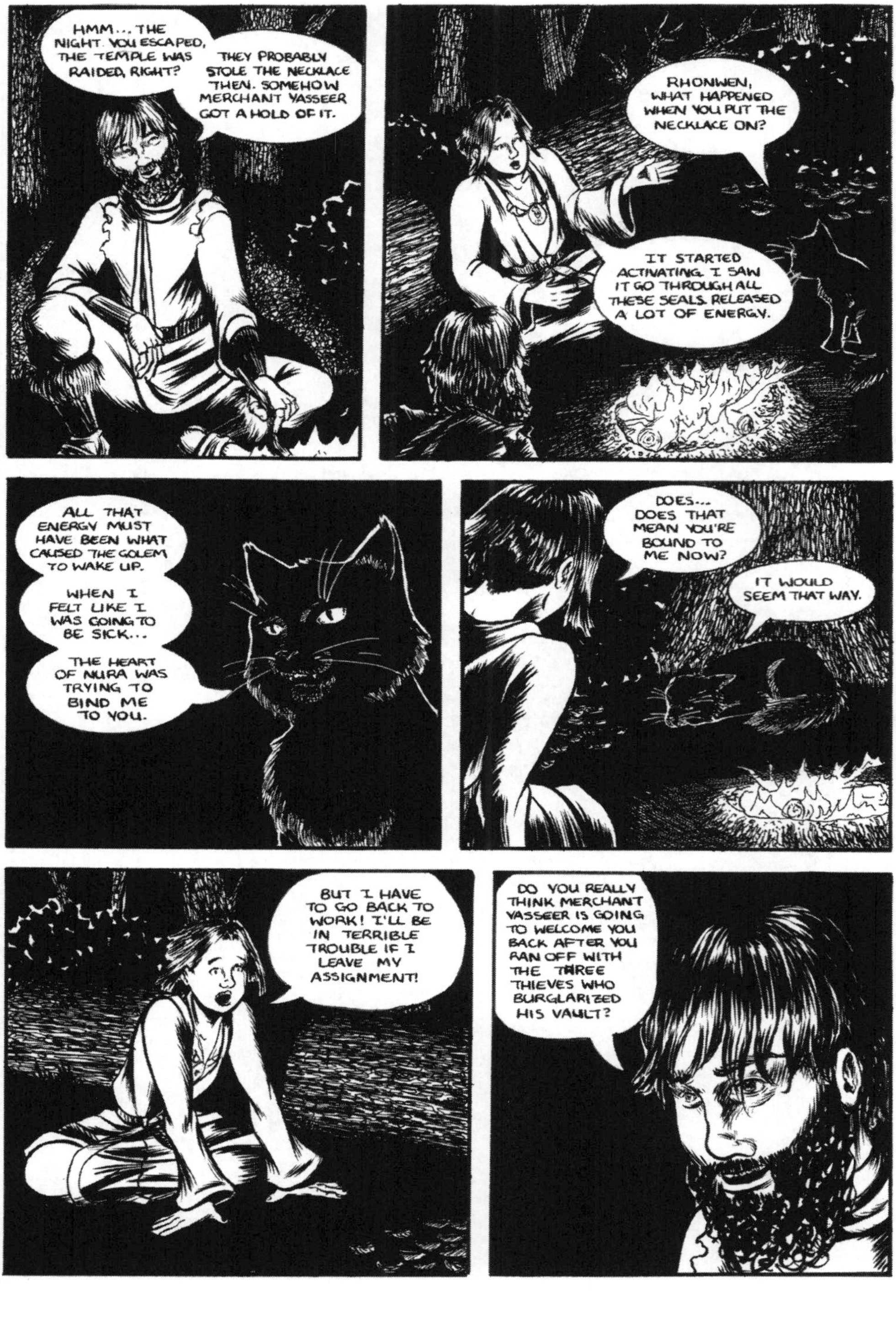
HMM... THE NIGHT YOU ESCAPED, THE TEMPLE WAS RAIDED, RIGHT?
THEY PROBABLY STOLE THE NECKLACE THEN. SOMEHOW MERCHANT VASSEER GOT A HOLD OF IT.
RHONWEN, WHAT HAPPENED WHEN YOU PUT THE NECKLACE ON?
IT STARTED ACTIVATING. I SAW IT GO THROUGH ALL THESE SEALS. RELEASED A LOT OF ENERGY.
ALL THAT ENERGY MUST HAVE BEEN WHAT CAUSED THE GOLEM TO WAKE UP.
WHEN I FELT LIKE I WAS GOING TO BE SICK...
THE HEART OF NURA WAS TRYING TO BIND ME TO YOU.
DOES... DOES THAT MEAN YOU'RE BOUND TO ME NOW?
IT WOULD SEEM THAT WAY.
BUT I HAVE TO GO BACK TO WORK! I'LL BE IN TERRIBLE TROUBLE IF I LEAVE MY ASSIGNMENT!
DO YOU REALLY THINK MERCHANT VASSEER IS GOING TO WELCOME YOU BACK AFTER YOU RAN OFF WITH THE THREE THIEVES WHO BURGLARIZED HIS VAULT?

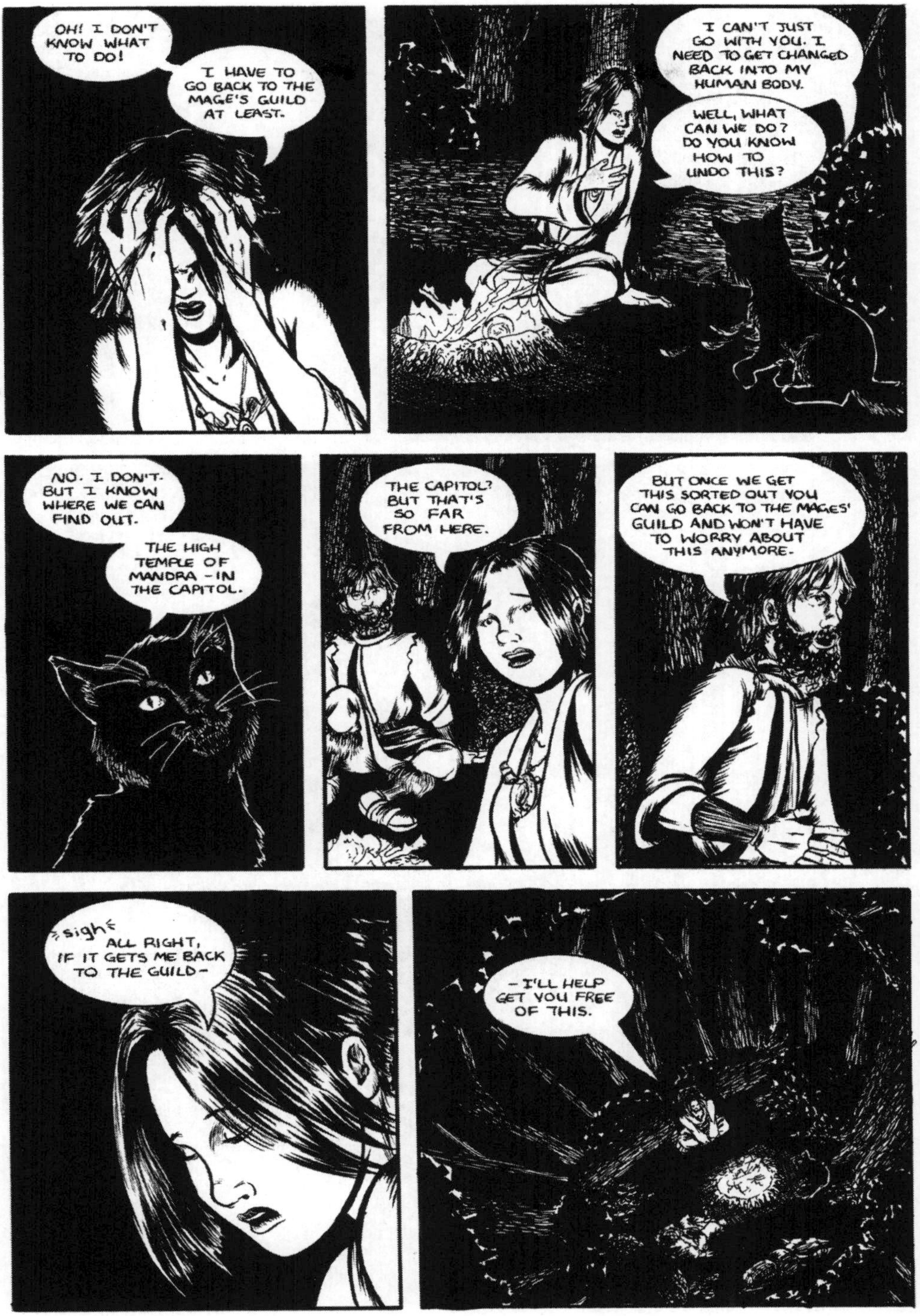
OH! I DON'T KNOW WHAT TO DO!
I HAVE TO GO BACK TO THE MAGE'S GUILD AT LEAST.
I CAN'T JUST GO WITH YOU. I NEED TO GET CHANGED BACK INTO MY HUMAN BODY.
WELL, WHAT CAN WE DO? DO YOU KNOW HOW TO UNDO THIS?
NO. I DON'T. BUT I KNOW WHERE WE CAN FIND OUT.
THE HIGH TEMPLE OF MANDRA - IN THE CAPITOL.
THE CAPITOL? BUT THAT'S SO FAR FROM HERE.
BUT ONCE WE GET THIS SORTED OUT YOU CAN GO BACK TO THE MAGES' GUILD AND WON'T HAVE TO WORRY ABOUT THIS ANYMORE.
sigh ALL RIGHT, IF IT GETS ME BACK TO THE GUILD-
-I'LL HELP GET YOU FREE OF THIS.

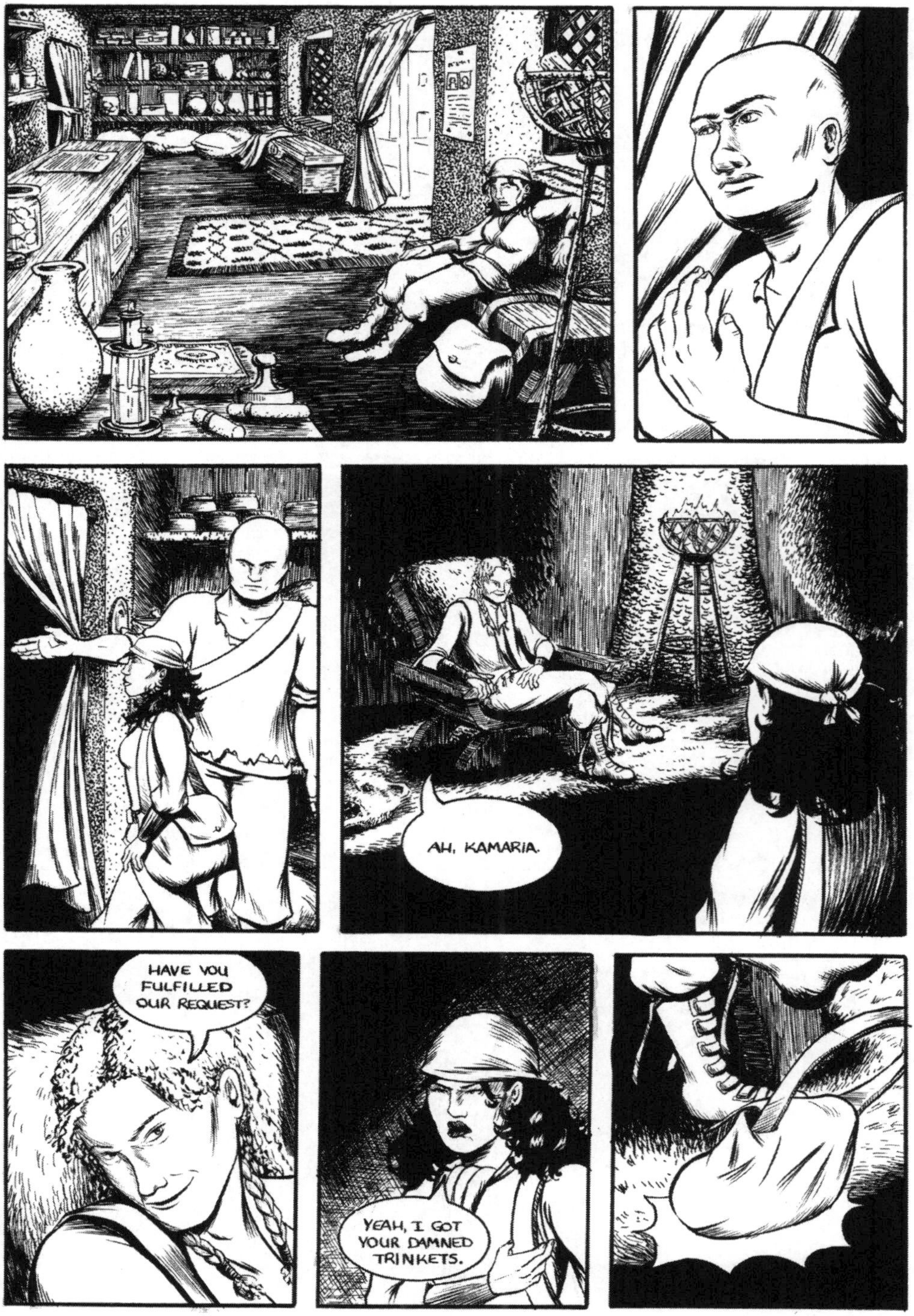
AH, KAMARIA.
HAVE YOU FULFILLED OUR REQUEST?
YEAH, I GOT YOUR DAMNED TRINKETS.

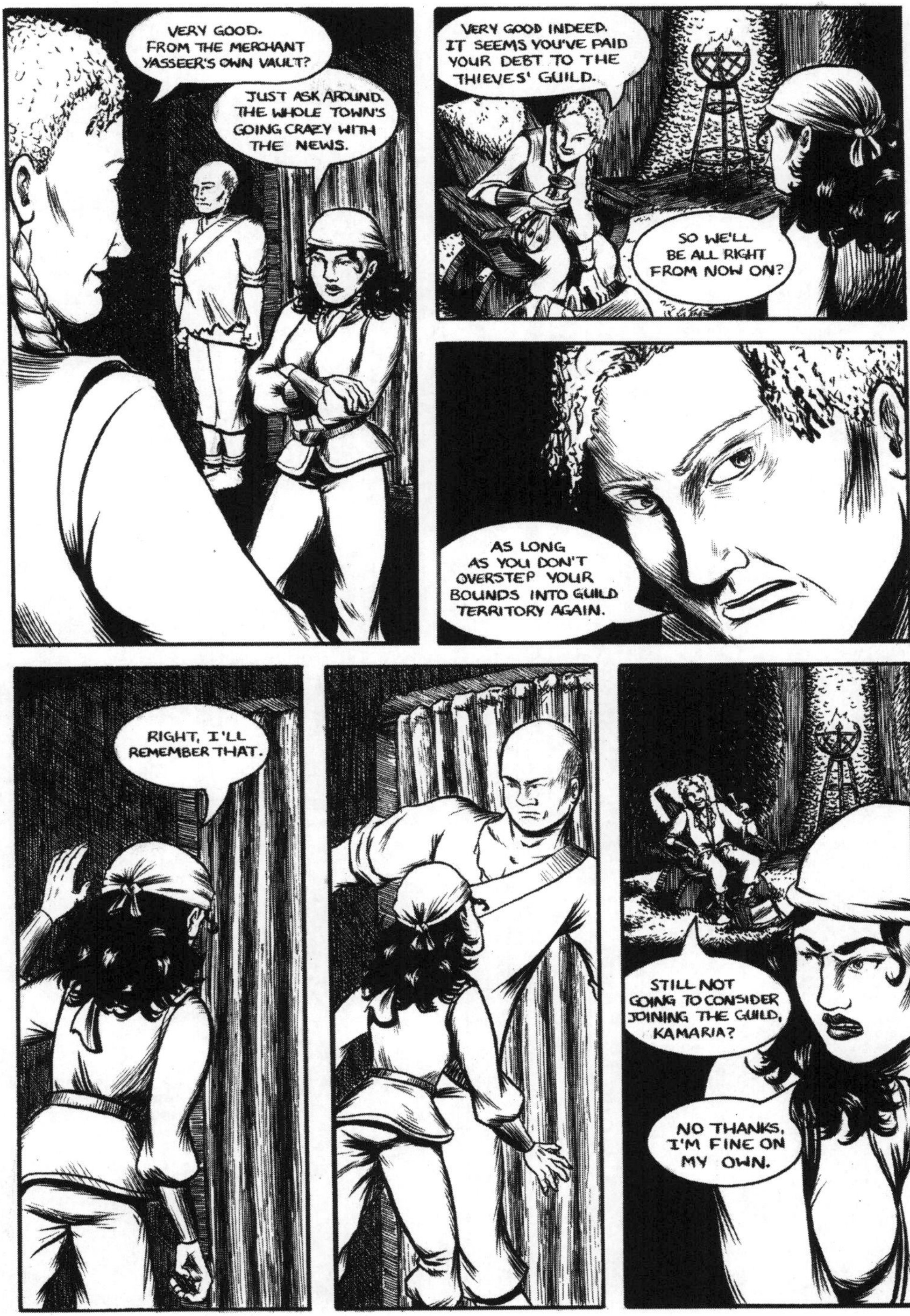
VERY GOOD. FROM THE MERCHANT YASSEER'S OWN VAULT?
JUST ASK AROUND. THE WHOLE TOWN'S GOING CRAZY WITH THE NEWS.
VERY GOOD INDEED. IT SEEMS YOU'VE PAID YOUR DEBT TO THE THIEVES' GUILD.
SO WE'LL BE ALL RIGHT FROM NOW ON?
AS LONG AS YOU DON'T OVERSTEP YOUR BOUNDS INTO GUILD TERRITORY AGAIN.
RIGHT, I'LL REMEMBER THAT.
STILL NOT GOING TO CONSIDER JOINING THE GUILD, KAMARIA?
NO THANKS, I'M FINE ON MY OWN.

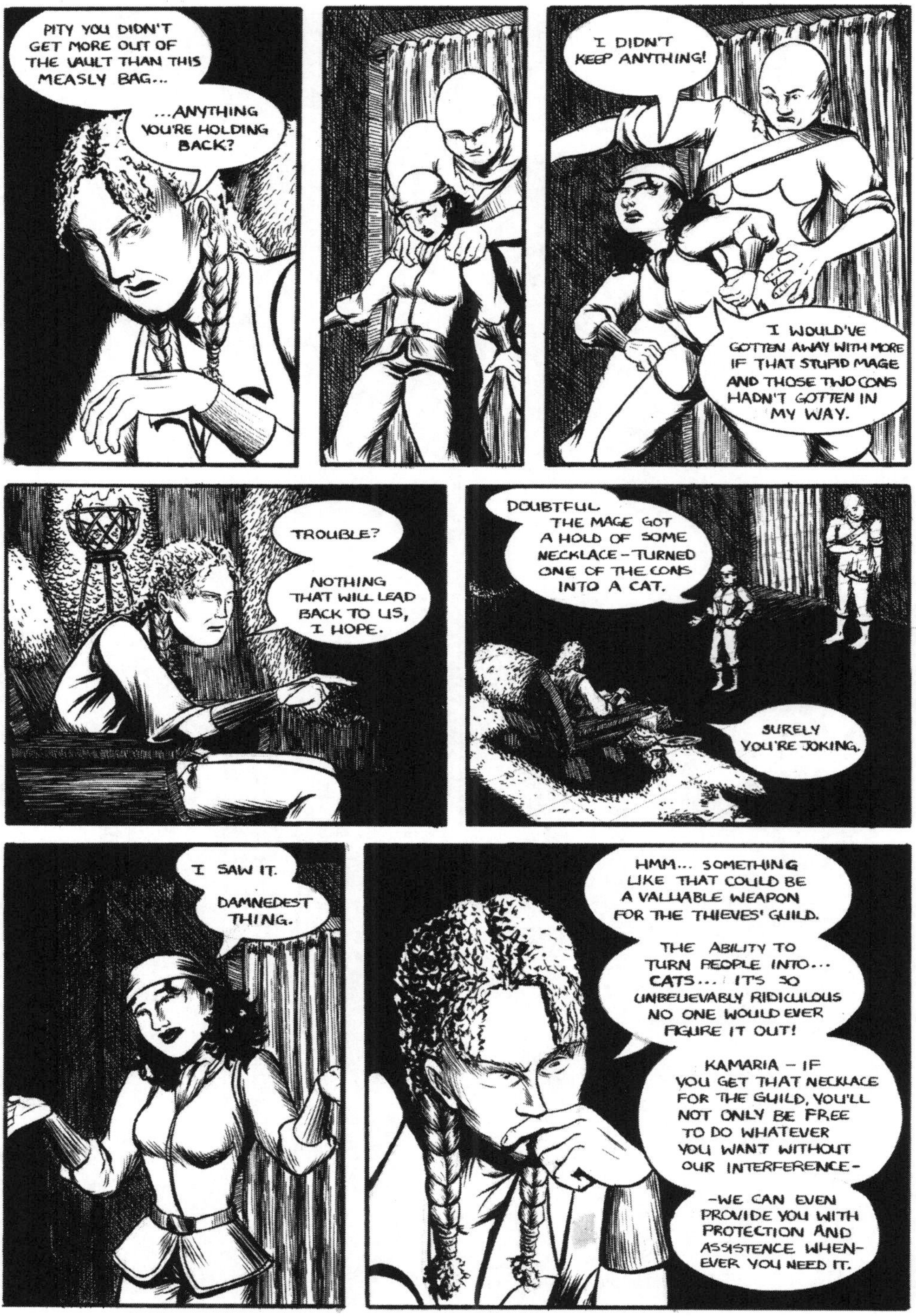
PITY YOU DIDN'T GET MORE OUT OF THE VAULT THAN THIS MEASLY BAG...
...ANYTHING YOU'RE HOLDING BACK?
I DIDN'T KEEP ANYTHING!
I WOULD'VE GOTTEN AWAY WITH MORE IF THAT STUPID MAGE AND THOSE TWO CONS HADN'T GOTTEN IN MY WAY.
TROUBLE?
NOTHING THAT WILL LEAD BACK TO US, I HOPE.
DOUBTFUL. THE MAGE GOT A HOLD OF SOME NECKLACE - TURNED ONE OF THE CONS INTO A CAT.
SURELY YOU'RE JOKING.
I SAW IT.
DAMNEDEST THING.
HMM... SOMETHING LIKE THAT COULD BE A VALUABLE WEAPON FOR THE THIEVES' GUILD.
THE ABILITY TO TURN PEOPLE INTO... CATS... IT'S SO UNBELIEVABLY RIDICULOUS NO ONE WOULD EVER FIGURE IT OUT!
KAMARIA - IF YOU GET THAT NECKLACE FOR THE GUILD, YOU'LL NOT ONLY BE FREE TO DO WHATEVER YOU WANT WITHOUT OUR INTERFERENCE-
-WE CAN EVEN PROVIDE YOU WITH PROTECTION AND ASSISTENCE WHEN-EVER YOU NEED IT.

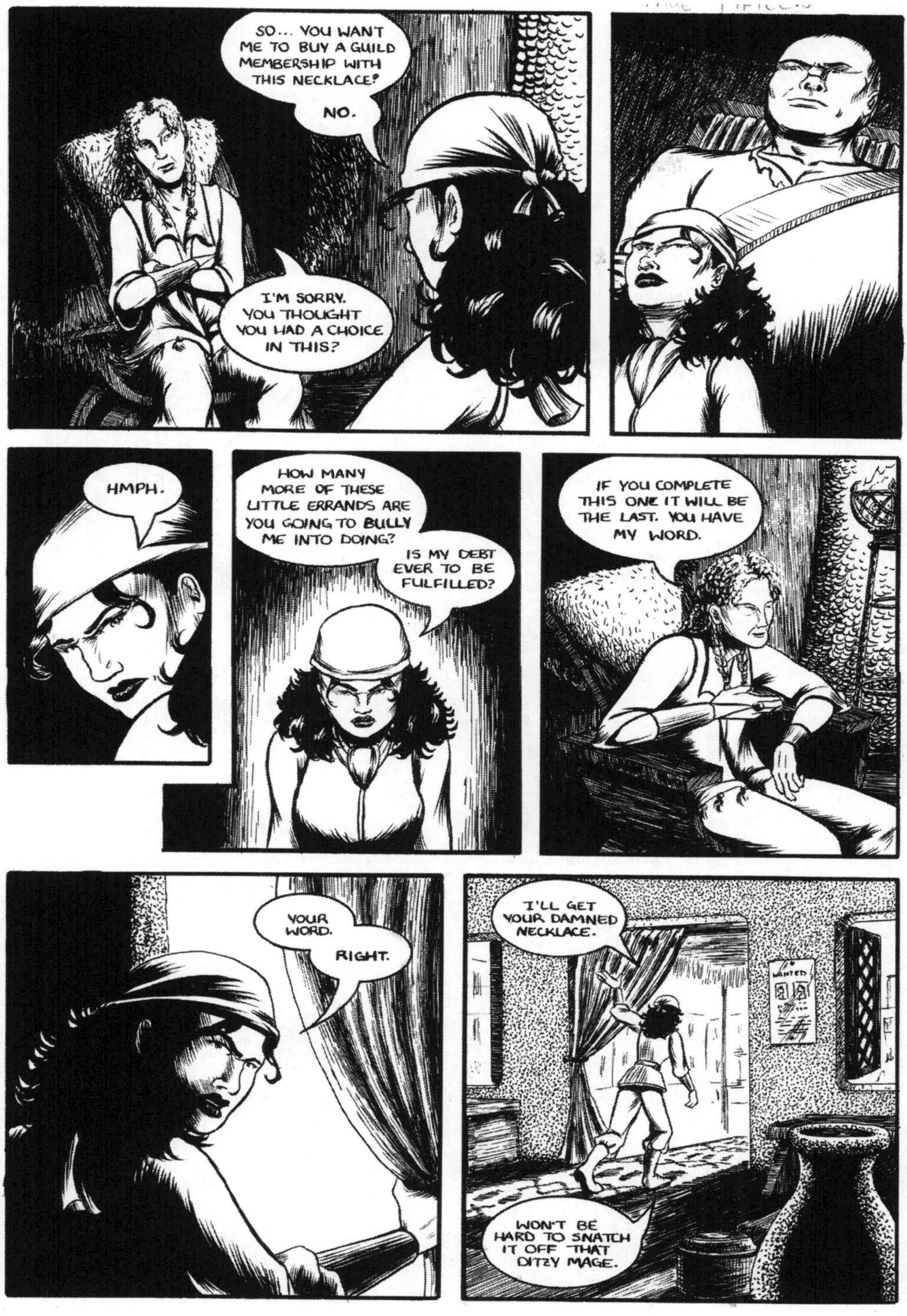
SO... YOU WANT ME TO BUY A GUILD MEMBERSHIP WITH THIS NECKLACE?
NO.
I'M SORRY. YOU THOUGHT YOU HAD A CHOICE IN THIS?
HMPH.
HOW MANY MORE OF THESE LITTLE ERRANDS ARE YOU GOING TO BULLY ME INTO DOING?
IS MY DEBT EVER TO BE FULFILLED?
IF YOU COMPLETE THIS ONE IT WILL BE THE LAST. YOU HAVE MY WORD.
YOUR WORD.
RIGHT.
I'LL GET YOUR DAMNED NECKLACE.
WANTED
WON'T BE HARD TO SNATCH IT OFF THAT DITZY MAGE.

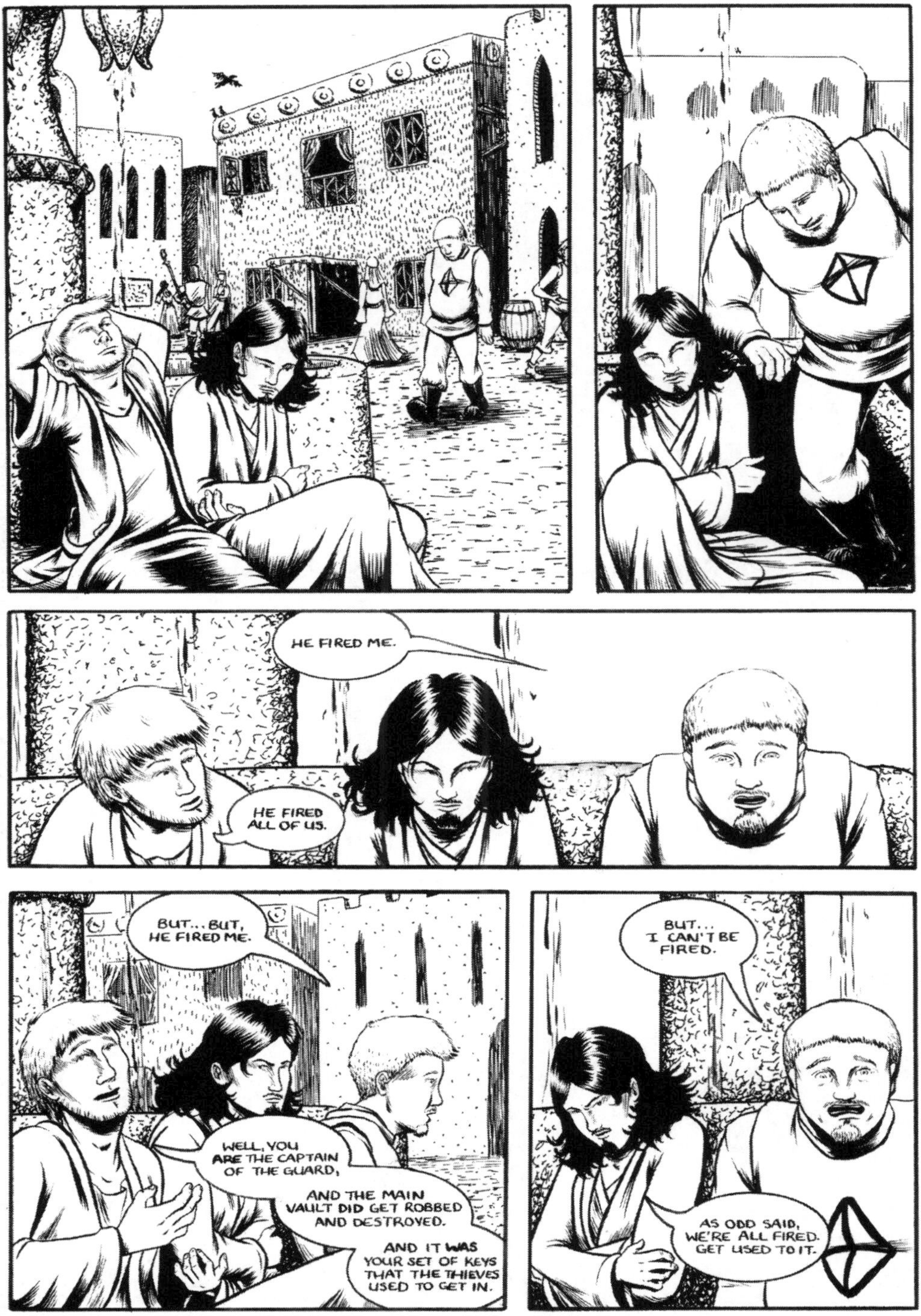
HE FIRED ME.
HE FIRED ALL OF US.
BUT... BUT, HE FIRED ME.
WELL, YOU ARE THE CAPTAIN OF THE GUARD,
AND THE MAIN VAULT DID GET ROBBED AND DESTROYED.
AND IT WAS YOUR SET OF KEYS THAT THE THIEVES USED TO GET IN.
BUT... I CAN'T BE FIRED.
AS ODD SAID, WE'RE ALL FIRED. GET USED TO IT.

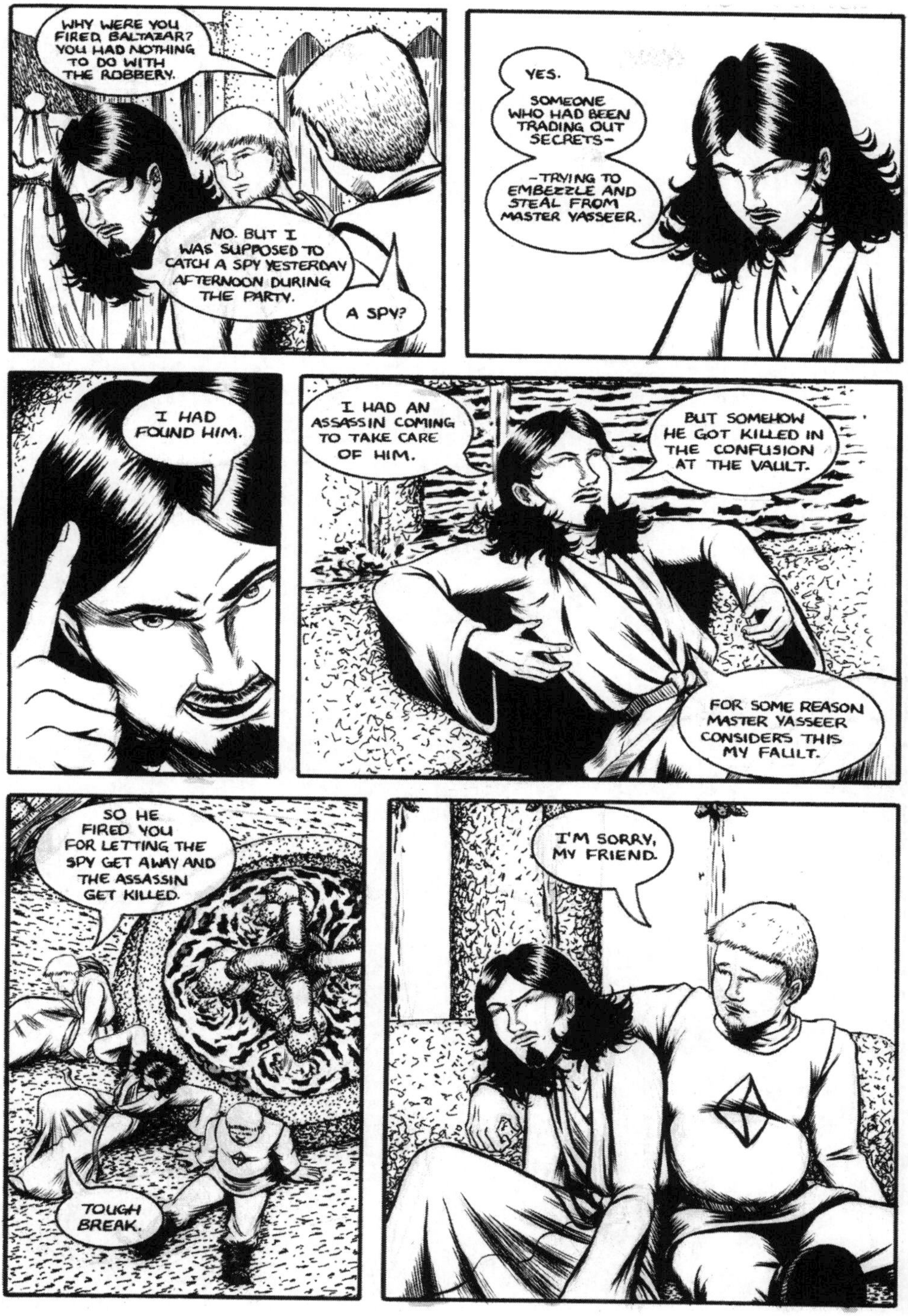
WHY WERE YOU FIRED BALTAZAR? YOU HAD NOTHING TO DO WITH THE ROBBERY.
NO. BUT I WAS SUPPOSED TO CATCH A SPY YESTERDAY AFTERNOON DURING THE PARTY.
A SPY?
YES.
SOMEONE WHO HAD BEEN TRADING OUT SECRETS-
-TRYING TO EMBEZZLE AND STEAL FROM MASTER YASSEER.
I HAD FOUND HIM.
I HAD AN ASSASSIN COMING TO TAKE CARE OF HIM.
BUT SOMEHOW HE GOT KILLED IN THE CONFUSION AT THE VAULT.
FOR SOME REASON MASTER YASSEER CONSIDERS THIS MY FAULT.
SO HE FIRED YOU FOR LETTING THE SPY GET AWAY AND THE ASSASSIN GET KILLED.
TOUGH BREAK.
I'M SORRY, MY FRIEND.

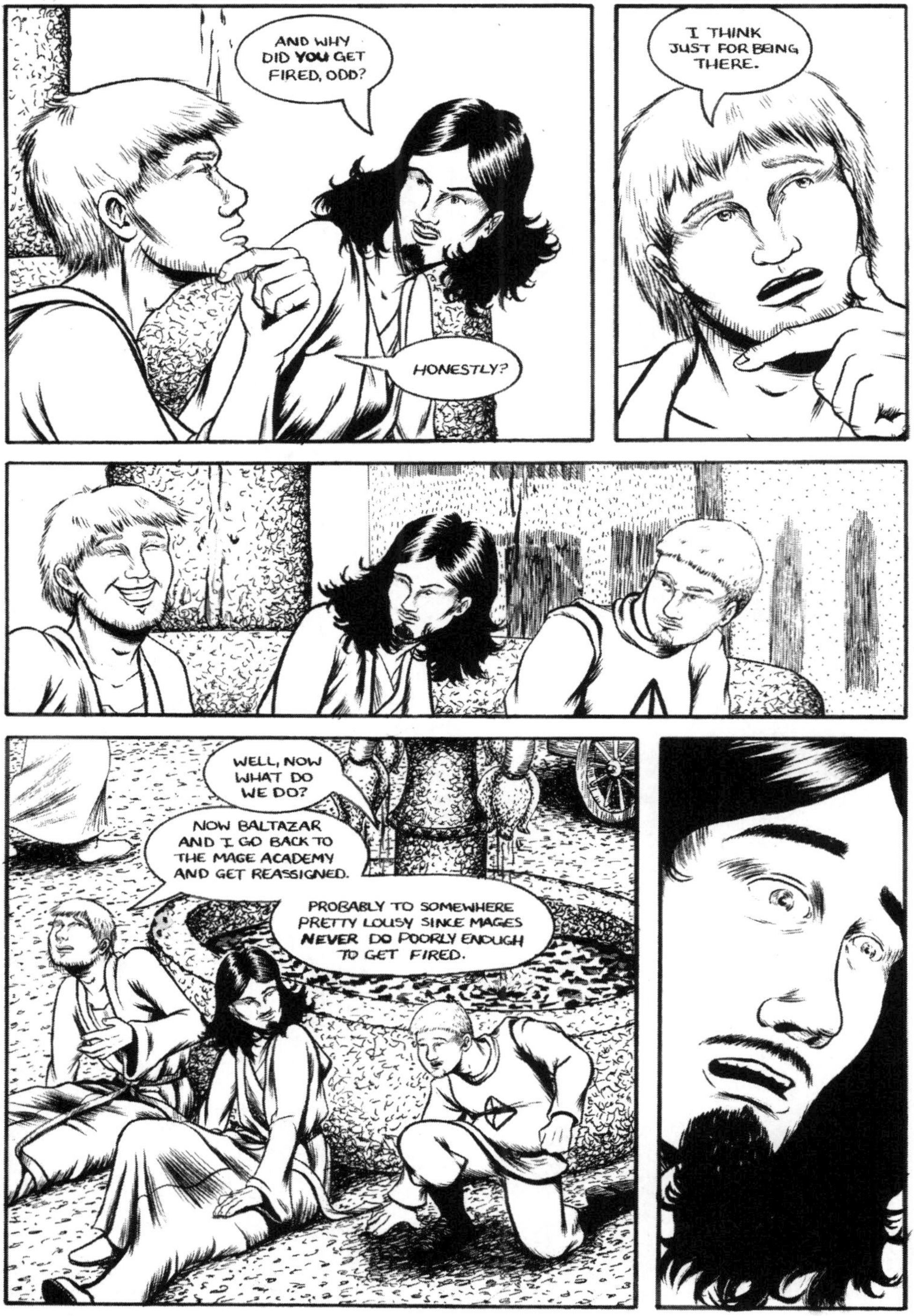
AND WHY DID **YOU** GET FIRED, ODD?
HONESTLY?
I THINK JUST FOR BEING THERE.
WELL, NOW WHAT DO WE DO?
NOW BALTAZAR AND I GO BACK TO THE MAGE ACADEMY AND GET REASSIGNED.
PROBABLY TO SOMEWHERE PRETTY LOUSY SINCE MAGES **NEVER** DO POORLY ENOUGH TO GET FIRED.

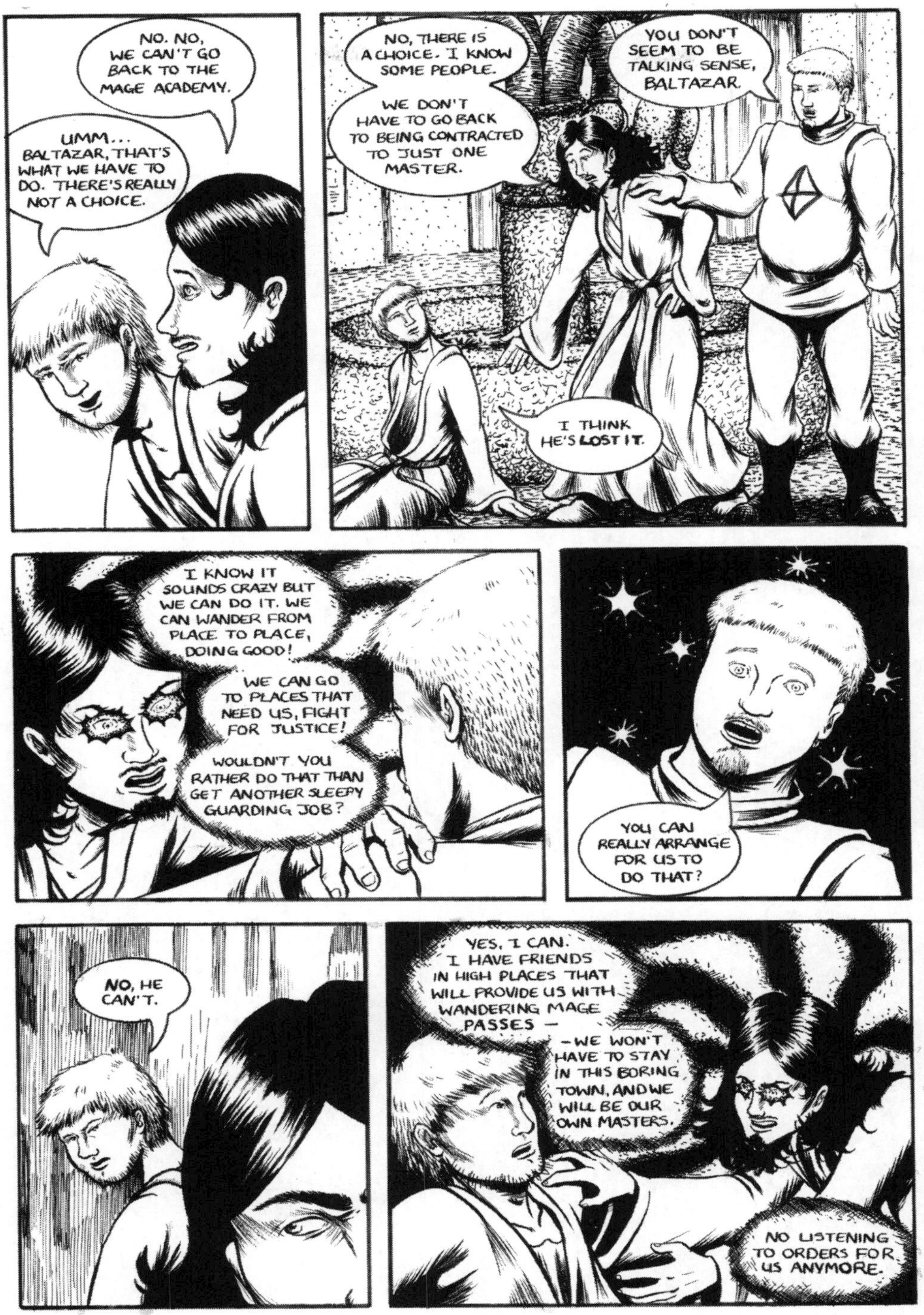
NO. NO, WE CAN'T GO BACK TO THE MAGE ACADEMY.
UMM... BALTAZAR, THAT'S WHAT WE HAVE TO DO. THERE'S REALLY NOT A CHOICE.
NO, THERE IS A CHOICE. I KNOW SOME PEOPLE.
WE DON'T HAVE TO GO BACK TO BEING CONTRACTED TO JUST ONE MASTER.
YOU DON'T SEEM TO BE TALKING SENSE, BALTAZAR.
I THINK HE'S LOST IT.
I KNOW IT SOUNDS CRAZY BUT WE CAN DO IT. WE CAN WANDER FROM PLACE TO PLACE, DOING GOOD!
WE CAN GO TO PLACES THAT NEED US, FIGHT FOR JUSTICE!
WOULDN'T YOU RATHER DO THAT THAN GET ANOTHER SLEEPY GUARDING JOB?
YOU CAN REALLY ARRANGE FOR US TO DO THAT?
NO, HE CAN'T.
YES, I CAN. I HAVE FRIENDS IN HIGH PLACES THAT WILL PROVIDE US WITH WANDERING MAGE PASSES —
— WE WON'T HAVE TO STAY IN THIS BORING TOWN, AND WE WILL BE OUR OWN MASTERS.
NO LISTENING TO ORDERS FOR US ANYMORE.

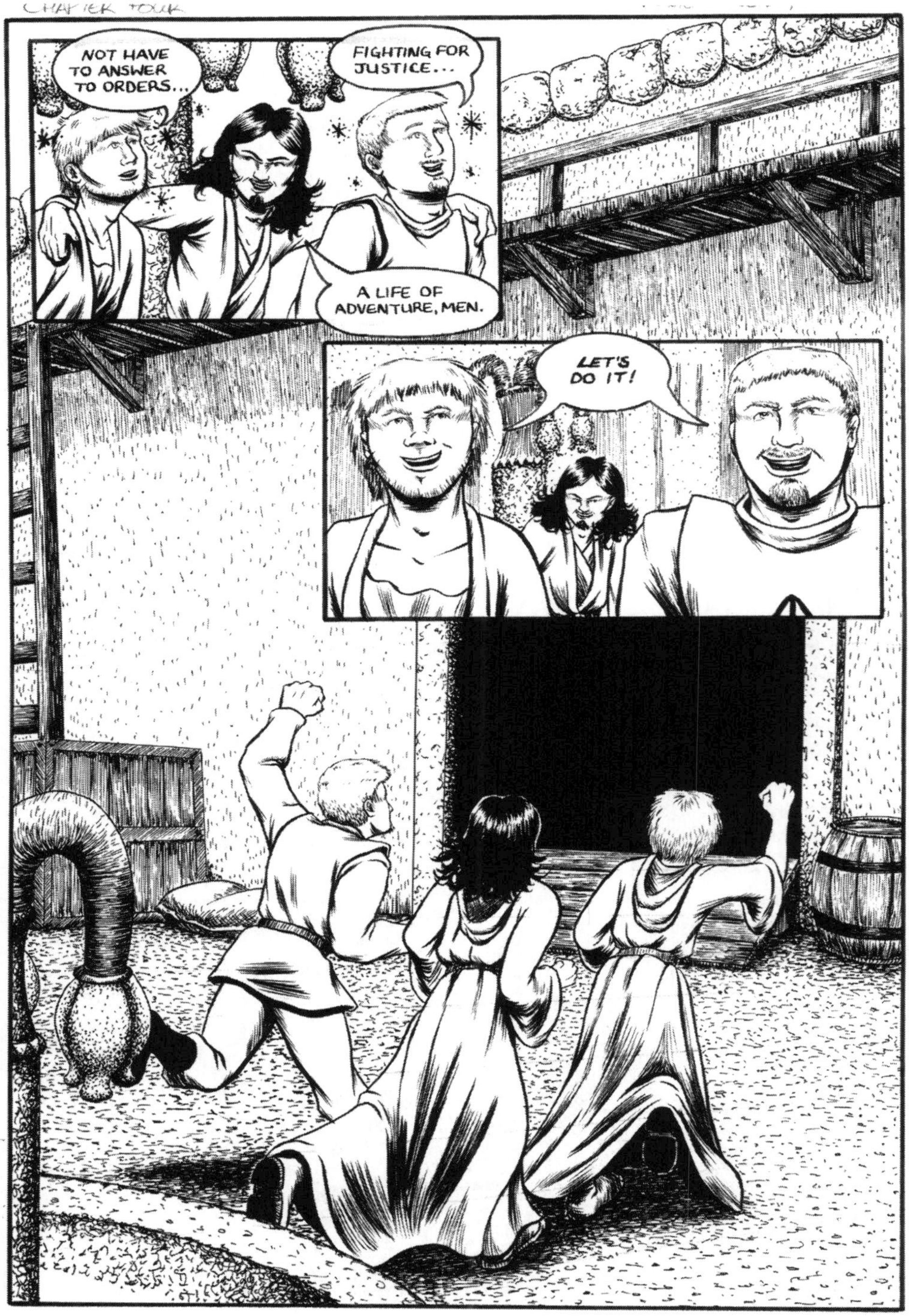
NOT HAVE TO ANSWER TO ORDERS...
FIGHTING FOR JUSTICE...
A LIFE OF ADVENTURE, MEN.
LET'S DO IT!

CHAPTER V

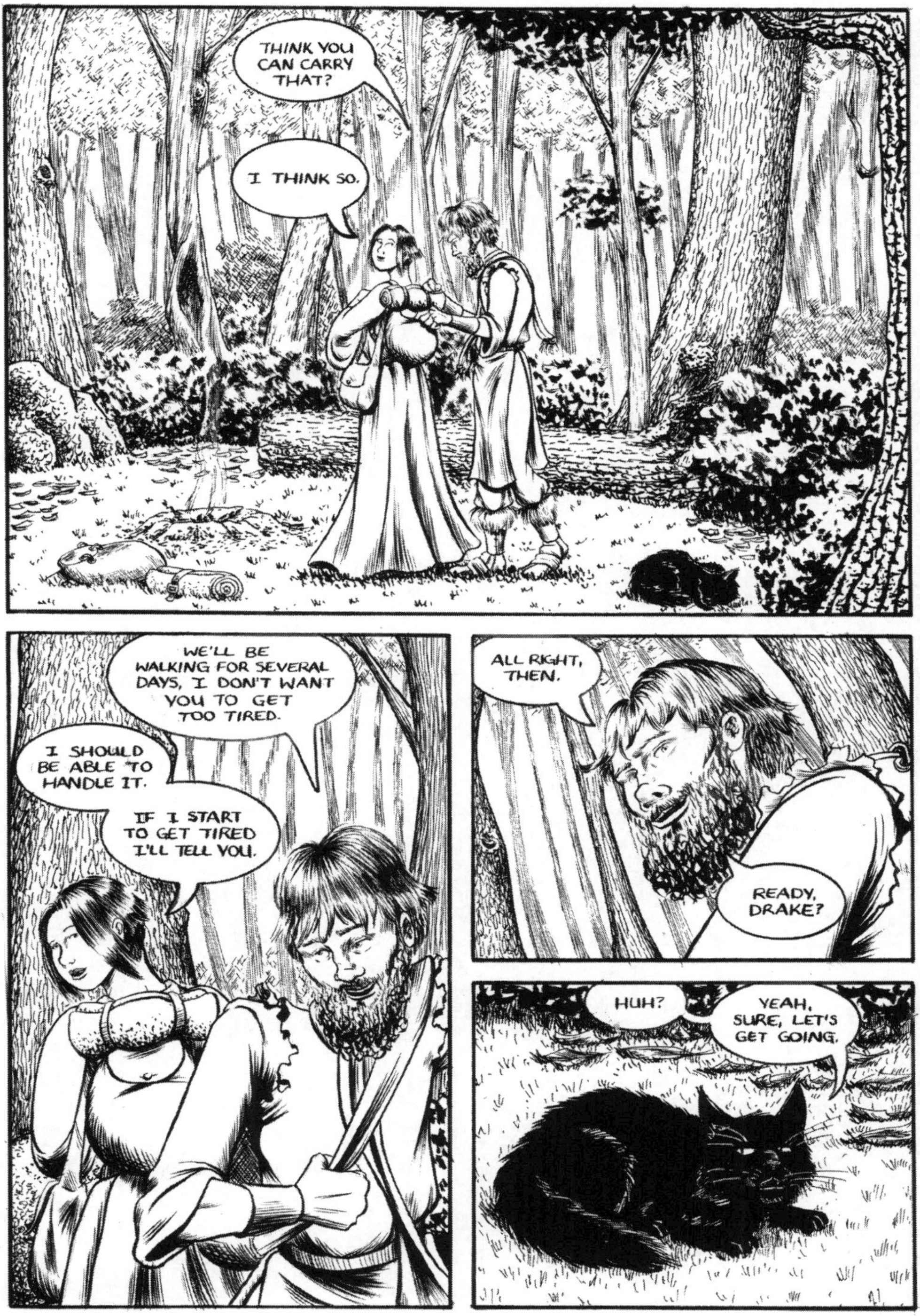
THINK YOU CAN CARRY THAT?
I THINK SO.
WE'LL BE WALKING FOR SEVERAL DAYS, I DON'T WANT YOU TO GET TOO TIRED.
I SHOULD BE ABLE TO HANDLE IT.
IF I START TO GET TIRED I'LL TELL YOU.
ALL RIGHT, THEN.
READY, DRAKE?
HUH?
YEAH, SURE, LET'S GET GOING.

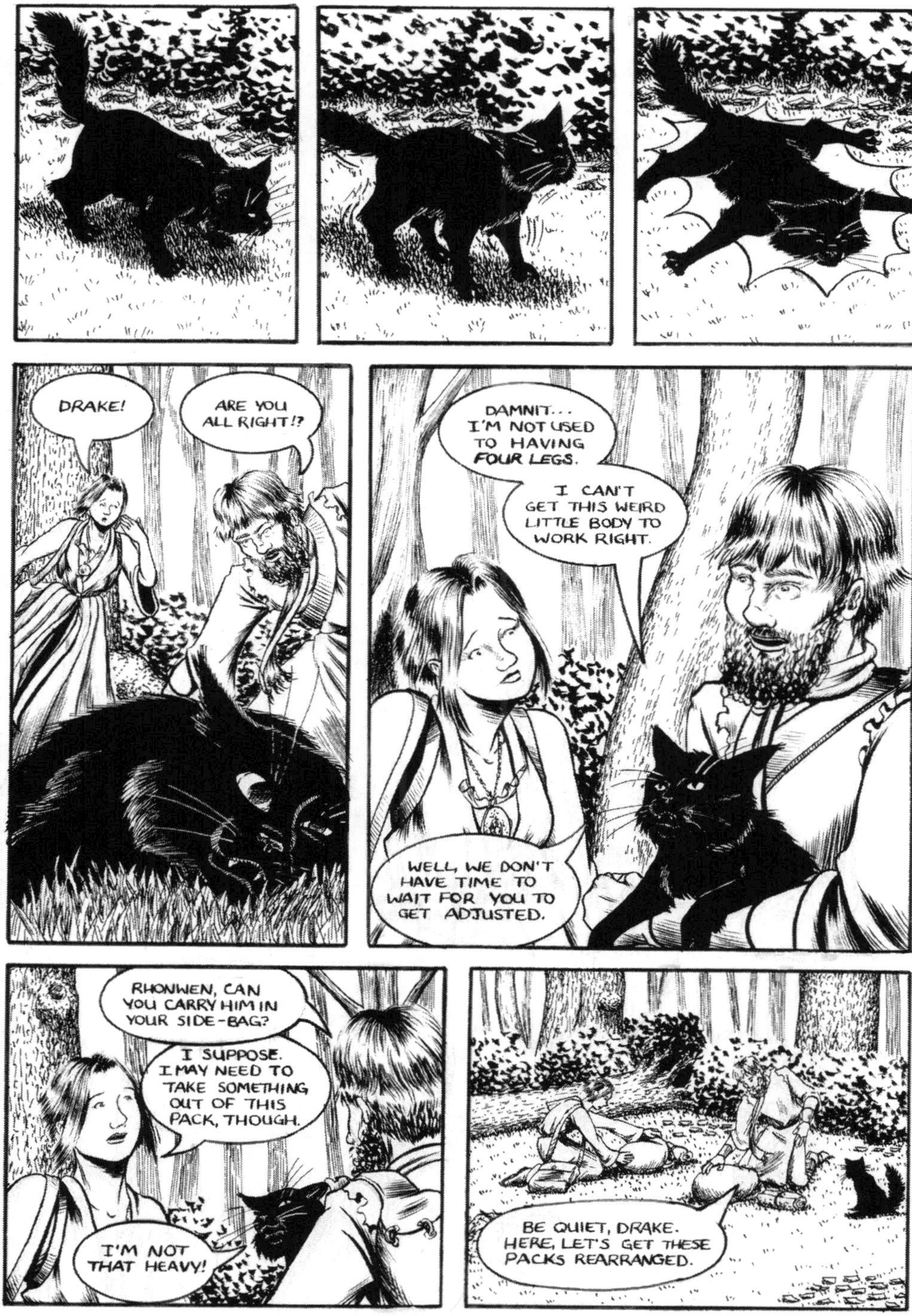
DRAKE!
ARE YOU ALL RIGHT!?
DAMNIT... I'M NOT USED TO HAVING FOUR LEGS.
I CAN'T GET THIS WEIRD LITTLE BODY TO WORK RIGHT.
WELL, WE DON'T HAVE TIME TO WAIT FOR YOU TO GET ADJUSTED.
RHONWEN, CAN YOU CARRY HIM IN YOUR SIDE-BAG?
I SUPPOSE. I MAY NEED TO TAKE SOMETHING OUT OF THIS PACK, THOUGH.
I'M NOT THAT HEAVY!
BE QUIET, DRAKE. HERE, LET'S GET THESE PACKS REARRANGED.

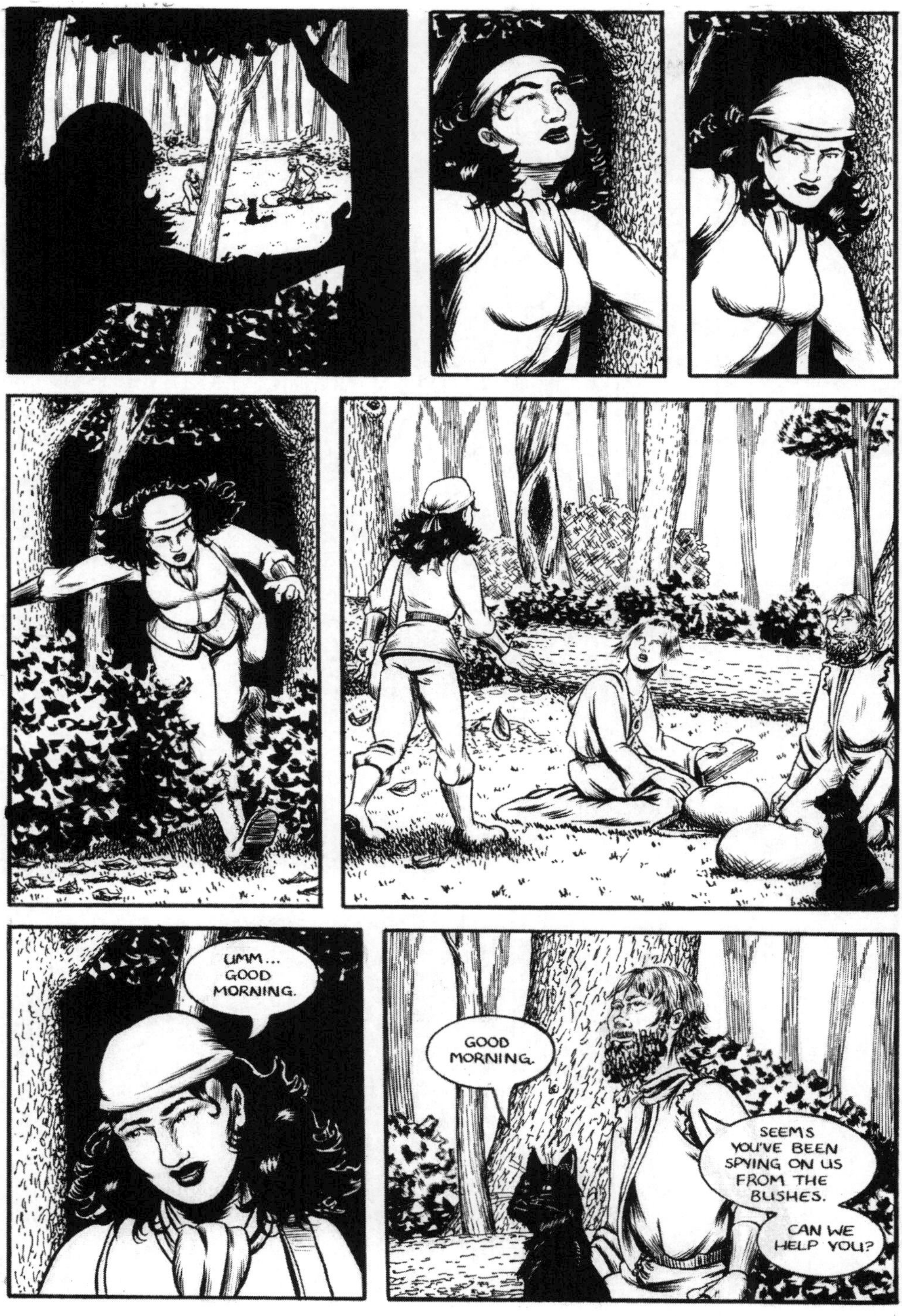
UMM... GOOD MORNING.
GOOD MORNING.
SEEMS YOU'VE BEEN SPYING ON US FROM THE BUSHES.
CAN WE HELP YOU?

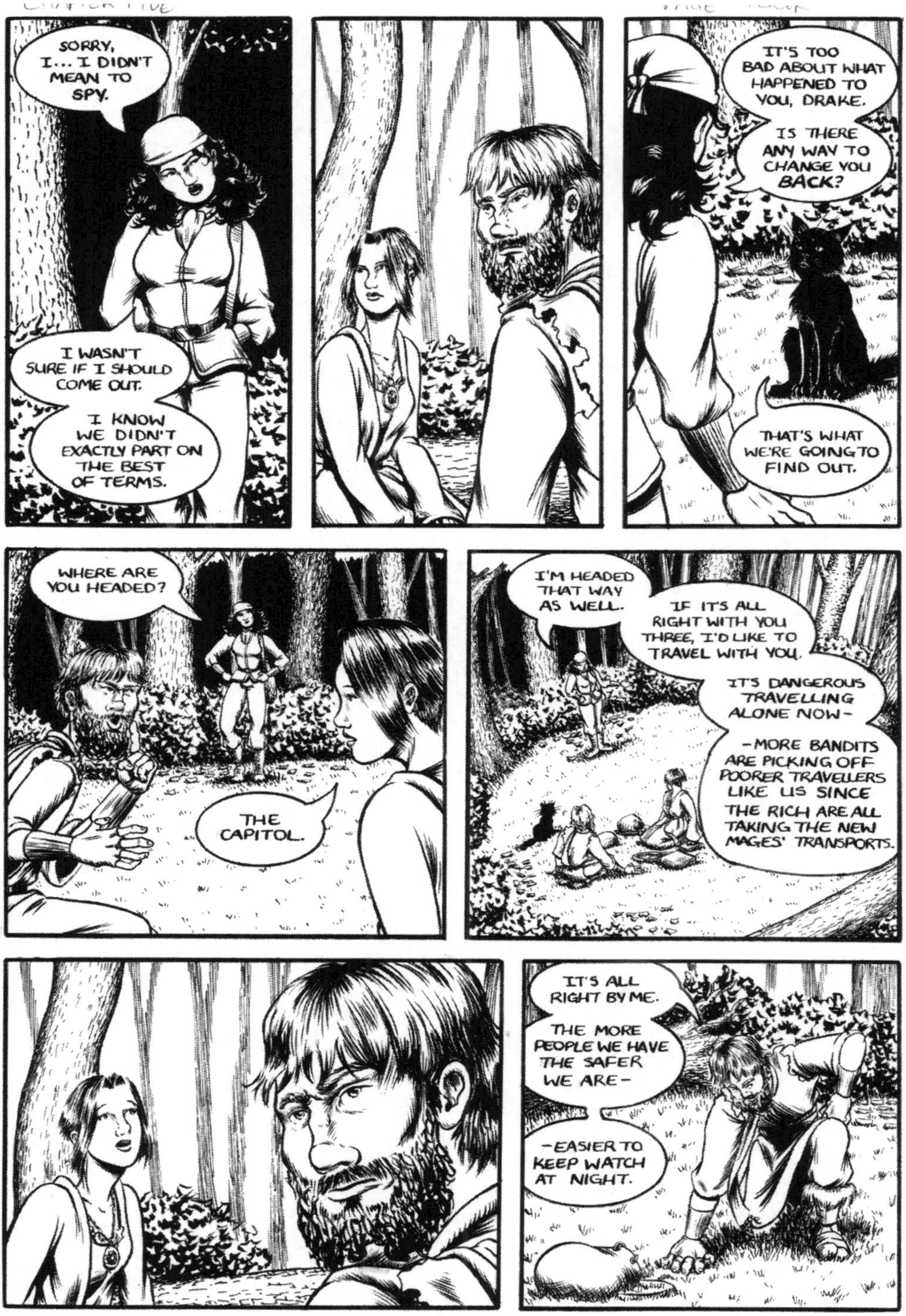
SORRY, I... I DIDN'T MEAN TO SPY.
I WASN'T SURE IF I SHOULD COME OUT.
I KNOW WE DIDN'T EXACTLY PART ON THE BEST OF TERMS.
IT'S TOO BAD ABOUT WHAT HAPPENED TO YOU, DRAKE.
IS THERE ANY WAY TO CHANGE YOU BACK?
THAT'S WHAT WE'RE GOING TO FIND OUT.
WHERE ARE YOU HEADED?
THE CAPITOL.
I'M HEADED THAT WAY AS WELL.
IF IT'S ALL RIGHT WITH YOU THREE, I'D LIKE TO TRAVEL WITH YOU.
IT'S DANGEROUS TRAVELLING ALONE NOW-
-MORE BANDITS ARE PICKING OFF POORER TRAVELLERS LIKE US SINCE THE RICH ARE ALL TAKING THE NEW MAGES' TRANSPORTS.
IT'S ALL RIGHT BY ME.
THE MORE PEOPLE WE HAVE THE SAFER WE ARE-
-EASIER TO KEEP WATCH AT NIGHT.

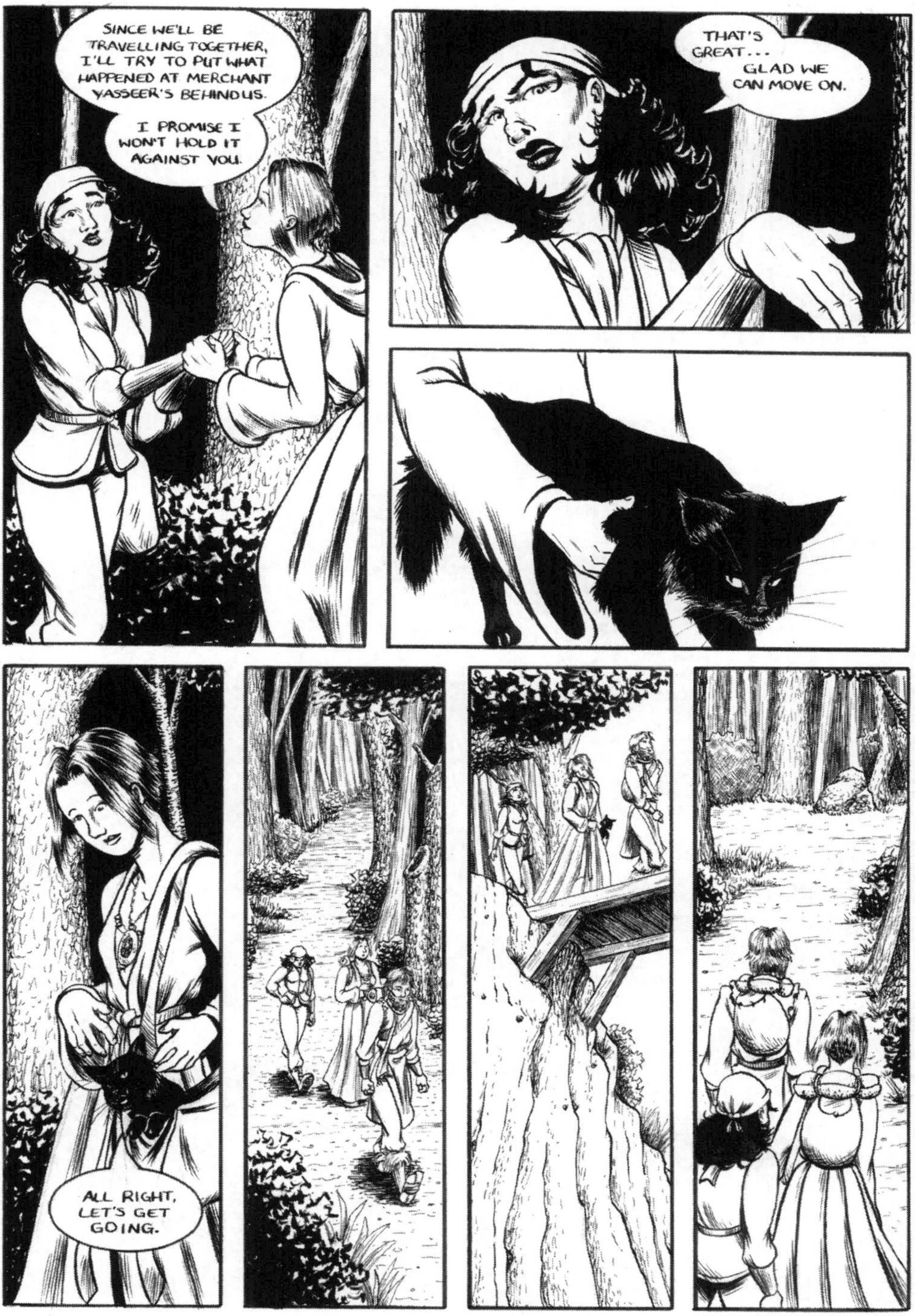
SINCE WE'LL BE TRAVELLING TOGETHER, I'LL TRY TO PUT WHAT HAPPENED AT MERCHANT YASSEER'S BEHIND US.
I PROMISE I WON'T HOLD IT AGAINST YOU.
THAT'S GREAT... GLAD WE CAN MOVE ON.
ALL RIGHT, LET'S GET GOING.

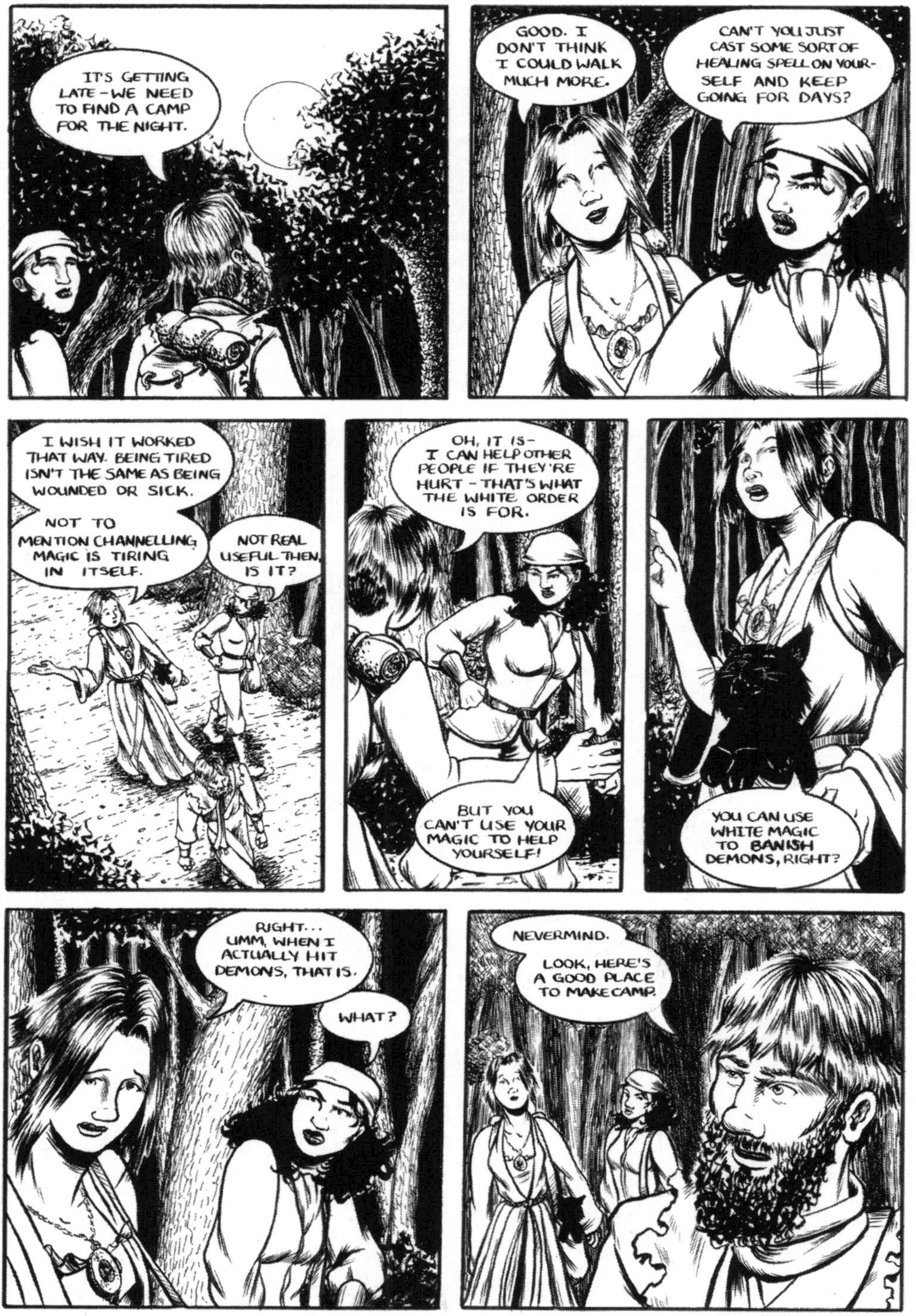
IT'S GETTING LATE-WE NEED TO FIND A CAMP FOR THE NIGHT.
GOOD. I DON'T THINK I COULD WALK MUCH MORE.
CAN'T YOU JUST CAST SOME SORT OF HEALING SPELL ON YOURSELF AND KEEP GOING FOR DAYS?
I WISH IT WORKED THAT WAY. BEING TIRED ISN'T THE SAME AS BEING WOUNDED OR SICK.
NOT TO MENTION CHANNELLING MAGIC IS TIRING IN ITSELF.
NOT REAL USEFUL THEN, IS IT?
OH, IT IS- I CAN HELP OTHER PEOPLE IF THEY'RE HURT - THAT'S WHAT THE WHITE ORDER IS FOR.
BUT YOU CAN'T USE YOUR MAGIC TO HELP YOURSELF!
YOU CAN USE WHITE MAGIC TO BANISH DEMONS, RIGHT?
RIGHT... UMM, WHEN I ACTUALLY HIT DEMONS, THAT IS.
WHAT?
NEVERMIND.
LOOK, HERE'S A GOOD PLACE TO MAKE CAMP.

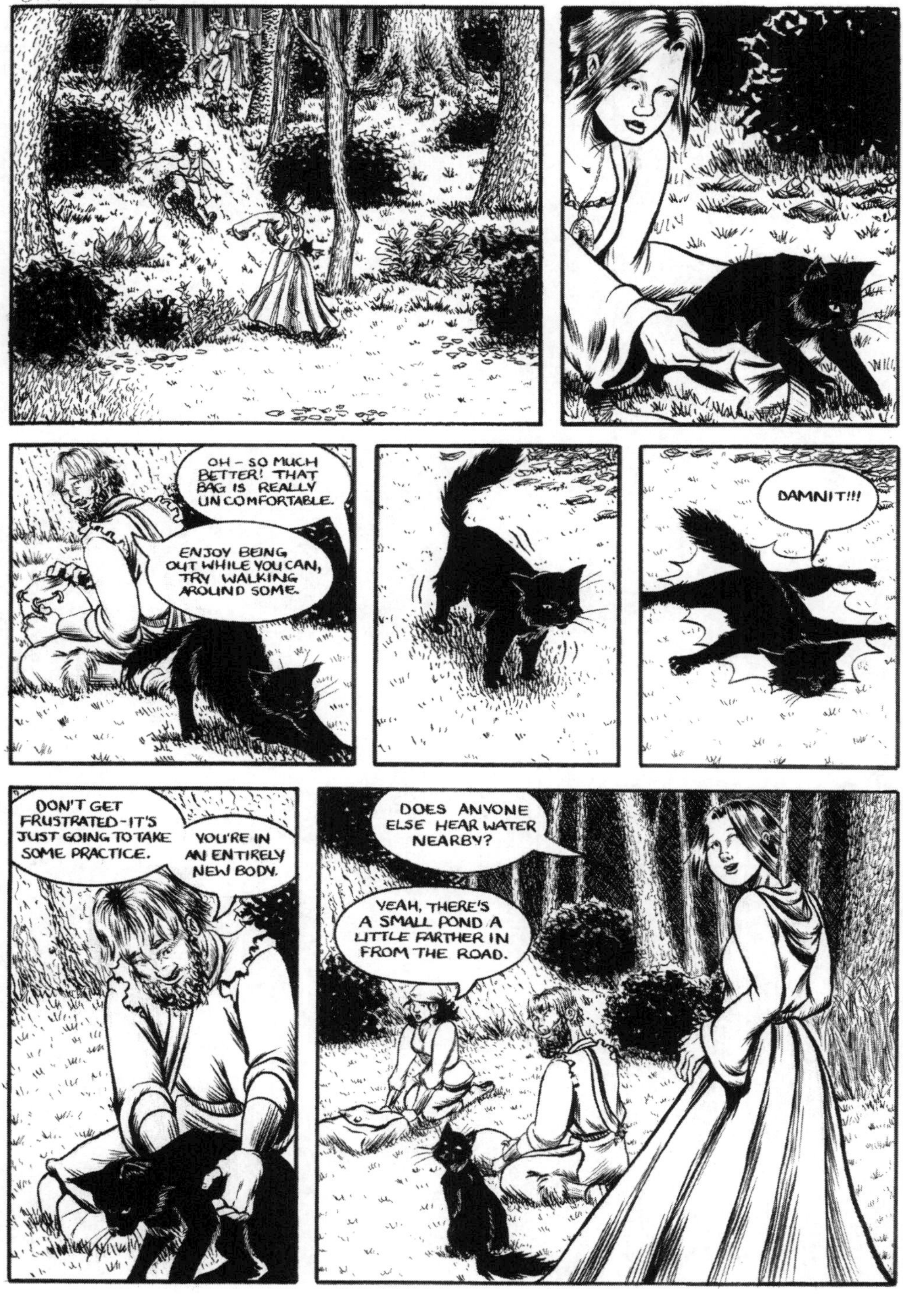
OH - SO MUCH BETTER! THAT BAG IS REALLY UNCOMFORTABLE.
ENJOY BEING OUT WHILE YOU CAN, TRY WALKING AROUND SOME.
DAMNIT!!!
DON'T GET FRUSTRATED - IT'S JUST GOING TO TAKE SOME PRACTICE.
YOU'RE IN AN ENTIRELY NEW BODY.
DOES ANYONE ELSE HEAR WATER NEARBY?
YEAH, THERE'S A SMALL POND A LITTLE FARTHER IN FROM THE ROAD.

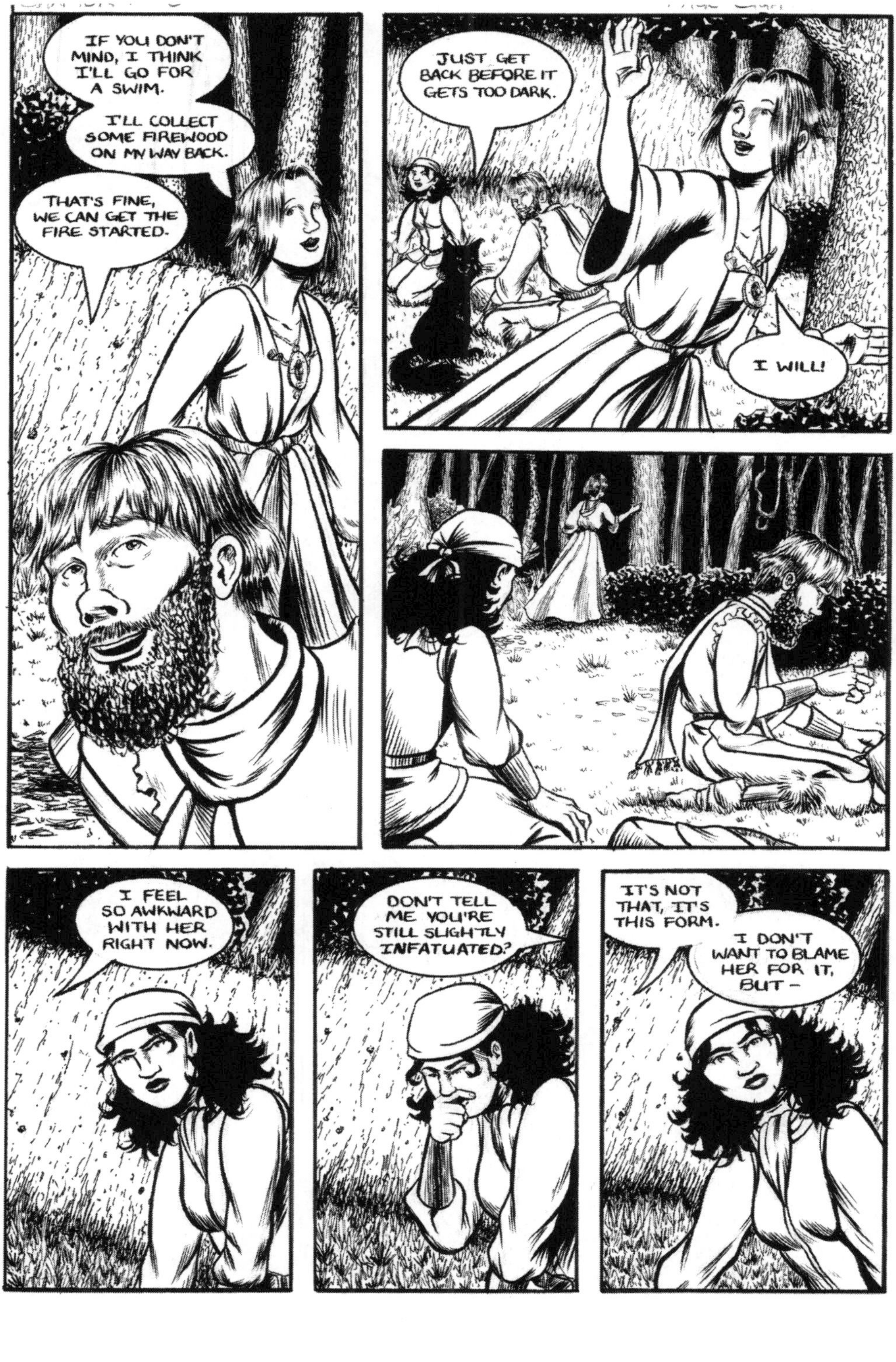
IF YOU DON'T MIND, I THINK I'LL GO FOR A SWIM.
I'LL COLLECT SOME FIREWOOD ON MY WAY BACK.
THAT'S FINE, WE CAN GET THE FIRE STARTED.
JUST GET BACK BEFORE IT GETS TOO DARK.
I WILL!
I FEEL SO AWKWARD WITH HER RIGHT NOW.
DON'T TELL ME YOU'RE STILL SLIGHTLY INFATUATED?
IT'S NOT THAT, IT'S THIS FORM.
I DON'T WANT TO BLAME HER FOR IT, BUT—

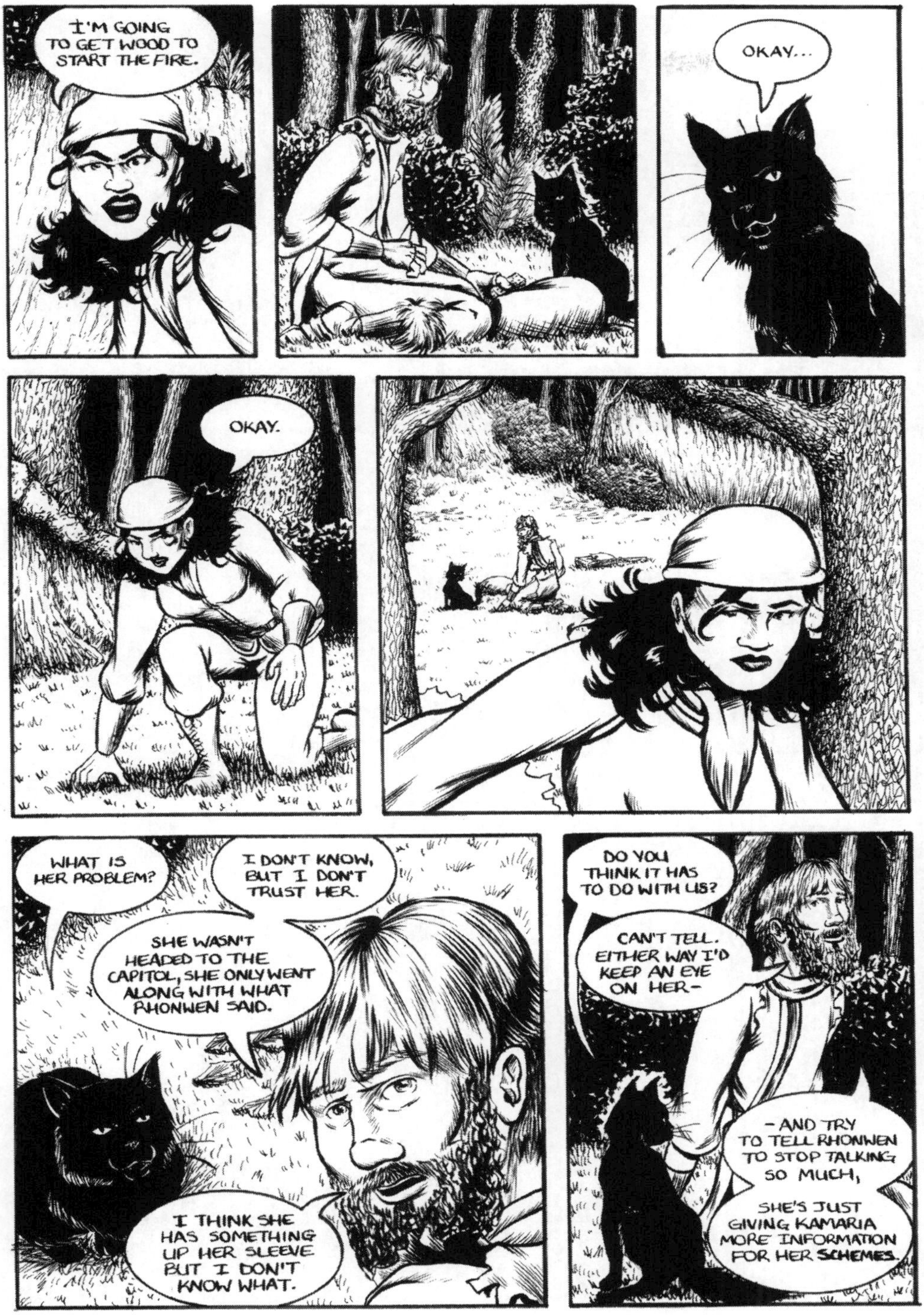
I'M GOING TO GET WOOD TO START THE FIRE.
OKAY...
OKAY.
WHAT IS HER PROBLEM?
I DON'T KNOW, BUT I DON'T TRUST HER.
SHE WASN'T HEADED TO THE CAPITOL, SHE ONLY WENT ALONG WITH WHAT RHONWEN SAID.
I THINK SHE HAS SOMETHING UP HER SLEEVE BUT I DON'T KNOW WHAT.
DO YOU THINK IT HAS TO DO WITH US?
CAN'T TELL. EITHER WAY I'D KEEP AN EYE ON HER-
-AND TRY TO TELL RHONWEN TO STOP TALKING SO MUCH,
SHE'S JUST GIVING KAMARIA MORE INFORMATION FOR HER SCHEMES.

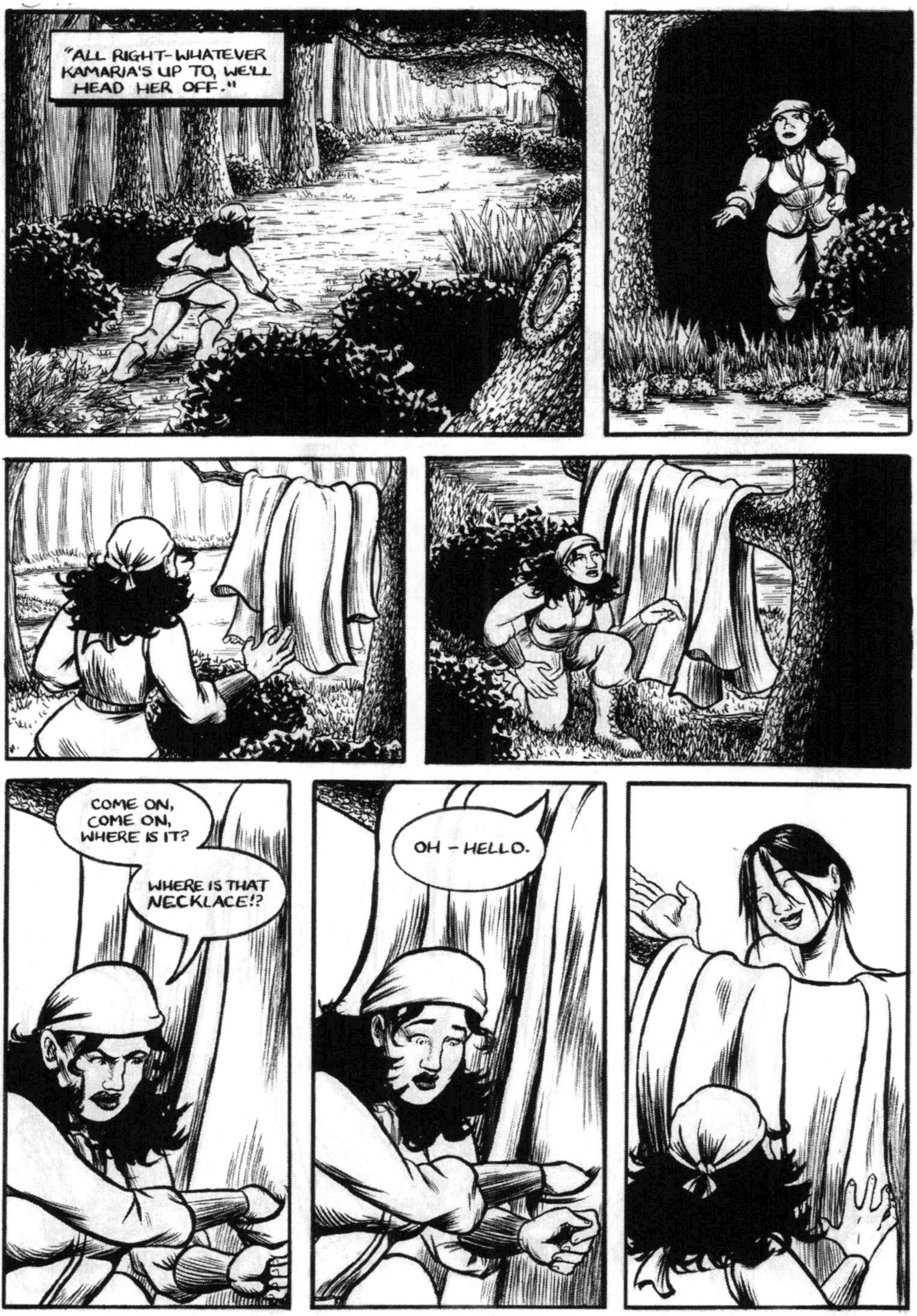
"ALL RIGHT- WHATEVER KAMARIA'S UP TO, WE'LL HEAD HER OFF."
COME ON, COME ON, WHERE IS IT?
WHERE IS THAT NECKLACE!?
OH - HELLO.

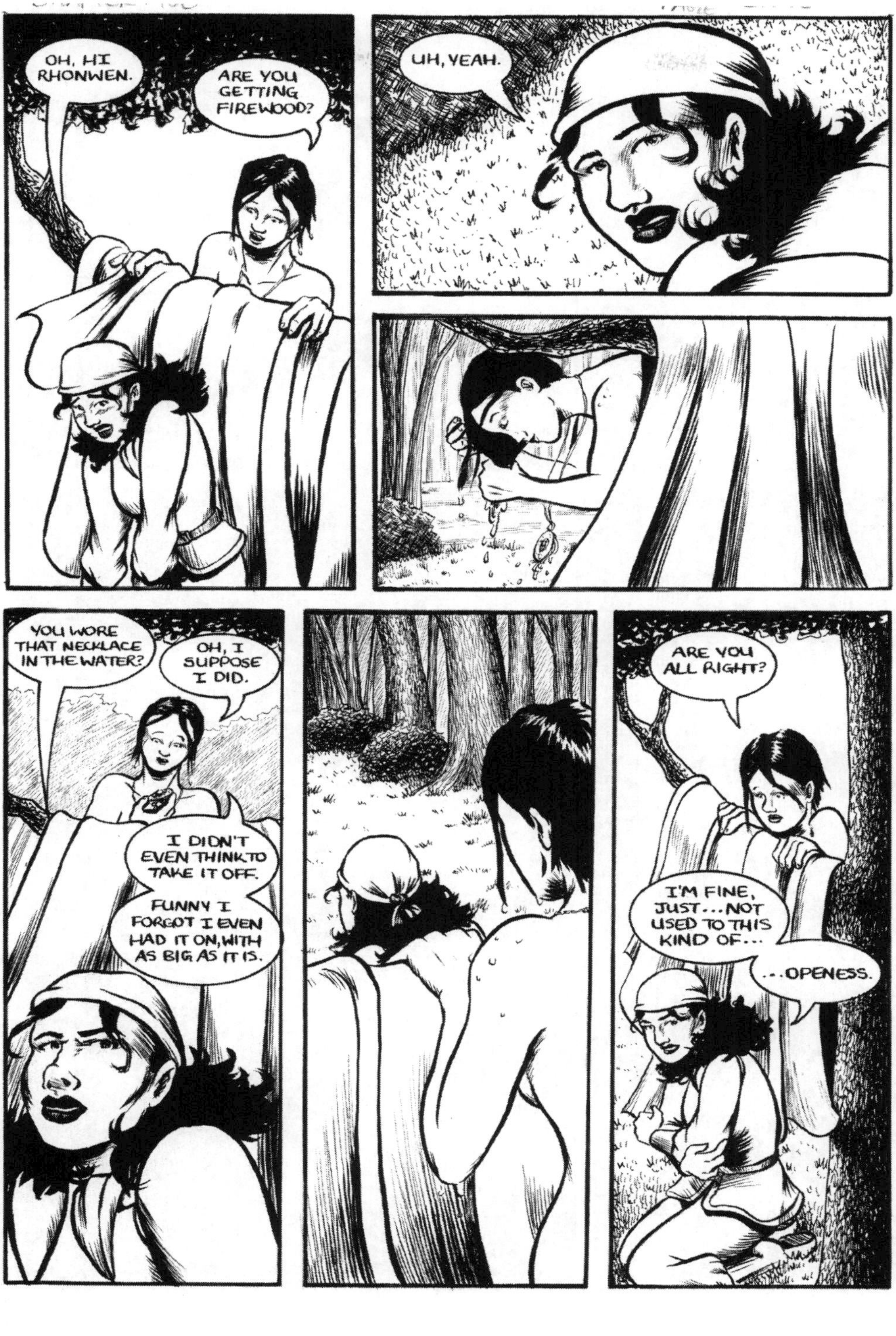

OH, HI RHONWEN.
ARE YOU GETTING FIREWOOD?
UH, YEAH.
YOU WORE THAT NECKLACE IN THE WATER?
OH, I SUPPOSE I DID.
I DIDN'T EVEN THINK TO TAKE IT OFF.
FUNNY I FORGOT I EVEN HAD IT ON, WITH AS BIG AS IT IS.
ARE YOU ALL RIGHT?
I'M FINE, JUST...NOT USED TO THIS KIND OF...
...OPENESS.

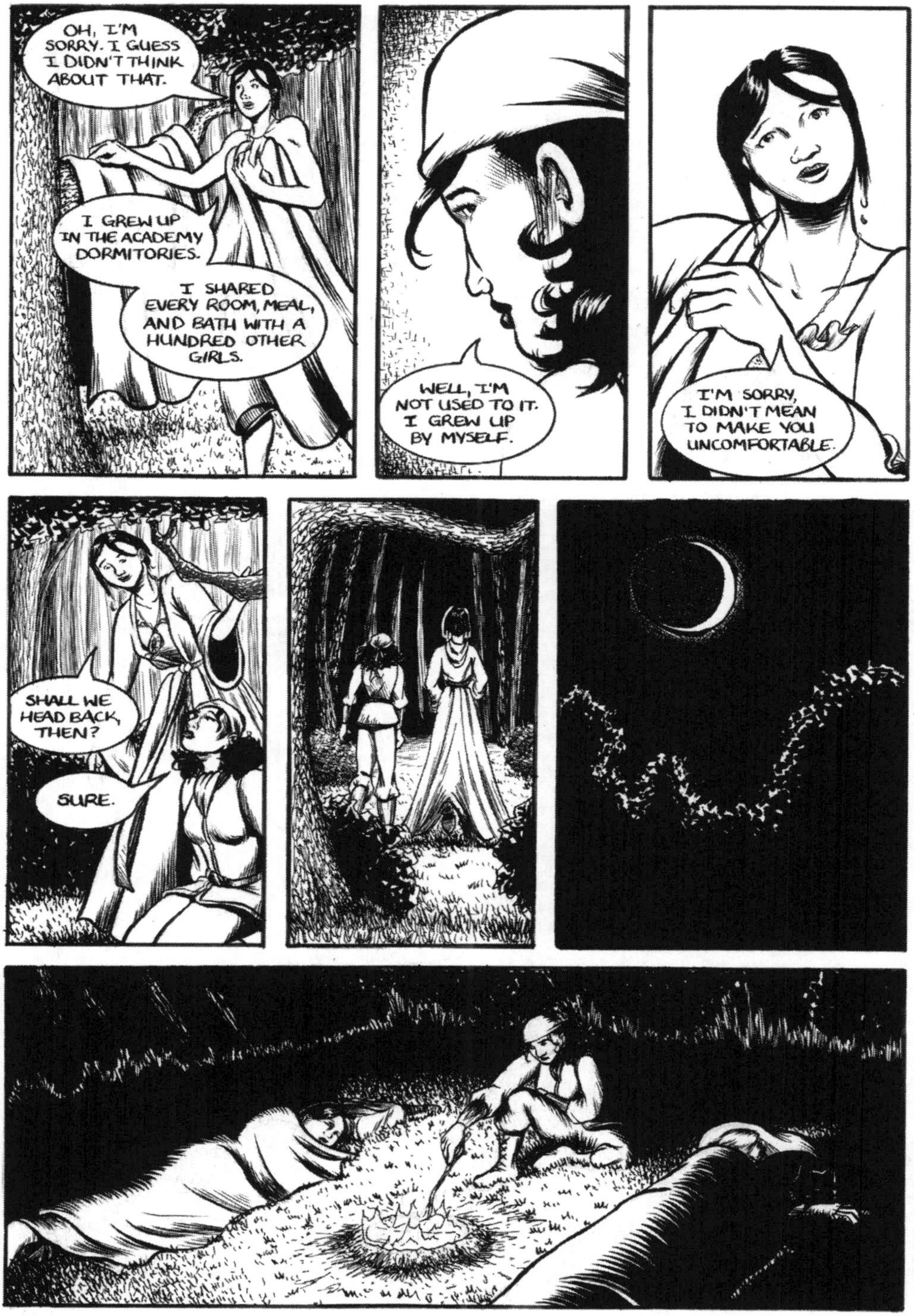
OH, I'M SORRY. I GUESS I DIDN'T THINK ABOUT THAT.
I GREW UP IN THE ACADEMY DORMITORIES.
I SHARED EVERY ROOM, MEAL, AND BATH WITH A HUNDRED OTHER GIRLS.
WELL, I'M NOT USED TO IT. I GREW UP BY MYSELF.
I'M SORRY, I DIDN'T MEAN TO MAKE YOU UNCOMFORTABLE.
SHALL WE HEAD BACK, THEN?
SURE.

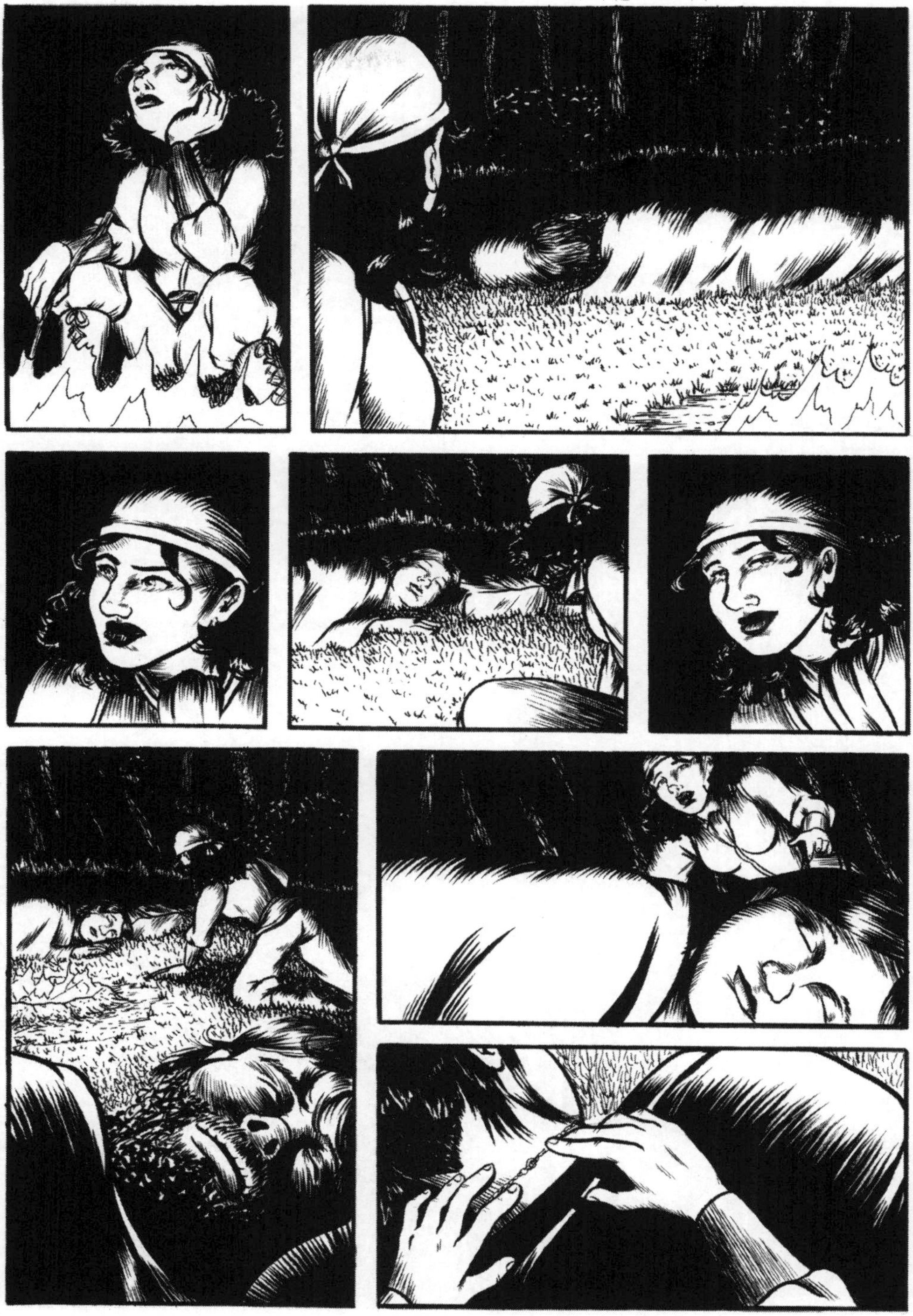

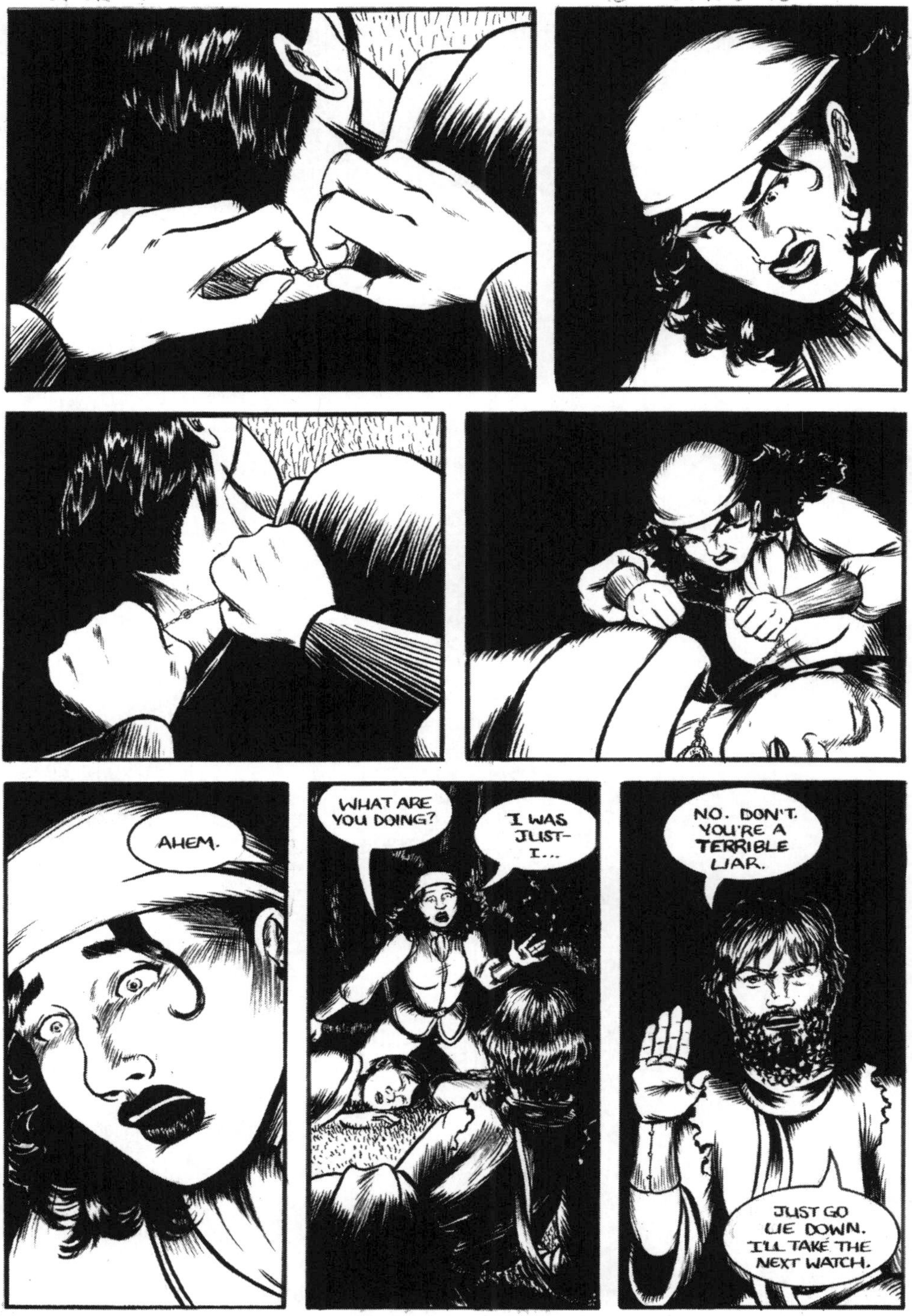
AHEM.
WHAT ARE YOU DOING?
I WAS JUST- I...
NO. DON'T. YOU'RE A TERRIBLE LIAR.
JUST GO LIE DOWN. I'LL TAKE THE NEXT WATCH.

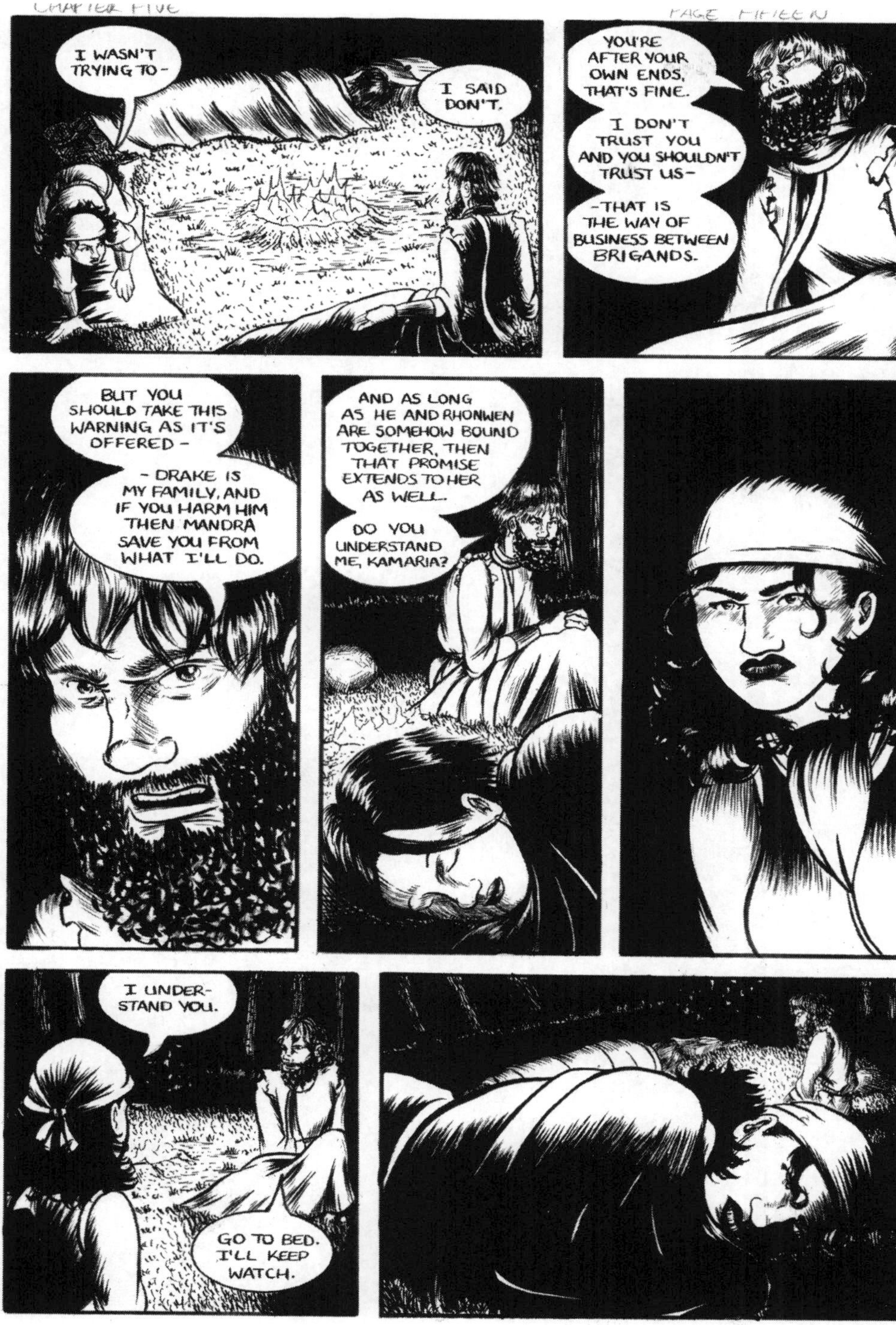
I WASN'T TRYING TO -
I SAID DON'T.
YOU'RE AFTER YOUR OWN ENDS, THAT'S FINE.
I DON'T TRUST YOU AND YOU SHOULDN'T TRUST US-
-THAT IS THE WAY OF BUSINESS BETWEEN BRIGANDS.
BUT YOU SHOULD TAKE THIS WARNING AS IT'S OFFERED -
- DRAKE IS MY FAMILY, AND IF YOU HARM HIM THEN MANDRA SAVE YOU FROM WHAT I'LL DO.
AND AS LONG AS HE AND RHONWEN ARE SOMEHOW BOUND TOGETHER, THEN THAT PROMISE EXTENDS TO HER AS WELL.
DO YOU UNDERSTAND ME, KAMARIA?
I UNDER-STAND YOU.
GO TO BED. I'LL KEEP WATCH.

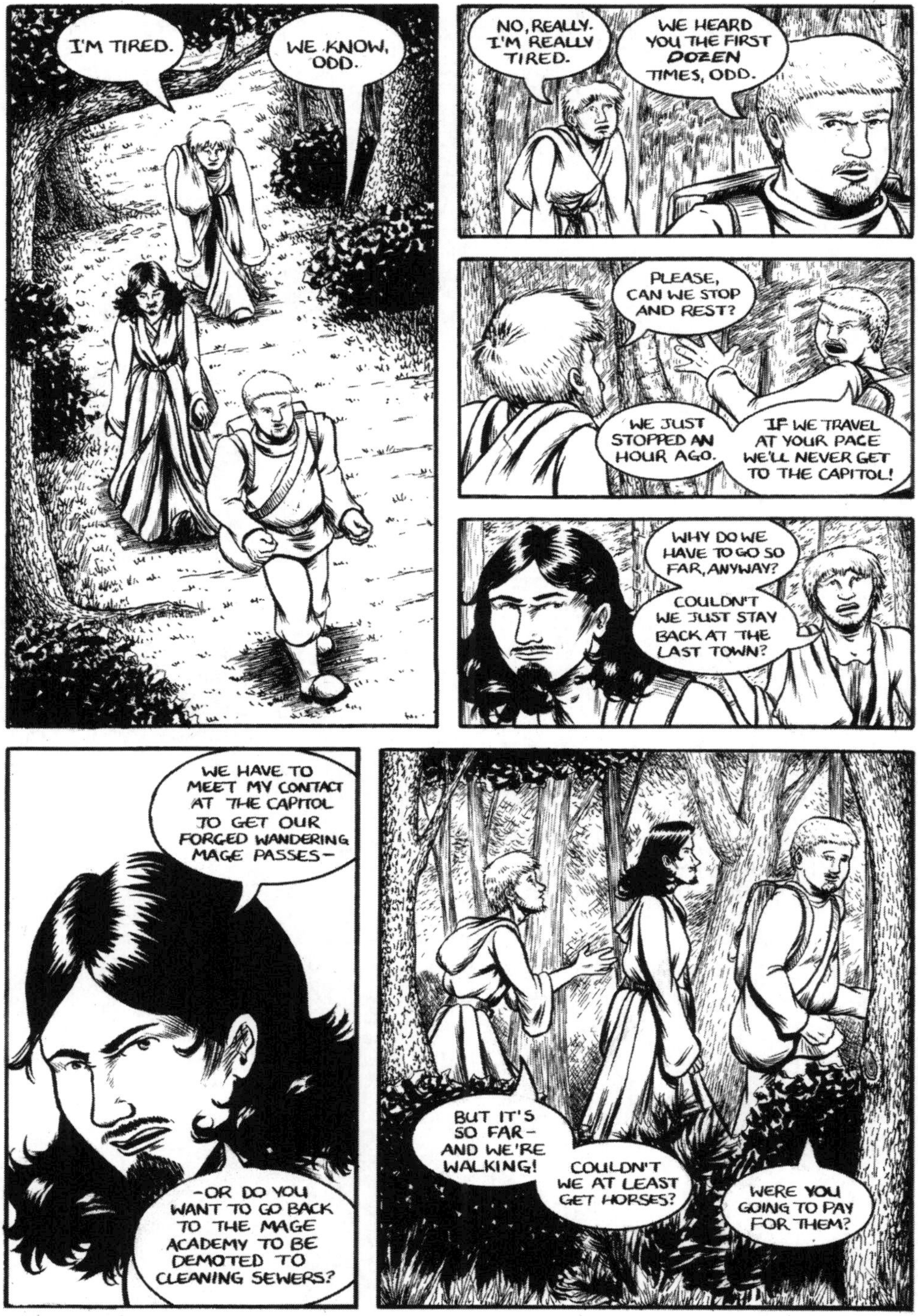
I'M TIRED.
WE KNOW, ODD.
NO, REALLY. I'M REALLY TIRED.
WE HEARD YOU THE FIRST DOZEN TIMES, ODD.
PLEASE, CAN WE STOP AND REST?
WE JUST STOPPED AN HOUR AGO.
IF WE TRAVEL AT YOUR PACE WE'LL NEVER GET TO THE CAPITOL!
WHY DO WE HAVE TO GO SO FAR, ANYWAY?
COULDN'T WE JUST STAY BACK AT THE LAST TOWN?
WE HAVE TO MEET MY CONTACT AT THE CAPITOL TO GET OUR FORGED WANDERING MAGE PASSES-
-OR DO YOU WANT TO GO BACK TO THE MAGE ACADEMY TO BE DEMOTED TO CLEANING SEWERS?
BUT IT'S SO FAR- AND WE'RE WALKING!
COULDN'T WE AT LEAST GET HORSES?
WERE YOU GOING TO PAY FOR THEM?

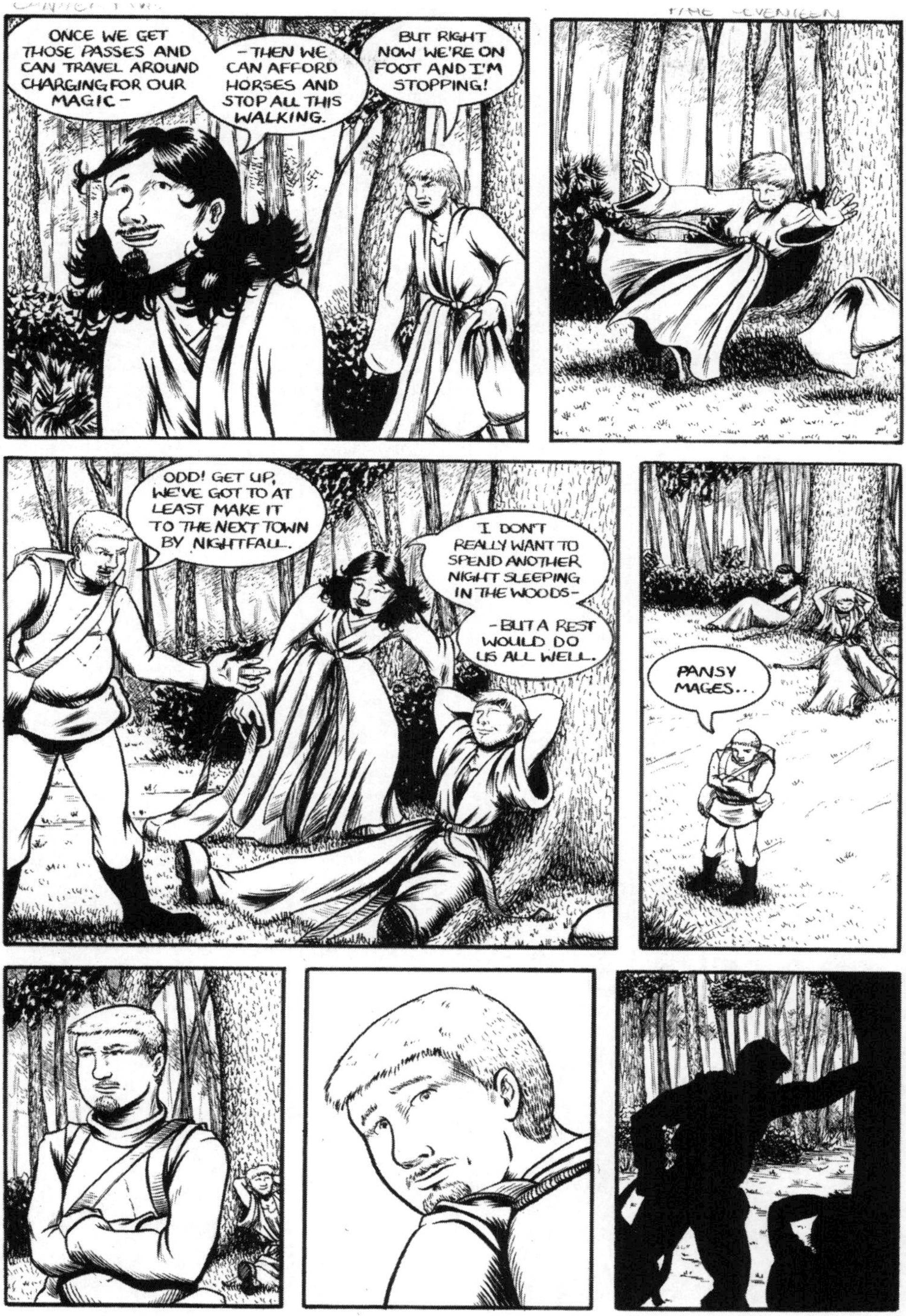
ONCE WE GET THOSE PASSES AND CAN TRAVEL AROUND CHARGING FOR OUR MAGIC -
- THEN WE CAN AFFORD HORSES AND STOP ALL THIS WALKING.
BUT RIGHT NOW WE'RE ON FOOT AND I'M STOPPING!
ODD! GET UP, WE'VE GOT TO AT LEAST MAKE IT TO THE NEXT TOWN BY NIGHTFALL.
I DON'T REALLY WANT TO SPEND ANOTHER NIGHT SLEEPING IN THE WOODS -
- BUT A REST WOULD DO US ALL WELL.
PANSY MAGES...

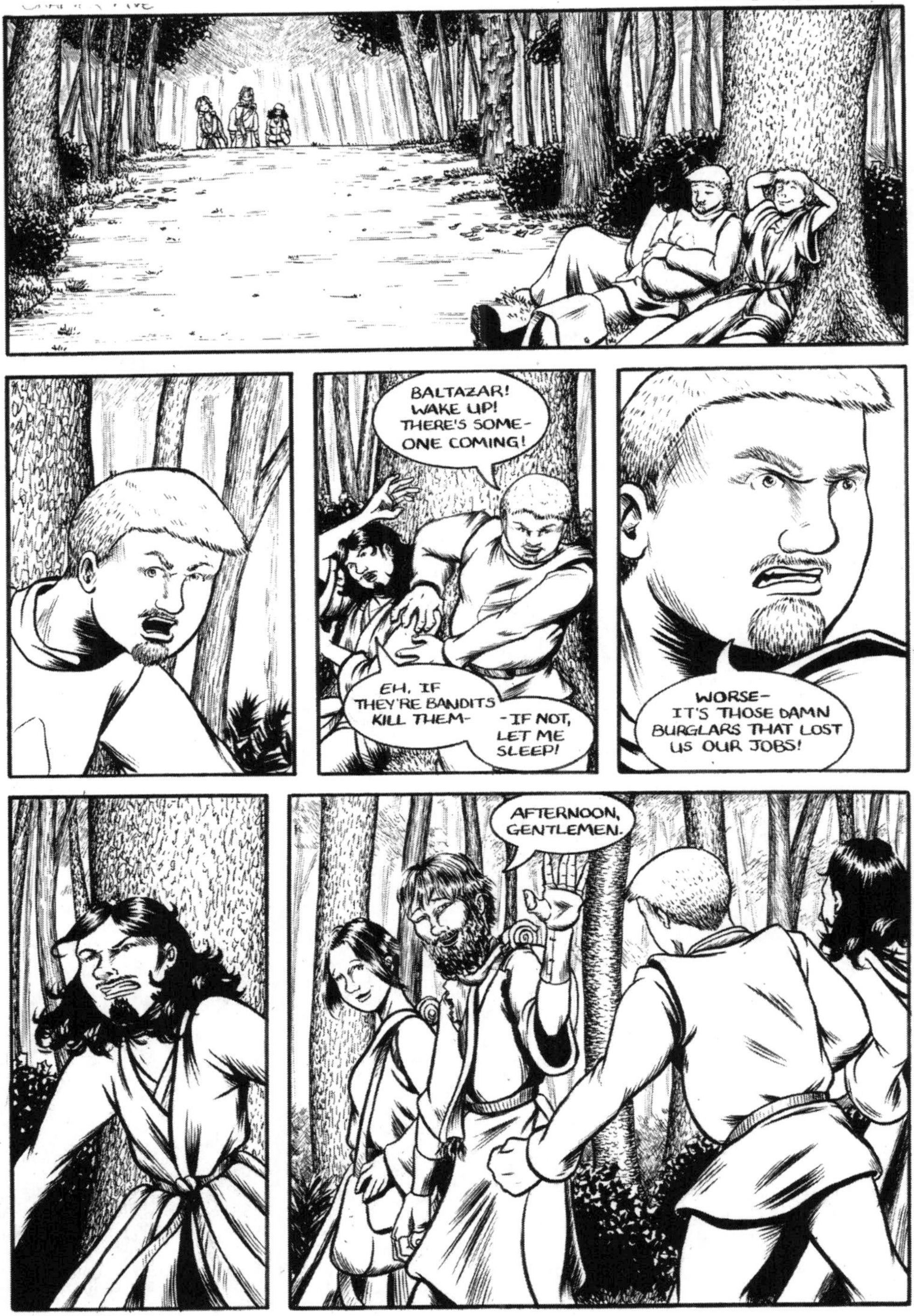
BALTAZAR! WAKE UP! THERE'S SOME-ONE COMING!
EH, IF THEY'RE BANDITS KILL THEM-
-IF NOT, LET ME SLEEP!
WORSE- IT'S THOSE DAMN BURGLARS THAT LOST US OUR JOBS!
AFTERNOON, GENTLEMEN.

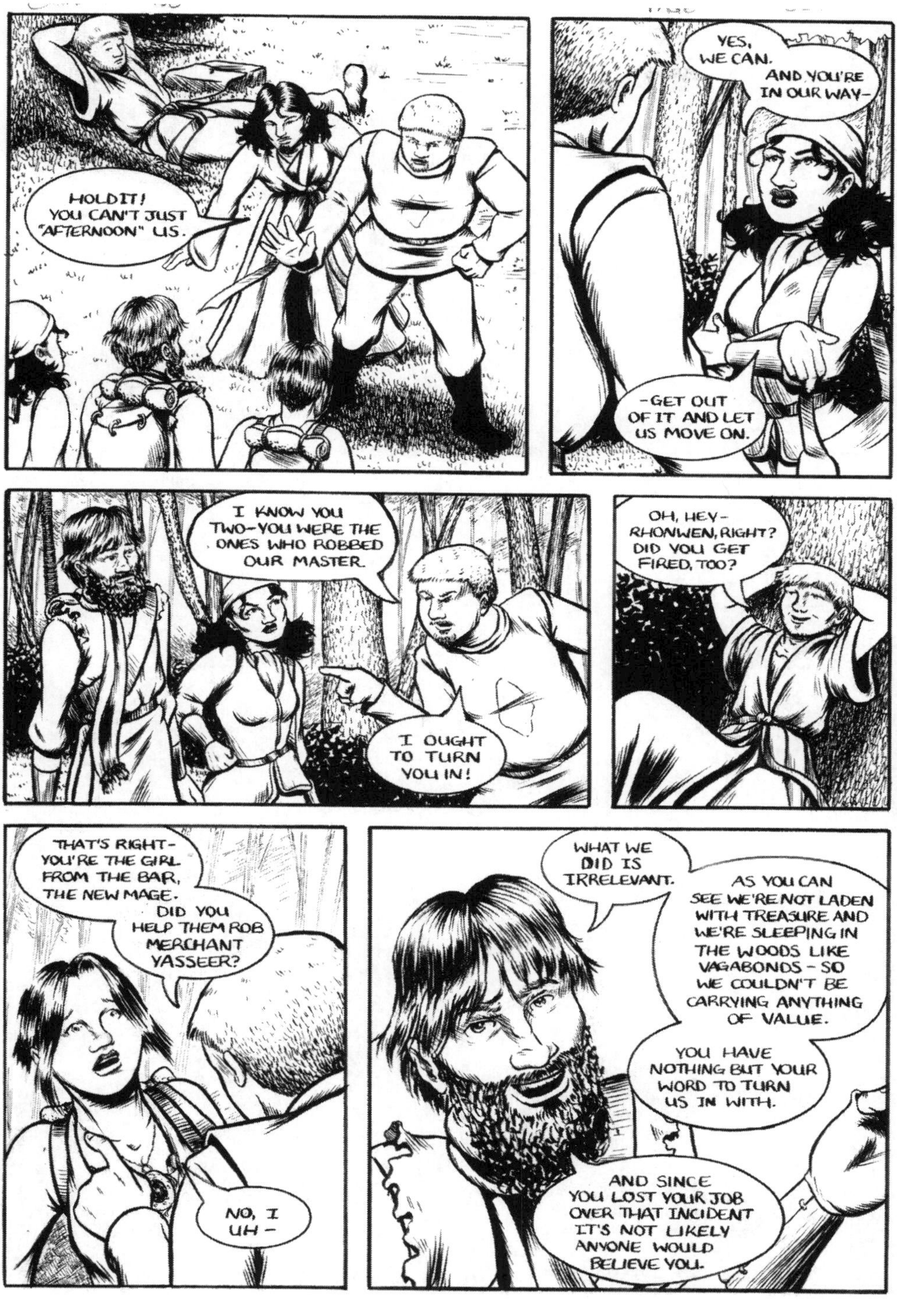
HOLD IT! YOU CAN'T JUST "AFTERNOON" US.
YES, WE CAN.
AND YOU'RE IN OUR WAY-
-GET OUT OF IT AND LET US MOVE ON.
I KNOW YOU TWO-YOU WERE THE ONES WHO ROBBED OUR MASTER.
I OUGHT TO TURN YOU IN!
OH, HEY- RHONWEN, RIGHT? DID YOU GET FIRED, TOO?
THAT'S RIGHT- YOU'RE THE GIRL FROM THE BAR, THE NEW MAGE.
DID YOU HELP THEM ROB MERCHANT YASSEER?
NO, I UH -
WHAT WE DID IS IRRELEVANT.
AS YOU CAN SEE WE'RE NOT LADEN WITH TREASURE AND WE'RE SLEEPING IN THE WOODS LIKE VAGABONDS - SO WE COULDN'T BE CARRYING ANYTHING OF VALUE.
YOU HAVE NOTHING BUT YOUR WORD TO TURN US IN WITH.
AND SINCE YOU LOST YOUR JOB OVER THAT INCIDENT IT'S NOT LIKELY ANYONE WOULD BELIEVE YOU.

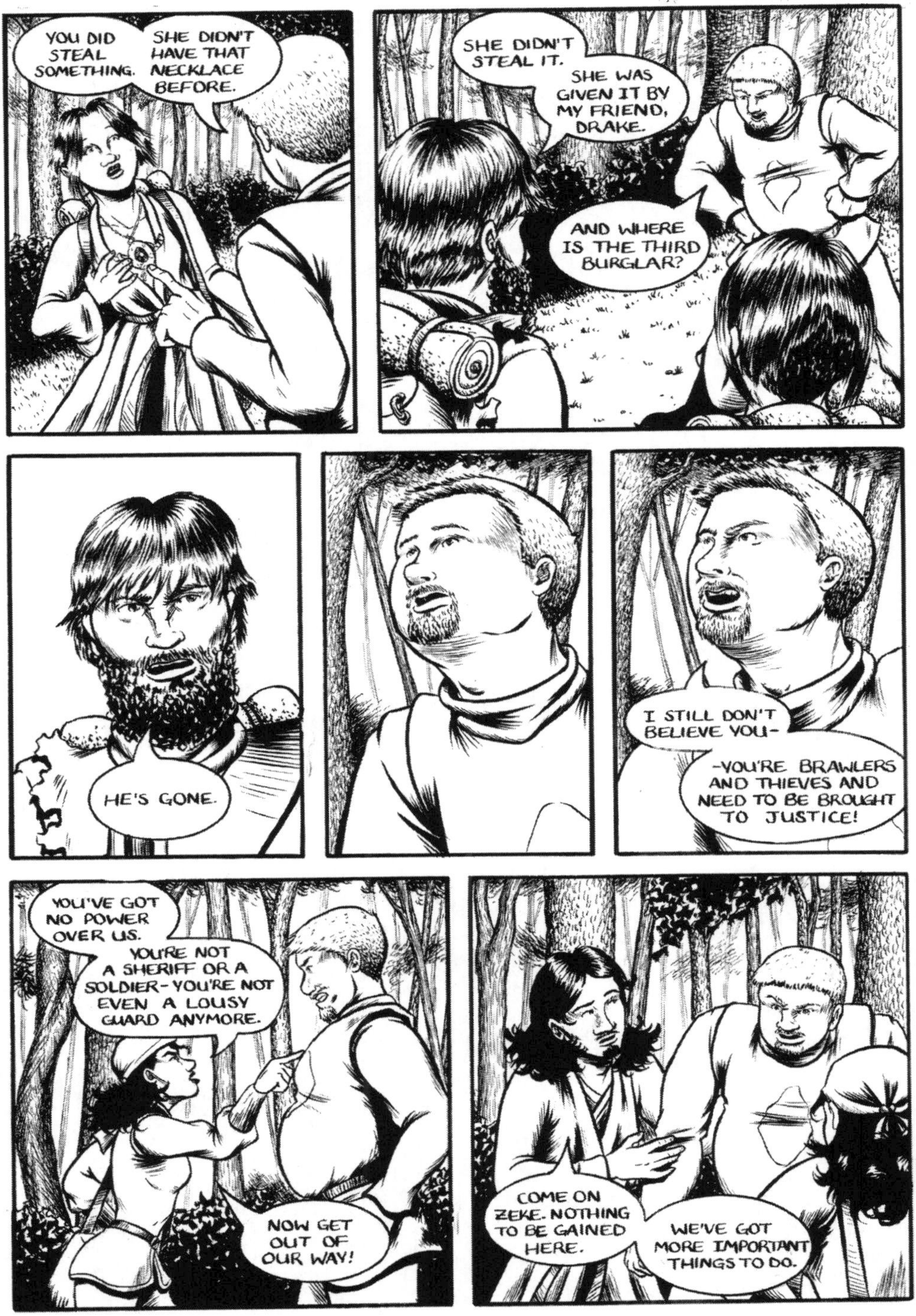
YOU DID STEAL SOMETHING.
SHE DIDN'T HAVE THAT NECKLACE BEFORE.
SHE DIDN'T STEAL IT.
SHE WAS GIVEN IT BY MY FRIEND, DRAKE.
AND WHERE IS THE THIRD BURGLAR?
HE'S GONE.
I STILL DON'T BELIEVE YOU-
-YOU'RE BRAWLERS AND THIEVES AND NEED TO BE BROUGHT TO JUSTICE!
YOU'VE GOT NO POWER OVER US.
YOU'RE NOT A SHERIFF OR A SOLDIER- YOU'RE NOT EVEN A LOUSY GUARD ANYMORE.
NOW GET OUT OF OUR WAY!
COME ON ZEKE. NOTHING TO BE GAINED HERE.
WE'VE GOT MORE IMPORTANT THINGS TO DO.

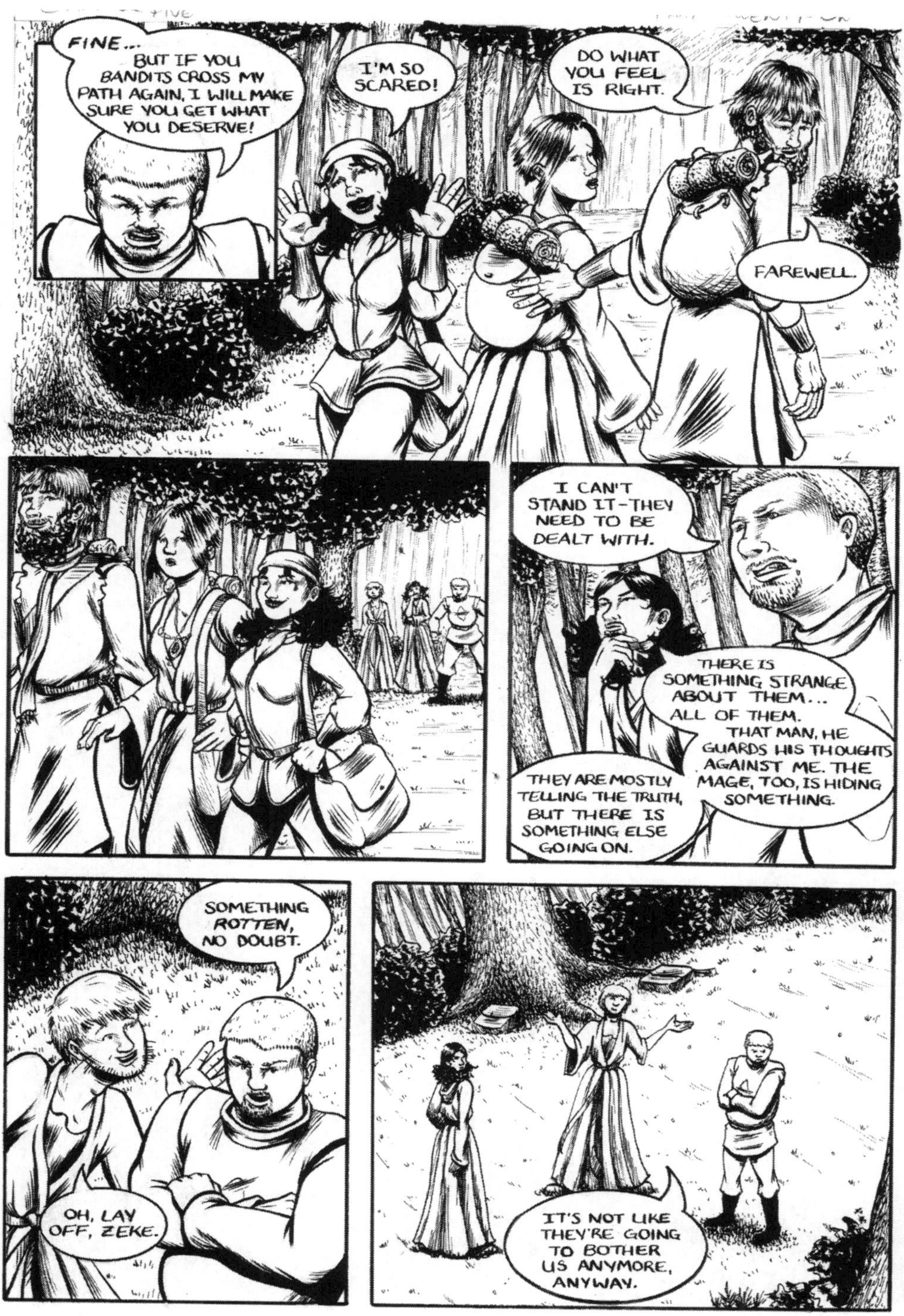
FINE... BUT IF YOU BANDITS CROSS MY PATH AGAIN, I WILL MAKE SURE YOU GET WHAT YOU DESERVE!
I'M SO SCARED!
DO WHAT YOU FEEL IS RIGHT.
FAREWELL.
I CAN'T STAND IT-THEY NEED TO BE DEALT WITH.
THERE IS SOMETHING STRANGE ABOUT THEM... ALL OF THEM. THAT MAN, HE GUARDS HIS THOUGHTS AGAINST ME. THE MAGE, TOO, IS HIDING SOMETHING.
THEY ARE MOSTLY TELLING THE TRUTH, BUT THERE IS SOMETHING ELSE GOING ON.
SOMETHING ROTTEN, NO DOUBT.
OH, LAY OFF, ZEKE.
IT'S NOT LIKE THEY'RE GOING TO BOTHER US ANYMORE, ANYWAY.

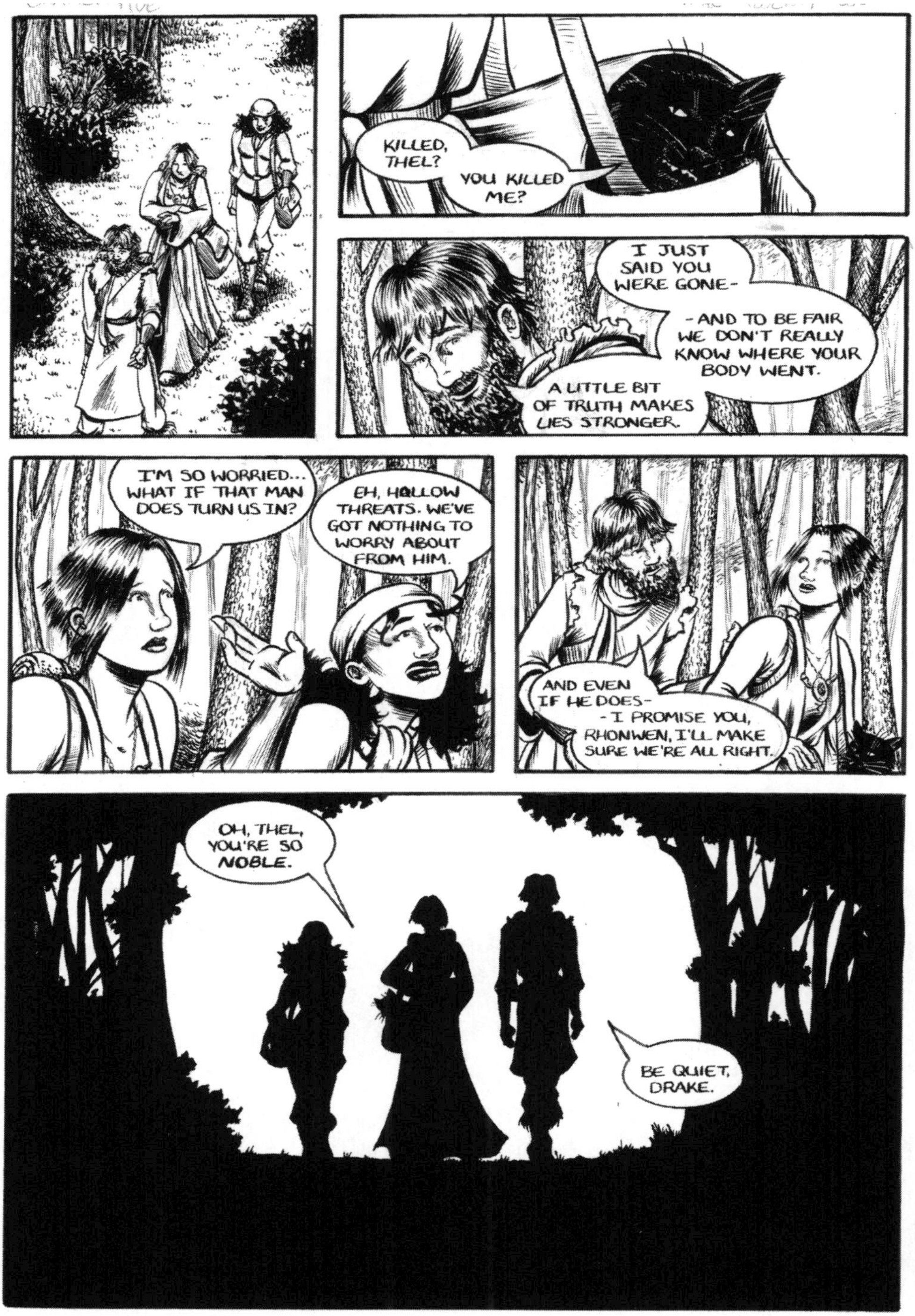
KILLED, THEL?
YOU KILLED ME?
I JUST SAID YOU WERE GONE-
-AND TO BE FAIR WE DON'T REALLY KNOW WHERE YOUR BODY WENT.
A LITTLE BIT OF TRUTH MAKES LIES STRONGER.
I'M SO WORRIED... WHAT IF THAT MAN DOES TURN US IN?
EH, HOLLOW THREATS. WE'VE GOT NOTHING TO WORRY ABOUT FROM HIM.
AND EVEN IF HE DOES-
-I PROMISE YOU, RHONWEN, I'LL MAKE SURE WE'RE ALL RIGHT.
OH, THEL, YOU'RE SO NOBLE.
BE QUIET, DRAKE.

CHAPTER VI

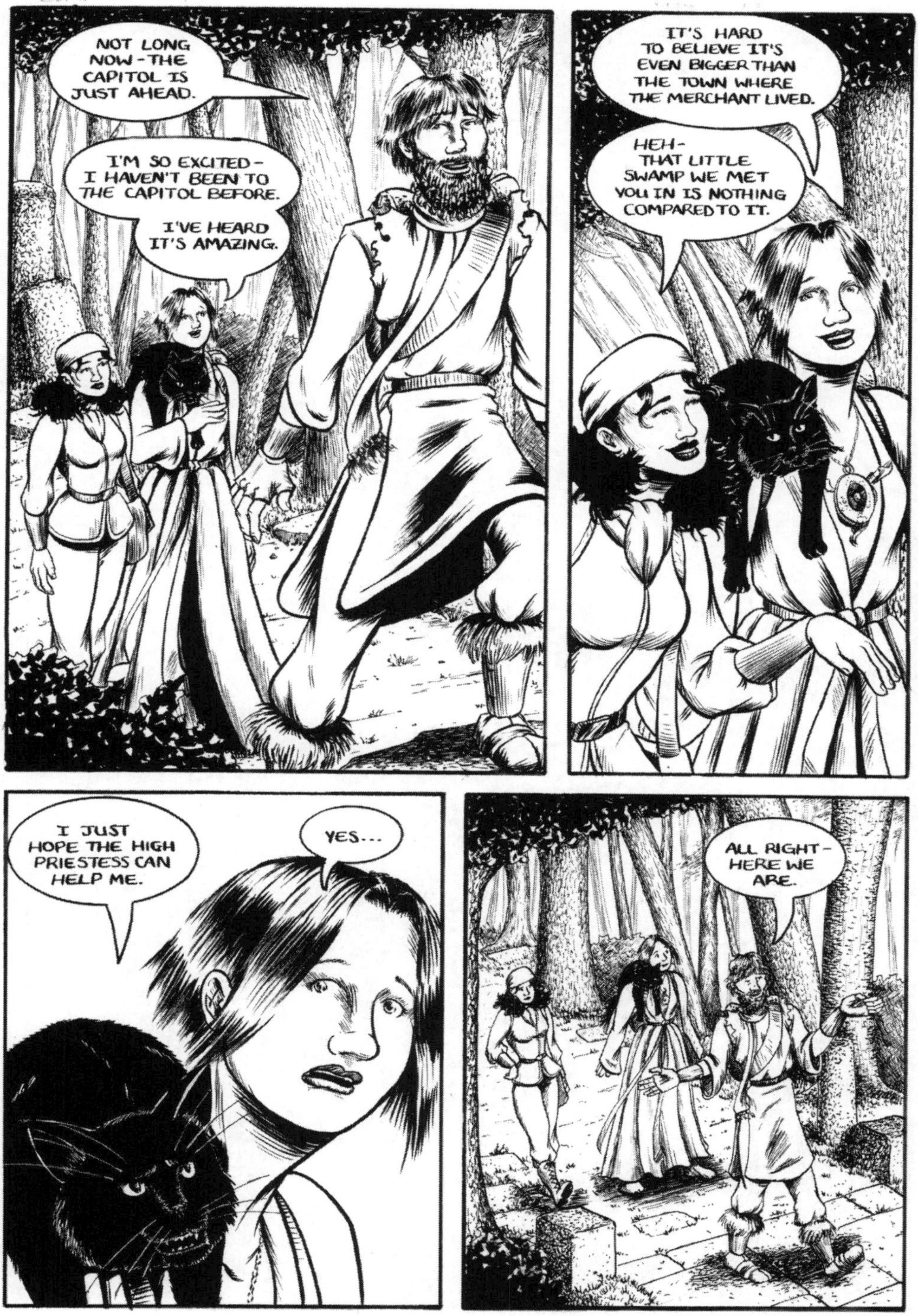
NOT LONG NOW - THE CAPITOL IS JUST AHEAD.
I'M SO EXCITED - I HAVEN'T BEEN TO THE CAPITOL BEFORE.
I'VE HEARD IT'S AMAZING.
IT'S HARD TO BELIEVE IT'S EVEN BIGGER THAN THE TOWN WHERE THE MERCHANT LIVED.
HEH- THAT LITTLE SWAMP WE MET YOU IN IS NOTHING COMPARED TO IT.
I JUST HOPE THE HIGH PRIESTESS CAN HELP ME.
YES...
ALL RIGHT - HERE WE ARE.

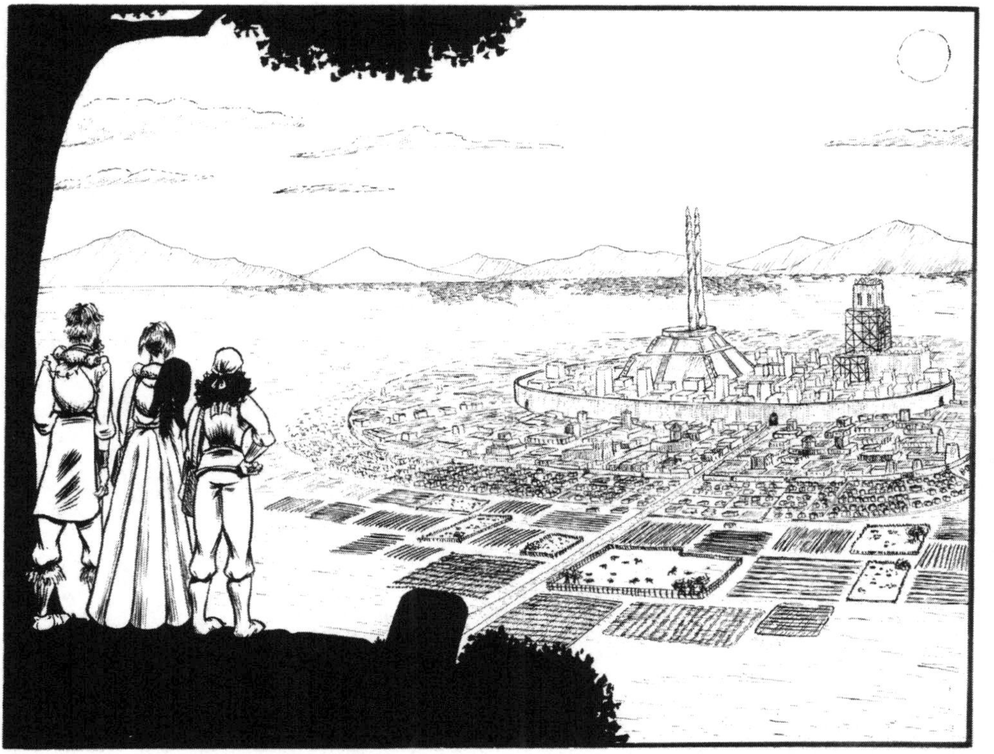

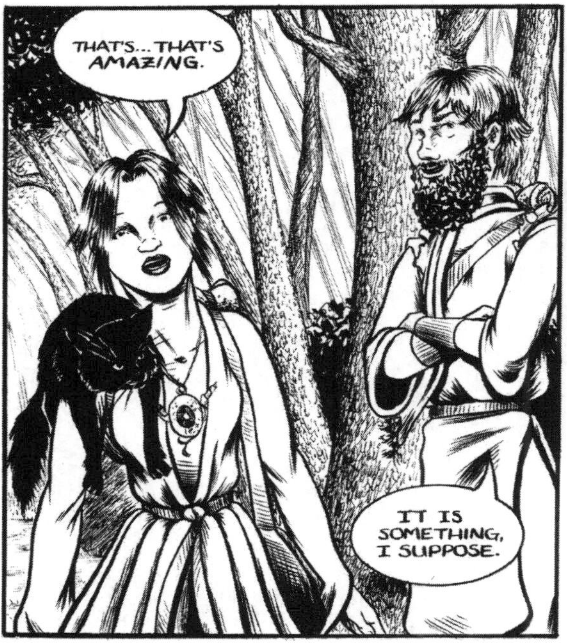
THAT'S... THAT'S AMAZING.
IT IS SOMETHING, I SUPPOSE.

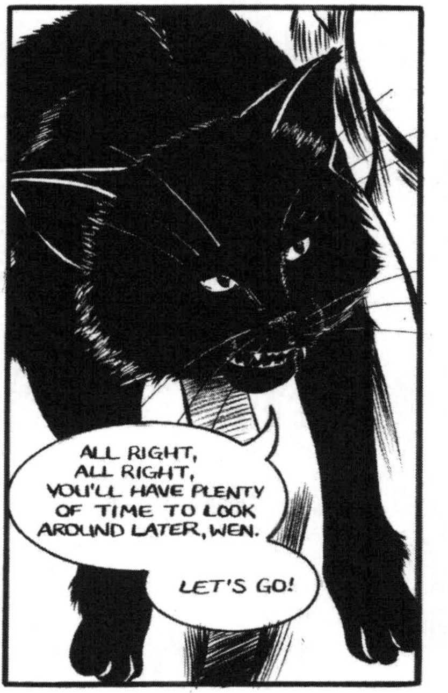
ALL RIGHT, ALL RIGHT, YOU'LL HAVE PLENTY OF TIME TO LOOK AROUND LATER, WEN.
LET'S GO!

DO YOU KNOW WHERE THE HIGH TEMPLE IS?

SHH!!! ASK THEL. I HAVE TO BE QUIET.

PEOPLE MIGHT JUST NOTICE A TALKING CAT, DON'T YOU THINK?

SORRY...

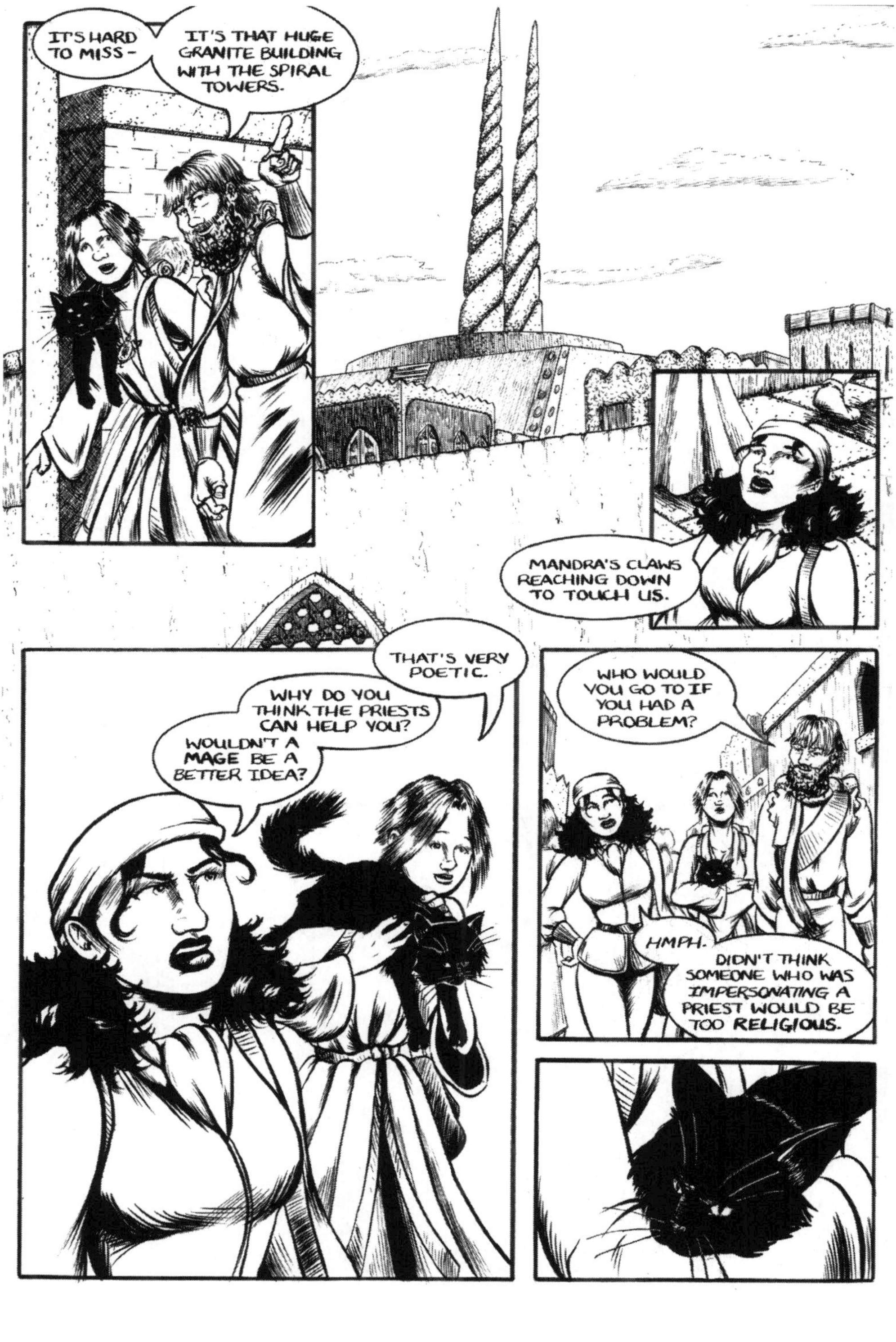
IT'S HARD TO MISS -
IT'S THAT HUGE GRANITE BUILDING WITH THE SPIRAL TOWERS.
MANDRA'S CLAWS REACHING DOWN TO TOUCH US.
THAT'S VERY POETIC.
WHY DO YOU THINK THE PRIESTS CAN HELP YOU?
WOULDN'T A MAGE BE A BETTER IDEA?
WHO WOULD YOU GO TO IF YOU HAD A PROBLEM?
HMPH.
DIDN'T THINK SOMEONE WHO WAS IMPERSONATING A PRIEST WOULD BE TOO RELIGIOUS.

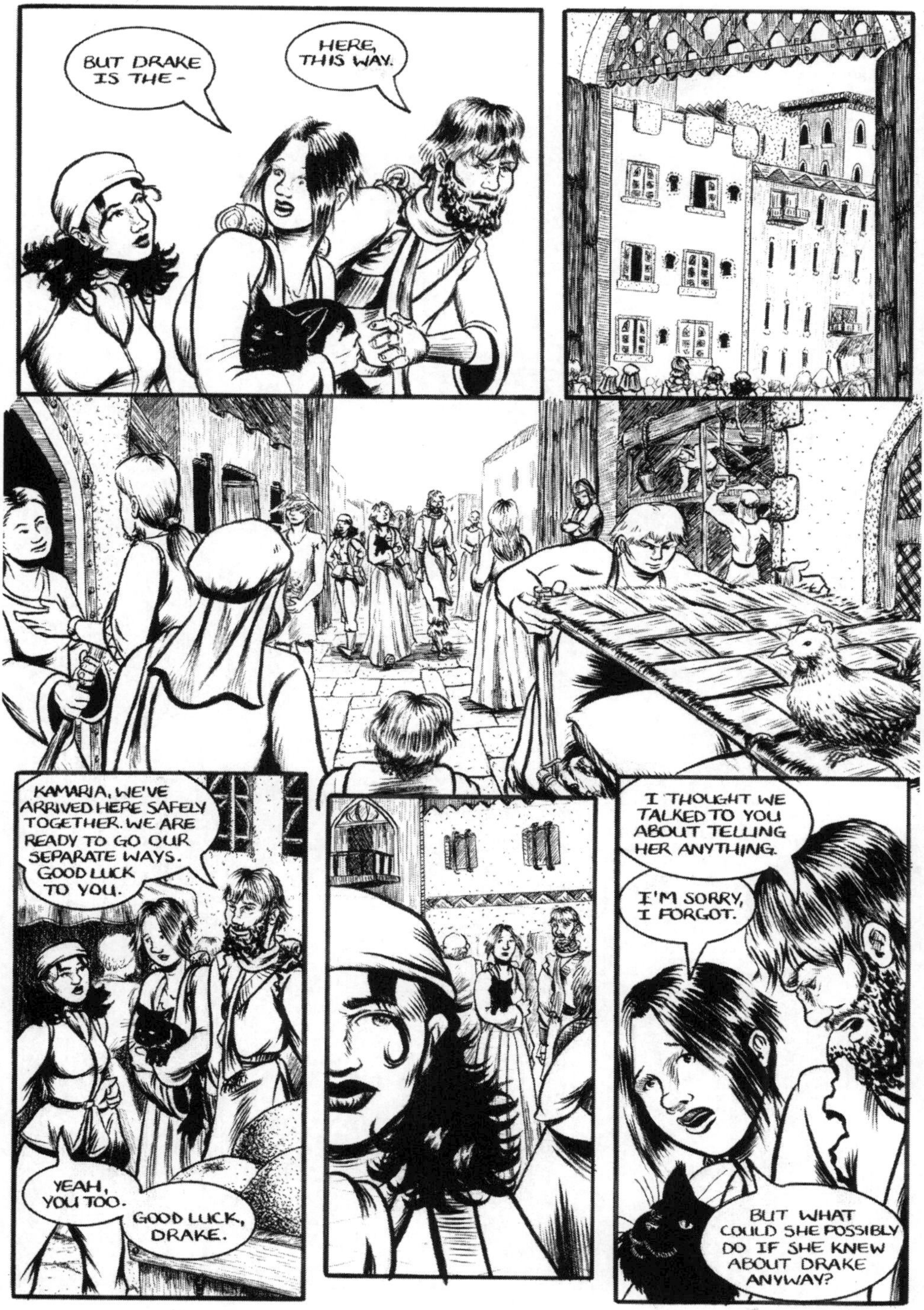
BUT DRAKE IS THE -
HERE, THIS WAY.
KAMARIA, WE'VE ARRIVED HERE SAFELY TOGETHER. WE ARE READY TO GO OUR SEPARATE WAYS. GOOD LUCK TO YOU.
YEAH, YOU TOO.
GOOD LUCK, DRAKE.
I THOUGHT WE TALKED TO YOU ABOUT TELLING HER ANYTHING.
I'M SORRY, I FORGOT.
BUT WHAT COULD SHE POSSIBLY DO IF SHE KNEW ABOUT DRAKE ANYWAY?

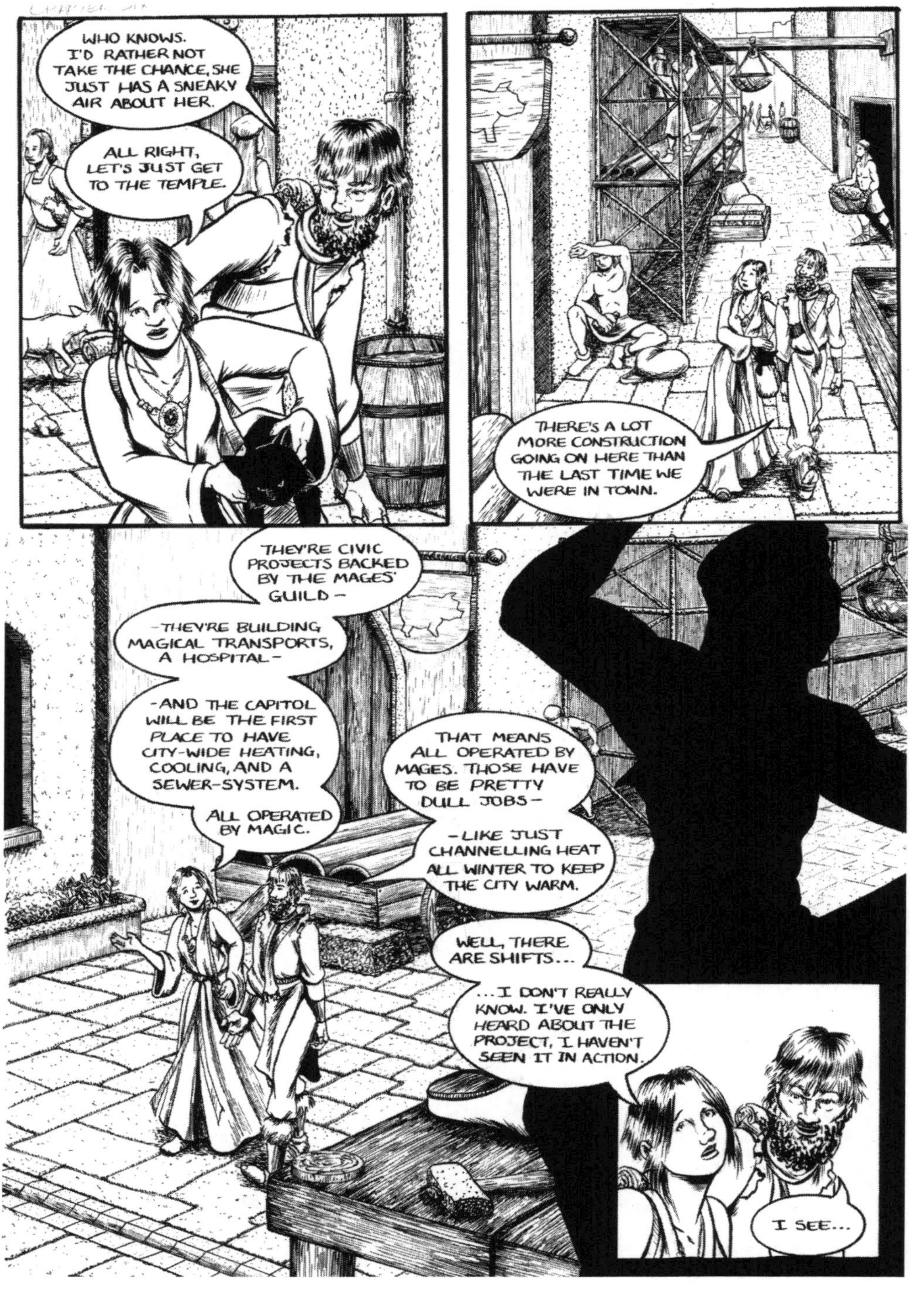
WHO KNOWS. I'D RATHER NOT TAKE THE CHANCE, SHE JUST HAS A SNEAKY AIR ABOUT HER.
ALL RIGHT, LET'S JUST GET TO THE TEMPLE.
THERE'S A LOT MORE CONSTRUCTION GOING ON HERE THAN THE LAST TIME WE WERE IN TOWN.
THEY'RE CIVIC PROJECTS BACKED BY THE MAGES' GUILD -
-THEY'RE BUILDING MAGICAL TRANSPORTS, A HOSPITAL-
-AND THE CAPITOL WILL BE THE FIRST PLACE TO HAVE CITY-WIDE HEATING, COOLING, AND A SEWER-SYSTEM.
ALL OPERATED BY MAGIC.
THAT MEANS ALL OPERATED BY MAGES. THOSE HAVE TO BE PRETTY DULL JOBS-
-LIKE JUST CHANNELLING HEAT ALL WINTER TO KEEP THE CITY WARM.
WELL, THERE ARE SHIFTS...
...I DON'T REALLY KNOW. I'VE ONLY HEARD ABOUT THE PROJECT, I HAVEN'T SEEN IT IN ACTION.
I SEE...

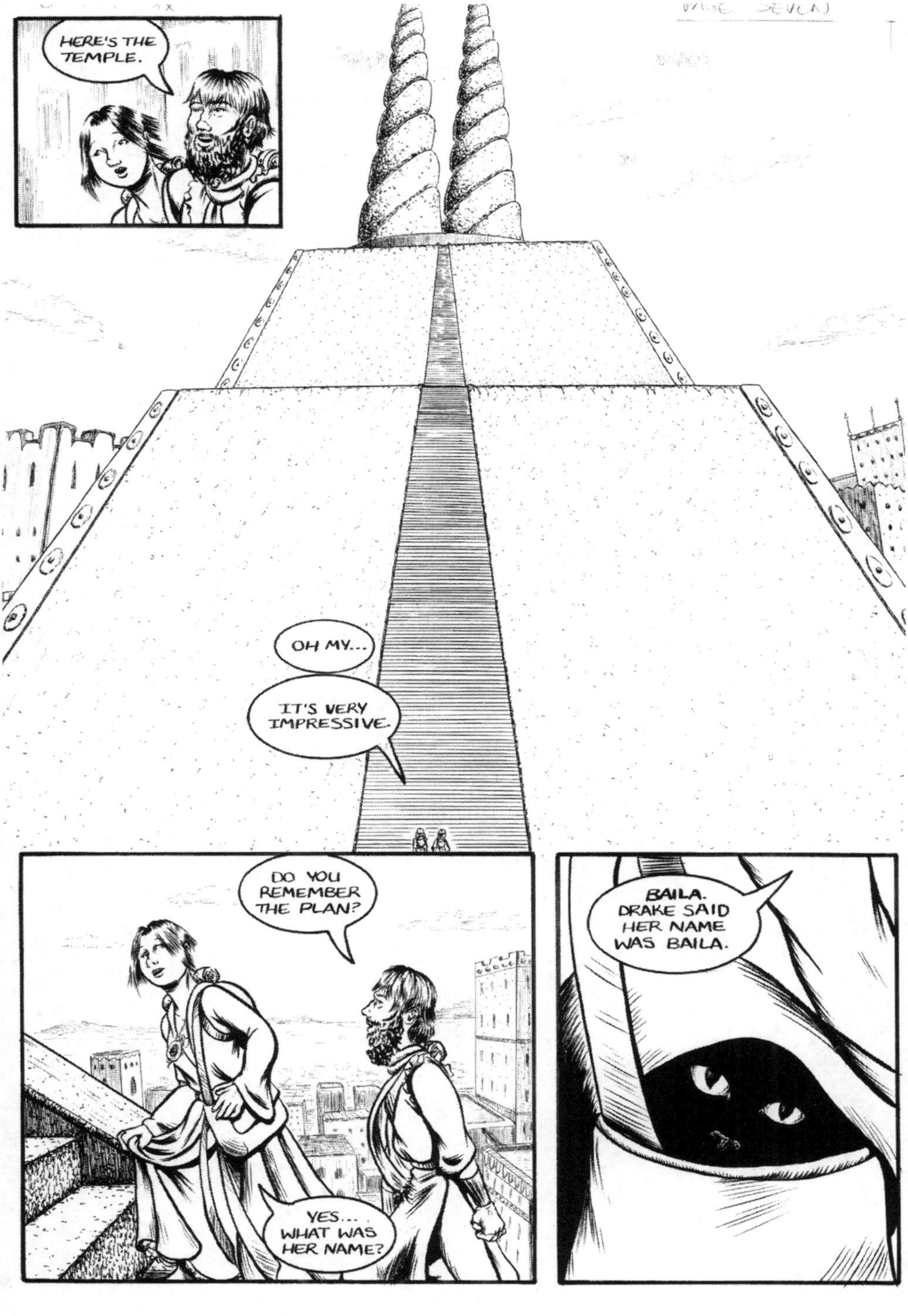
HERE'S THE TEMPLE.
OH MY...
IT'S VERY IMPRESSIVE.
DO YOU REMEMBER THE PLAN?
YES... WHAT WAS HER NAME?
BAILA. DRAKE SAID HER NAME WAS BAILA.

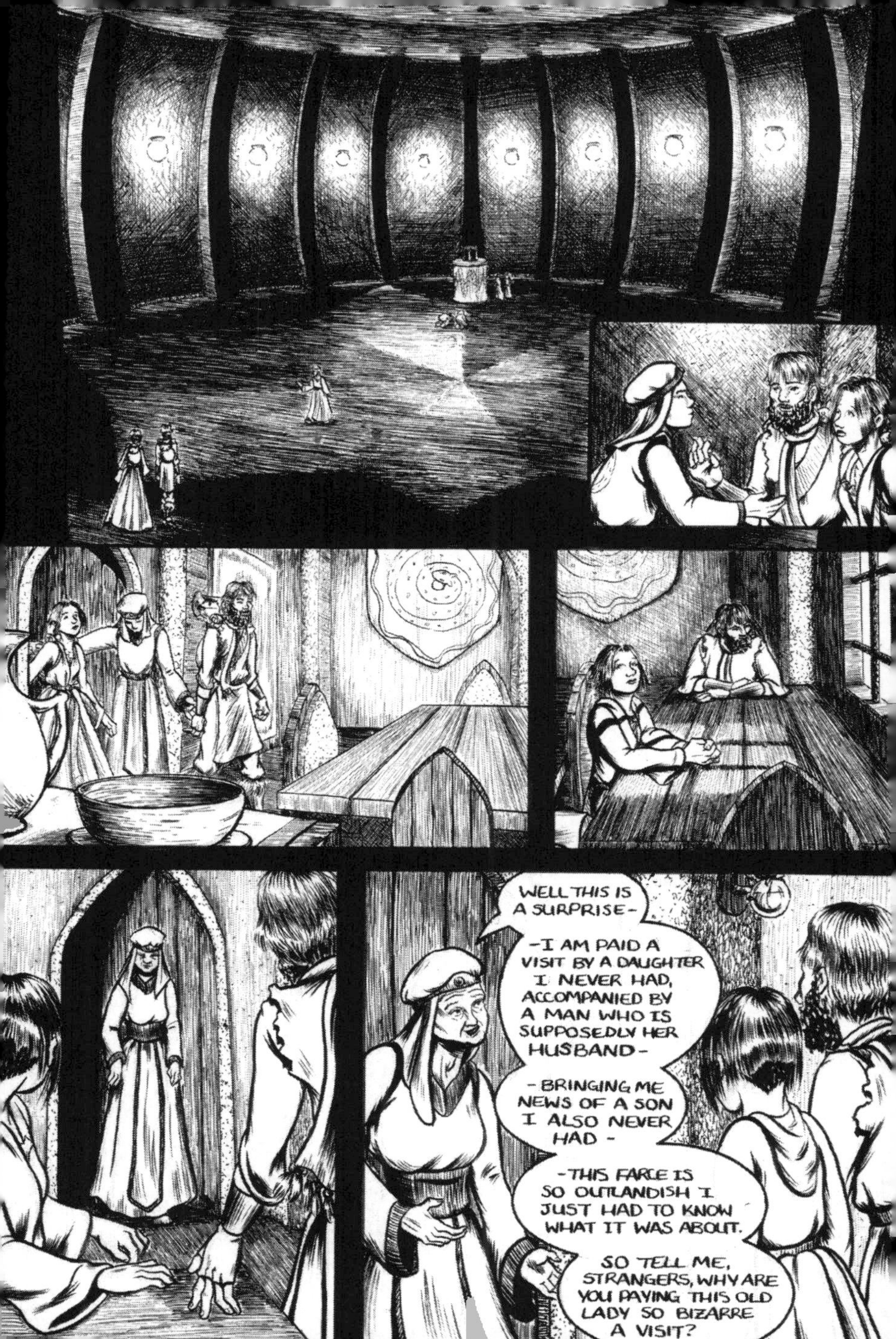
WELL THIS IS A SURPRISE-
-I AM PAID A VISIT BY A DAUGHTER I NEVER HAD, ACCOMPANIED BY A MAN WHO IS SUPPOSEDLY HER HUSBAND-
- BRINGING ME NEWS OF A SON I ALSO NEVER HAD -
-THIS FARCE IS SO OUTLANDISH I JUST HAD TO KNOW WHAT IT WAS ABOUT.
SO TELL ME, STRANGERS, WHY ARE YOU PAYING THIS OLD LADY SO BIZARRE A VISIT?

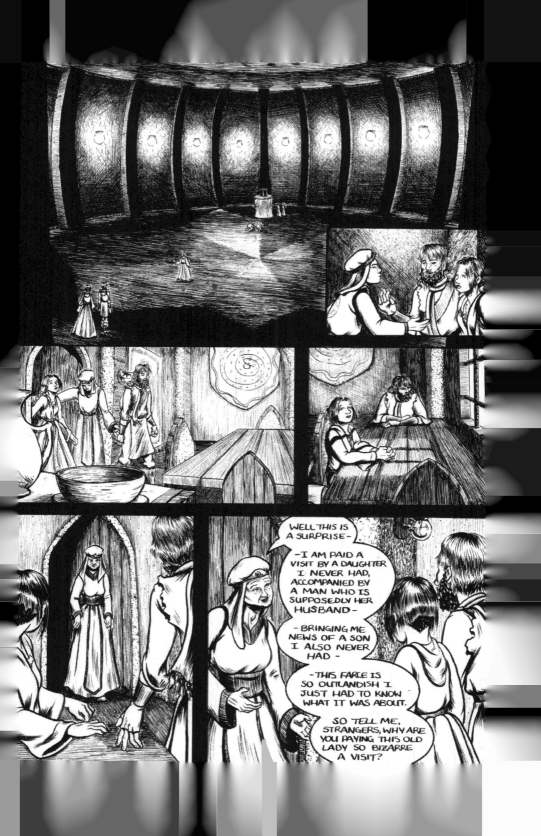

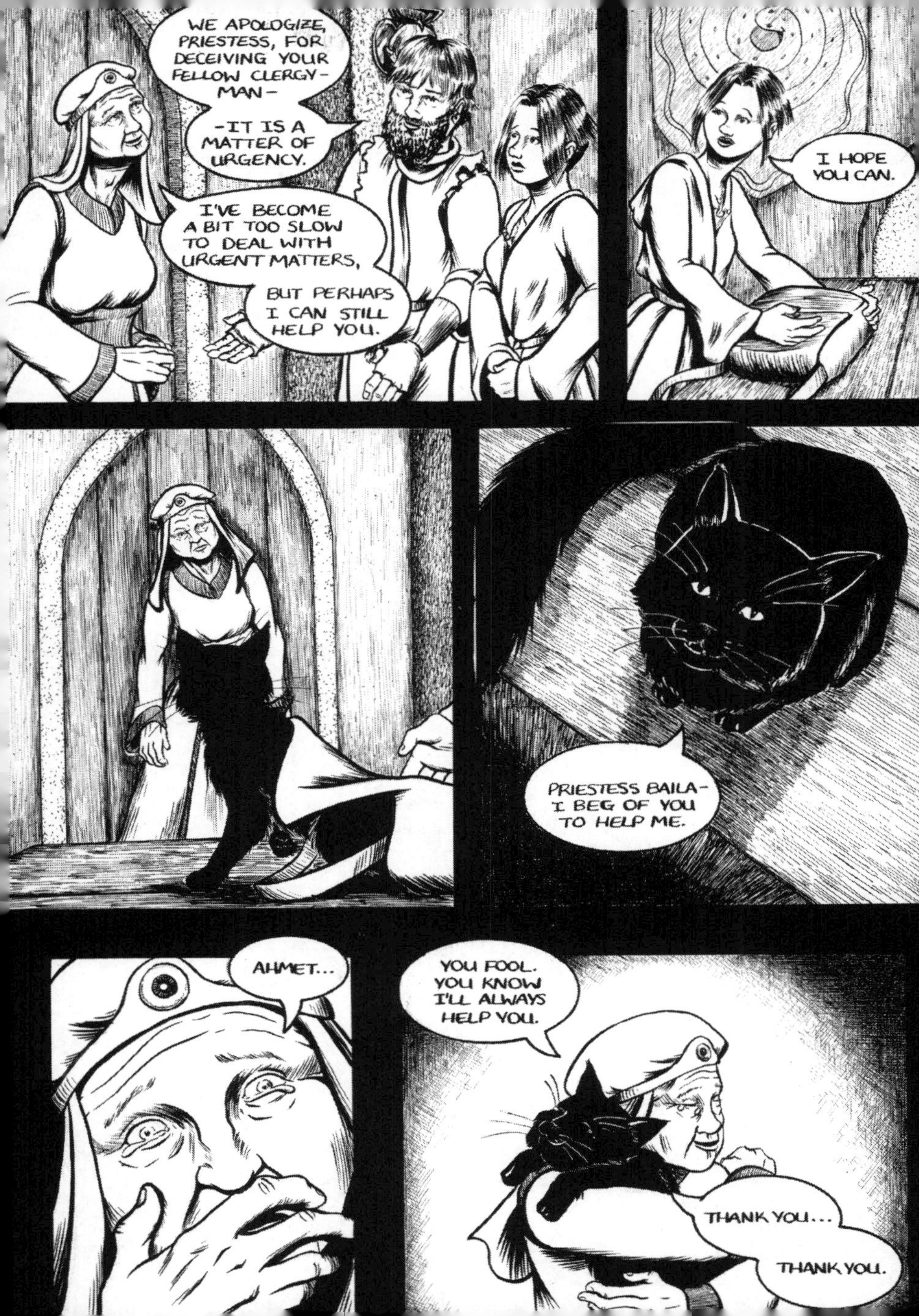
WE APOLOGIZE, PRIESTESS, FOR DECEIVING YOUR FELLOW CLERGY-MAN-
-IT IS A MATTER OF URGENCY.
I'VE BECOME A BIT TOO SLOW TO DEAL WITH URGENT MATTERS,
BUT PERHAPS I CAN STILL HELP YOU.
I HOPE YOU CAN.
PRIESTESS BAILA-I BEG OF YOU TO HELP ME.
AHMET...
YOU FOOL. YOU KNOW I'LL ALWAYS HELP YOU.
THANK YOU...
THANK YOU.

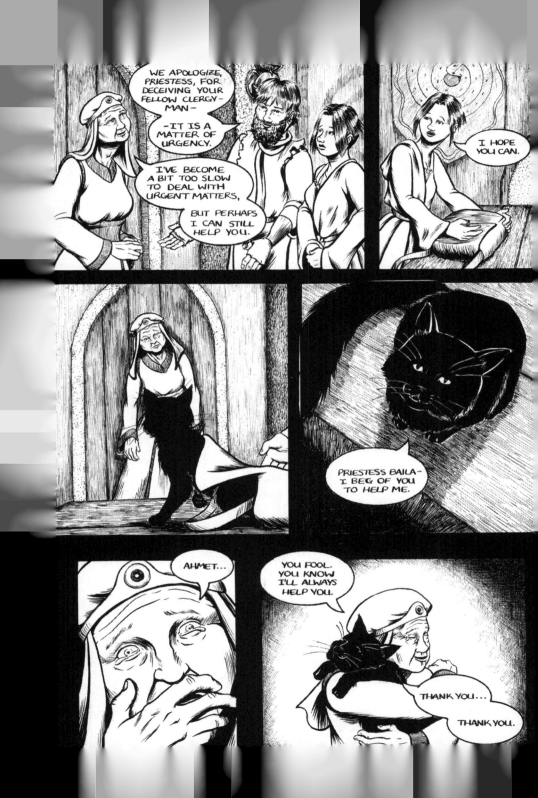

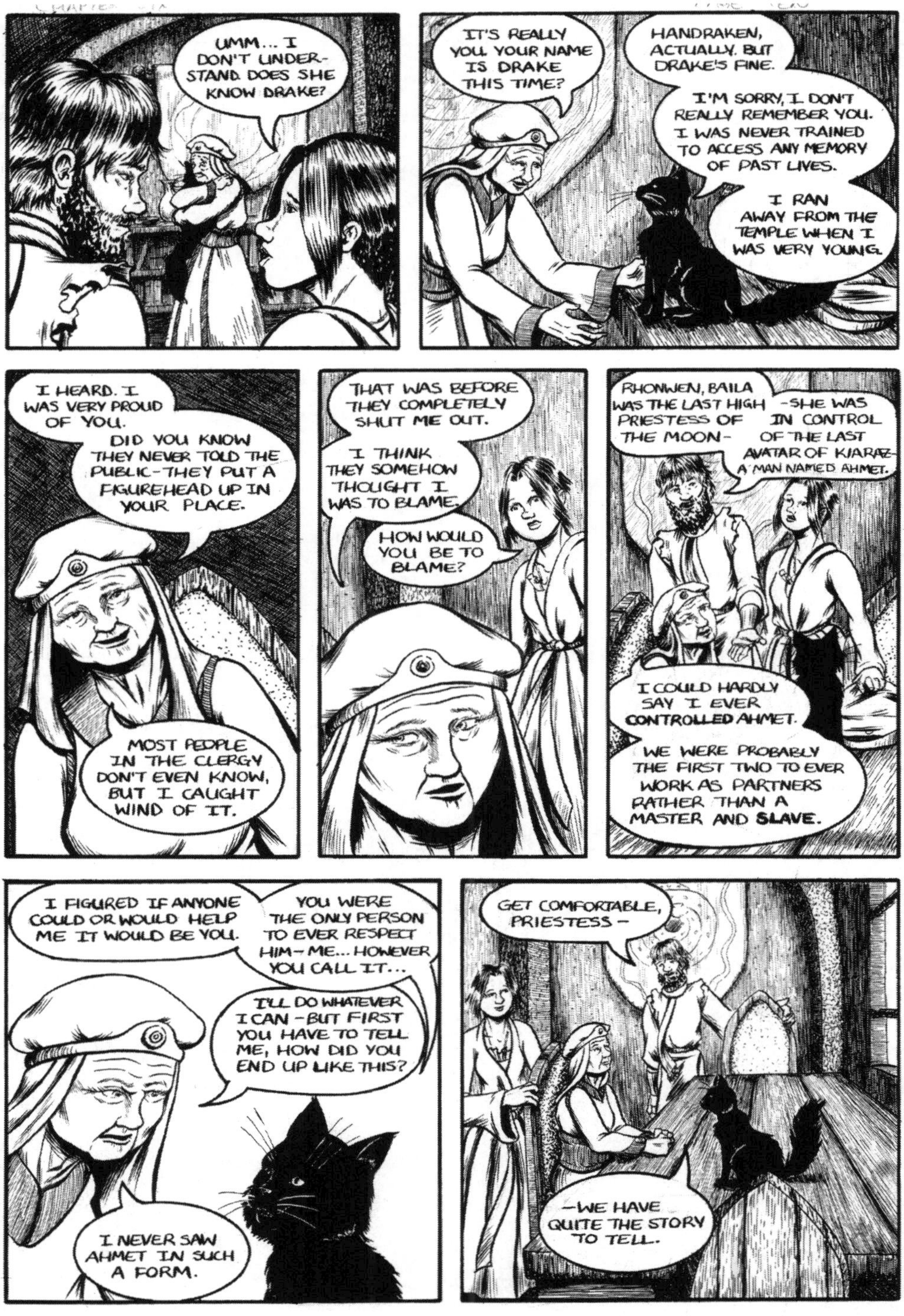
UMM... I DON'T UNDERSTAND. DOES SHE KNOW DRAKE?
IT'S REALLY YOU. YOUR NAME IS DRAKE THIS TIME?
HANDRAKEN, ACTUALLY. BUT DRAKE'S FINE.
I'M SORRY, I DON'T REALLY REMEMBER YOU. I WAS NEVER TRAINED TO ACCESS ANY MEMORY OF PAST LIVES.
I RAN AWAY FROM THE TEMPLE WHEN I WAS VERY YOUNG.
I HEARD. I WAS VERY PROUD OF YOU.
DID YOU KNOW THEY NEVER TOLD THE PUBLIC-THEY PUT A FIGUREHEAD UP IN YOUR PLACE.
MOST PEOPLE IN THE CLERGY DON'T EVEN KNOW, BUT I CAUGHT WIND OF IT.
THAT WAS BEFORE THEY COMPLETELY SHUT ME OUT.
I THINK THEY SOMEHOW THOUGHT I WAS TO BLAME.
HOW WOULD YOU BE TO BLAME?
RHONWEN, BAILA WAS THE LAST HIGH PRIESTESS OF THE MOON-
-SHE WAS IN CONTROL OF THE LAST AVATAR OF KIARAE-A MAN NAMED AHMET.
I COULD HARDLY SAY I EVER CONTROLLED AHMET.
WE WERE PROBABLY THE FIRST TWO TO EVER WORK AS PARTNERS RATHER THAN A MASTER AND SLAVE.
I FIGURED IF ANYONE COULD OR WOULD HELP ME IT WOULD BE YOU.
YOU WERE THE ONLY PERSON TO EVER RESPECT HIM-ME... HOWEVER YOU CALL IT...
I'LL DO WHATEVER I CAN-BUT FIRST YOU HAVE TO TELL ME, HOW DID YOU END UP LIKE THIS?
I NEVER SAW AHMET IN SUCH A FORM.
GET COMFORTABLE, PRIESTESS-
-WE HAVE QUITE THE STORY TO TELL.

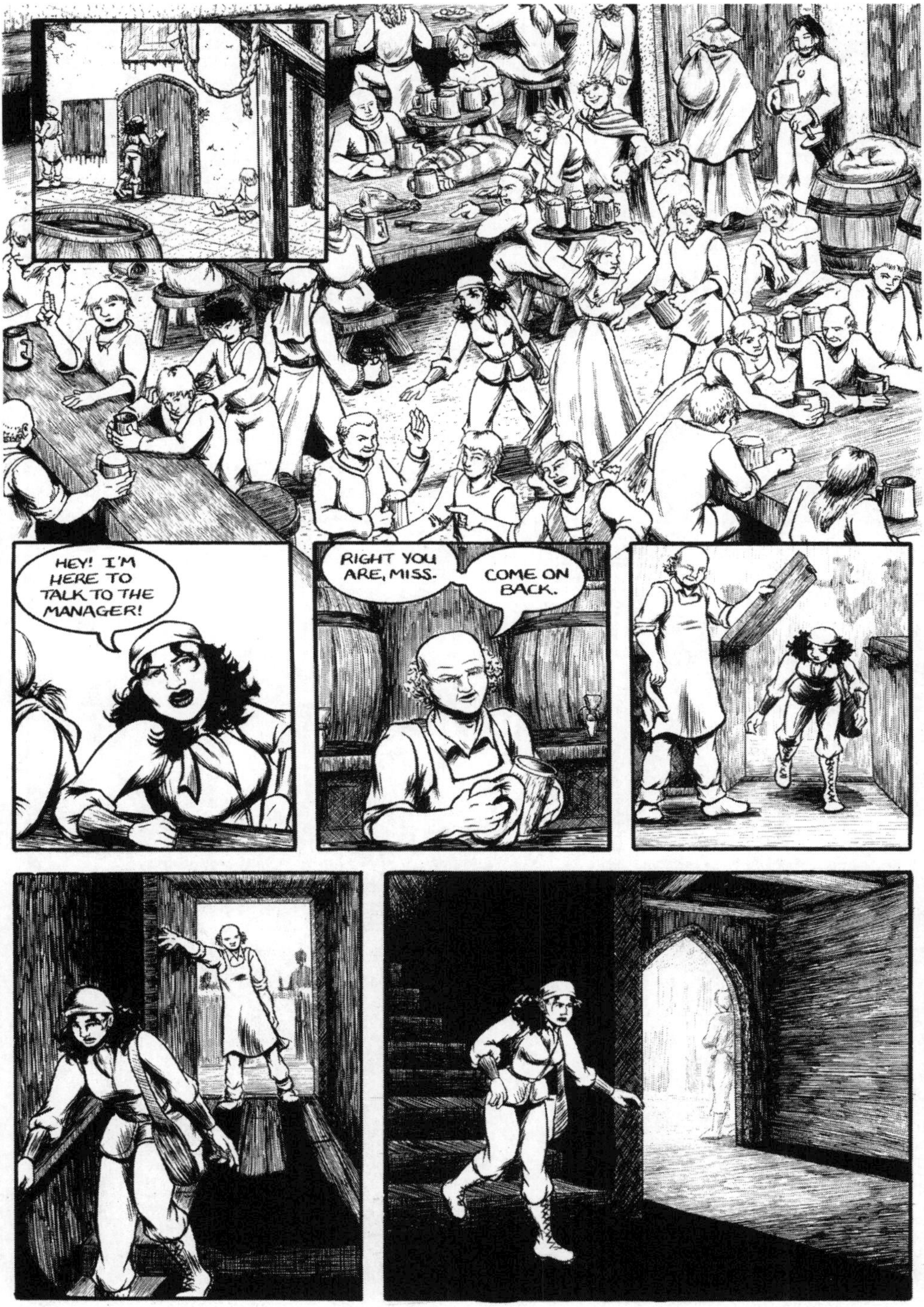
HEY! I'M HERE TO TALK TO THE MANAGER!
RIGHT YOU ARE, MISS.
COME ON BACK.

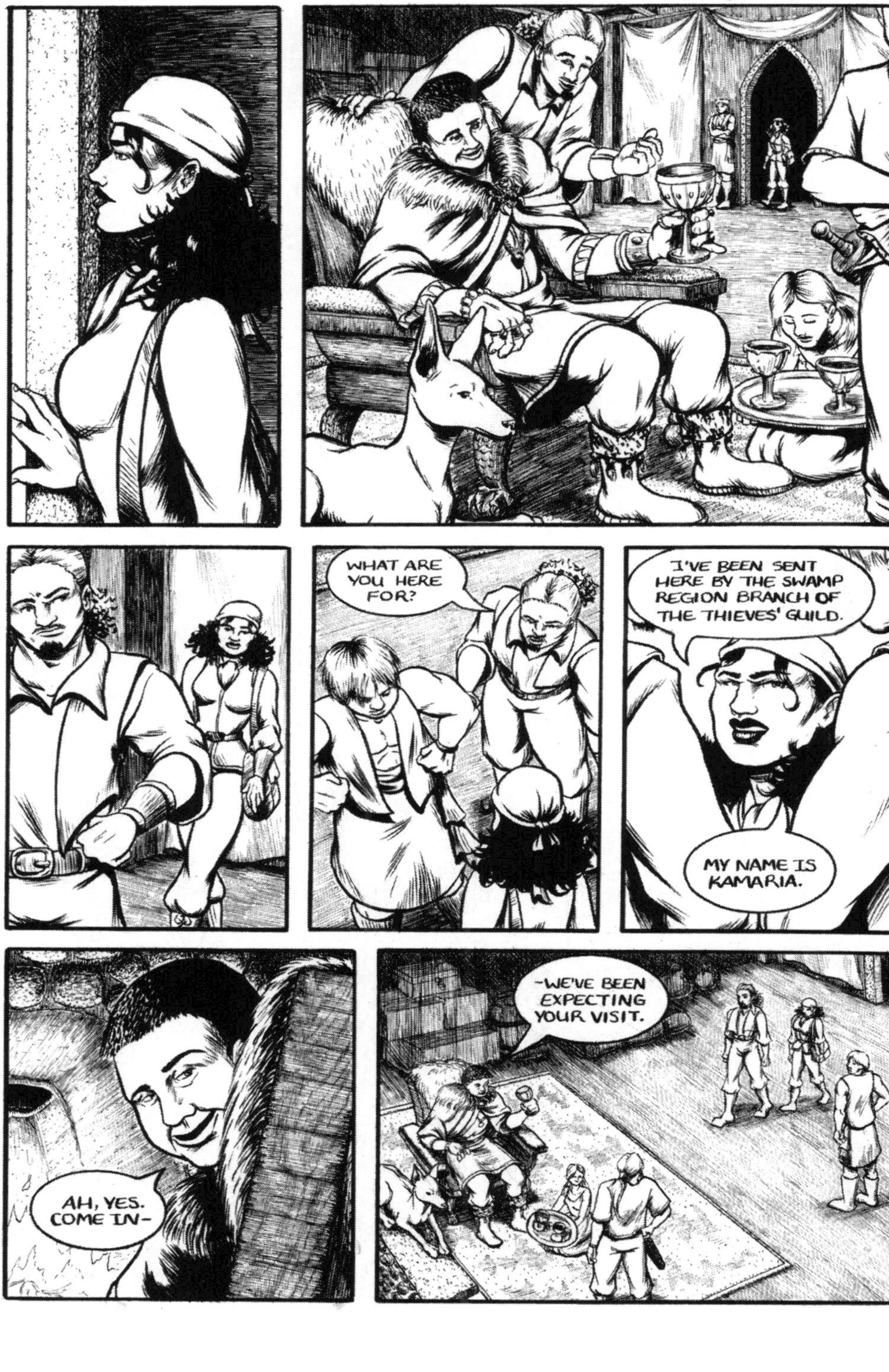
WHAT ARE YOU HERE FOR?
I'VE BEEN SENT HERE BY THE SWAMP REGION BRANCH OF THE THIEVES' GUILD.
MY NAME IS KAMARIA.
AH, YES. COME IN-
-WE'VE BEEN EXPECTING YOUR VISIT.

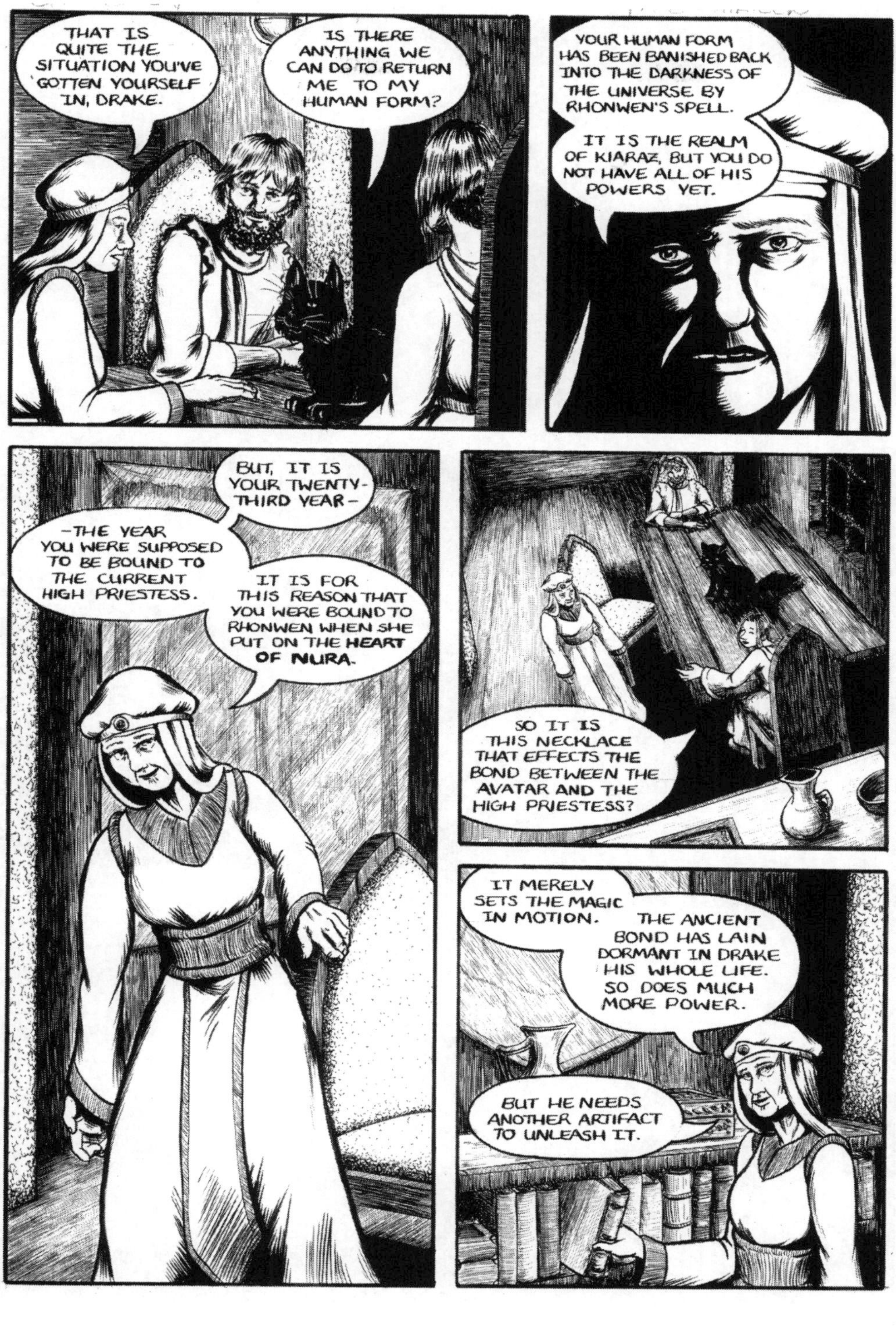
THAT IS QUITE THE SITUATION YOU'VE GOTTEN YOURSELF IN, DRAKE.
IS THERE ANYTHING WE CAN DO TO RETURN ME TO MY HUMAN FORM?
YOUR HUMAN FORM HAS BEEN BANISHED BACK INTO THE DARKNESS OF THE UNIVERSE BY RHONWEN'S SPELL.
IT IS THE REALM OF KIARAZ, BUT YOU DO NOT HAVE ALL OF HIS POWERS YET.
BUT, IT IS YOUR TWENTY-THIRD YEAR-
-THE YEAR YOU WERE SUPPOSED TO BE BOUND TO THE CURRENT HIGH PRIESTESS.
IT IS FOR THIS REASON THAT YOU WERE BOUND TO RHONWEN WHEN SHE PUT ON THE HEART OF NURA.
SO IT IS THIS NECKLACE THAT EFFECTS THE BOND BETWEEN THE AVATAR AND THE HIGH PRIESTESS?
IT MERELY SETS THE MAGIC IN MOTION.
THE ANCIENT BOND HAS LAIN DORMANT IN DRAKE HIS WHOLE LIFE. SO DOES MUCH MORE POWER.
BUT HE NEEDS ANOTHER ARTIFACT TO UNLEASH IT.

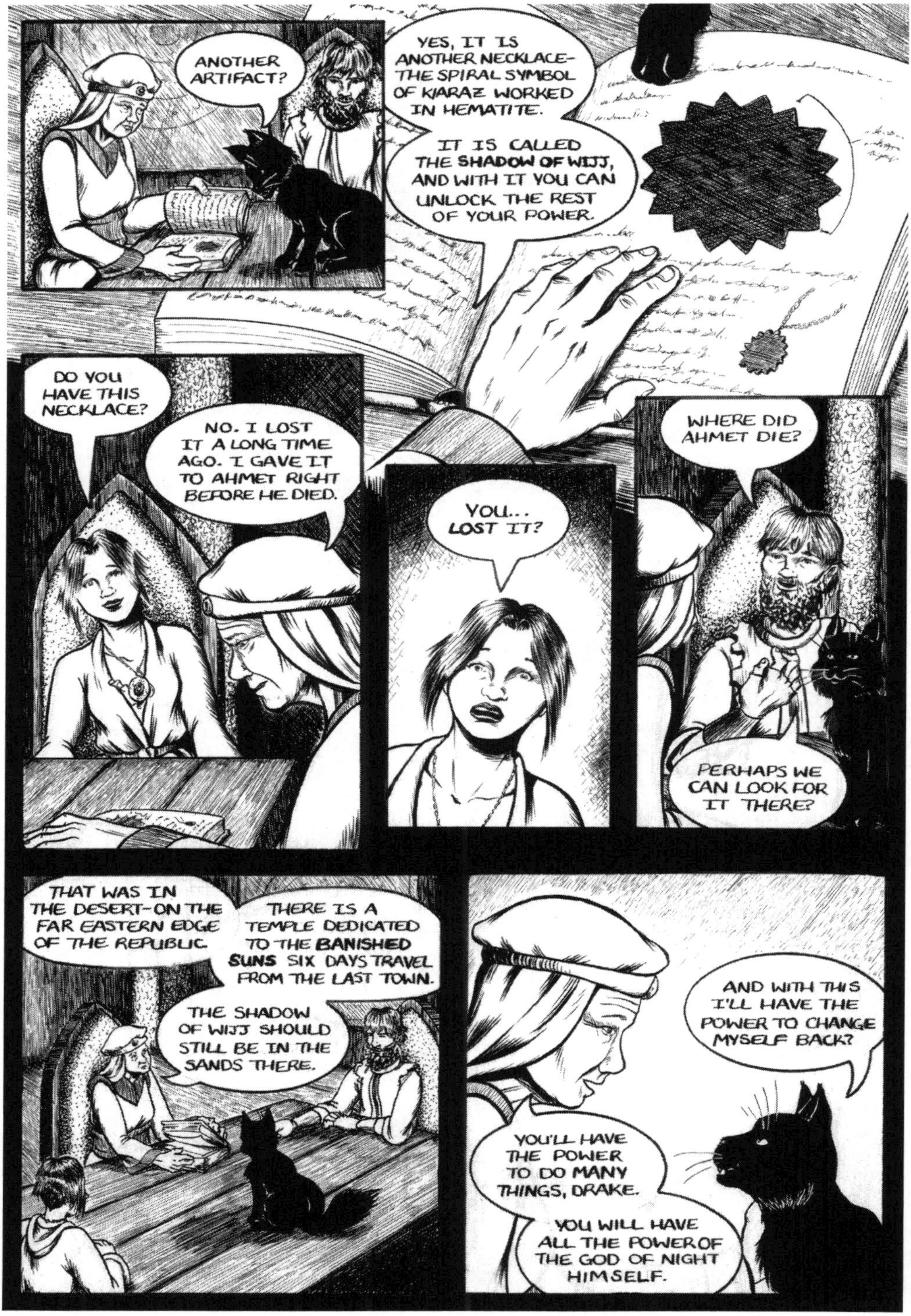
ANOTHER ARTIFACT?
YES, IT IS ANOTHER NECKLACE- THE SPIRAL SYMBOL OF KIARAZ WORKED IN HEMATITE.
IT IS CALLED THE SHADOW OF WIJJ, AND WITH IT YOU CAN UNLOCK THE REST OF YOUR POWER.
DO YOU HAVE THIS NECKLACE?
NO. I LOST IT A LONG TIME AGO. I GAVE IT TO AHMET RIGHT BEFORE HE DIED.
YOU... LOST IT?
WHERE DID AHMET DIE?
PERHAPS WE CAN LOOK FOR IT THERE?
THAT WAS IN THE DESERT-ON THE FAR EASTERN EDGE OF THE REPUBLIC.
THERE IS A TEMPLE DEDICATED TO THE BANISHED SUNS SIX DAYS TRAVEL FROM THE LAST TOWN.
THE SHADOW OF WIJJ SHOULD STILL BE IN THE SANDS THERE.
AND WITH THIS I'LL HAVE THE POWER TO CHANGE MYSELF BACK?
YOU'LL HAVE THE POWER TO DO MANY THINGS, DRAKE.
YOU WILL HAVE ALL THE POWER OF THE GOD OF NIGHT HIMSELF.

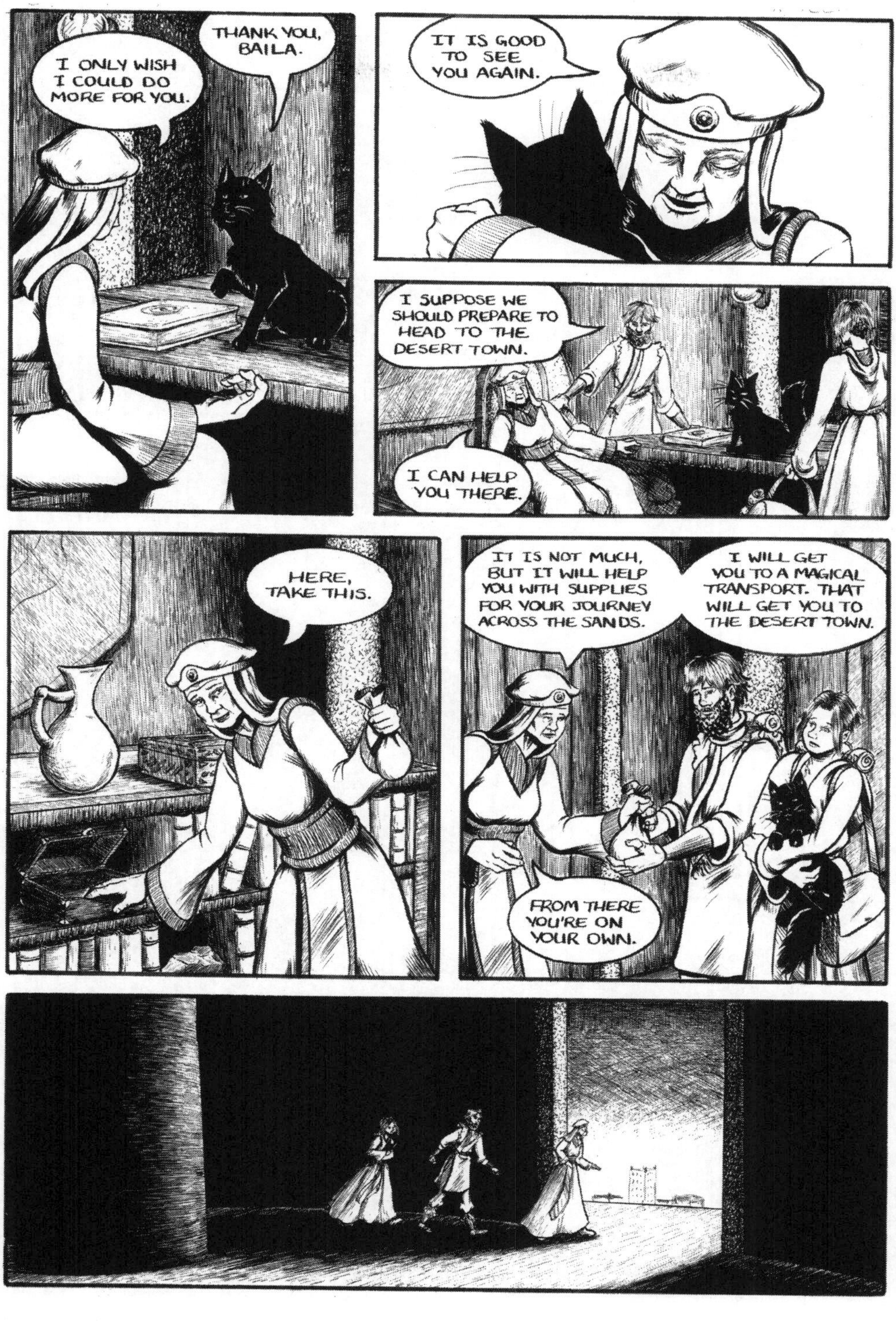
I ONLY WISH I COULD DO MORE FOR YOU.
THANK YOU, BAILA.
IT IS GOOD TO SEE YOU AGAIN.
I SUPPOSE WE SHOULD PREPARE TO HEAD TO THE DESERT TOWN.
I CAN HELP YOU THERE.
HERE, TAKE THIS.
IT IS NOT MUCH, BUT IT WILL HELP YOU WITH SUPPLIES FOR YOUR JOURNEY ACROSS THE SANDS.
I WILL GET YOU TO A MAGICAL TRANSPORT. THAT WILL GET YOU TO THE DESERT TOWN.
FROM THERE YOU'RE ON YOUR OWN.

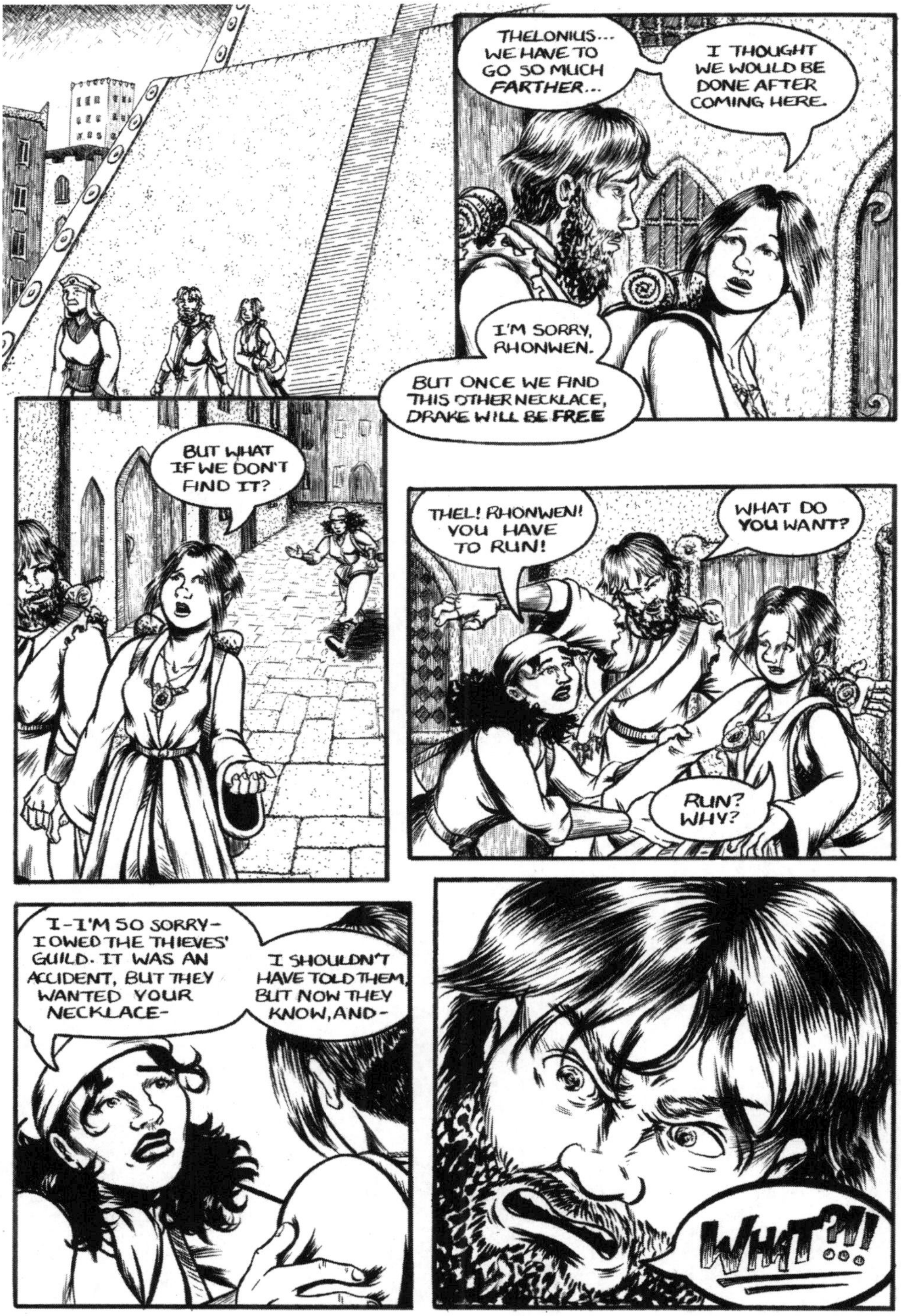
THELONIUS... WE HAVE TO GO SO MUCH FARTHER...
I THOUGHT WE WOULD BE DONE AFTER COMING HERE.
I'M SORRY, RHONWEN.
BUT ONCE WE FIND THIS OTHER NECKLACE, DRAKE WILL BE FREE
BUT WHAT IF WE DON'T FIND IT?
THEL! RHONWEN! YOU HAVE TO RUN!
WHAT DO YOU WANT?
RUN? WHY?
I-I'M SO SORRY- I OWED THE THIEVES' GUILD. IT WAS AN ACCIDENT, BUT THEY WANTED YOUR NECKLACE-
I SHOULDN'T HAVE TOLD THEM, BUT NOW THEY KNOW, AND-
WHAT?!!

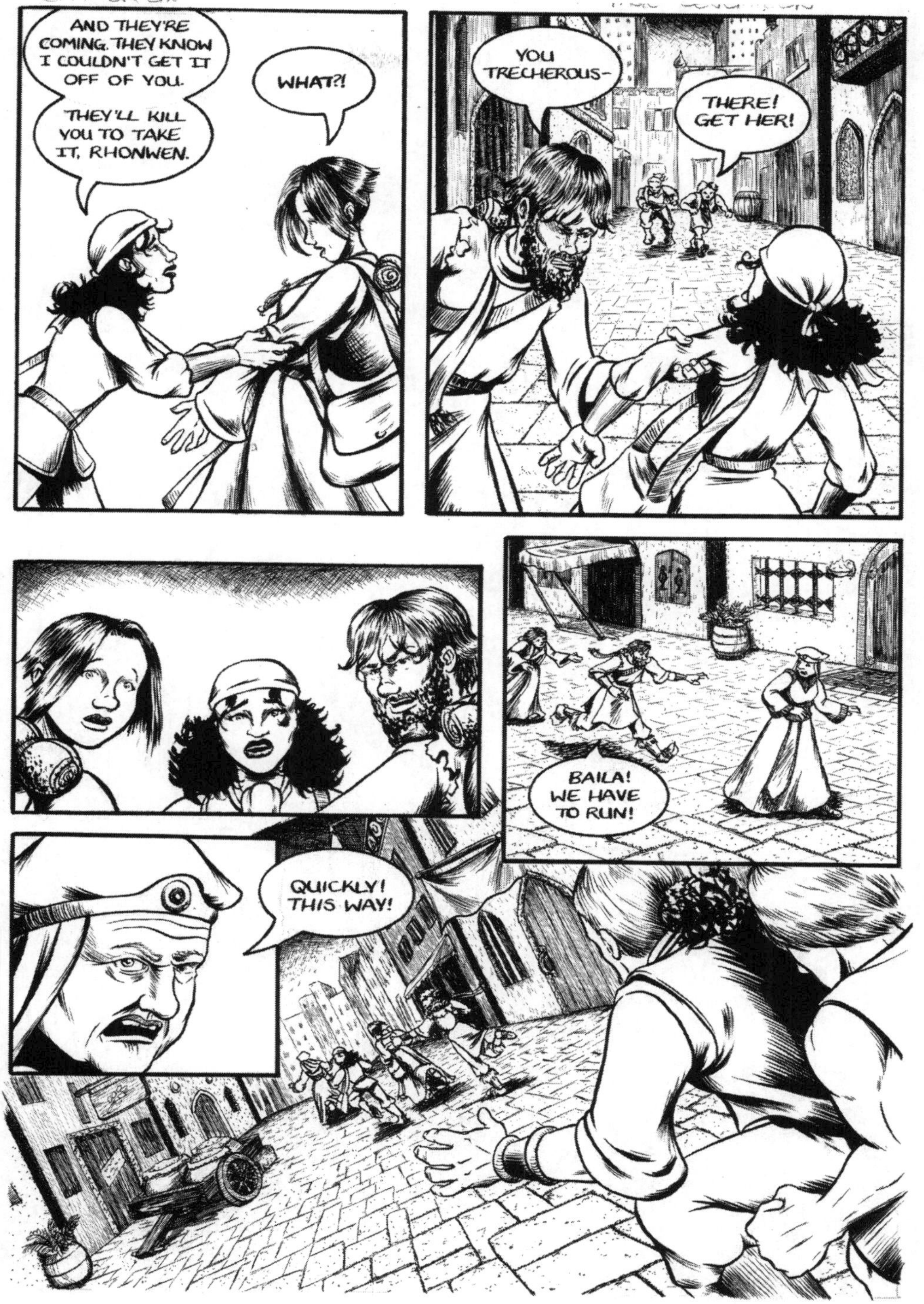
AND THEY'RE COMING. THEY KNOW I COULDN'T GET IT OFF OF YOU.
THEY'LL KILL YOU TO TAKE IT, RHONWEN.
WHAT?!
YOU TRECHEROUS-
THERE! GET HER!
BAILA! WE HAVE TO RUN!
QUICKLY! THIS WAY!

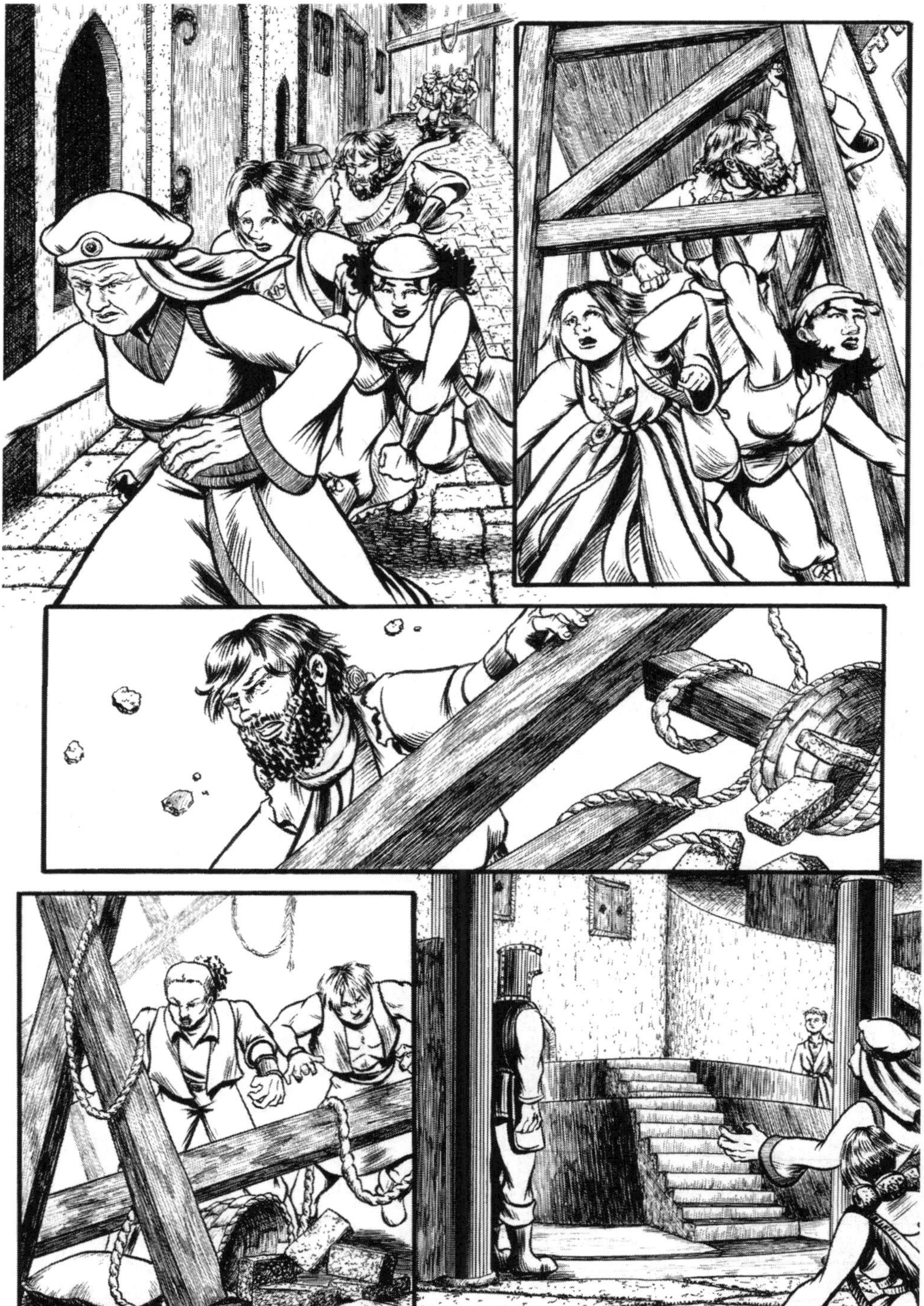

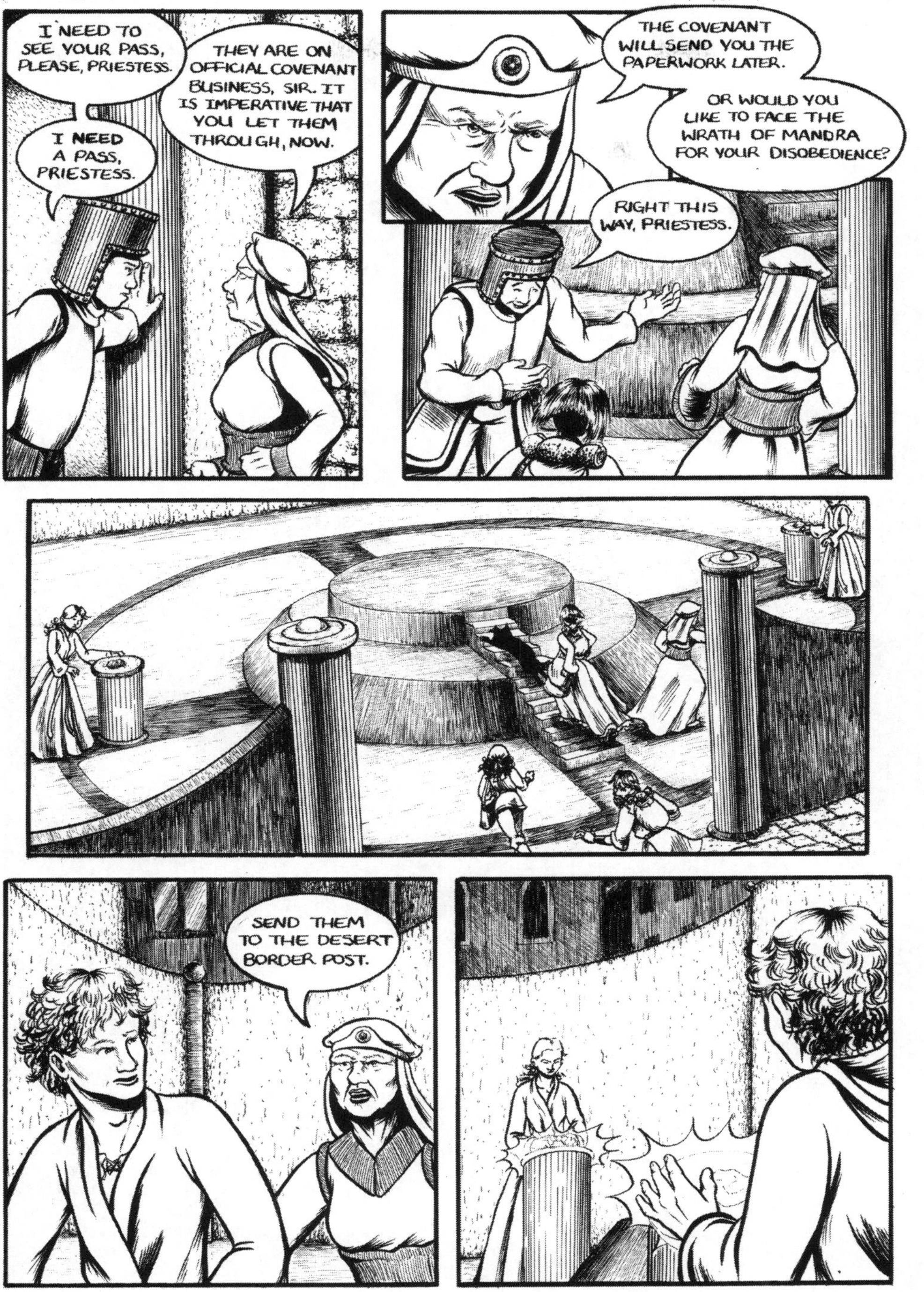
I NEED TO SEE YOUR PASS, PLEASE, PRIESTESS.
I NEED A PASS, PRIESTESS.
THEY ARE ON OFFICIAL COVENANT BUSINESS, SIR. IT IS IMPERATIVE THAT YOU LET THEM THROUGH, NOW.
THE COVENANT WILL SEND YOU THE PAPERWORK LATER.
OR WOULD YOU LIKE TO FACE THE WRATH OF MANDRA FOR YOUR DISOBEDIENCE?
RIGHT THIS WAY, PRIESTESS.
SEND THEM TO THE DESERT BORDER POST.

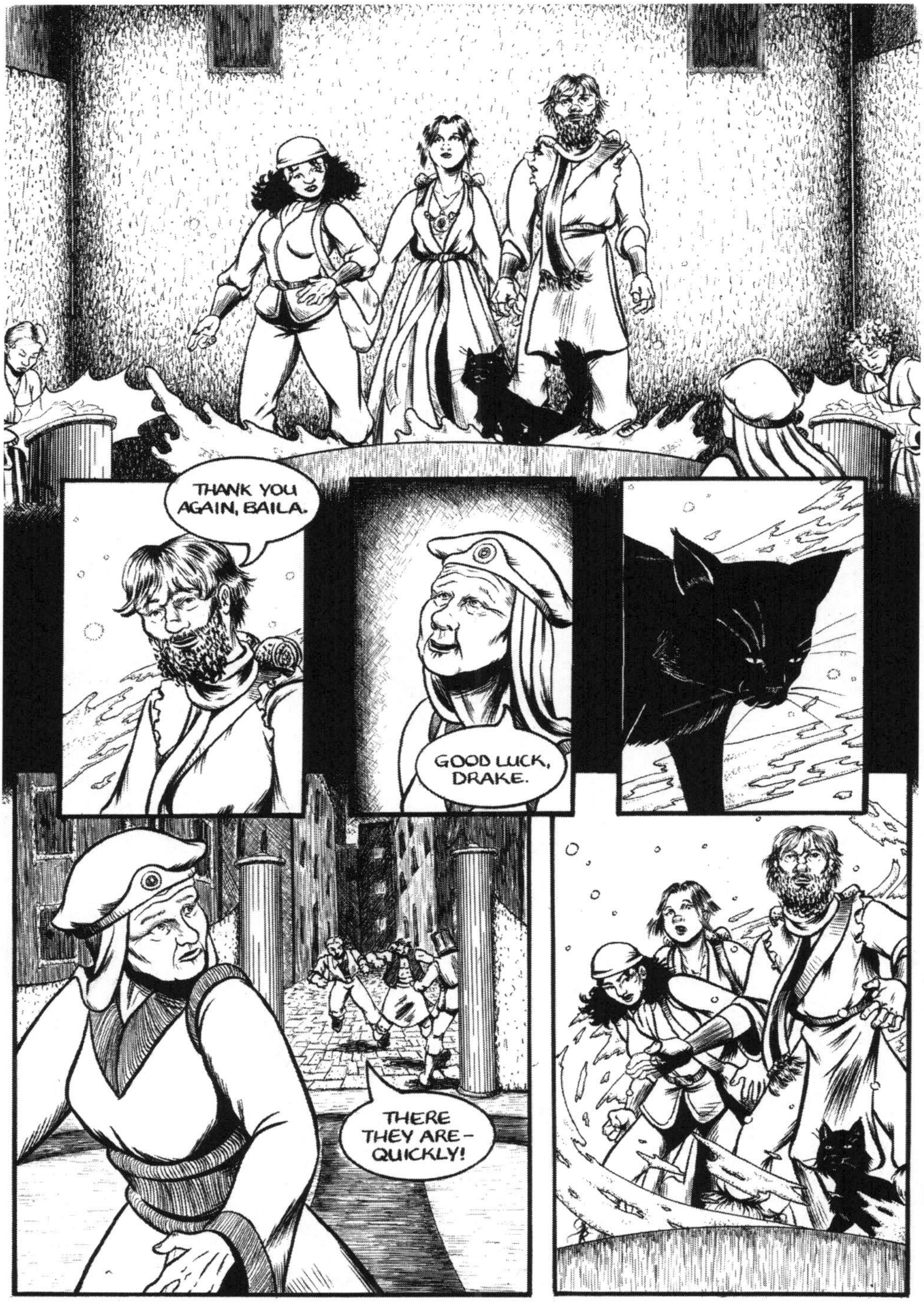
THANK YOU AGAIN, BAILA.
GOOD LUCK, DRAKE.
THERE THEY ARE- QUICKLY!

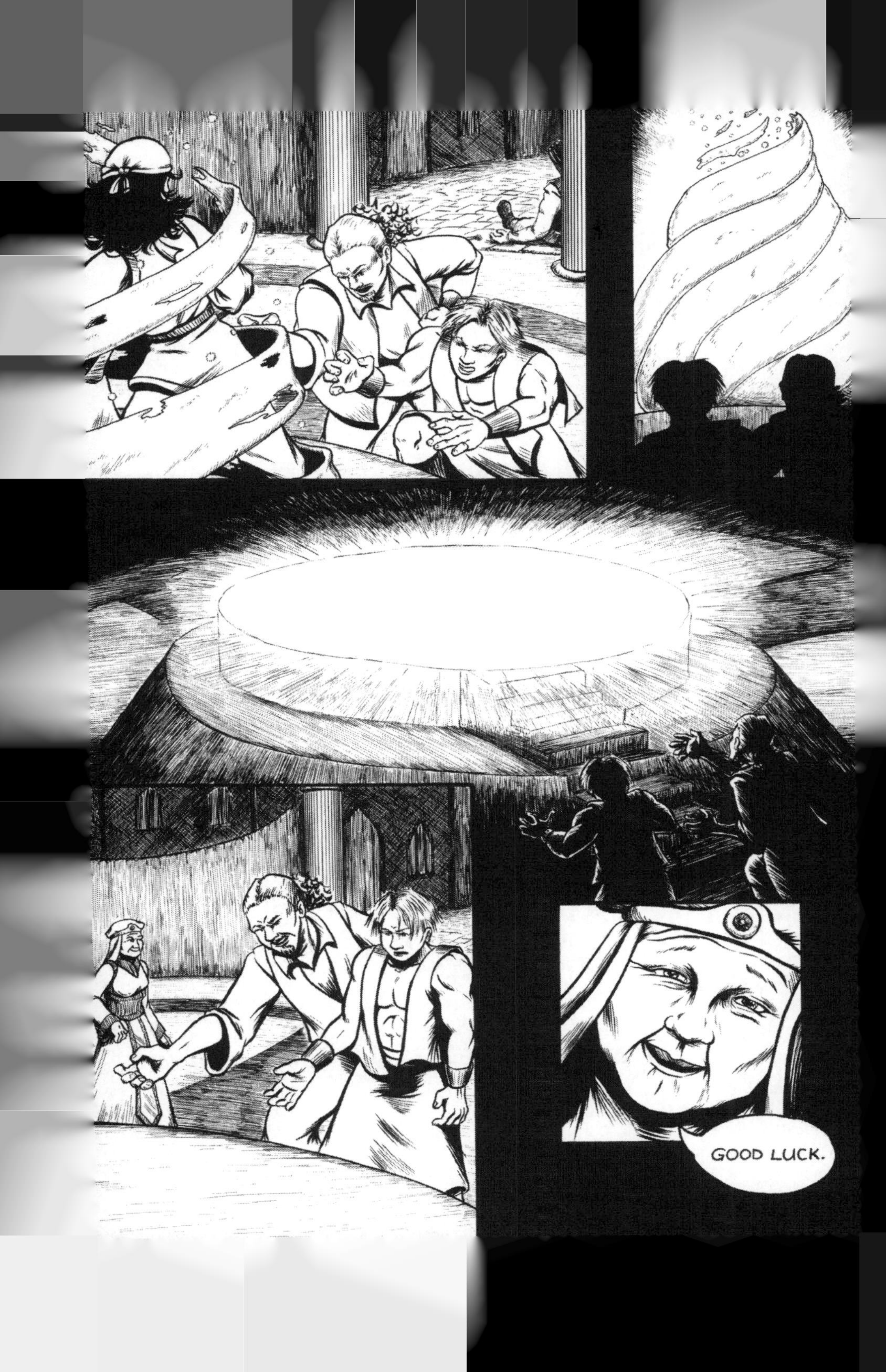
GOOD LUCK.

CHAPTER VII

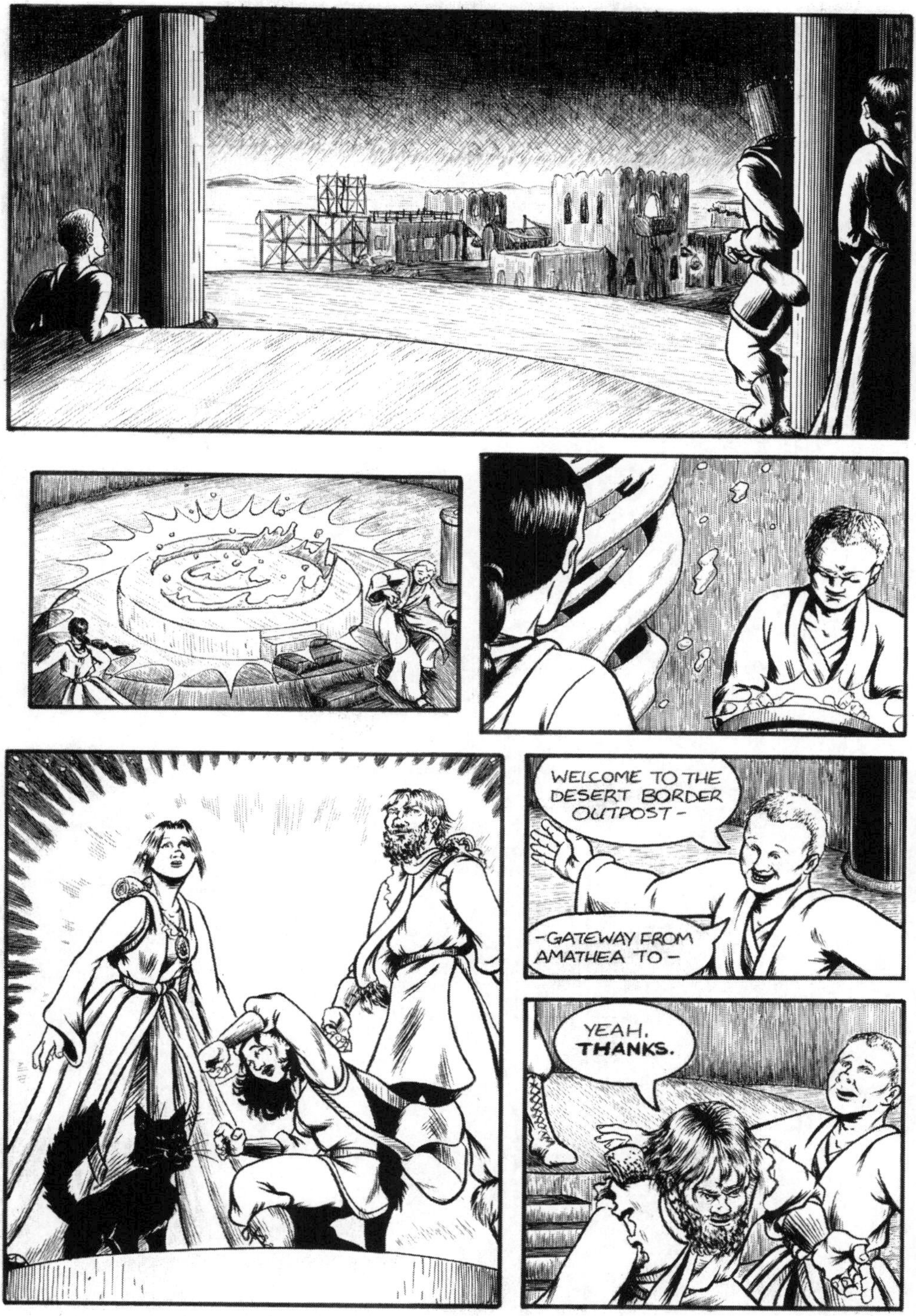
WELCOME TO THE DESERT BORDER OUTPOST -
- GATEWAY FROM AMATHEA TO -
YEAH, THANKS.

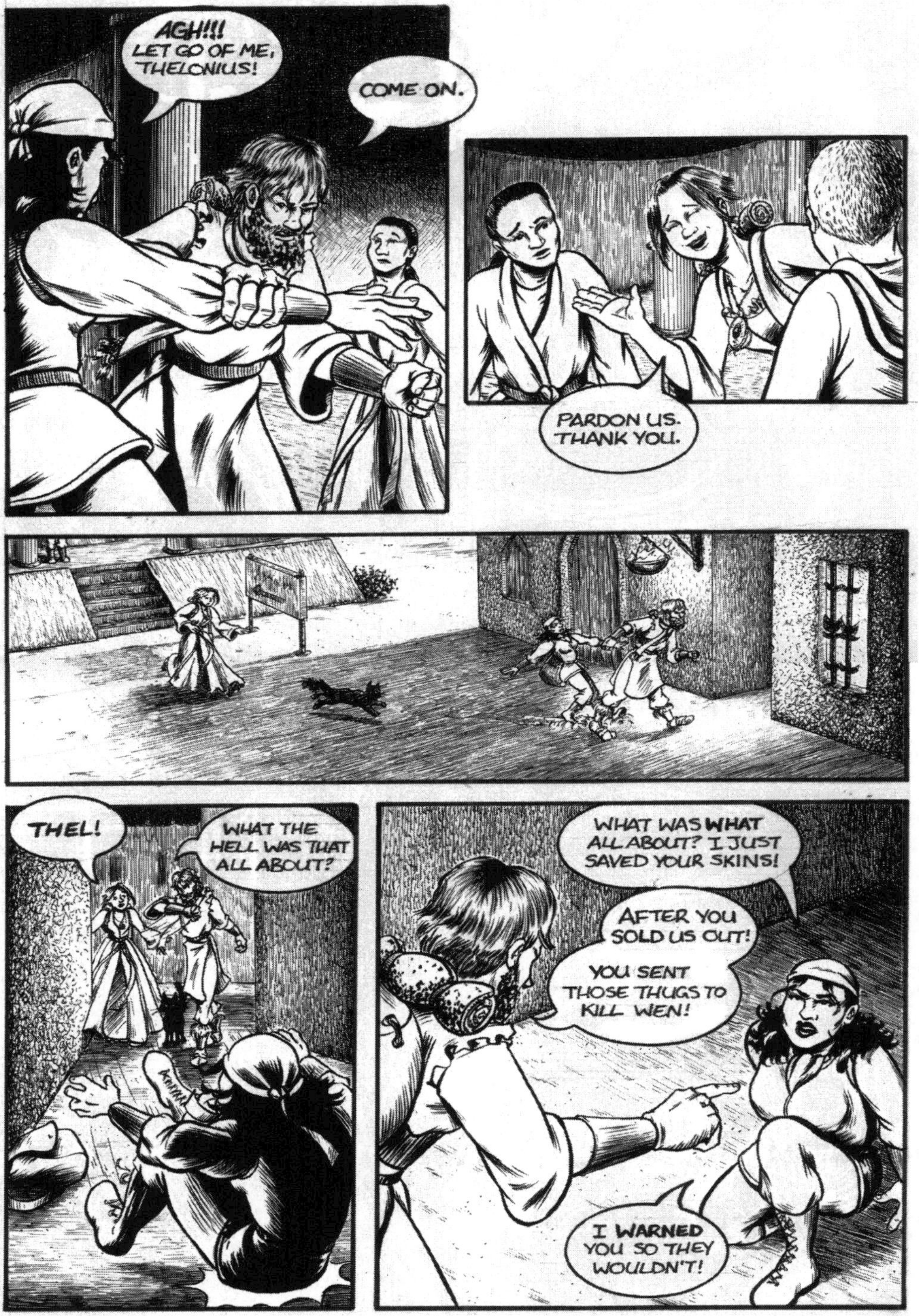
AGH!!! LET GO OF ME, THELONIUS!
COME ON.
PARDON US. THANK YOU.
THEL!
WHAT THE HELL WAS THAT ALL ABOUT?
WHAT WAS WHAT ALL ABOUT? I JUST SAVED YOUR SKINS!
AFTER YOU SOLD US OUT!
YOU SENT THOSE THUGS TO KILL WEN!
I WARNED YOU SO THEY WOULDN'T!

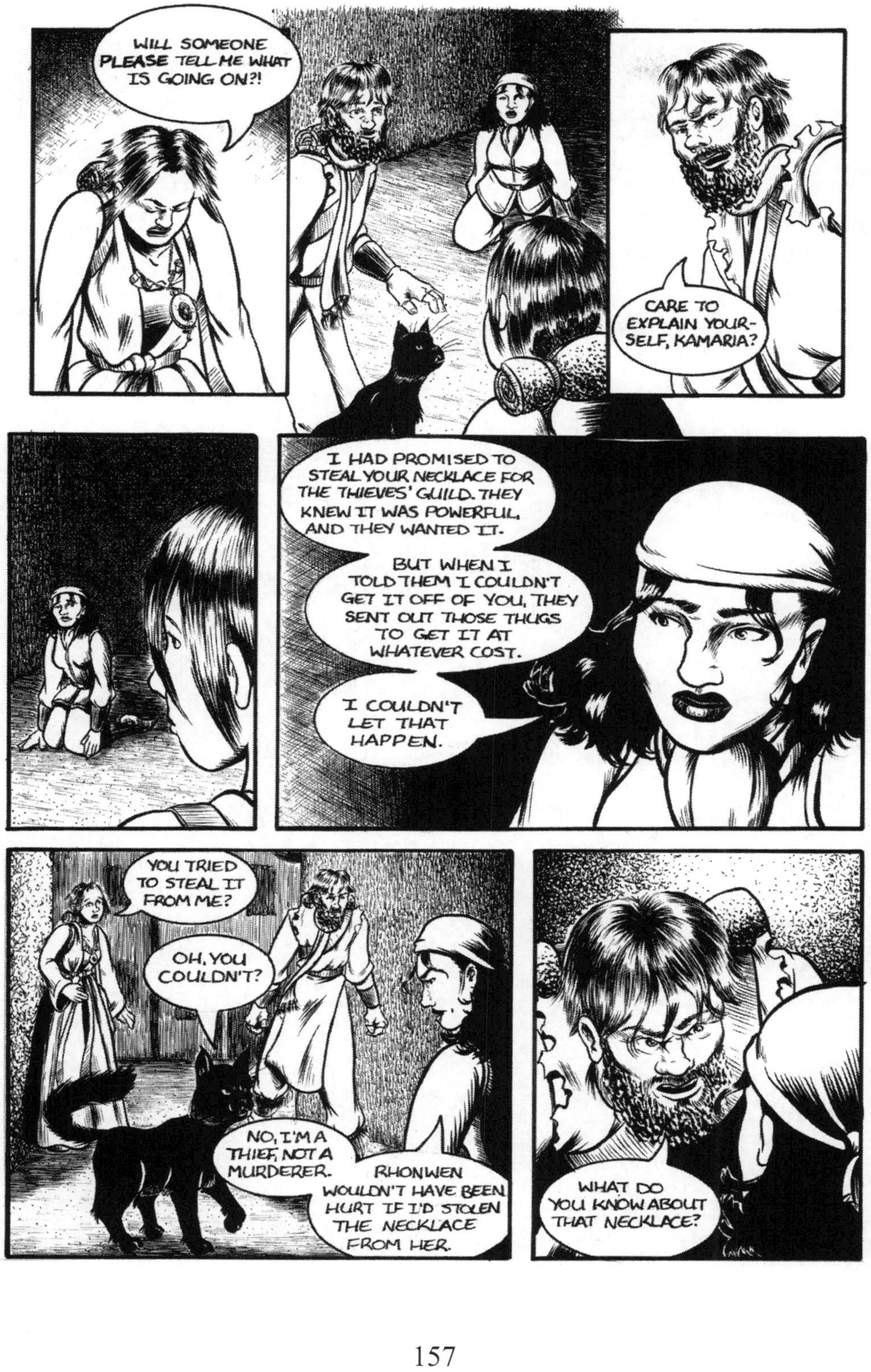
WILL SOMEONE PLEASE TELL ME WHAT IS GOING ON?!
CARE TO EXPLAIN YOURSELF, KAMARIA?
I HAD PROMISED TO STEAL YOUR NECKLACE FOR THE THIEVES' GUILD. THEY KNEW IT WAS POWERFUL, AND THEY WANTED IT.
BUT WHEN I TOLD THEM I COULDN'T GET IT OFF OF YOU, THEY SENT OUT THOSE THUGS TO GET IT AT WHATEVER COST.
I COULDN'T LET THAT HAPPEN.
YOU TRIED TO STEAL IT FROM ME?
OH, YOU COULDN'T?
NO, I'M A THIEF, NOT A MURDERER.
RHONWEN WOULDN'T HAVE BEEN HURT IF I'D STOLEN THE NECKLACE FROM HER.
WHAT DO YOU KNOW ABOUT THAT NECKLACE?

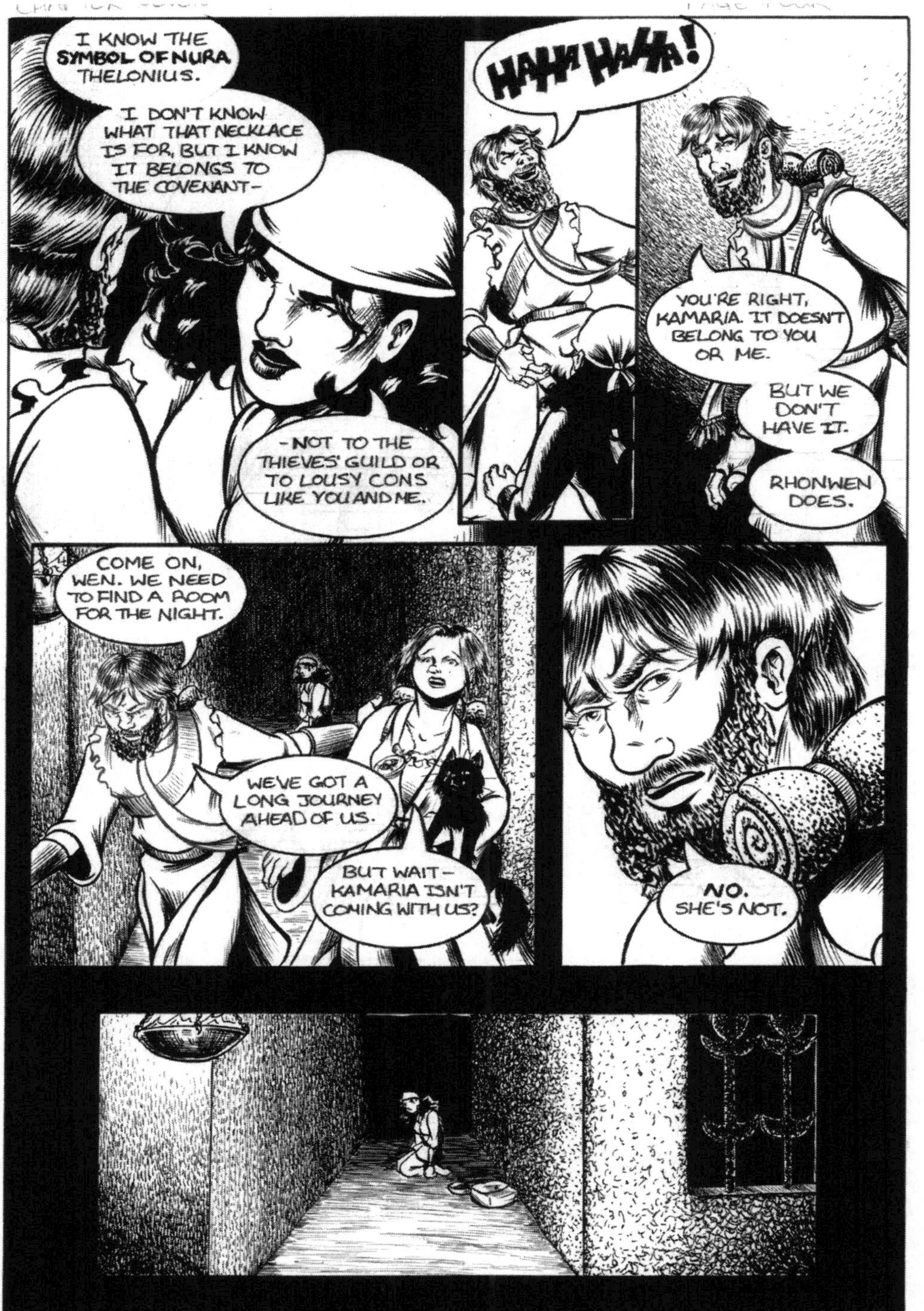
I KNOW THE SYMBOL OF NURA THELONIUS.
I DON'T KNOW WHAT THAT NECKLACE IS FOR, BUT I KNOW IT BELONGS TO THE COVENANT-
-NOT TO THE THIEVES' GUILD OR TO LOUSY CONS LIKE YOU AND ME.
HAHA HAHA!
YOU'RE RIGHT, KAMARIA. IT DOESN'T BELONG TO YOU OR ME.
BUT WE DON'T HAVE IT.
RHONWEN DOES.
COME ON, WEN. WE NEED TO FIND A ROOM FOR THE NIGHT.
WE'VE GOT A LONG JOURNEY AHEAD OF US.
BUT WAIT- KAMARIA ISN'T COMING WITH US?
NO. SHE'S NOT.

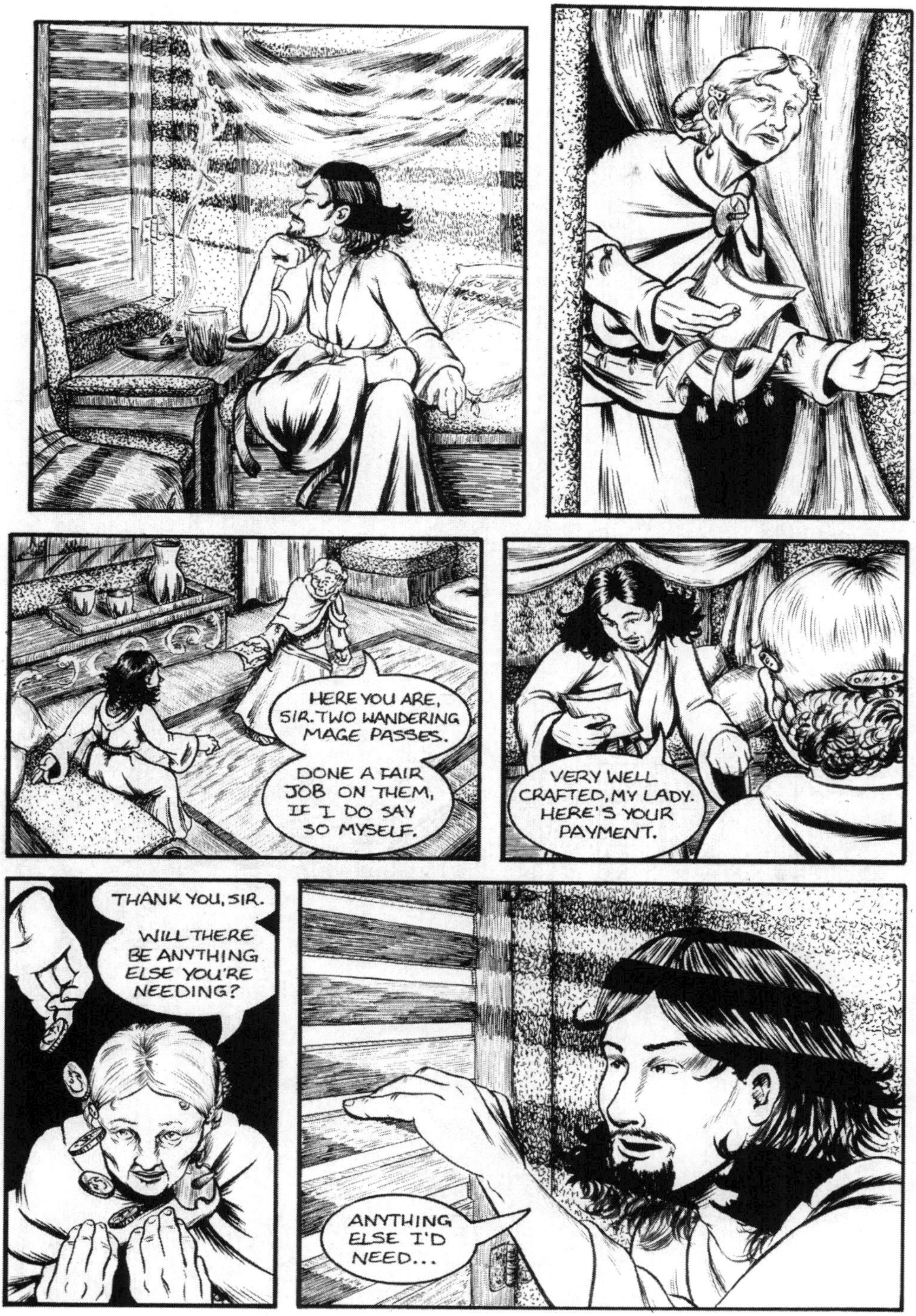
HERE YOU ARE, SIR. TWO WANDERING MAGE PASSES.
DONE A FAIR JOB ON THEM, IF I DO SAY SO MYSELF.
VERY WELL CRAFTED, MY LADY. HERE'S YOUR PAYMENT.
THANK YOU, SIR.
WILL THERE BE ANYTHING ELSE YOU'RE NEEDING?
ANYTHING ELSE I'D NEED...

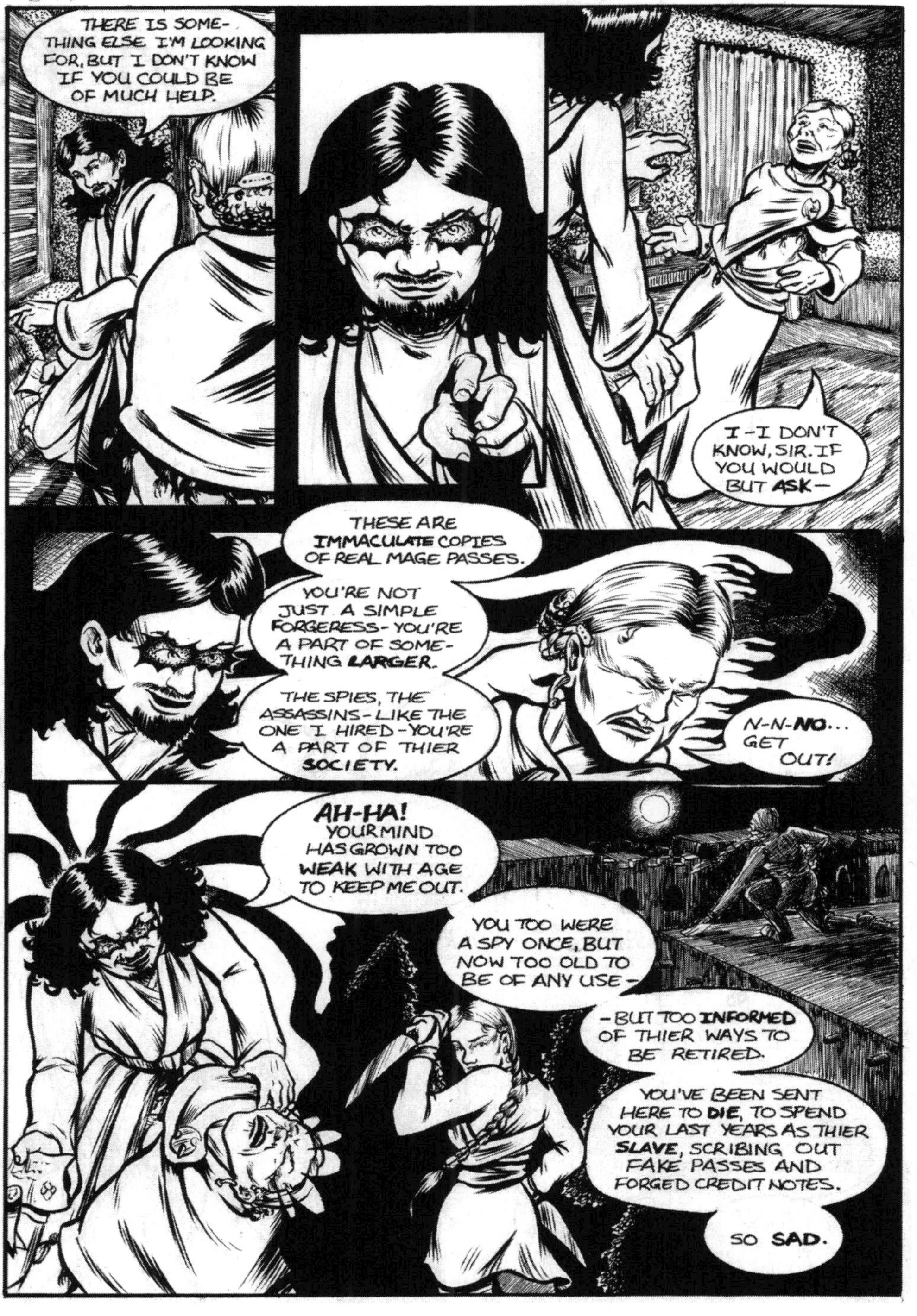
THERE IS SOME-THING ELSE I'M LOOKING FOR, BUT I DON'T KNOW IF YOU COULD BE OF MUCH HELP.
I-I DON'T KNOW, SIR. IF YOU WOULD BUT ASK—
THESE ARE IMMACULATE COPIES OF REAL MAGE PASSES.
YOU'RE NOT JUST A SIMPLE FORGERESS- YOU'RE A PART OF SOME-THING LARGER.
THE SPIES, THE ASSASSINS- LIKE THE ONE I HIRED - YOU'RE A PART OF THIER SOCIETY.
N-N-NO... GET OUT!
AH-HA! YOUR MIND HAS GROWN TOO WEAK WITH AGE TO KEEP ME OUT.
YOU TOO WERE A SPY ONCE, BUT NOW TOO OLD TO BE OF ANY USE—
—BUT TOO INFORMED OF THIER WAYS TO BE RETIRED.
YOU'VE BEEN SENT HERE TO DIE, TO SPEND YOUR LAST YEARS AS THIER SLAVE, SCRIBING OUT FAKE PASSES AND FORGED CREDIT NOTES.
SO SAD.

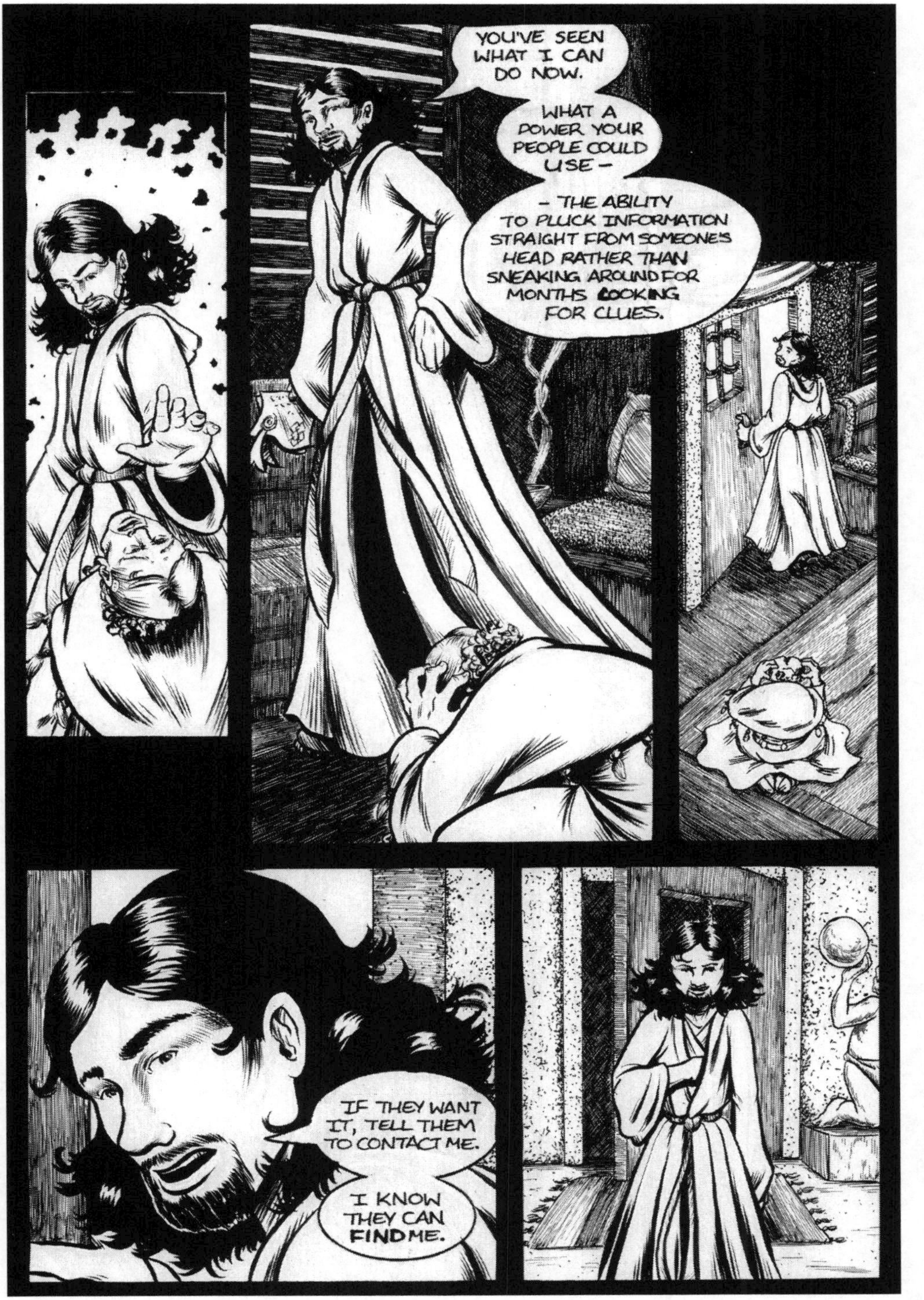
YOU'VE SEEN WHAT I CAN DO NOW.
WHAT A POWER YOUR PEOPLE COULD USE –
– THE ABILITY TO PLUCK INFORMATION STRAIGHT FROM SOMEONE'S HEAD RATHER THAN SNEAKING AROUND FOR MONTHS LOOKING FOR CLUES.
IF THEY WANT IT, TELL THEM TO CONTACT ME.
I KNOW THEY CAN FIND ME.

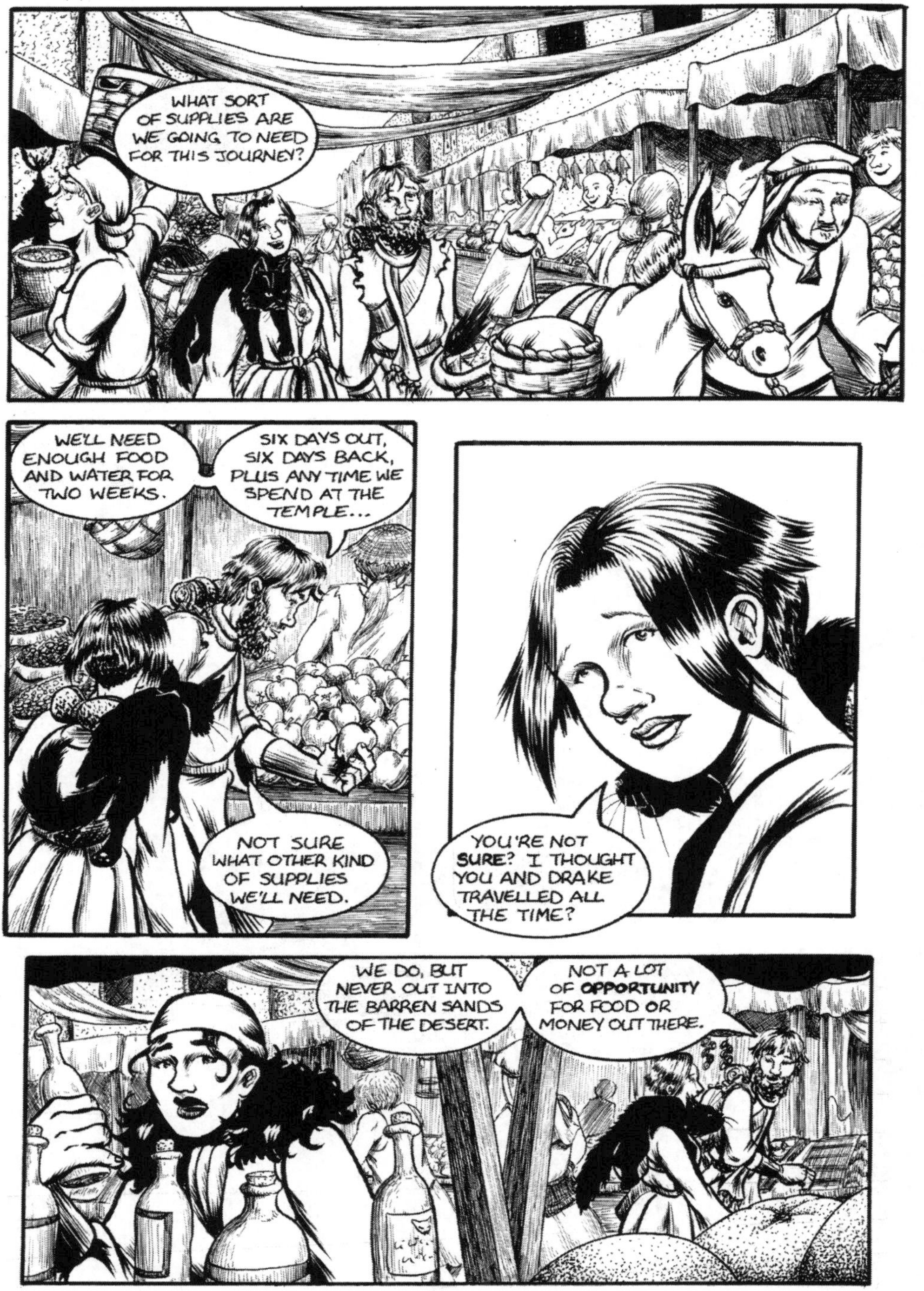
WHAT SORT OF SUPPLIES ARE WE GOING TO NEED FOR THIS JOURNEY?
WE'LL NEED ENOUGH FOOD AND WATER FOR TWO WEEKS.
SIX DAYS OUT, SIX DAYS BACK, PLUS ANY TIME WE SPEND AT THE TEMPLE...
NOT SURE WHAT OTHER KIND OF SUPPLIES WE'LL NEED.
YOU'RE NOT **SURE**? I THOUGHT YOU AND DRAKE TRAVELLED ALL THE TIME?
WE DO, BUT NEVER OUT INTO THE BARREN SANDS OF THE DESERT.
NOT A LOT OF **OPPORTUNITY** FOR FOOD OR MONEY OUT THERE.

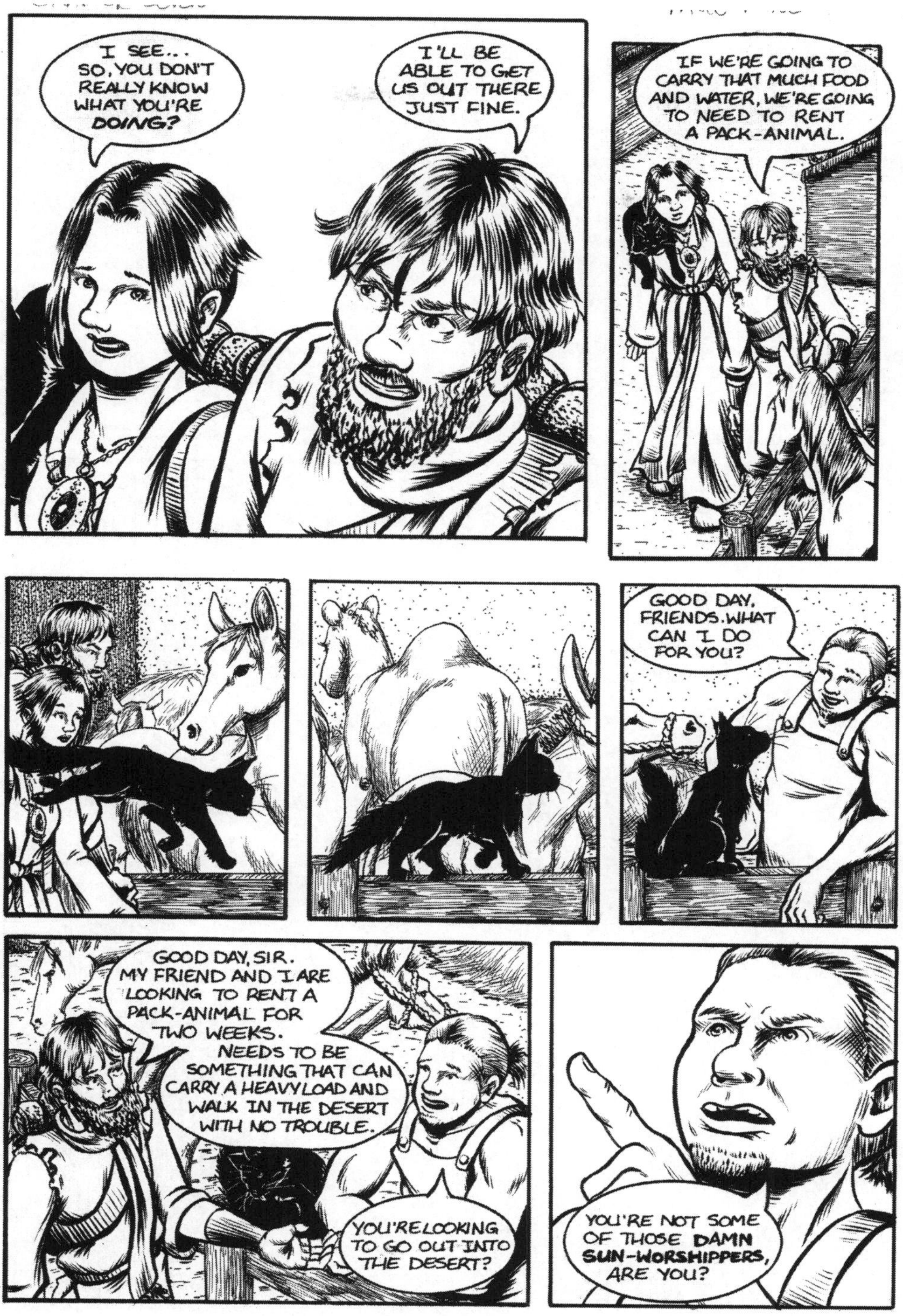
I SEE... SO, YOU DON'T REALLY KNOW WHAT YOU'RE **DOING?**
I'LL BE ABLE TO GET US OUT THERE JUST FINE.
IF WE'RE GOING TO CARRY THAT MUCH FOOD AND WATER, WE'RE GOING TO NEED TO RENT A PACK-ANIMAL.
GOOD DAY, FRIENDS. WHAT CAN I DO FOR YOU?
GOOD DAY, SIR. MY FRIEND AND I ARE LOOKING TO RENT A PACK-ANIMAL FOR TWO WEEKS.
NEEDS TO BE SOMETHING THAT CAN CARRY A HEAVY LOAD AND WALK IN THE DESERT WITH NO TROUBLE.
YOU'RE LOOKING TO GO OUT INTO THE DESERT?
YOU'RE NOT SOME OF THOSE **DAMN SUN-WORSHIPPERS,** ARE YOU?

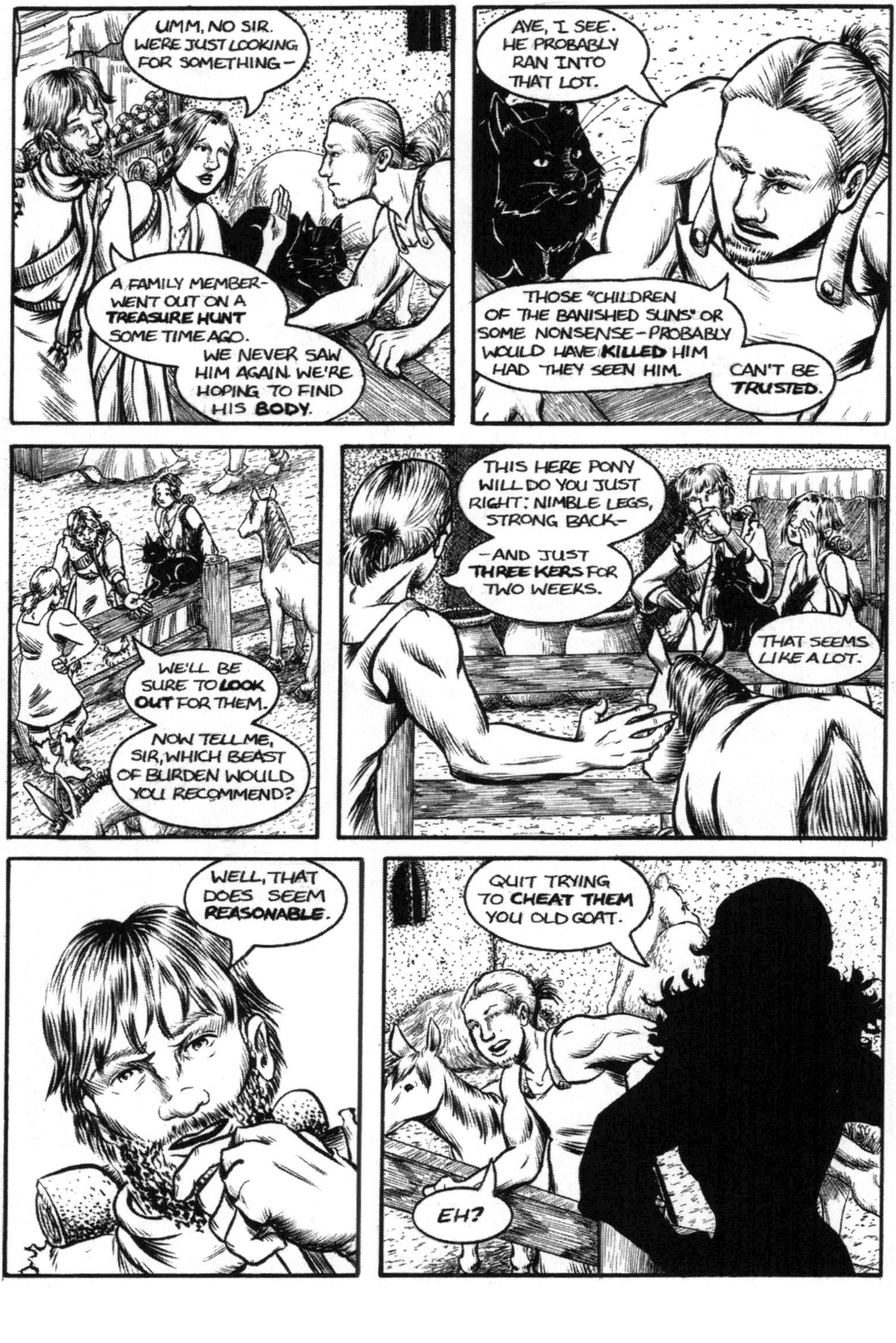
UMM, NO SIR. WERE JUST LOOKING FOR SOMETHING—
A FAMILY MEMBER WENT OUT ON A TREASURE HUNT SOME TIME AGO.
WE NEVER SAW HIM AGAIN. WE'RE HOPING TO FIND HIS BODY.
AYE, I SEE. HE PROBABLY RAN INTO THAT LOT.
THOSE "CHILDREN OF THE BANISHED SUNS" OR SOME NONSENSE—PROBABLY WOULD HAVE KILLED HIM HAD THEY SEEN HIM.
CAN'T BE TRUSTED.
WE'LL BE SURE TO LOOK OUT FOR THEM.
NOW TELL ME, SIR, WHICH BEAST OF BURDEN WOULD YOU RECOMMEND?
THIS HERE PONY WILL DO YOU JUST RIGHT: NIMBLE LEGS, STRONG BACK—
—AND JUST THREE KERS FOR TWO WEEKS.
THAT SEEMS LIKE A LOT.
WELL, THAT DOES SEEM REASONABLE.
QUIT TRYING TO CHEAT THEM YOU OLD GOAT.
EH?

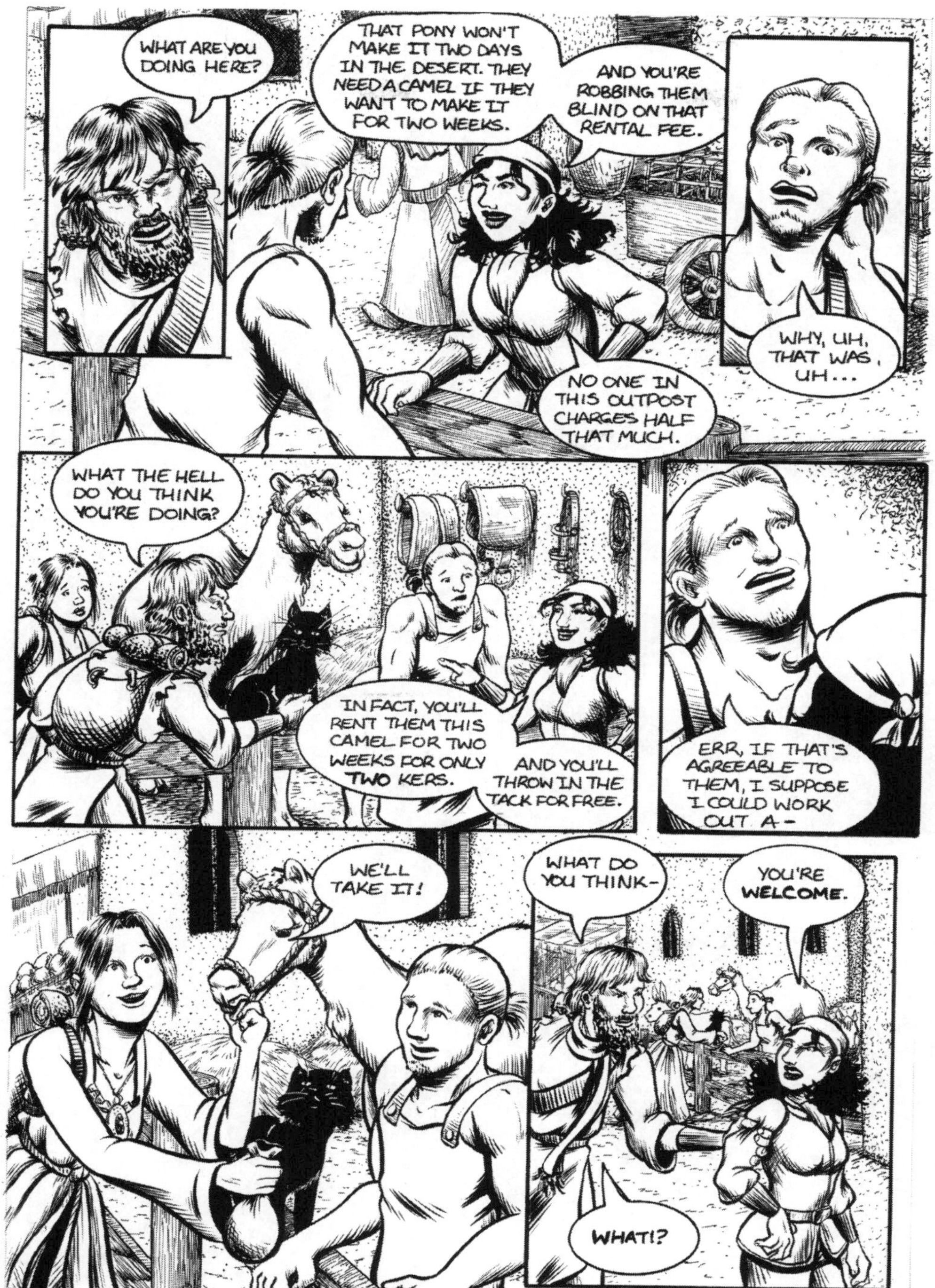
WHAT ARE YOU DOING HERE?
THAT PONY WON'T MAKE IT TWO DAYS IN THE DESERT. THEY NEED A CAMEL IF THEY WANT TO MAKE IT FOR TWO WEEKS.
AND YOU'RE ROBBING THEM BLIND ON THAT RENTAL FEE.
WHY, UH, THAT WAS, UH...
NO ONE IN THIS OUTPOST CHARGES HALF THAT MUCH.
WHAT THE HELL DO YOU THINK YOU'RE DOING?
IN FACT, YOU'LL RENT THEM THIS CAMEL FOR TWO WEEKS FOR ONLY **TWO KERS.**
AND YOU'LL THROW IN THE TACK FOR FREE.
ERR, IF THAT'S AGREEABLE TO THEM, I SUPPOSE I COULD WORK OUT A-
WE'LL TAKE IT!
WHAT DO YOU THINK-
YOU'RE **WELCOME.**
WHAT!?

YOU NEEDED **SAVING** THERE AGAIN, IT SEEMED.

LET ME GUESS, **DRAKE** USED TO MAKE ALL THE **DEALS** WHEN HE WAS STILL **HUMAN**.

YOU'RE SIDING WITH **HER**!?

MISS KAMARIA! ARE YOU COMING WITH US AGAIN?

YOU NEED SOMEONE WHO KNOWS HOW TO **SURVIVE** OUT IN THE **DESERT**.

YOU DO?

I CAN SURVIVE JUST ABOUT **ANYWHERE**. I LEARNED A LOT OF THAT WHEN I WAS STILL A KID.

IS IT ALL RIGHT IF SHE COMES ALONG, THELONIUS?

SEEMS WE **DO** NEED HER HELP.

166

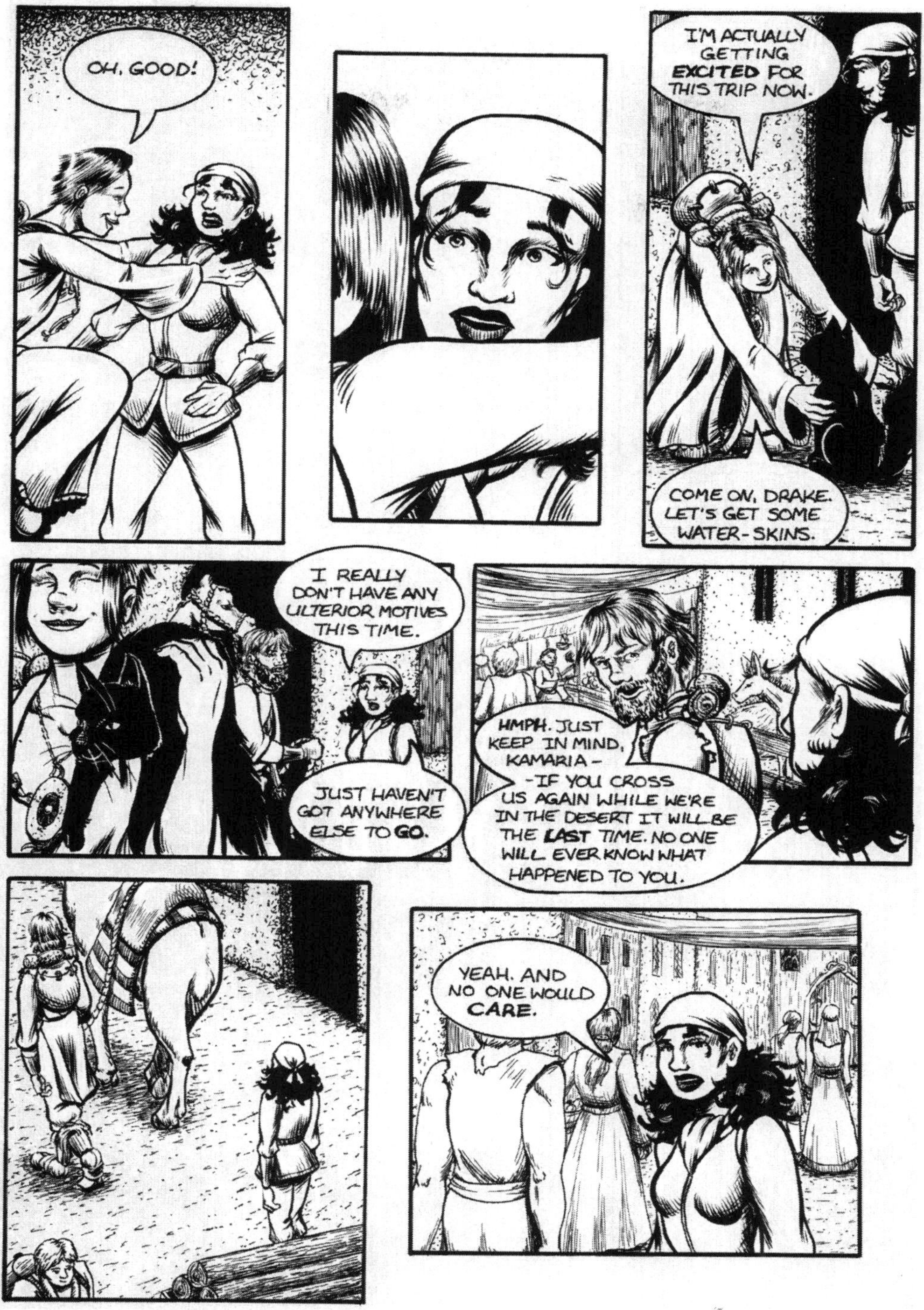
OH, GOOD!
I'M ACTUALLY GETTING EXCITED FOR THIS TRIP NOW.
COME ON, DRAKE. LET'S GET SOME WATER-SKINS.
I REALLY DON'T HAVE ANY ULTERIOR MOTIVES THIS TIME.
JUST HAVEN'T GOT ANYWHERE ELSE TO GO.
HMPH. JUST KEEP IN MIND, KAMARIA -
-IF YOU CROSS US AGAIN WHILE WE'RE IN THE DESERT IT WILL BE THE LAST TIME. NO ONE WILL EVER KNOW WHAT HAPPENED TO YOU.
YEAH. AND NO ONE WOULD CARE.

GET ANY OF THAT AMINIAN ALE, YET?

NO SHIPMENTS FROM AMINIA IN WEEKS - WHOLE TOWN'S IN QUARANTINE.

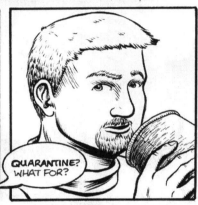

QUARANTINE? WHAT FOR?

SOME KIND OF INFECTION'S RAGING THROUGH ALL THEIR FARMS.

NO ONE'S BEEN ALLOWED TO TRADE WITH THEM SINCE IT STARTED ABOUT A MONTH AGO.

SURE HOPE IT DOESN'T KILL THEIR BARLEY - THAT'S A GREAT ALE THEY MAKE.

AYE, IT IS. I'LL LET YOU KNOW IF I GET ANY MORE IN.

GOTTA FIND BALTAZAR...

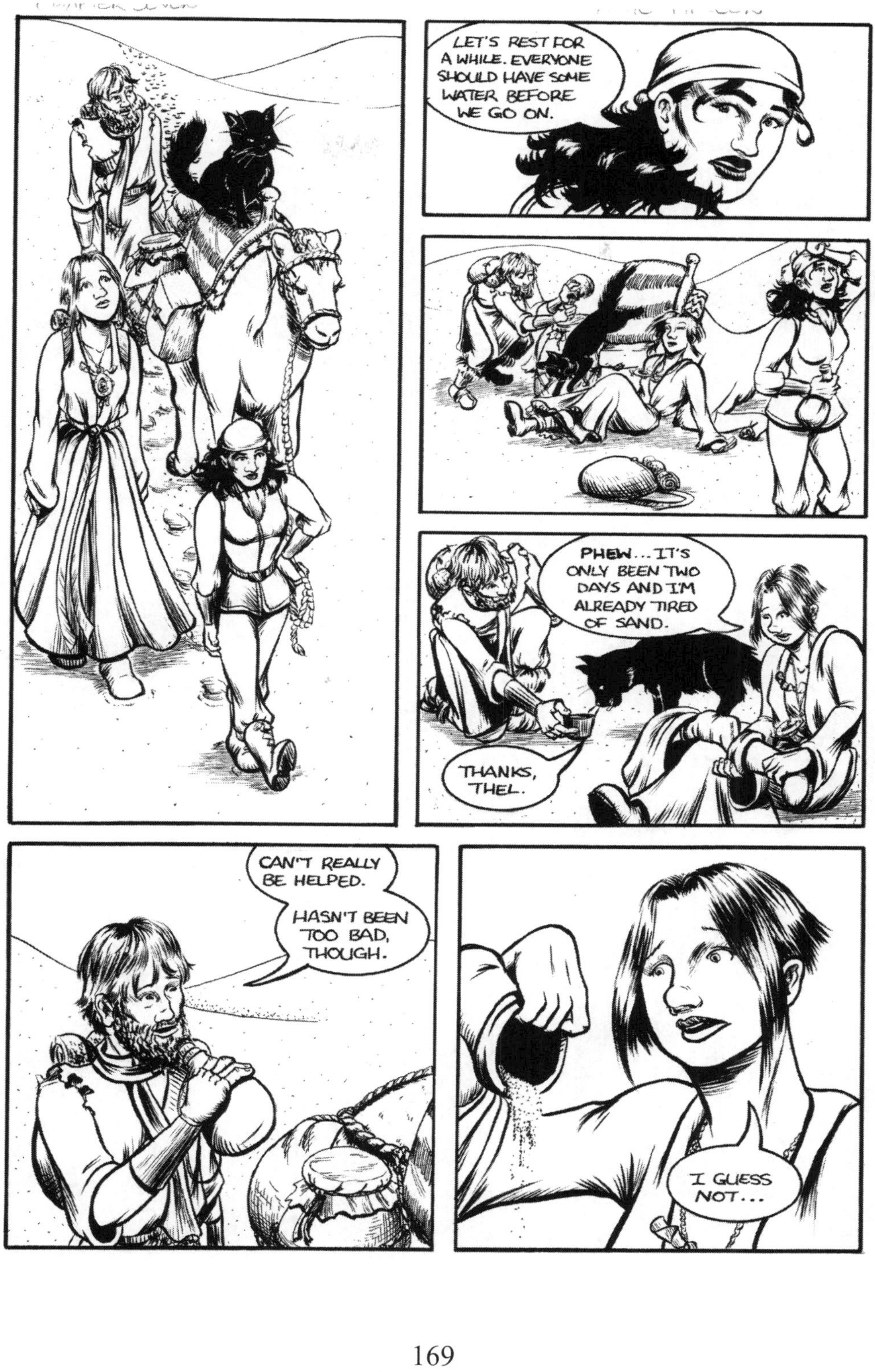
LET'S REST FOR A WHILE. EVERYONE SHOULD HAVE SOME WATER BEFORE WE GO ON.
PHEW... IT'S ONLY BEEN TWO DAYS AND I'M ALREADY TIRED OF SAND.
THANKS, THEL.
CAN'T REALLY BE HELPED.
HASN'T BEEN TOO BAD, THOUGH.
I GUESS NOT...

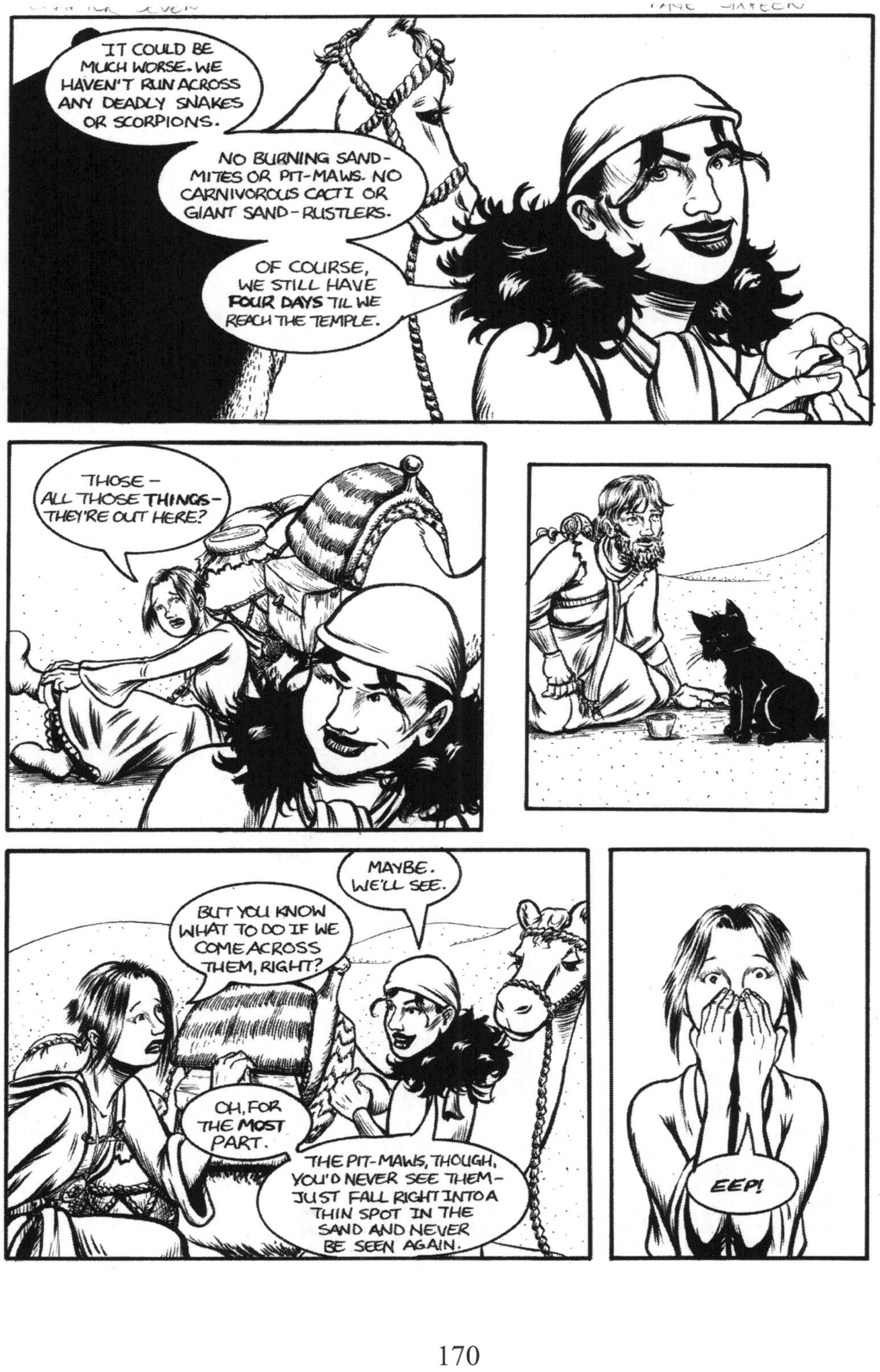
IT COULD BE MUCH WORSE. WE HAVEN'T RUN ACROSS ANY DEADLY SNAKES OR SCORPIONS.
NO BURNING SAND-MITES OR PIT-MAWS. NO CARNIVOROUS CACTI OR GIANT SAND-RUSTLERS.
OF COURSE, WE STILL HAVE **FOUR DAYS** TIL WE REACH THE TEMPLE.
THOSE - ALL THOSE **THINGS** - THEY'RE OUT HERE?
MAYBE. WE'LL SEE.
BUT YOU KNOW WHAT TO DO IF WE COME ACROSS THEM, RIGHT?
OH, FOR THE **MOST** PART.
THE PIT-MAWS, THOUGH, YOU'D NEVER SEE THEM - JUST FALL RIGHT INTO A THIN SPOT IN THE SAND AND NEVER BE SEEN AGAIN.
EEP!

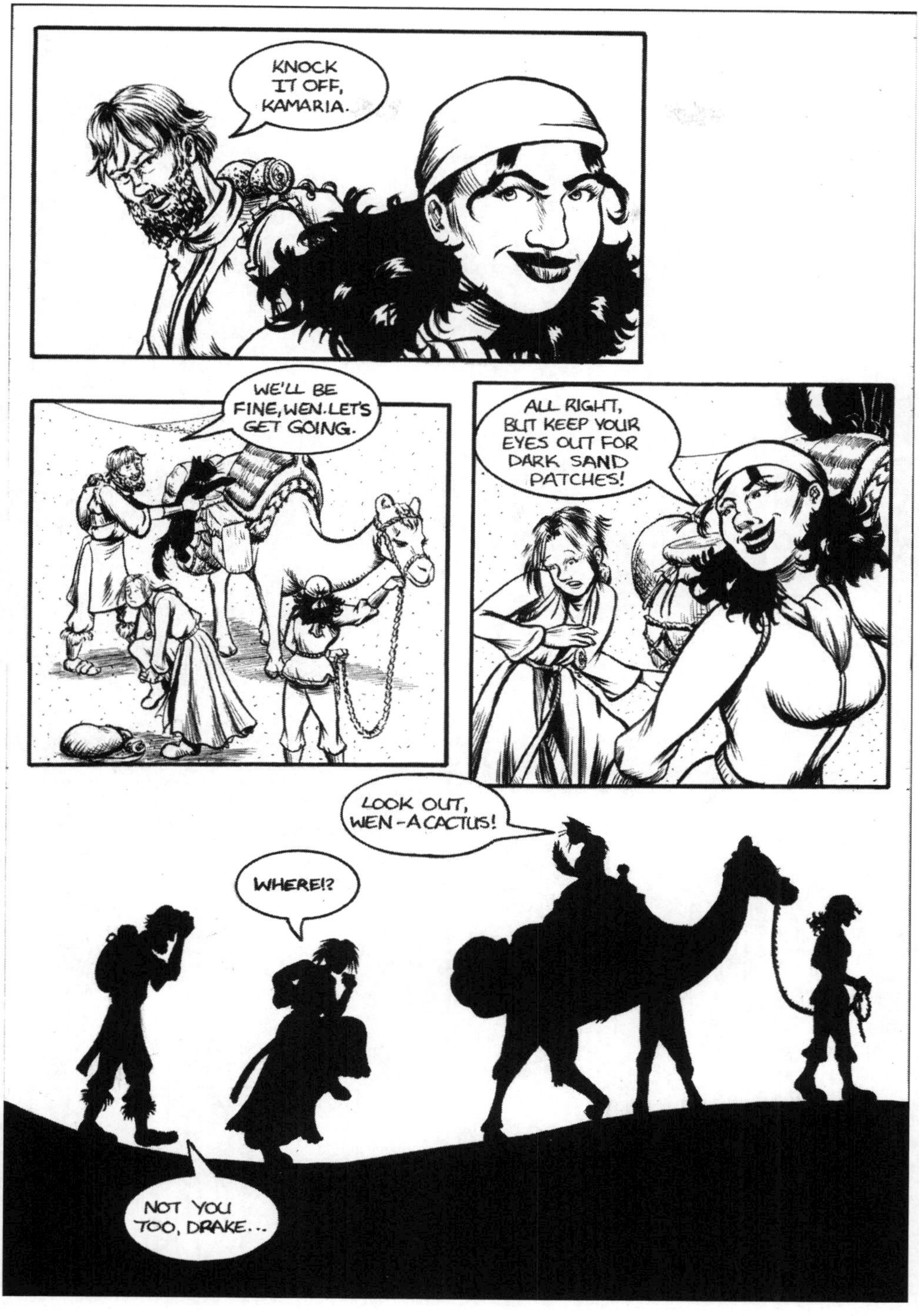
KNOCK IT OFF, KAMARIA.
WE'LL BE FINE, WEN. LET'S GET GOING.
ALL RIGHT, BUT KEEP YOUR EYES OUT FOR DARK SAND PATCHES!
LOOK OUT, WEN-A CACTUS!
WHERE!?
NOT YOU TOO, DRAKE...

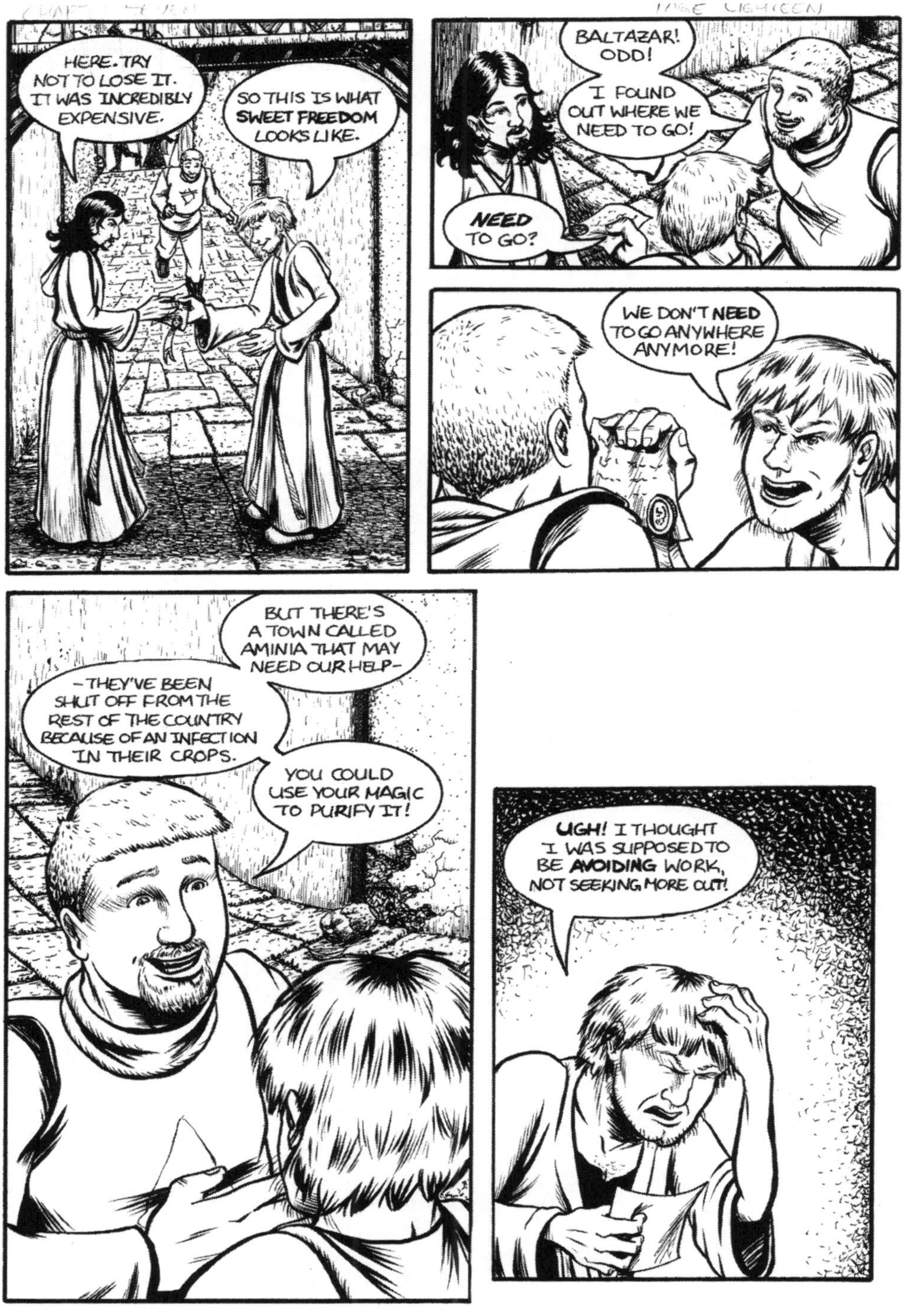
HERE. TRY NOT TO LOSE IT. IT WAS INCREDIBLY EXPENSIVE.
SO THIS IS WHAT SWEET FREEDOM LOOKS LIKE.
BALTAZAR! ODD!
I FOUND OUT WHERE WE NEED TO GO!
NEED TO GO?
WE DON'T NEED TO GO ANYWHERE ANYMORE!
BUT THERE'S A TOWN CALLED AMINIA THAT MAY NEED OUR HELP-
-THEY'VE BEEN SHUT OFF FROM THE REST OF THE COUNTRY BECAUSE OF AN INFECTION IN THEIR CROPS.
YOU COULD USE YOUR MAGIC TO PURIFY IT!
UGH! I THOUGHT I WAS SUPPOSED TO BE AVOIDING WORK, NOT SEEKING MORE OUT!

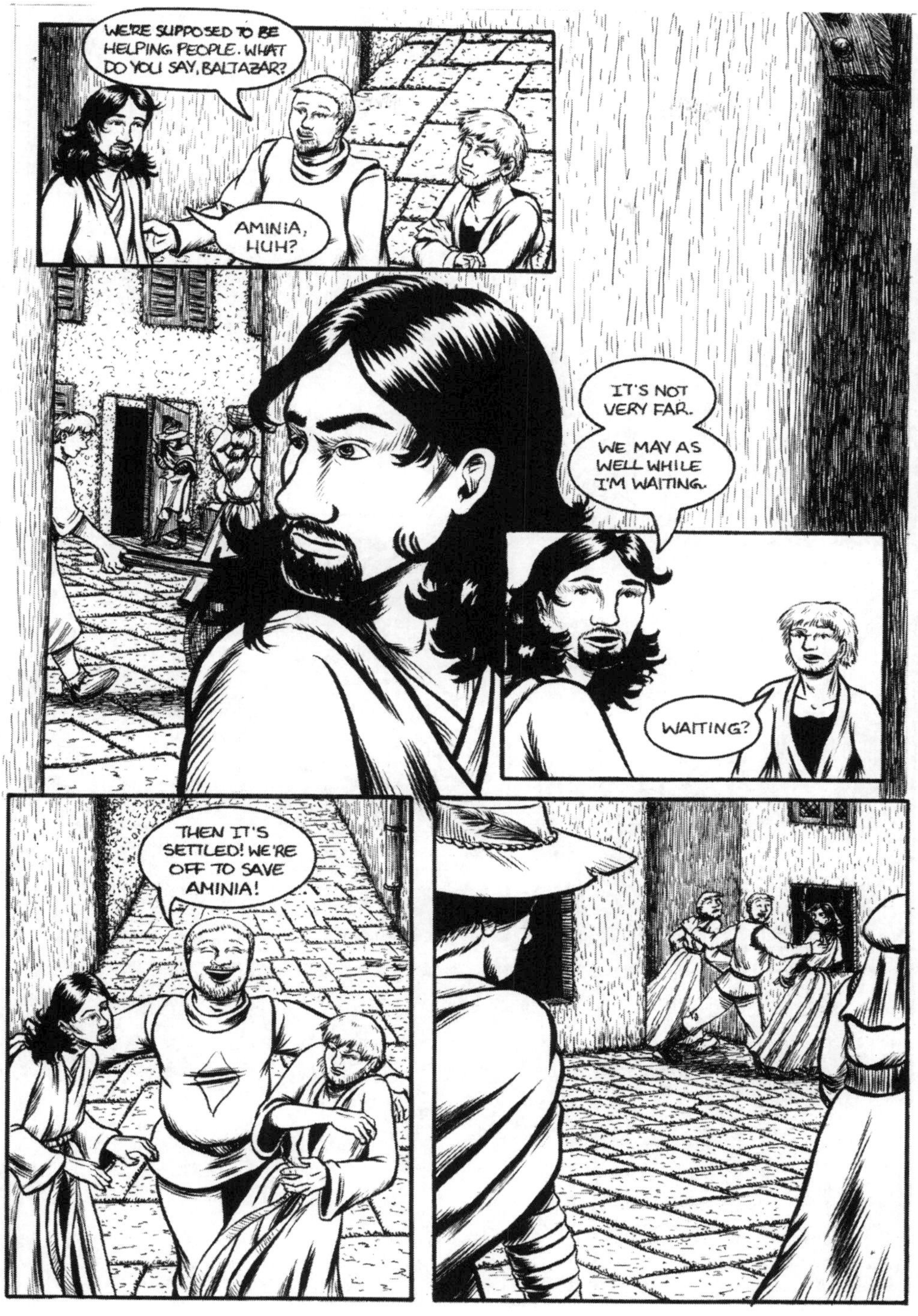
WE'RE SUPPOSED TO BE HELPING PEOPLE. WHAT DO YOU SAY, BALTAZAR?
AMINIA, HUH?
IT'S NOT VERY FAR.
WE MAY AS WELL WHILE I'M WAITING.
WAITING?
THEN IT'S SETTLED! WE'RE OFF TO SAVE AMINIA!

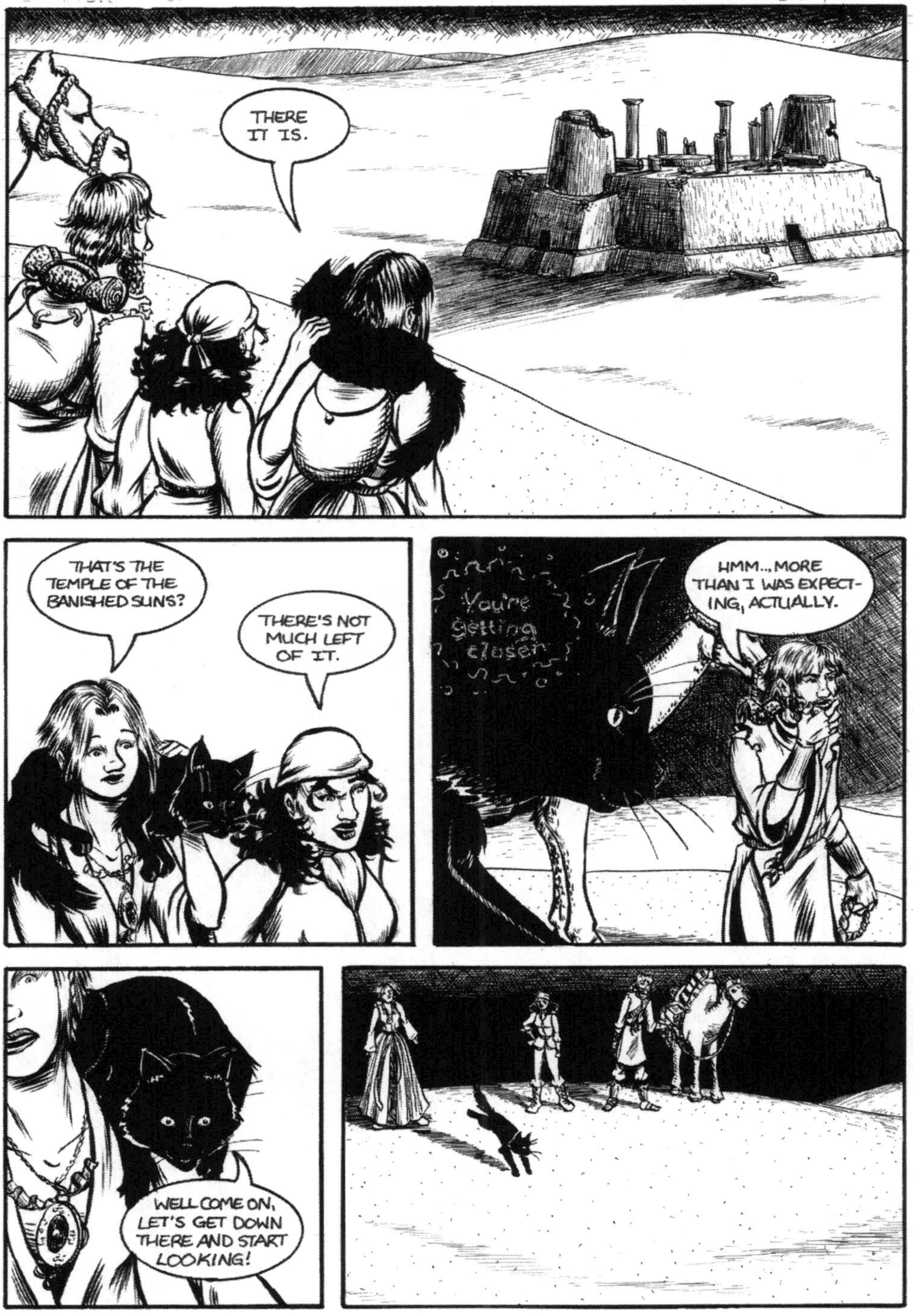
THERE IT IS.
THAT'S THE TEMPLE OF THE BANISHED SUNS?
THERE'S NOT MUCH LEFT OF IT.
You're getting closer
HMM... MORE THAN I WAS EXPECTING, ACTUALLY.
WELL COME ON, LET'S GET DOWN THERE AND START LOOKING!

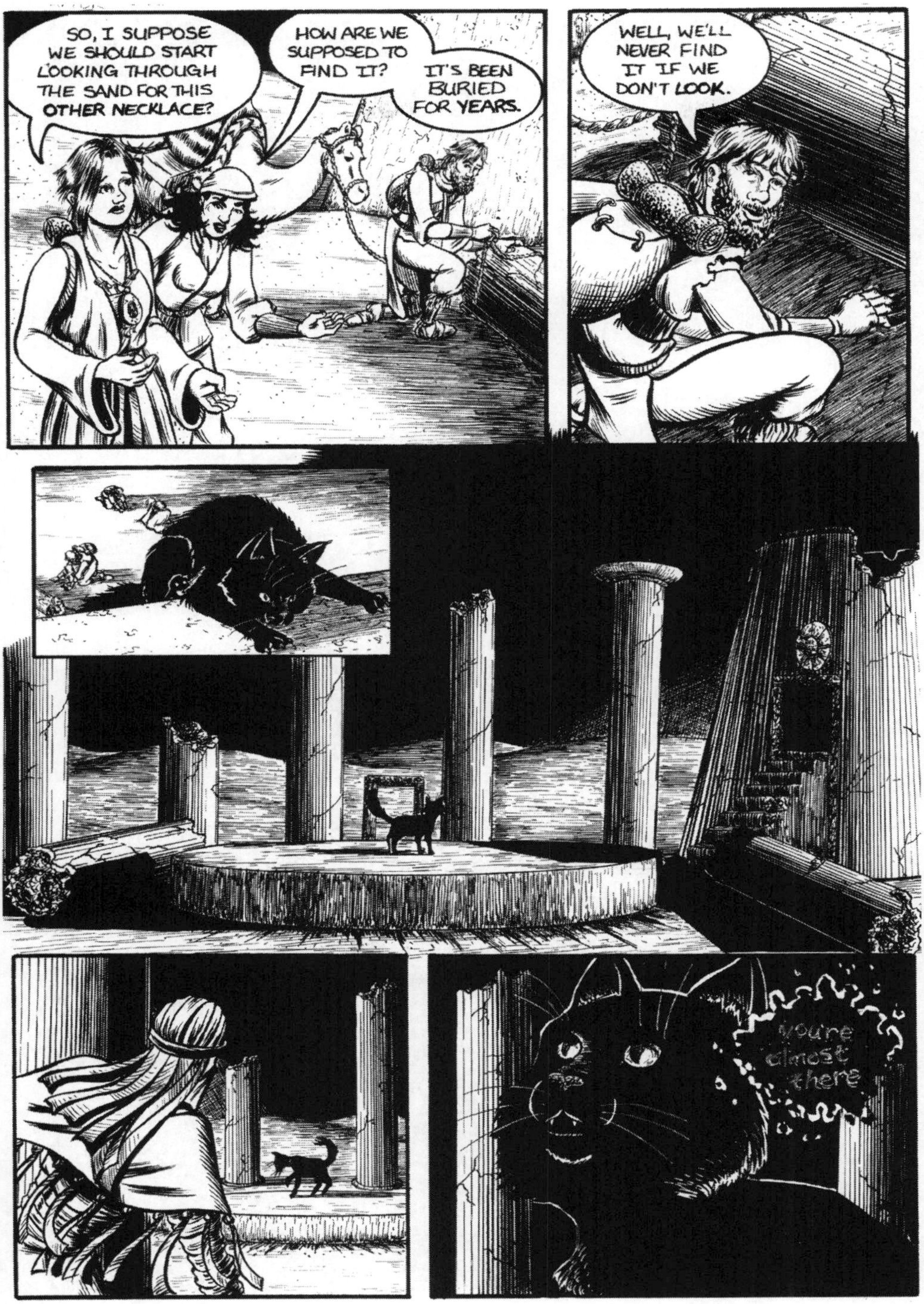
SO, I SUPPOSE WE SHOULD START LOOKING THROUGH THE SAND FOR THIS OTHER NECKLACE?
HOW ARE WE SUPPOSED TO FIND IT?
IT'S BEEN BURIED FOR YEARS.
WELL, WE'LL NEVER FIND IT IF WE DON'T LOOK.
you're almost there

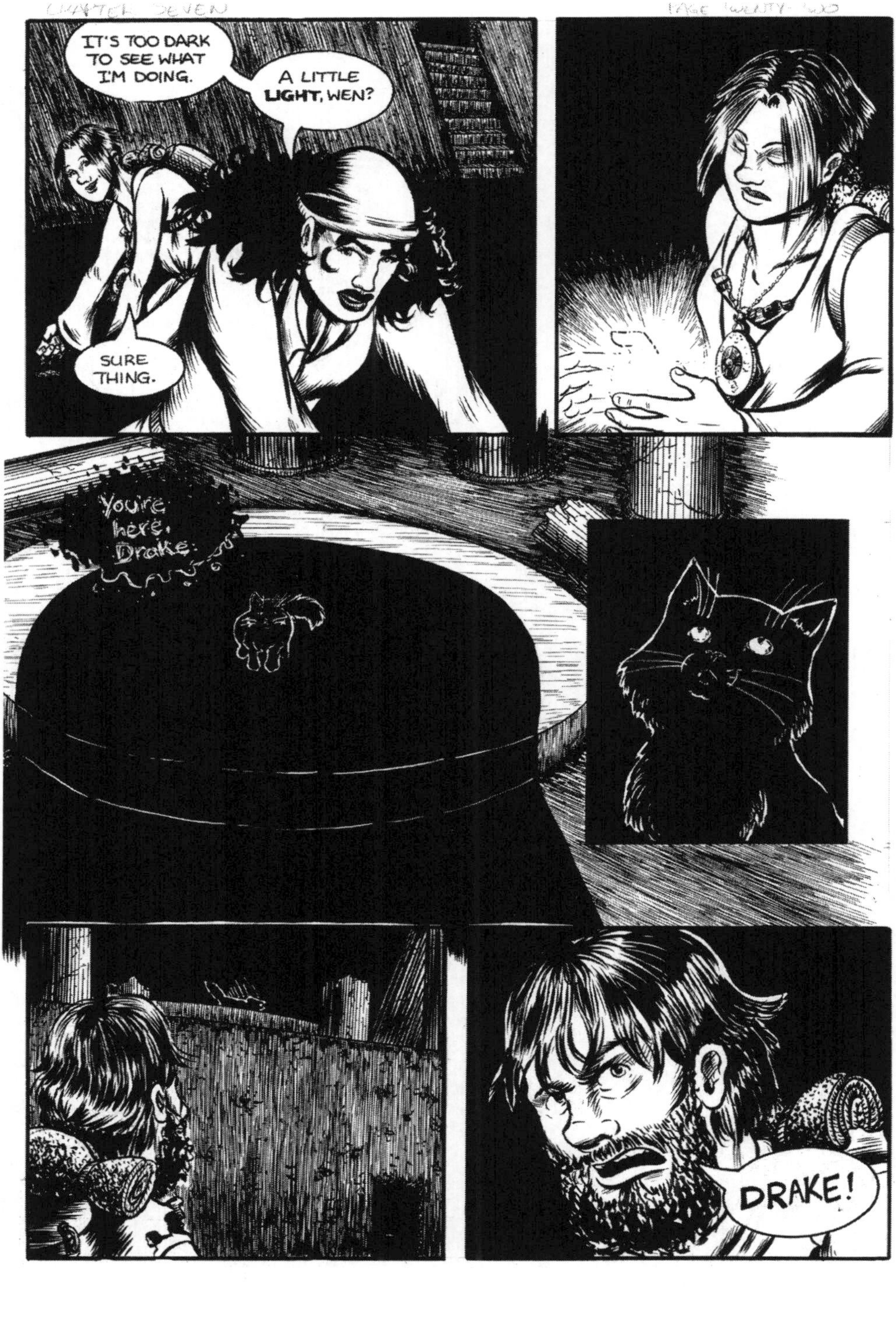
IT'S TOO DARK TO SEE WHAT I'M DOING.
A LITTLE LIGHT, WEN?
SURE THING.
You're here, Drake.
DRAKE!

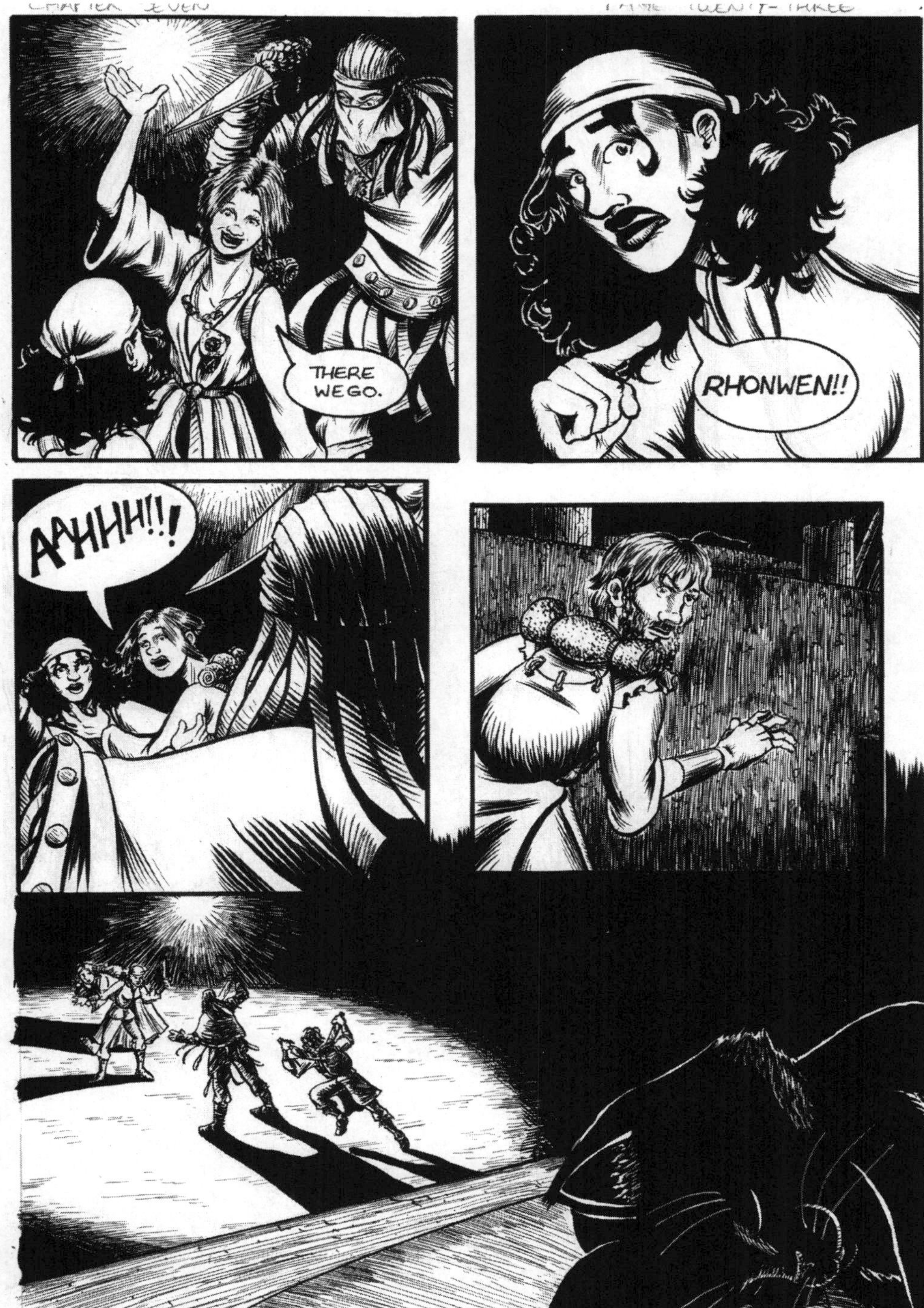
THERE WEGO.
RHONWEN!!
AAHHH!!!

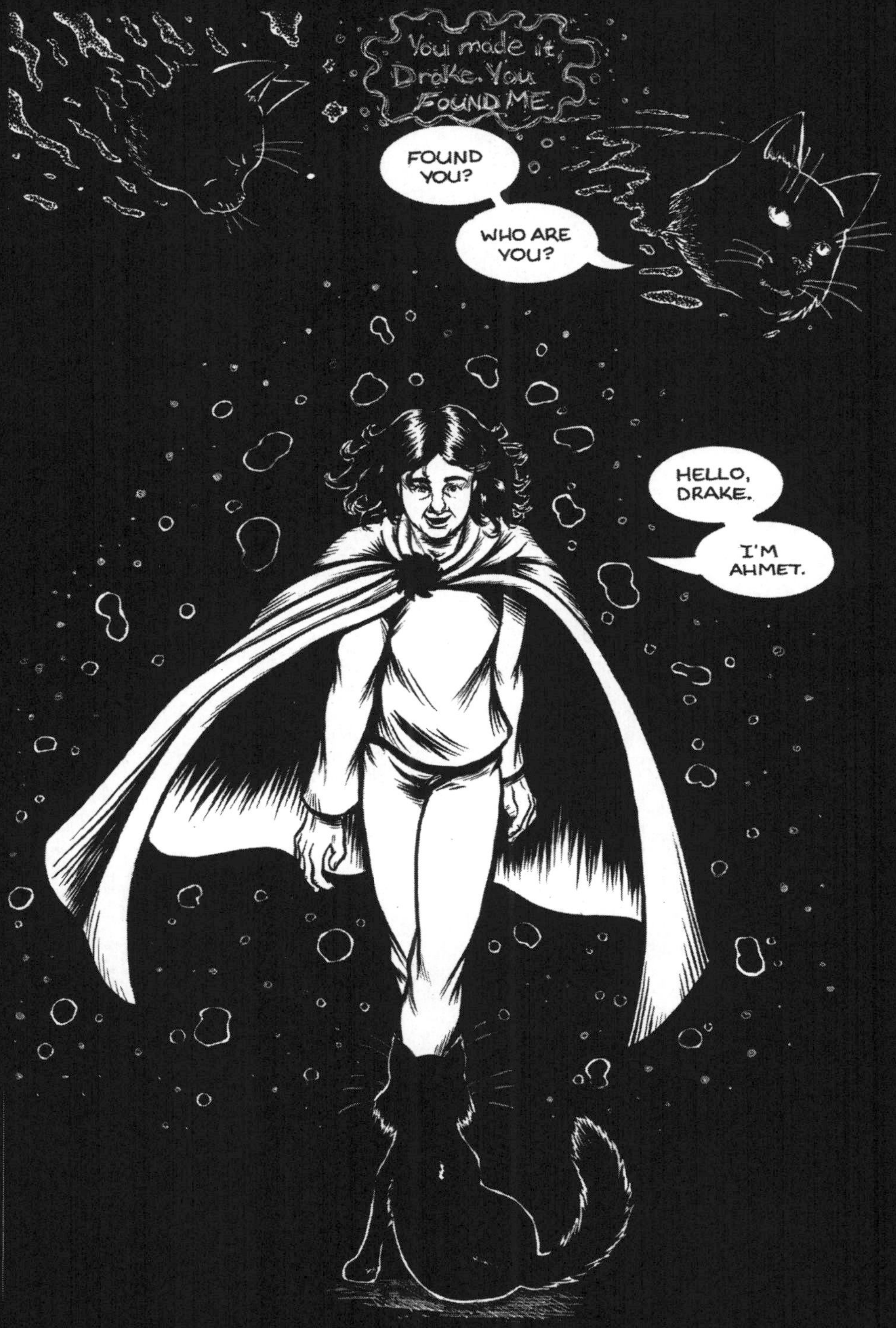
You made it, Drake. You FOUND ME.
FOUND YOU?
WHO ARE YOU?
HELLO, DRAKE.
I'M AHMET.

Sketches and Process Work

Character Sketches

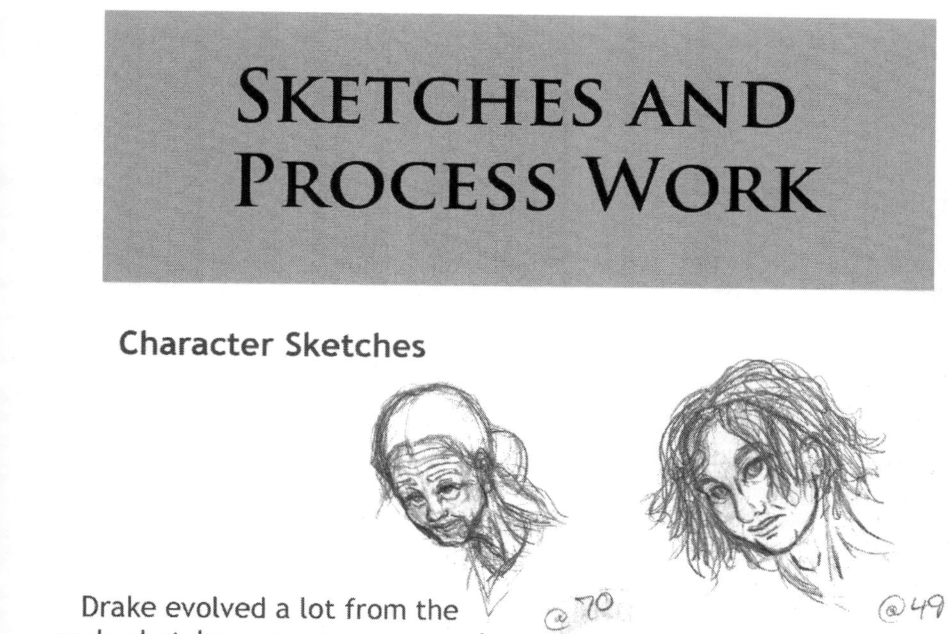

@70
@49

Drake evolved a lot from the early sketches - as you can see, I also couldn't decide if he wanted facial hair or not, hence the final decision to have him eternally 5 o'clock shadowed.

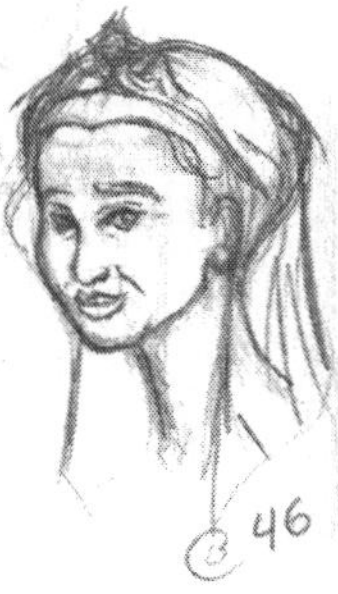

@46

Ahmet and Baila

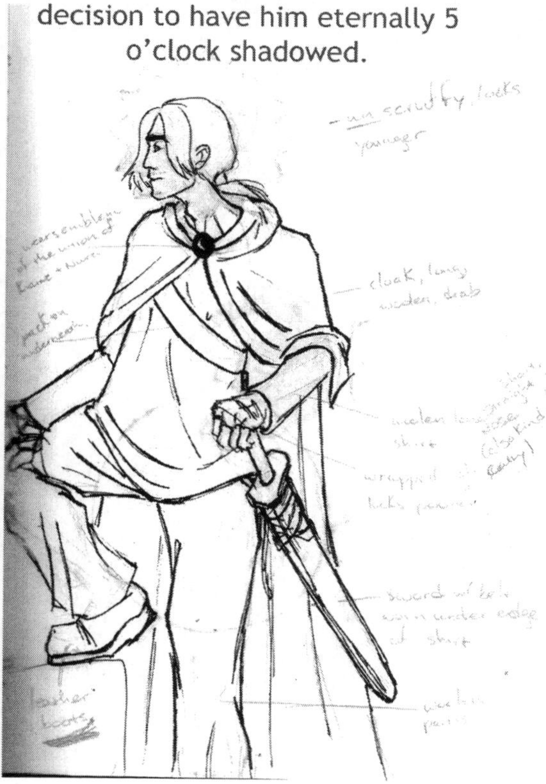

cloak, long, woolen, drab

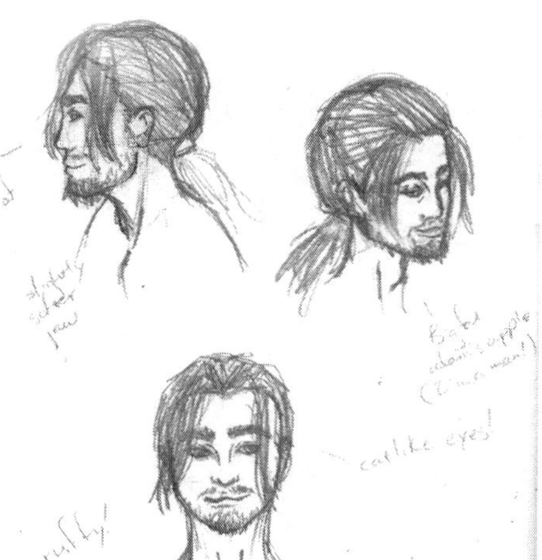

catlike eyes!
scruffy!
Drake!

Baltazar, Odd, and Zeke

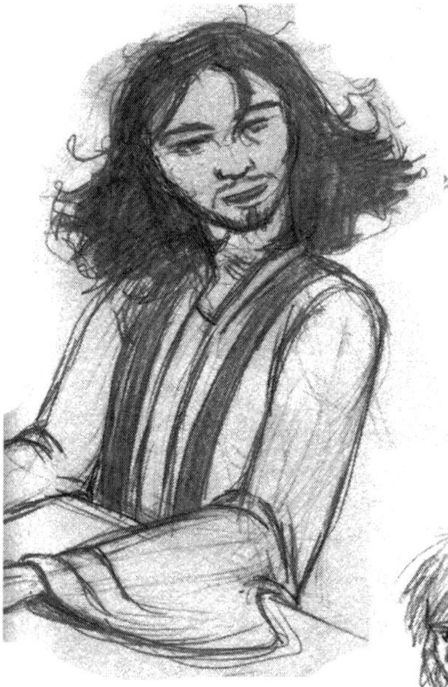

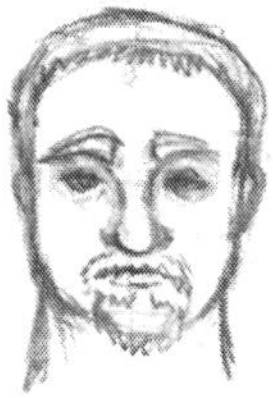

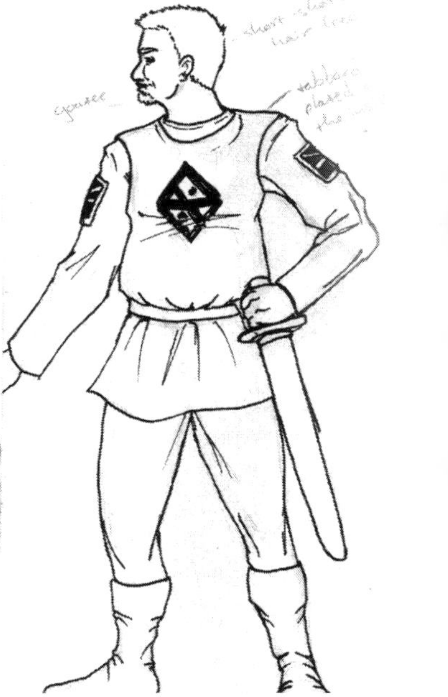

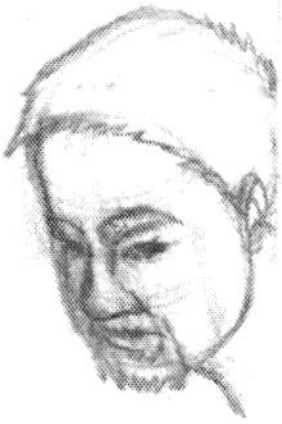

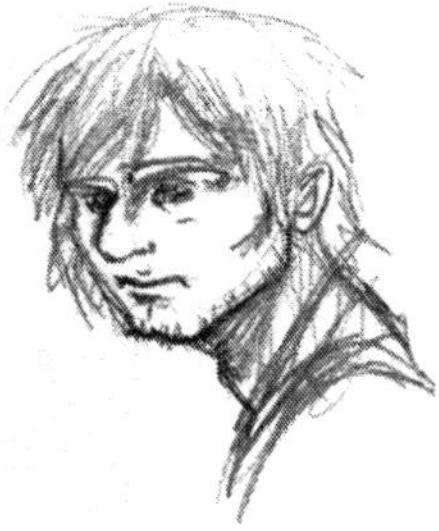

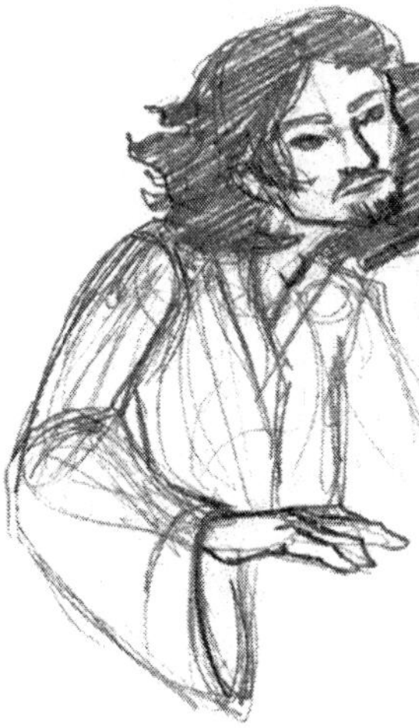

These three didn't take as much work - they are based on a notorious trio of my friends.

Ultimately, Drake came out like this:

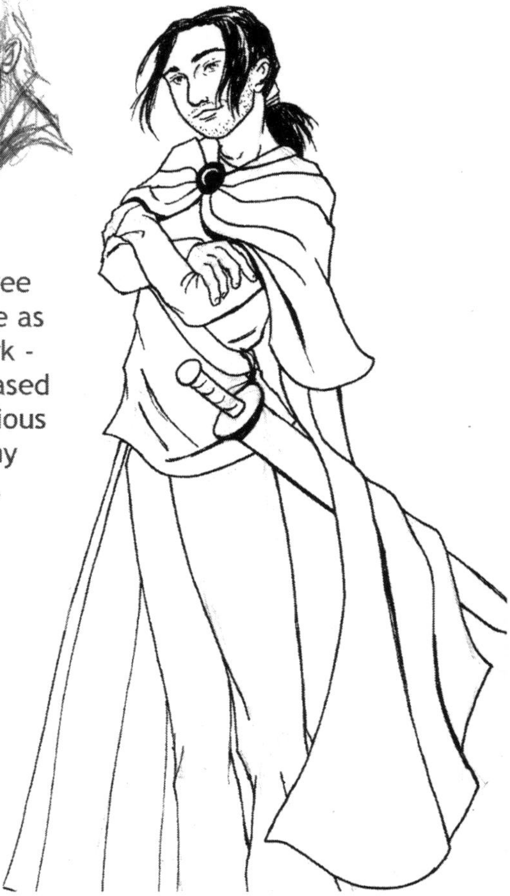

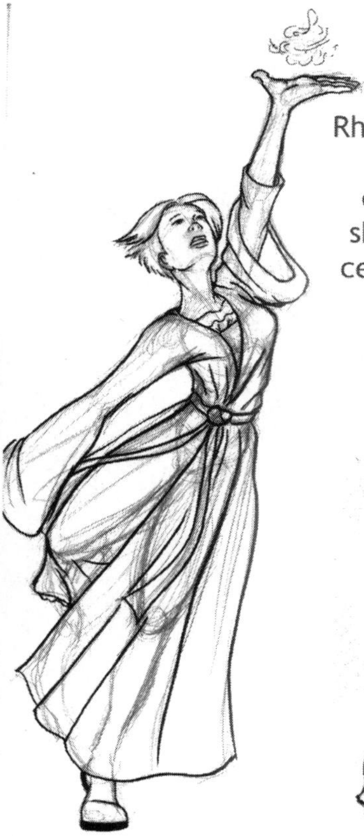

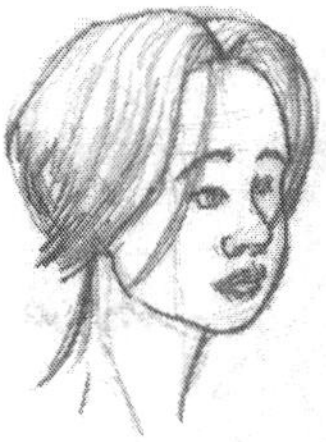

Rhonwen didn't change much throughout her design, either. I latched onto the short hair and round, innocent face really early on - it just suits her so well!

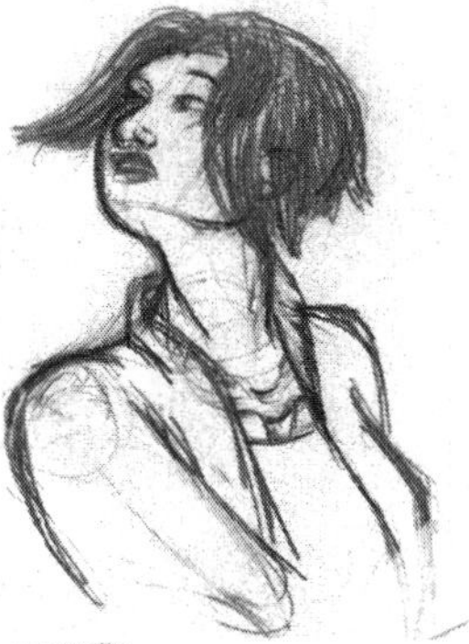

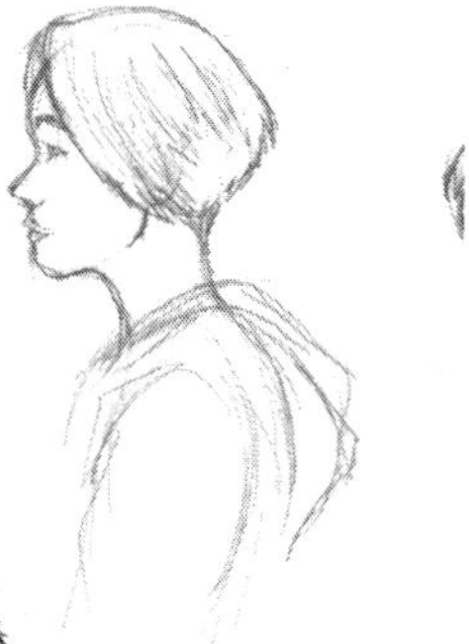

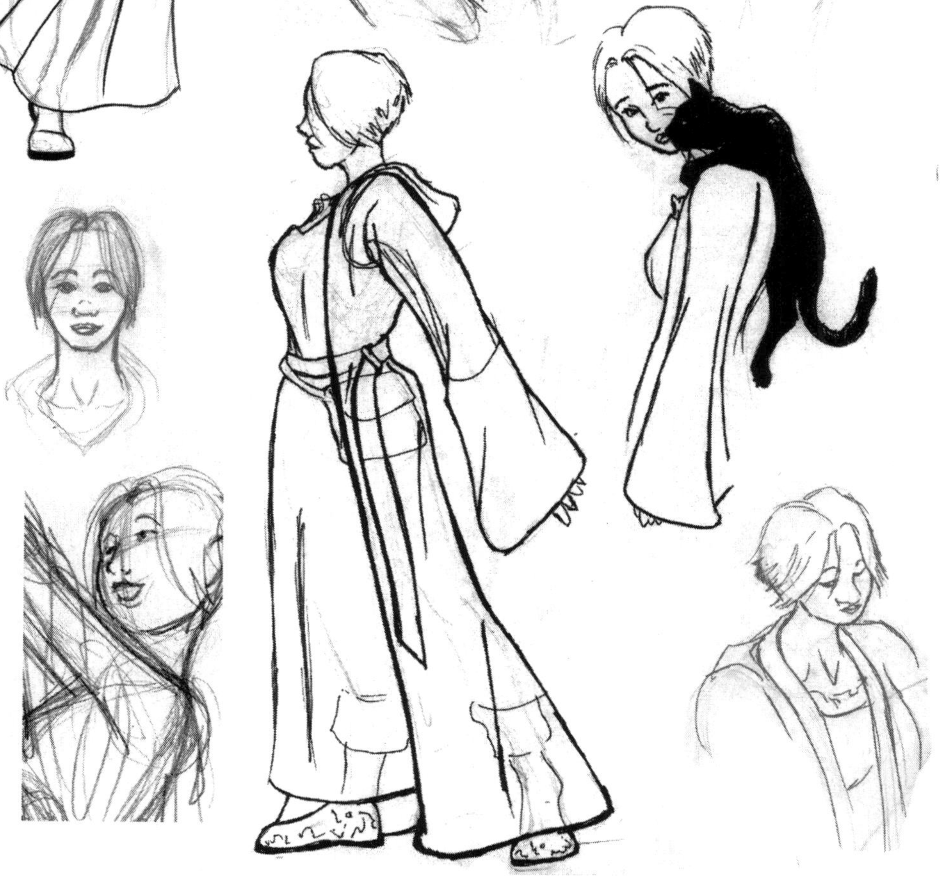

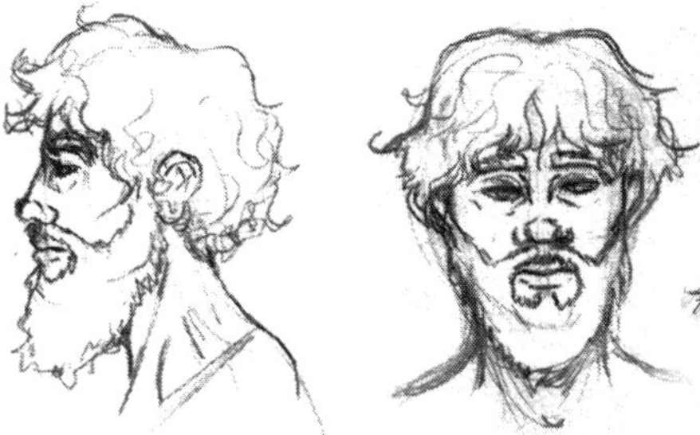

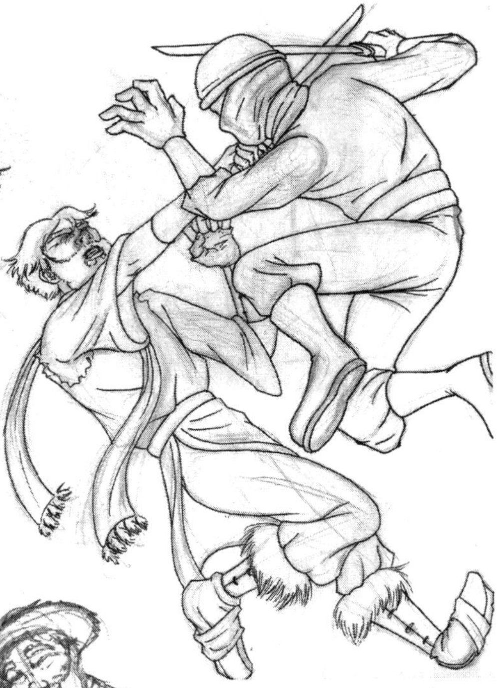

Thelonious was designed with the idea of looking like a farmer - simple rural clothes to hide his true nature. His physical appearance was also based on a roomate I had in college, I liked the idea of using his scruffy hair and bushy beard on a main character - it's usually a look you see more in side or single-appearance characters.

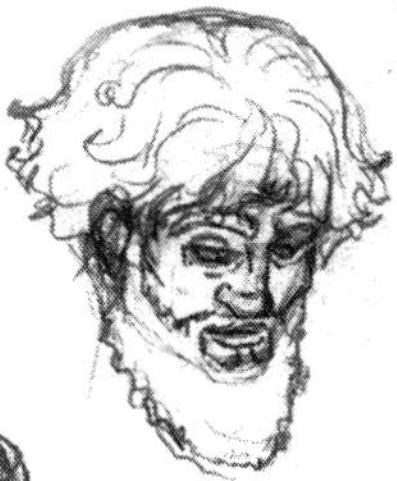

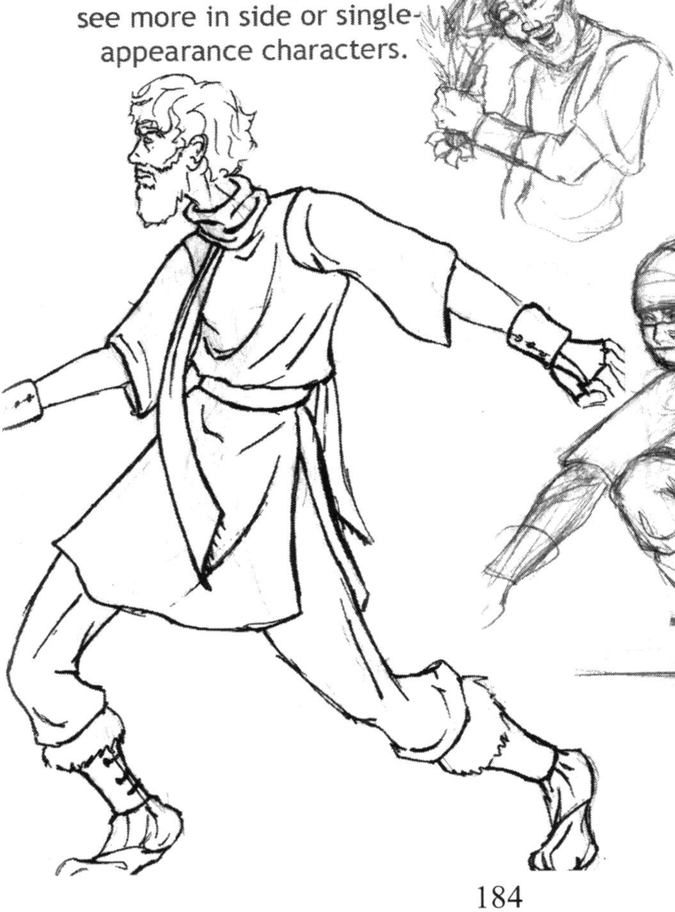

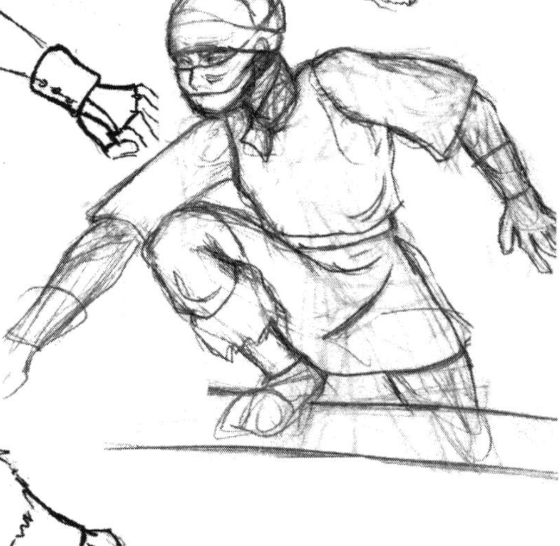

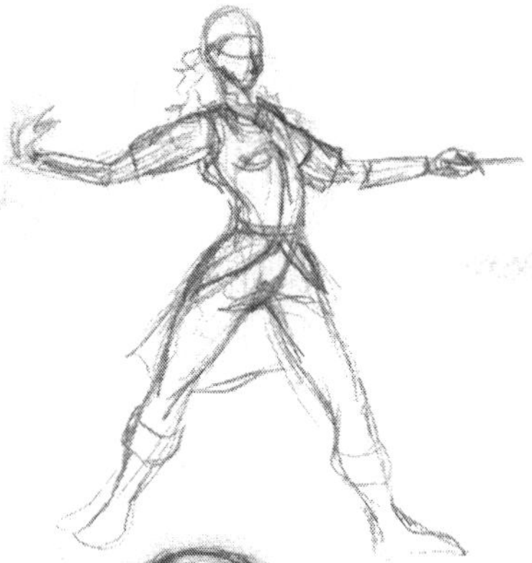

Kamaria's design was a challenge - I was trying to balance her androgenous dress with classically beautiful features (and a serious scowl.)

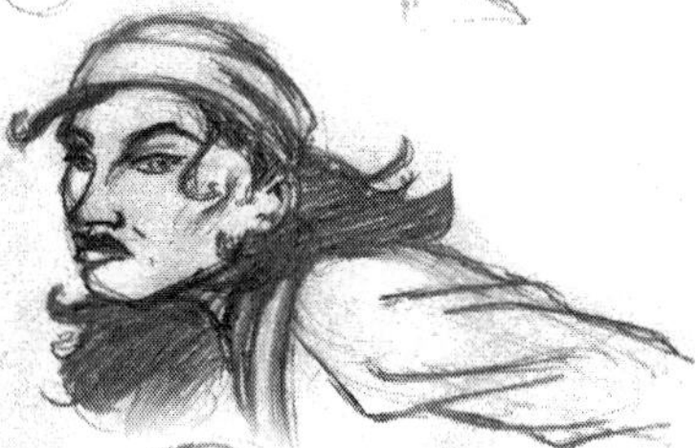

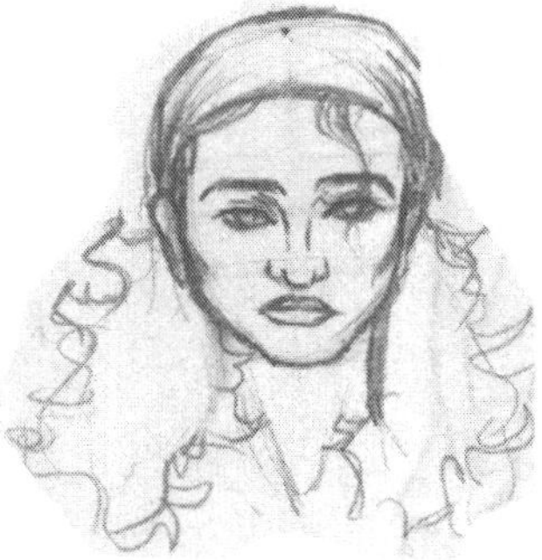

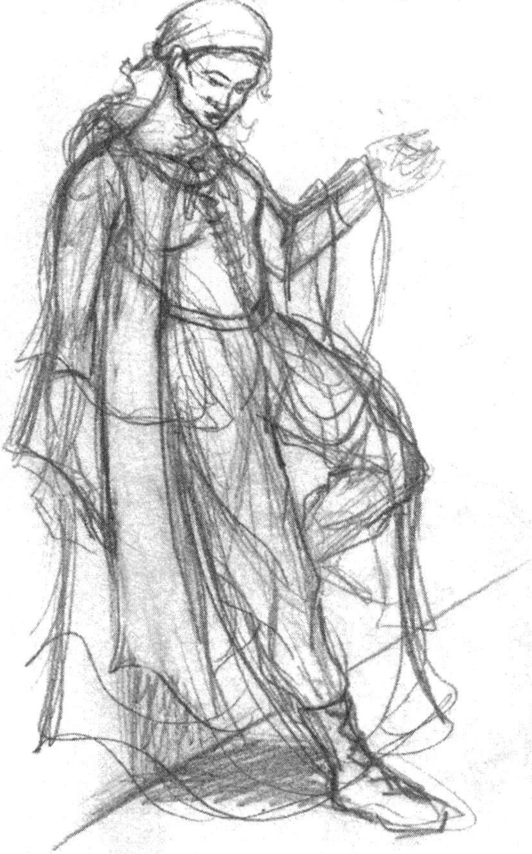

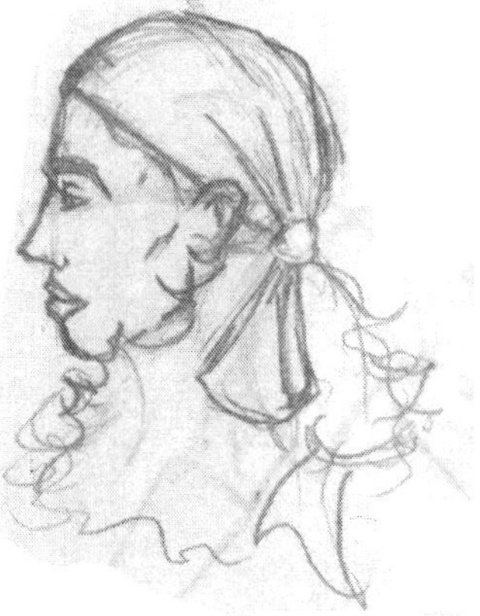

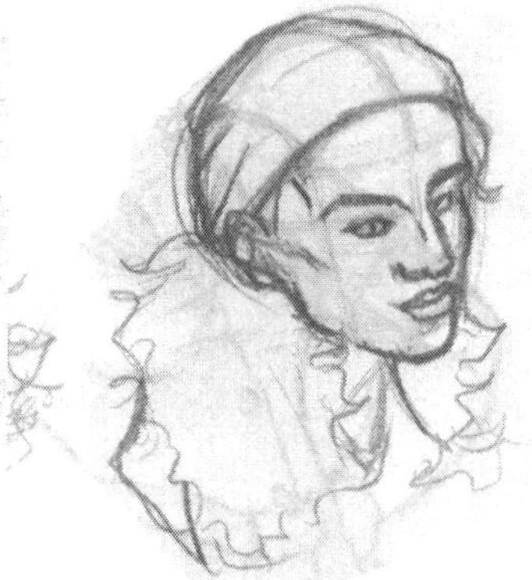

Some initial sketches for priests, priestesses, and guards for the Covenant of Mandra

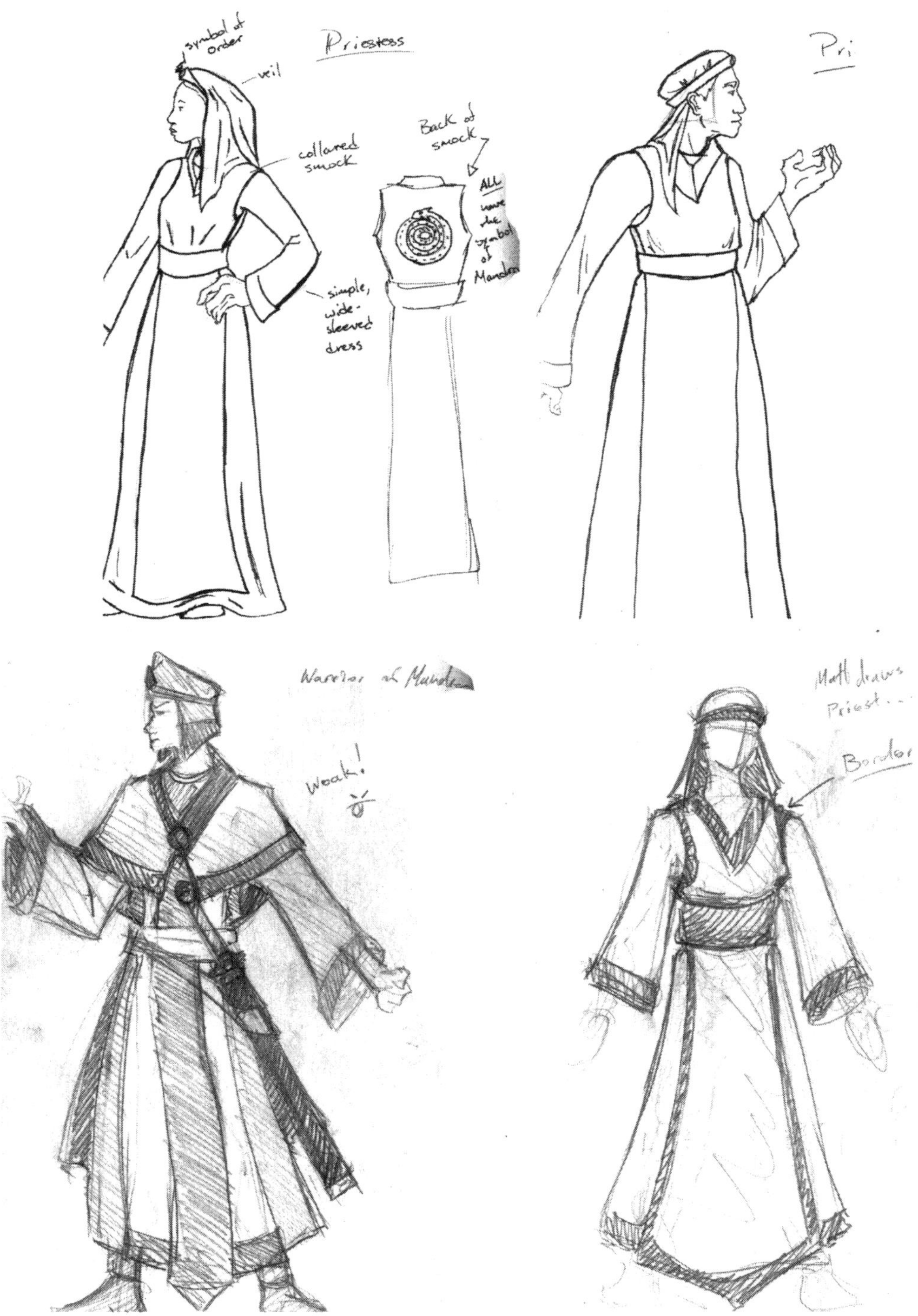
symbol of order
Priestess
veil
collared smock
Back of smock
ALL have the symbol of Mandra
simple, wide-sleeved dress
Woak!
Matt draws Priest...
Border

The two basic character sketches for the spy/assassin character from chapters two and three. For characters that are only going to appear once or twice, I usually just do a quick sketch to solidify their design in my head.

The spy's civillian outfit is a good example of the kind of "Arabian Nights" feel I was going for with a lot of the cultural design. Ultimately, a lot of the world ended up evolving in different directions, but early on it was a little more apparent in some of my designs.

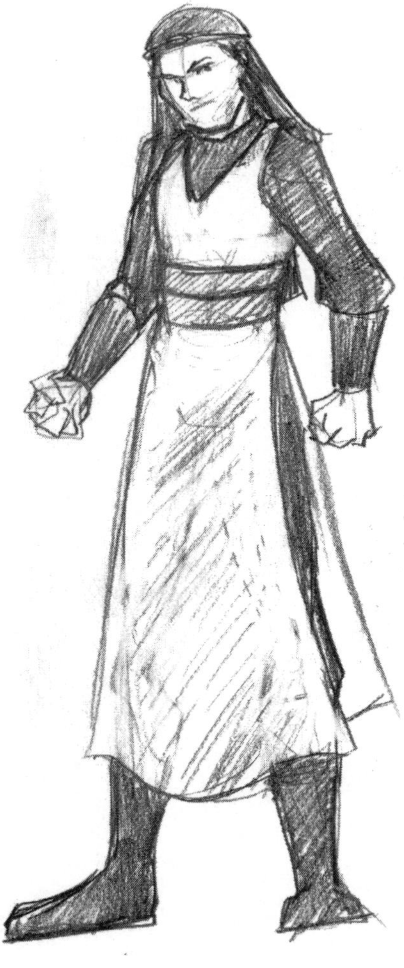

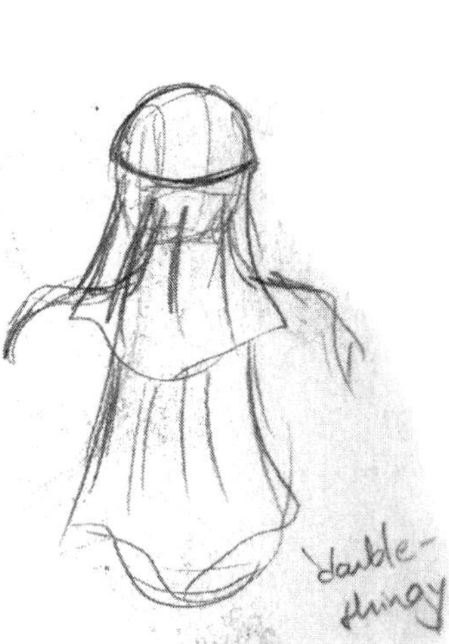
double-thingy

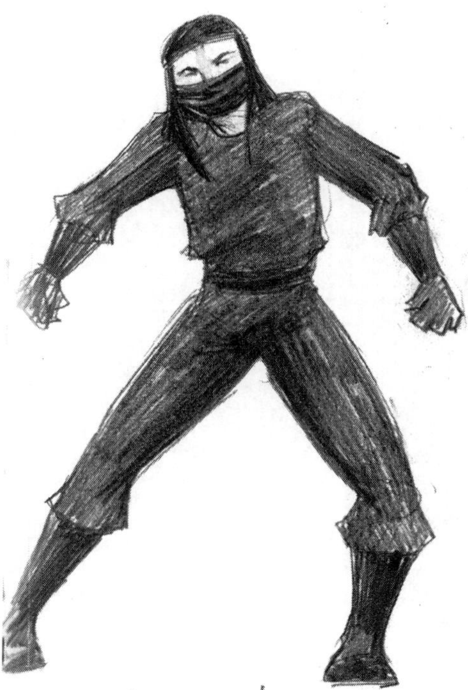
NINJING!

The designs for the Temple of the Banished Suns and the worshippers who maintain it.

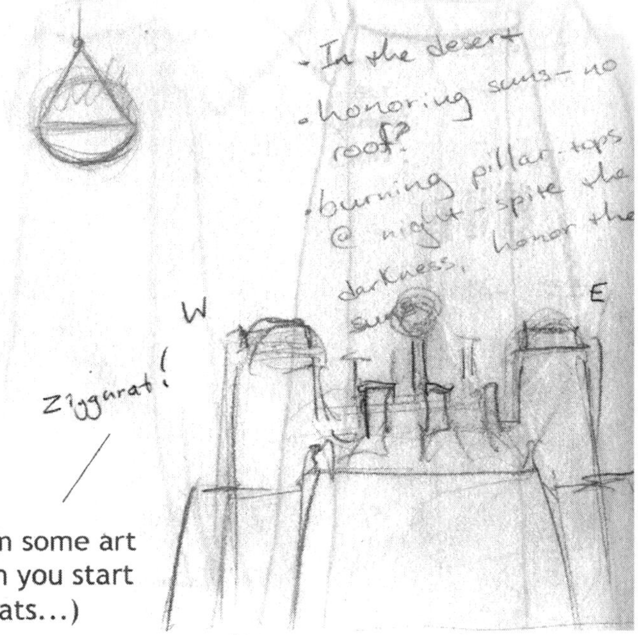

- In the desert
- honoring suns – no roof?
- burning pillar-tops @ night – spire the darkness, honor the suns
W
E
Ziggurat!

A lot more is learned about the Children of the Banished Suns in the next story-arc, but they were important to figure out early since the first scene of the whole story starts with them!

(Clearly you've taken some art history courses when you start designing ziggurats...)

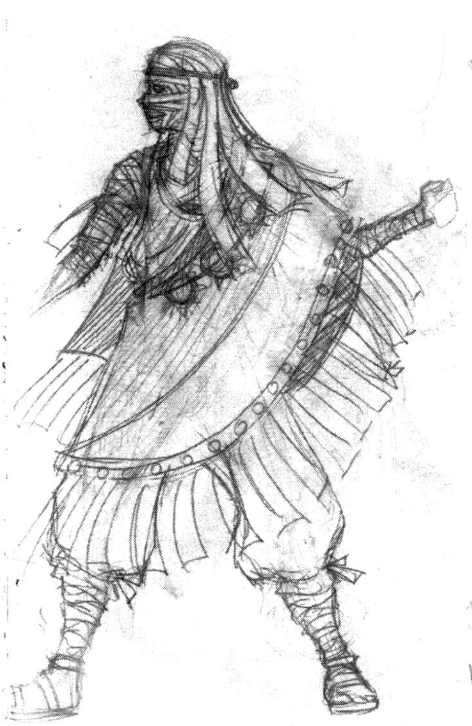

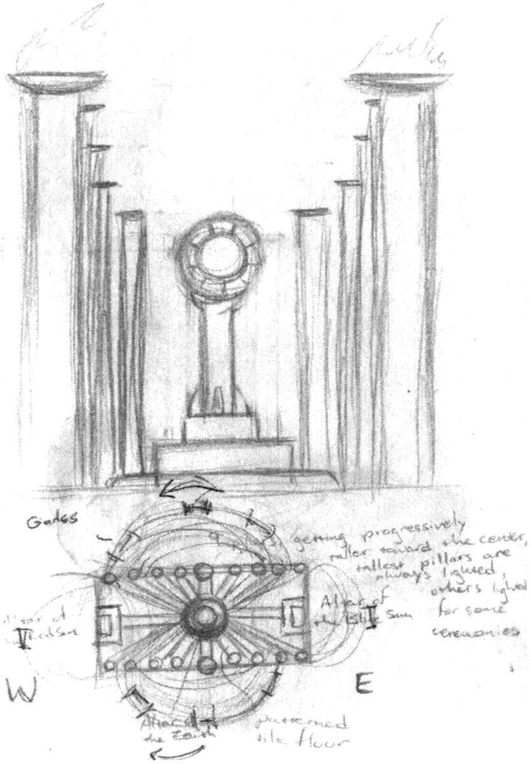

Gates
getting progressively taller toward the center, tallest pillars are always lighted, others lighted for some ceremonies
W
E
patterned tile floor

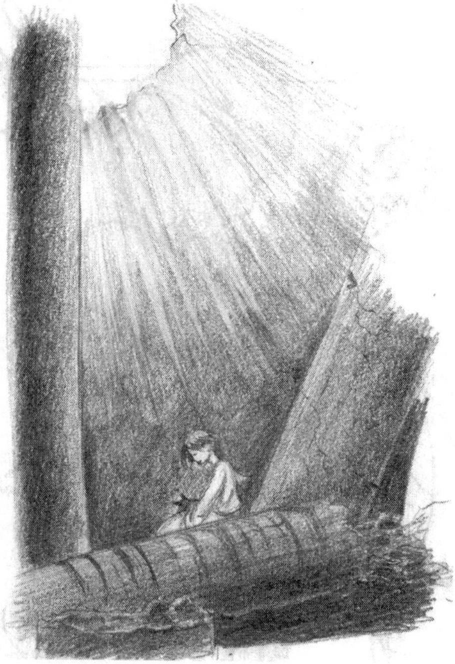

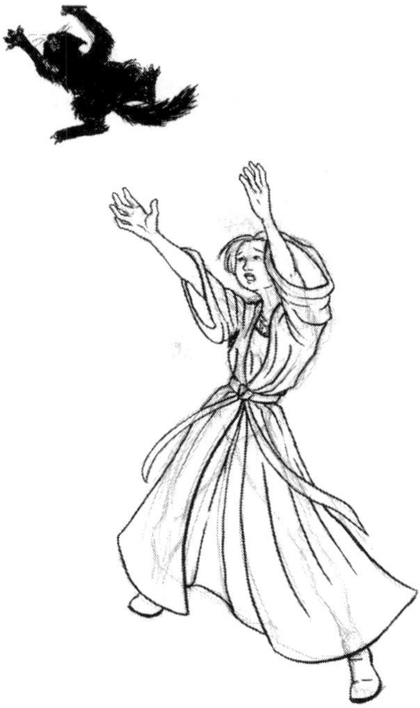

Temple of Mandra where Drake was raised

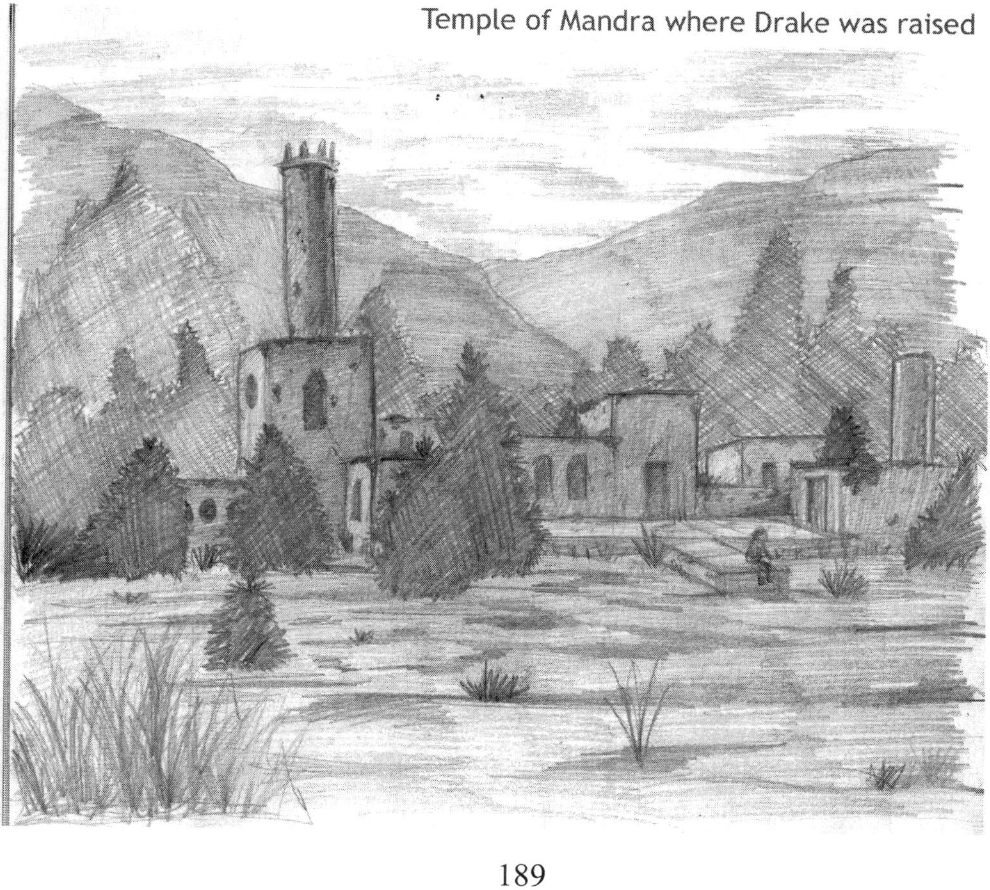

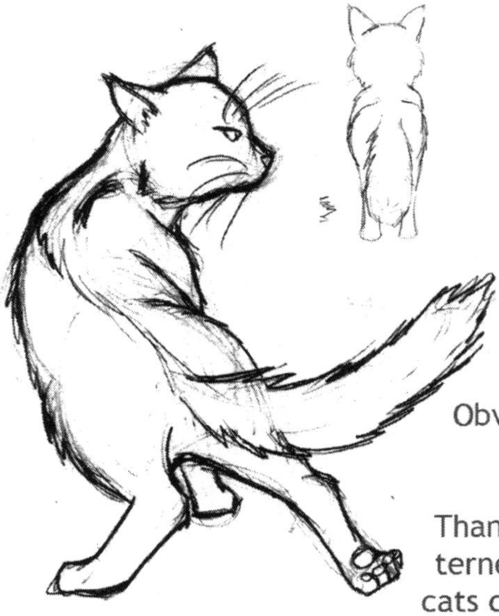

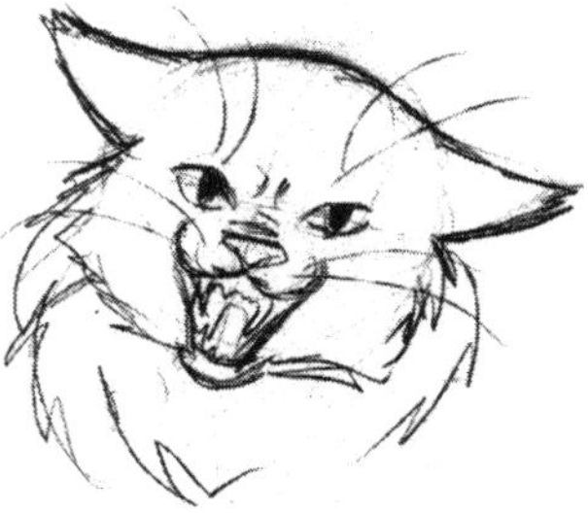

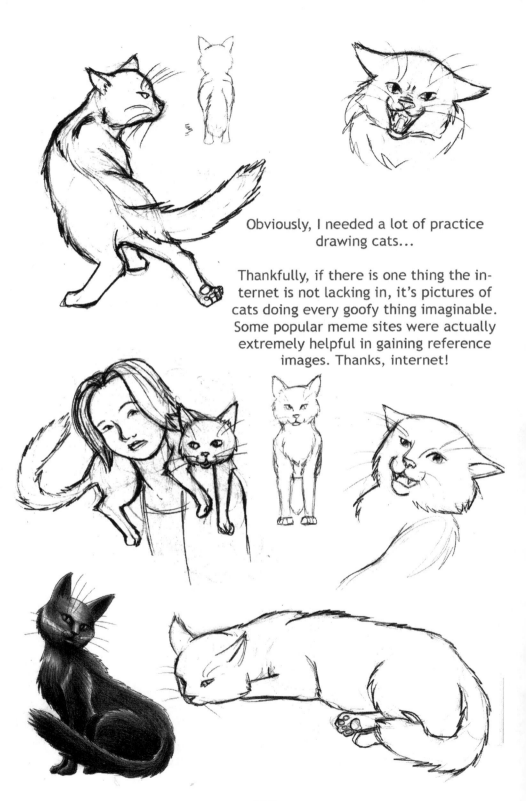

Obviously, I needed a lot of practice drawing cats...

Thankfully, if there is one thing the internet is not lacking in, it's pictures of cats doing every goofy thing imaginable. Some popular meme sites were actually extremely helpful in gaining reference images. Thanks, internet!

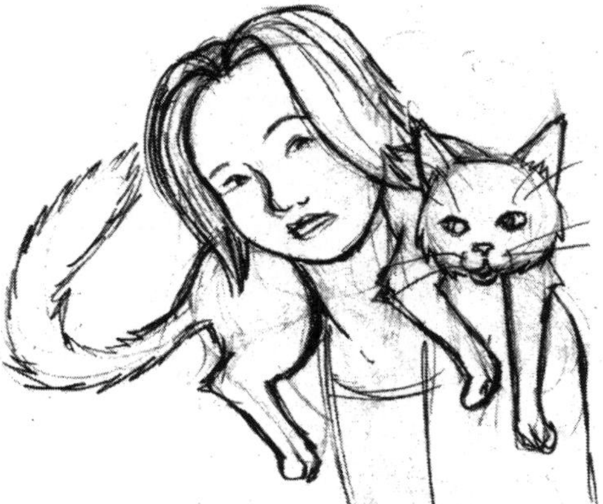

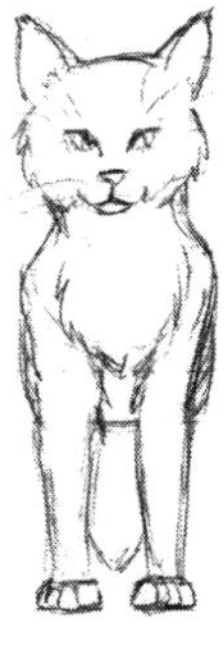

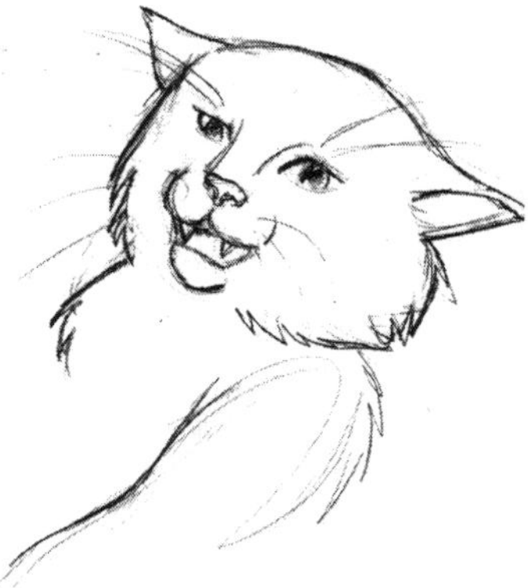

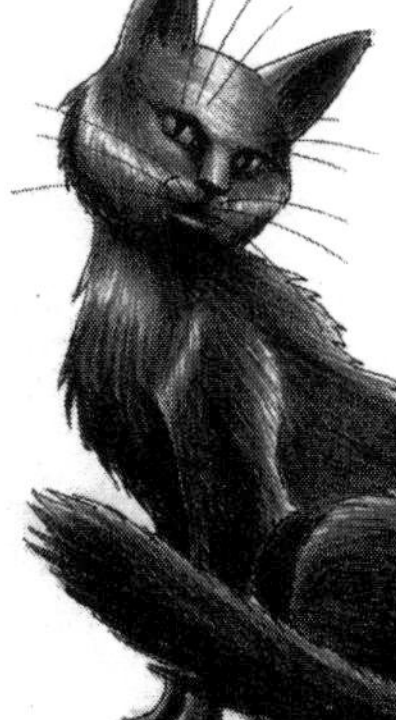

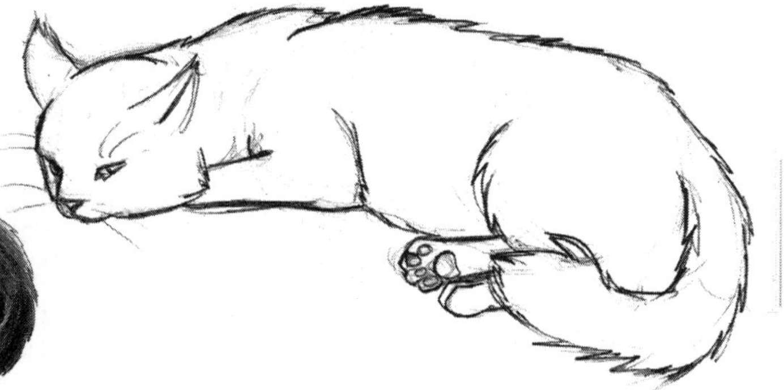

BONUS SHORT STORY

This story is supposed to happen on the group's way out into the desert. While I had planned it from early on, it ended up not fitting into the flow of chapter seven. Thankfully, this fun little short was still able to make it to you!

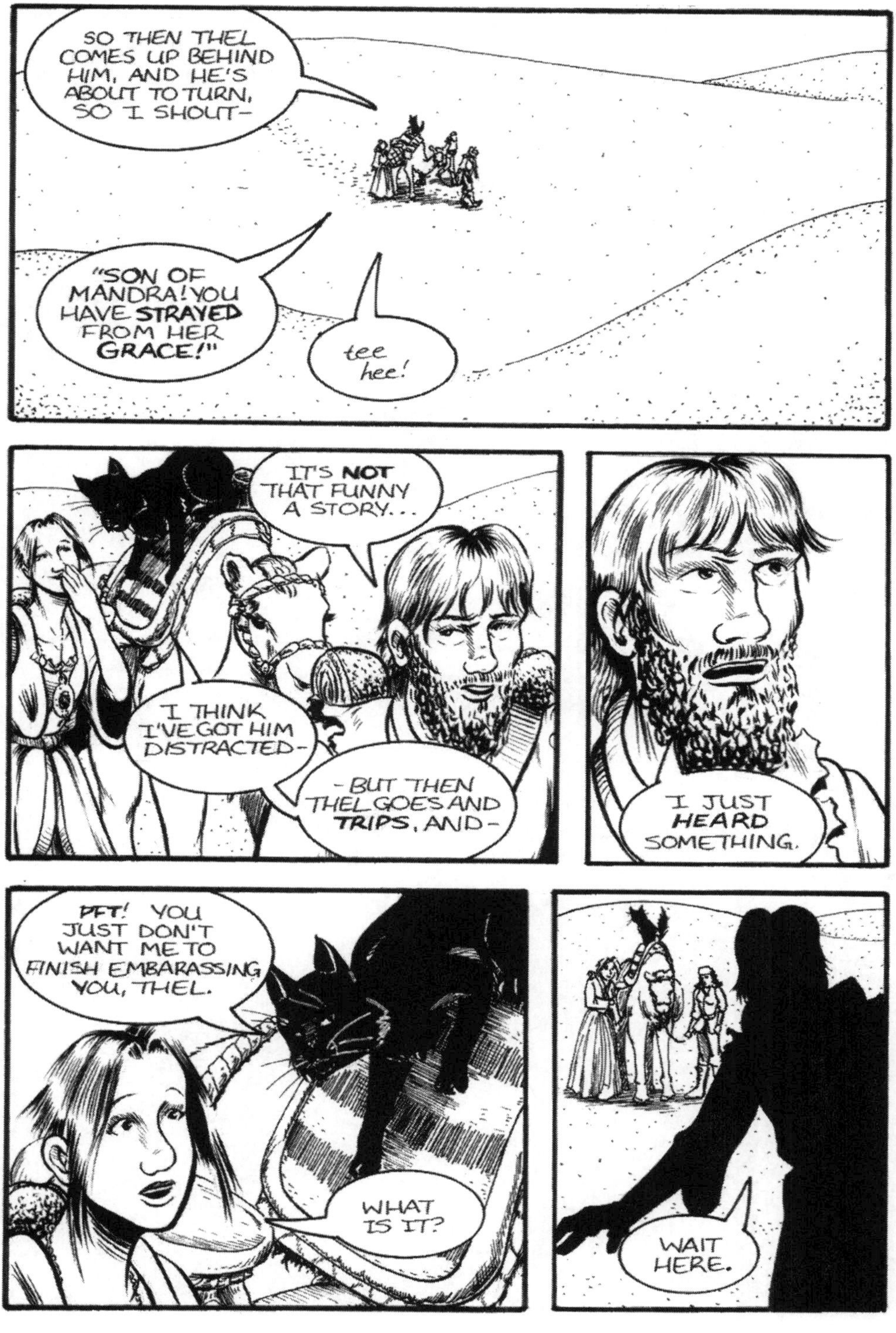
SO THEN THEL COMES UP BEHIND HIM, AND HE'S ABOUT TO TURN, SO I SHOUT-
"SON OF MANDRA! YOU HAVE STRAYED FROM HER GRACE!"
tee hee!
IT'S NOT THAT FUNNY A STORY...
I THINK I'VE GOT HIM DISTRACTED-
-BUT THEN THEL GOES AND TRIPS, AND-
I JUST HEARD SOMETHING.
PFT! YOU JUST DON'T WANT ME TO FINISH EMBARASSING YOU, THEL.
WHAT IS IT?
WAIT HERE.

WHERE'S HE GOING?

WHAT HAVE YOU FOUND?

I DON'T KNOW. SOME **FEARSOME** DESERT BEAST— TAKE A LOOK.

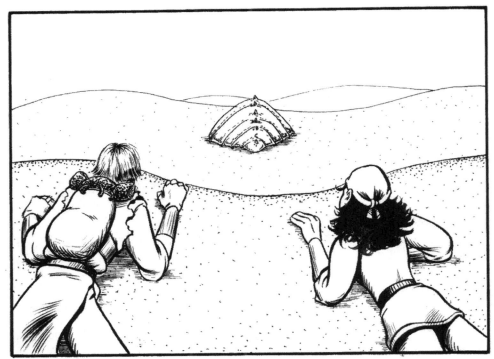

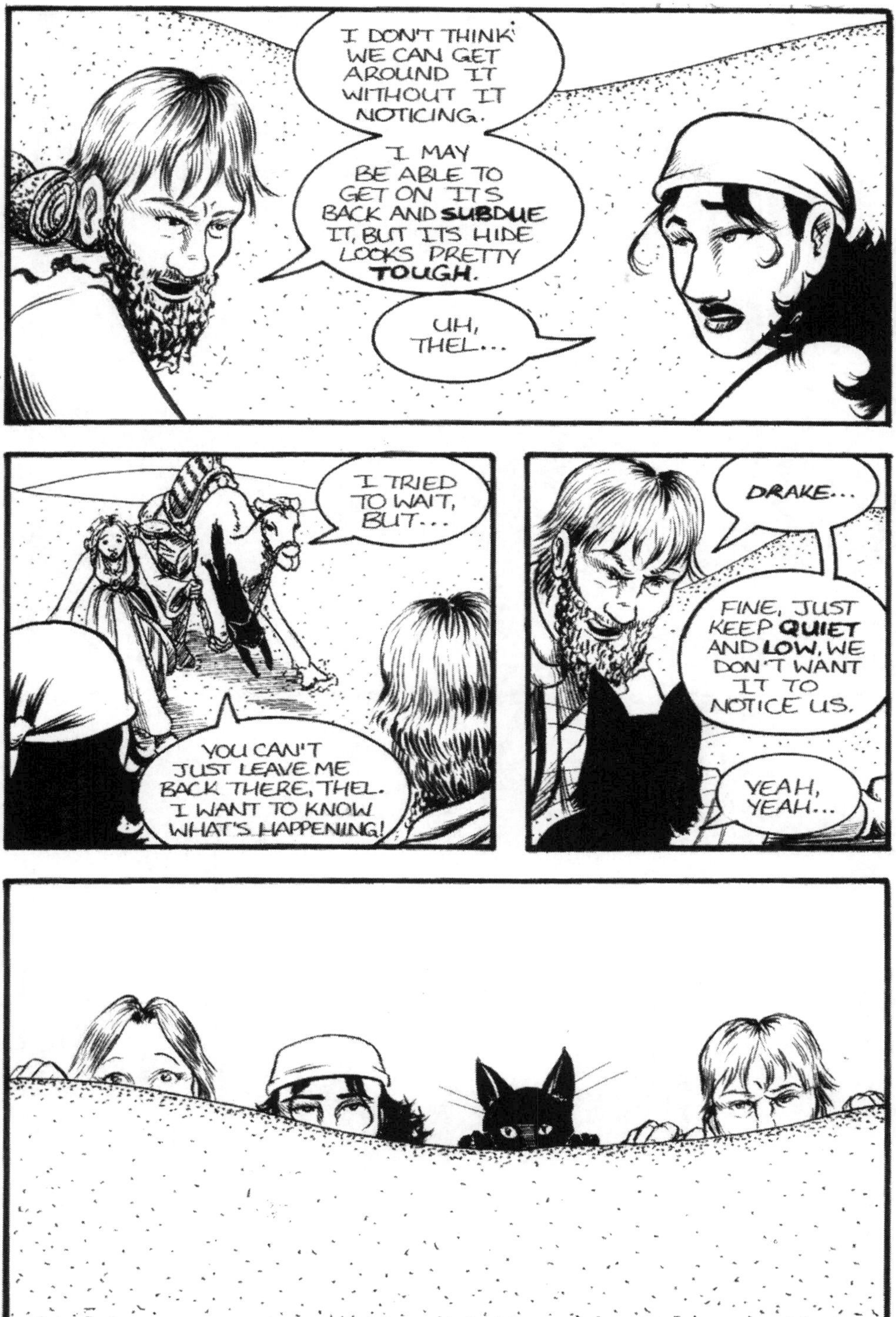
I DON'T THINK WE CAN GET AROUND IT WITHOUT IT NOTICING.
I MAY BE ABLE TO GET ON ITS BACK AND SUBDUE IT, BUT ITS HIDE LOOKS PRETTY TOUGH.
UH, THEL...
I TRIED TO WAIT, BUT...
YOU CAN'T JUST LEAVE ME BACK THERE, THEL. I WANT TO KNOW WHAT'S HAPPENING!
DRAKE...
FINE, JUST KEEP QUIET AND LOW, WE DON'T WANT IT TO NOTICE US.
YEAH, YEAH...

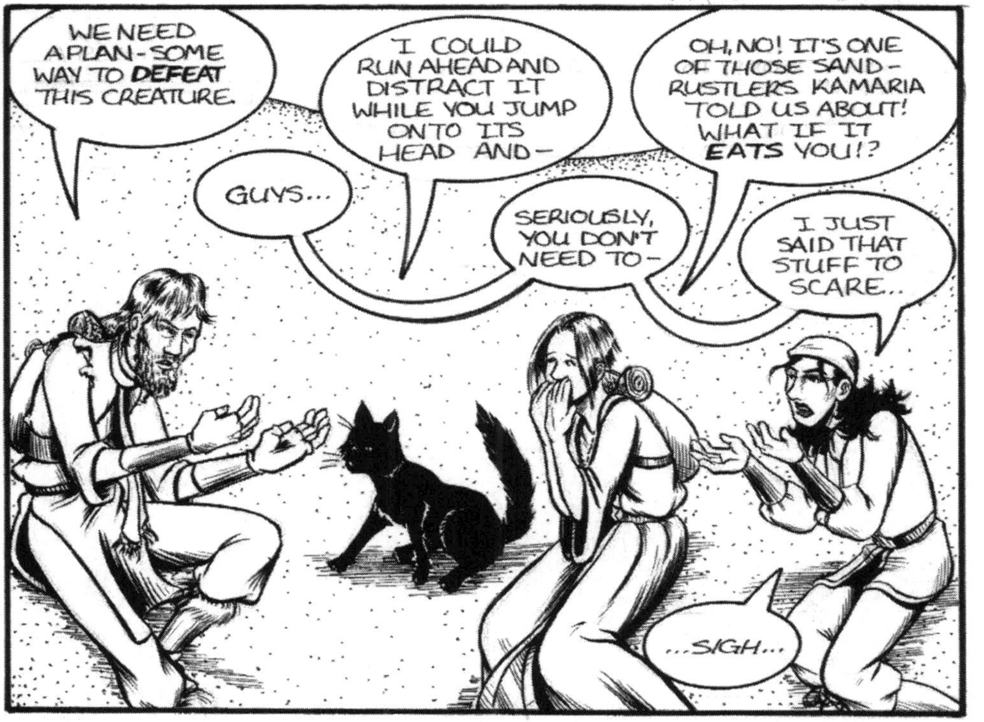
WE NEED A PLAN - SOME WAY TO **DEFEAT** THIS CREATURE.
I COULD RUN AHEAD AND DISTRACT IT WHILE YOU JUMP ONTO ITS HEAD AND-
OH, NO! IT'S ONE OF THOSE SAND-RUSTLERS KAMARIA TOLD US ABOUT! WHAT IF IT **EATS** YOU!?
GUYS...
SERIOUSLY, YOU DON'T NEED TO-
I JUST SAID THAT STUFF TO SCARE..
...SIGH...

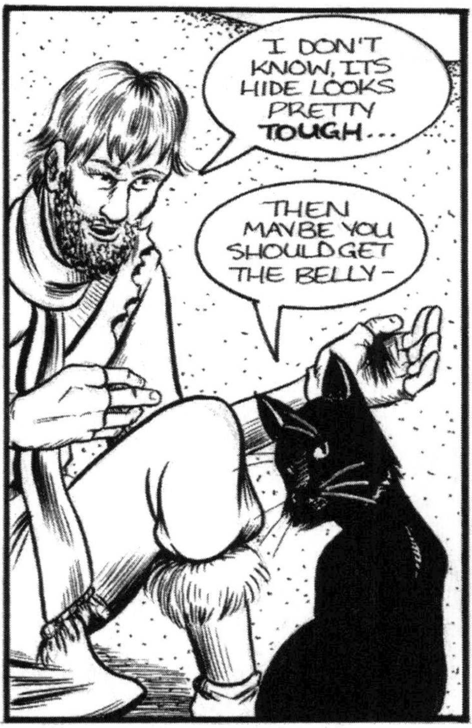
I DON'T KNOW, ITS HIDE LOOKS PRETTY **TOUGH**...
THEN MAYBE YOU SHOULD GET THE BELLY-

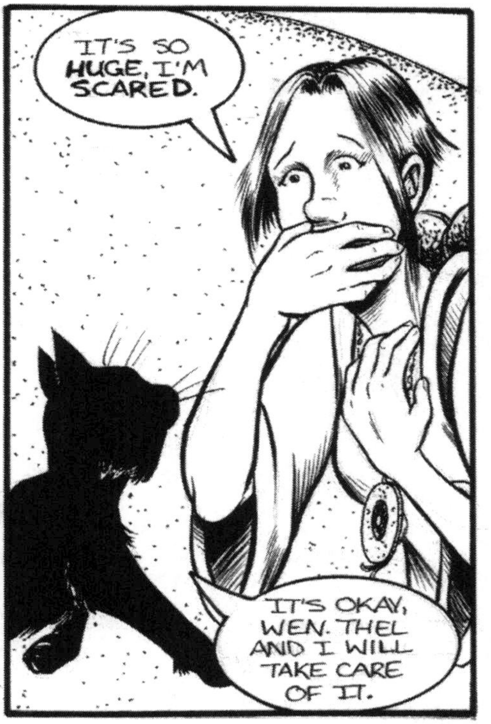
IT'S SO **HUGE**, I'M **SCARED**.
IT'S OKAY, WEN. THEL AND I WILL TAKE CARE OF IT.

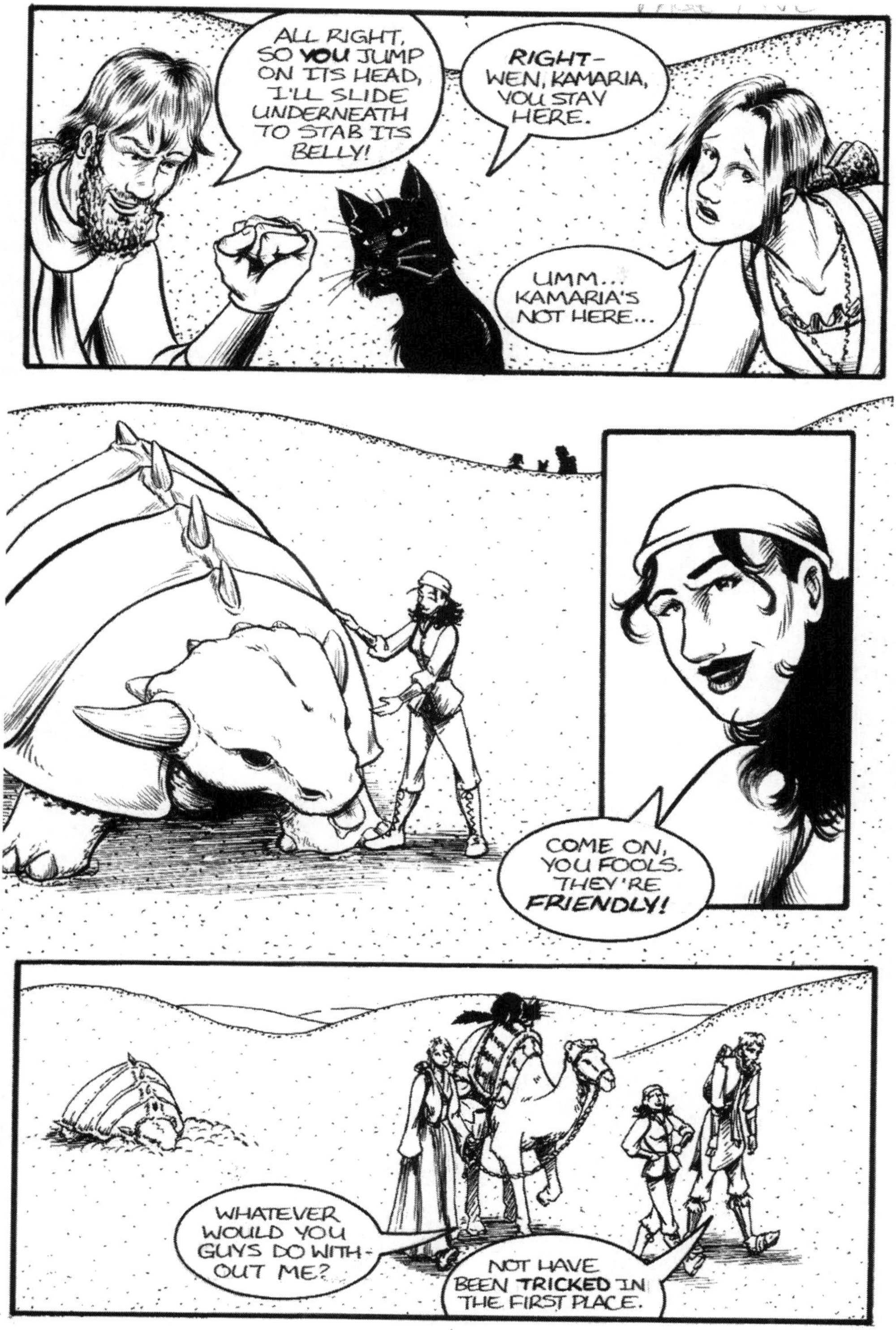
ALL RIGHT, SO YOU JUMP ON ITS HEAD, I'LL SLIDE UNDERNEATH TO STAB ITS BELLY!
RIGHT- WEN, KAMARIA, YOU STAY HERE.
UMM... KAMARIA'S NOT HERE...
COME ON, YOU FOOLS. THEY'RE FRIENDLY!
WHATEVER WOULD YOU GUYS DO WITH-OUT ME?
NOT HAVE BEEN TRICKED IN THE FIRST PLACE.

THEOLOGY FEATURE: MANDRA

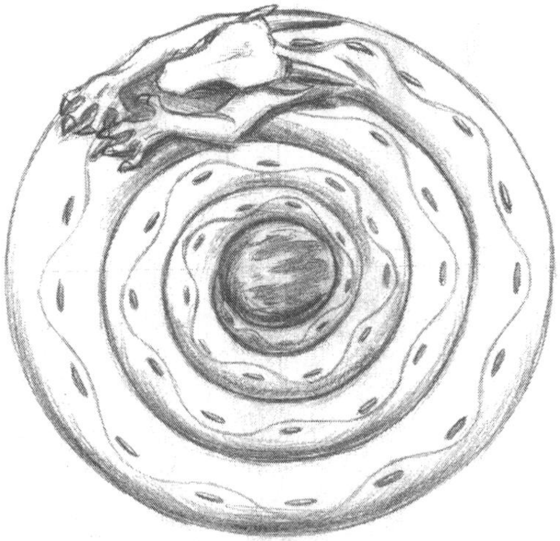

Mandra is the primary deity and central figure of the Covenant of Mandra - the main faith in the world of *Age of Night*. Mandra is said to have created the planet of Wijj by reaching into the river of time and pulling out seven jewels covered in mud, which became the heart and earth of the planet.

Mandra is represented as a dragon coiled around Wijj, protecting and guarding it. She is said to guide the lives of her children - all of the people of Wijj - and to judge their deeds and delegate reward and punishment during and after their lives.

The Covenant of Mandra claims to recieve edicts directly from Mandra through their High Priest, the Blessed of Mandra. The position, like many in the Covenant, is determined by divination at the leader's birth.

Mandra is traditionally said to be female, but some leaders in the mostly patriarchal society of Amathea have proposed that Mandra may be genderless or hermaphroditic.

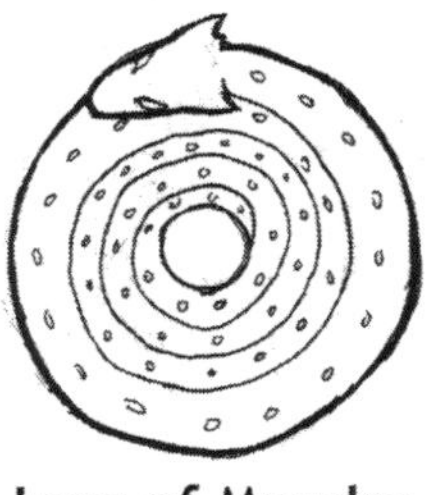

Icon of Mandra

Character Profile: Drake

Handraken (who always goes by Drake) is the main character of *Age of Night*. He was born into the Covenant of Mandra to priest and priestess parents and was immediately recognized by the Covenant diviners as the next incarnation of the God of Night - Kiaraz. Drake was then raised by the whole temple clergy instead of his parents, and was being prepared to assume his official role once he came of age.

Early on, Drake was dissatisfied with his lot - being treated like a dog by many of the clergy. While the Avatar of Kiaraz is feared for his power, he is not well respected by the rest of the Covenant, since Kiaraz is the God of chaos, revelry, and destruction. Drake's connection to Kiaraz is what prompted him to leave the temple and run away when he was only eight years old. While he was scared and uncertain what to do with himself, having never lived outside the aegis of the temple, he was happier to have his freedom.

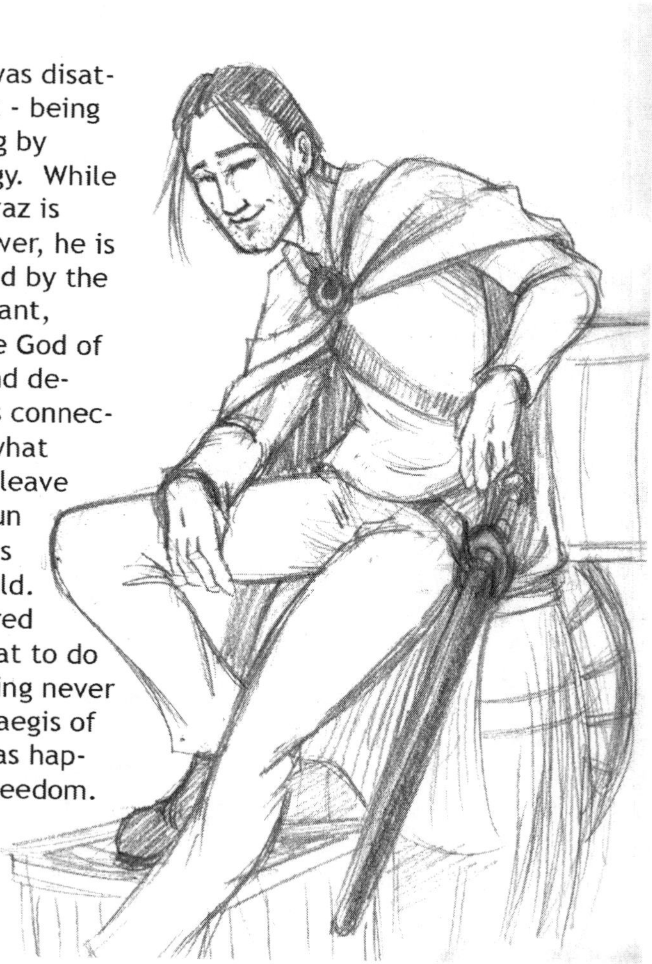

Shortly after running away, Drake met up with Thelonious - another recent runaway who was a few years older than him. The two quickly became close friends, learning from each other how to survive on the road. They spent many years enjoying the vagabond lifestyle - sleeping wherever they could, stealing, conning, and (very rarely) working for their meals.

While the two became skilled conmen they were careful to never take too much of value from anyone in need. Free stays at inns, free meals, a coin here or there - never outright robbery of any large amount of money or belongings, and certainly not from folks already in need.

Drake's acrimonious history and early training with the Covenant allowed him a certain advantage in these cons. He still posed as a priest (which he technically was by birth) and used this appearance to gain people's trust and occasionally secure "donations to the temple." Also, at some point he stole an emblem and cloak from the Servants of the Union of Nura and Kiaraz. This order specializes in marriages, which Drake very often performed for people (for a small fee, of course.) While he knew how to do everything correctly, these marriages were not strictly speaking legal. Not that any of the people he did it for would ever need to know that...

Drake's primary goal in life is enjoying himself - spending time with his friend Thel, partaking of good food, good drink, and good company (especially the ladies.) After many years on the road, he felt safe that he had escaped his fate to take his place in the Covenant and be bound to the High Priestess of Nura in his twenty-third year.

Union of Nura and Kiaraz

Kiaraz

200

My sincerest thanks to you for reading this book. Telling this story has been my greatest passion, and I hope to keep telling it for years to come.

You can continue the journey with me. Follow *Age of Night* online at www.ageofnight.com. New pages are uploaded twice a week.

Thank you again, and I hope to see you there.

- A.

Made in the USA
Middletown, DE
03 May 2015